GOLDIE

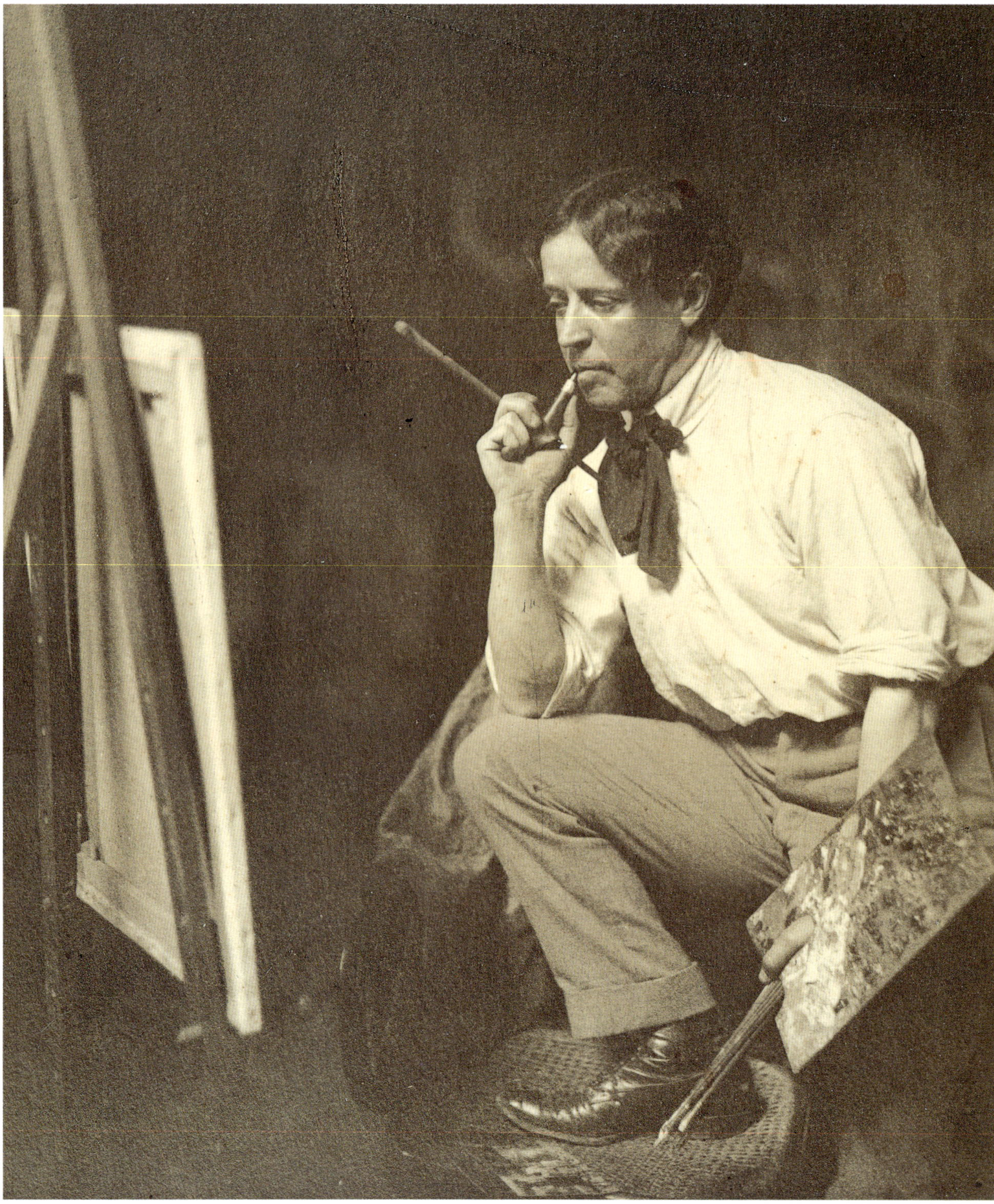

GOLDIE

ROGER BLACKLEY

AUCKLAND ART GALLERY
TOI O TĀMAKI

David Bateman

First published in 1997 by
Auckland Art Gallery Toi o Tāmaki
P. O. Box 5449, Auckland 1, New Zealand

in association with
David Bateman Ltd
30 Tarndale Grove, Albany Business Park
Albany, Auckland, New Zealand

Reprinted 1997,1999, 2000

ISBN 1 86953 340 2 (hardback)
ISBN 1 86953 352 6 (paperback)

Design by Gerrard Malcolm, Auckland
Editorial services by Michael Gifkins and Associates
Printed in China by Everbest Printing Co.

Photography: John McIver and Jennifer French, Auckland Art Gallery Toi o Tāmaki. Additional photography: Russell-Cotes Art Gallery and Museum, Bournemouth, pp.90, 91; University of York, England, pp.64, 75; David Hankey, Edenbridge, p.143; Matt Pia, London, p.133; Fine Arts Museums of San Francisco, p.8; State Library of New South Wales, Sydney, p.viii; Art Gallery of South Australia, Adelaide, p.149; Richard Stringer, Brisbane, pp.72, 77; Museum of New Zealand Te Papa Tongarewa, pp.12, 100, 101, 111, 148, 162; Alexander Turnbull Library, pp.10, 48; Auckland Museum, pp.18, 21, 35; Richard Wotton, Sarjeant Gallery, p.78; Michael Hall, Wellington, p.163; Lloyd Park, Christchurch, pp.98, 173 (top); Martin Hunter, p.43; David J. Wise, pp.124, 125.

Published on the occasion of the exhibition *GOLDIE*
Auckland Art Gallery Toi o Tāmaki, 28 June – 28 October 1997
proudly sponsored by ERNST & YOUNG

Frontispiece: Goldie at the easel, around 1908 (Auckland Art Gallery Toi o Tāmaki)

foreword

The portraits of Māori by Charles F. Goldie are the most widely recognised images of New Zealand art history. They continue to fire the popular imagination with their emotional resonance and sheer technical virtuosity, however contested the actual or symbolic 'truth' of their representation. Popularly revered by Māori and Pākehā alike, Goldie's work has nonetheless felt the full weight of critical scorn. Indeed, this dynamic tension between acclaim and disdain has few, if any, equals in New Zealand art. *GOLDIE* examines and re-assesses that phenomenon.

The ambitious scope of *GOLDIE* has relied upon the confidence of the project's principal sponsor, Ernst & Young. Their long-standing commitment to the Gallery has focused on the art of New Zealand and, on this occasion, has extended to directly underwriting the research development of *GOLDIE*. In addition to supporting the project in Auckland, they have also assisted its tour to Sydney, Dunedin, Christchurch and the Museum of New Zealand Te Papa Tongarewa, Wellington. The Gallery greatly appreciates the generous support of Ernst & Young and that of the participating venues.

Haerewa, the Gallery's iwi liaison group, established in 1995 and chaired by Elizabeth Ellis, has played a critical role in preparing the way for this project. Their counsel on issues concerning Goldie's portraits of Māori has been invaluable. Haerewa also guided the work of Mamae Takerei, Iwi Liaison Consultant, who took on the complex role of establishing contact with the many descendants of Goldie's models. This challenging task was generously supported by Creative New Zealand, Arts Council of New Zealand *Toi Aotearoa*.

In co-publishing *GOLDIE* with David Bateman, the Gallery is ensuring the widest possible audience for a book which will have a life and readership well beyond *GOLDIE*, the exhibition. The contributors to the publication, Roger Blackley, Ngahuia Te Awekotuku, Leonard Bell and David Wise, provide a long-awaited re-evaluation of Goldie's work. The Gallery is indebted to each of them for their insights into the art of Charles F. Goldie.

The driving force behind *GOLDIE* has been Roger Blackley, Curator of Historical New Zealand Art. The publication and exhibition have benefited from his curatorial acumen and capacity to win the confidence of lenders. *GOLDIE* is much the richer for his unflagging enthusiasm. Danielle Tolson, assisting with curatorial research, and Gallery photographers John McIver and Jennifer French, also made an exceptional contribution to the project.

Finally, the Gallery acknowledges the wide public interest which has followed the development of *GOLDIE*. Appeals for information have been very generously answered, assisting the placement of Goldie in a new context. We are grateful to the many institutional and private lenders to the exhibition, especially the Goldie family, whose willingness to share their works with a wider public has made this project possible.

Chris Saines
Director, Auckland Art Gallery Toi o Tāmaki

acknowledgements

My greatest debt is to Charles Goldie's extended family. Mr and Mrs S. J. Cooper of Melbourne provided access to Olive Goldie's papers and gave permission for Goldie's works to be reproduced in this book. Goldie family members in New Zealand were equally supportive of the project, providing access to family papers and to the works of art in their possession. Particular thanks are due to Ken, Ruth, Betty, Fay and Helen.

Thanks are also due to the staff of art galleries, museums and libraries who have assisted this work, particularly Auckland City Library, Auckland Museum, Waikato Museum of Art and History, Hawke's Bay Museum, Sarjeant Gallery, Alexander Turnbull Library, Museum of New Zealand Te Papa Tongarewa, Robert McDougall Art Gallery, Canterbury Public Library, Aigantighe Art Gallery, Dunedin Public Art Gallery, Otago Early Settlers' Museum, State Library of New South Wales, Art Gallery of South Australia, Russell-Cotes Art Gallery and Museum (Bournemouth) and the Thyssen-Bornemisza Collection (Lugano). I am also grateful to Alister Taylor.

Roger Bhatnager and many other private owners of Goldie's works have assisted in this project. Thanks to all who agreed to the inclusion of their treasures in this book and the associated exhibition. Special thanks to the Goldie family.

Auckland Art Gallery under Christopher Johnstone, former director, and current director Chris Saines, has strongly supported the Goldie project. I would like to acknowledge all my colleagues at the Gallery, especially Danielle Tolson for her work as Goldie Exhibition Coordinator. As sponsors of the Goldie exhibition, Ernst & Young supported much of the research for this publication.

The following individuals provided invaluable assistance: Leonard Bell, Jack and Jeanie Blackley, Eamonn Bolger, Ron Brownson, Johanne Buchanan, Janice Chong, Grahame Chote, Fiona Ciaran, Roger Collins, David Colquhoun, Tipa Compain, Sophie Coupland, Anna Crighton, Jeremy Dart, William Dart, Frances Davies, Chaz Doherty, Ellen Ellis, Terry Firkin, Kathleen Fogarty, Yves Forest, Jennifer French, Brenda Gamble, Shaun Garner, John Gow, Theresa Graham, Michael Graham-Stewart, Nicolas Greis, Julia Gresson, Elaine Gurian, Penny Hacking, Wharehuia Hemara, Sarah Hillary, Kerry Howe, Merv Hutchinson, Jane Hylton, Tame Iti, Martyn Johns, Alexa Johnston, Julie King, Suzanne Knight, Nicholas Lambourne, Louis Le Vaillant, Pauline Lellman, Amanda Lillie, Joan McCracken, John McIver, Rod Macleod, Gordon Maitland, Hinureina Mangan, Ngahiraka Mason, Marian Minson, Roger Neich, Richard Neville, Justine Olsen, Nello Pasquini, Neil Roberts, Malcolm Ross, Sarah Shieff, Bronwyn Simes, Damian Skinner, Ross Somerville, Oliver Stead, Caleb Stuart, Jane Sutherland, Chris Szekely, Mamae Takerei, Ngahuia Te Awekotuku, Helen Telford, Evelyn Tobin, Celia Thompson, Richard Thompson, Jo Torr, Tim Walker, Ann and Peter Webb, Genevieve Webb, John Webster, Ian Wedde, Jane Wild, Rodney Wilson, Andrea Wise, David Wise, Nicola Woodhouse.

Hei kōrero whakamutunga, ngā mihi ki a koutou, ngā uri whakatupu o ngā rangatira kua whakaahuatia e Hāre Kōri.

Roger Blackley

Auckland, January 1997

contents

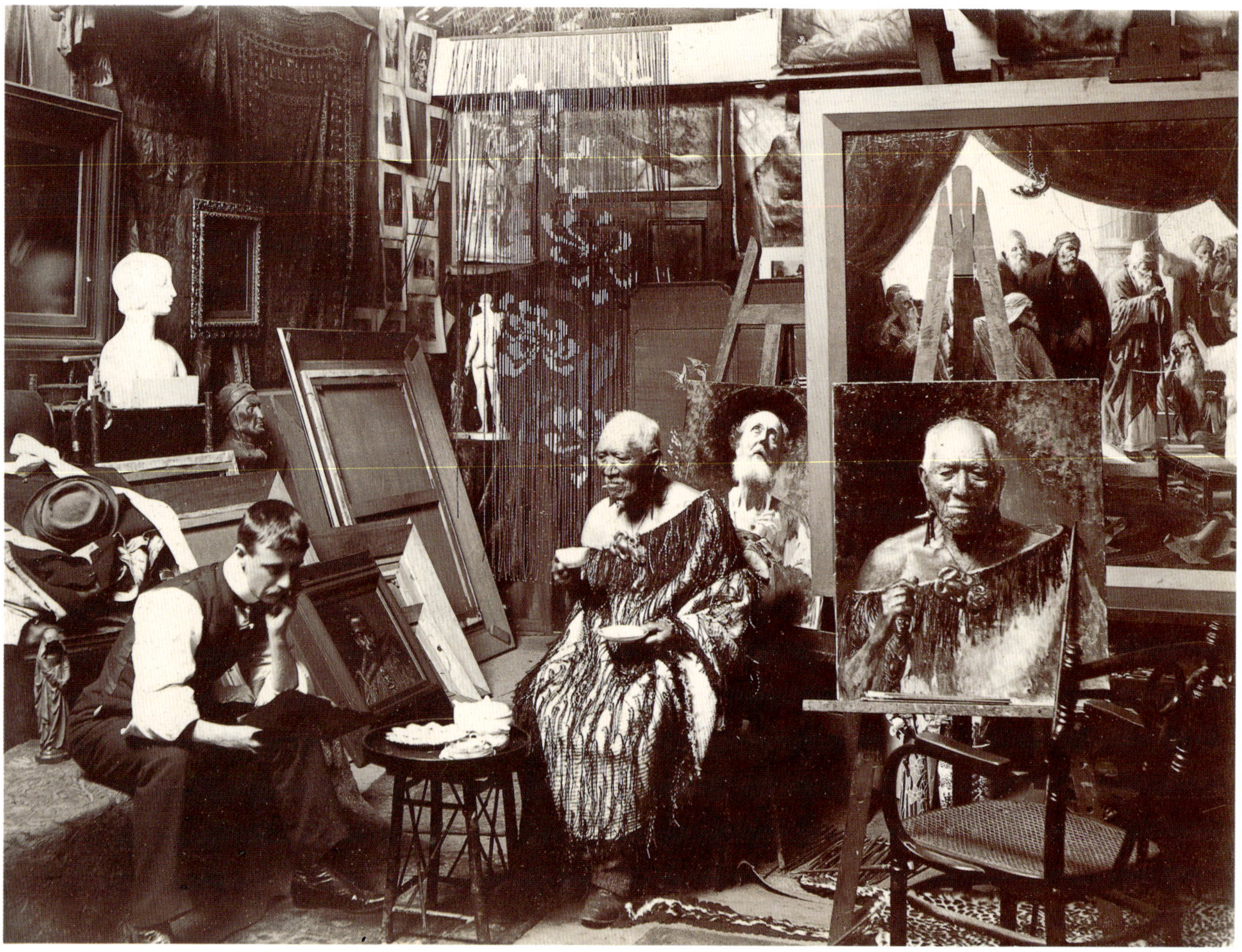

the art of charles f. goldie

Charles F. Goldie is probably New Zealand's best-known artist. His popular fame has been fed by a constant stream of newspaper reports documenting record-shattering prices, thefts, vandalisms and forgeries. Descendants of Goldie's models revere the depictions of their ancestors, while others have denounced the paintings as documents of colonial racism. Yet the story of the artist and his career is embedded in a thick accretion of myth, where dubious anecdotes rub shoulders with strongly opposing opinions. Researching an article on Goldie for the *Woman's Weekly* in 1958, Florence Roberts found it difficult to trace accurate information about the artist and his career.

> [Goldie] did a great service in recording the Maori of his day but it seems that no one has done him a similar service. For in an endeavour to find out a few facts about the painter I discovered how very little had ever been written about him in the past or present.[1]

Roberts referred to this phenomenon as 'that dangerous quagmire of familiarity where everybody "knows" the man yet nothing about him. Facts are hard to separate from this daub of opinion and impression.' Over the four subsequent decades, Goldie's mystique has only intensified. One culprit is undoubtedly the popular media and their sensationalising reports. Another is the neglect inflicted by Pākehā scholarship.

Suffering from spells of ill-health and depression, Goldie spent his later years as a virtual recluse in his Remuera home. Apart from ordering the memorabilia of his artistic career into a sequence of albums, now housed in the library of the Auckland Museum, he left no written account of his life and art. The art establishment firmly turned its back on the artist, regarding the New Zealand public's fixation with his work as one more unfortunate element of popular taste that required correction. The intellectual and physical neglect suffered by Goldie's paintings throughout the modernist period must in part be regarded as a form of revenge for this public renown. In the 1950s, when Auckland Art Gallery consigned Goldie's original frames to the scrapheap, the artist's handwritten labels went with them.

The only significant publications on Goldie's career are Alister Taylor's opulent limited-edition volumes of 1977 and 1979, written in collaboration with Jan Glen. These extraordinary books came not from a museum or academic source but from an entrepreneurial publisher effectively creating investment items linked to Goldie's popularity in the marketplace. Taylor's books were avidly collected (most of the first volume went to subscribers) and today are traded by art dealers rather than second-hand booksellers. Taylor and Glen revealed a sizeable *œuvre* of several hundred works, certainly larger than anyone had previously suspected, and the books served well in delivering provenances for the saleroom. Inevitably, they also provided models for some of the forgers who, with varying degrees of success, have been enlarging

Goldie and his model Pātara Te Tuhi enjoying a cup of tea in the studio, photographed in 1901 by R. Love of Edwards' Studio (from the album Maoriland Photographs, *Mitchell Library, State Library of New South Wales, Sydney).*

Goldie's *œuvre.* In terms of colour plates and scholarly research into Goldie and his models, Taylor's volumes represented a significant advance on any previous publication on an individual New Zealand artist. These books will remain an essential resource for anyone interested in Goldie, his works and the people he depicted.

As recently as the early 1980s, Auckland Art Gallery's Goldie paintings inhabited motley frames for which they were never intended. Works that Goldie framed as ovals had become rectangles, with unfinished corners visible. Even the gigantic *The Arrival of the Maoris in New Zealand* had been reduced to a thin modern frame. Although fitfully on display, Auckland Art Gallery's Goldie paintings were usually found in the storeroom. The catalyst for change was the exhibition *Te Maori – Te hokinga mai: The return home* in 1987, when modern replicas of Goldie's trademark moulding were placed on the portraits, and an ornate gilded frame fitted to *The Arrival of the Maoris.* The presence of a sizeable Māori audience highlighted the radically conflicting attitudes towards Goldie and his works, especially the contrast between the respect expressed by many Māori and the widespread denigration on the part of many 'politically correct' Pākehā. Even more fascinating was the gulf between 'informed' or 'expert' opinion and the enthusiasms of the public at large, as recorded in the Gallery's visitors' book.

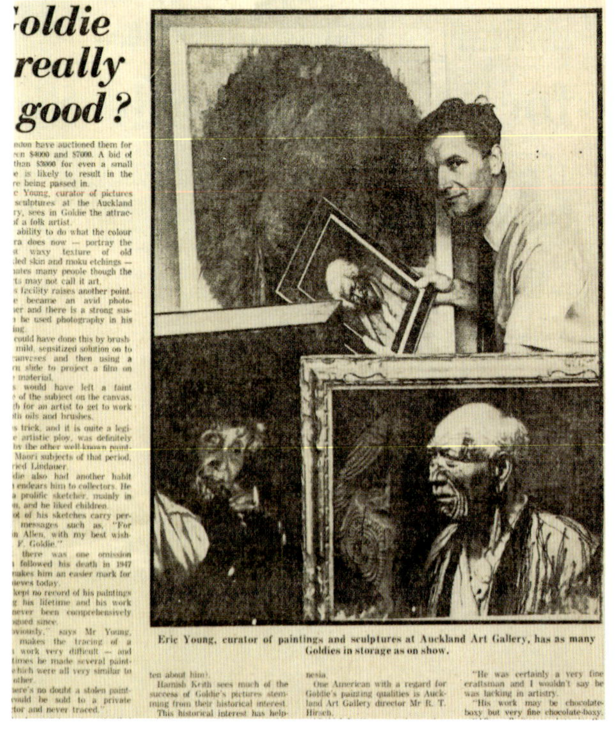
'oldie really good?

Eric Young, curator of paintings and sculptures at Auckland Art Gallery, has as many Goldies in storage as on show.

ten about him).
Hamish Keith sees much of the success of Goldie's pictures stemming from their historical interest.
This historical interest has help-

nesia.
One American with a regard for Goldie's painting qualities is Auckland Art Gallery director Mr R. T. Hirsch.

"He was certainly a very fine craftsman and I wouldn't say he was lacking in artistry.
"His work may be chocolate-boxy but very fine chocolate-boxy.

The massive controversy that erupted late in 1990 over the National Art Gallery's $900,000 acquisition of two important Goldie paintings graphically demonstrated Goldie's paradoxical status: a painter of immense popular renown familiar to both Māori and Pākehā New Zealanders, whose precise value as an artist seemed decidedly uncertain. Art-historical scholarship, driven by a modernist agenda, still continued to downplay Goldie's true stature. At the same time, the controversy served to enhance the artist's profile with the 'general' public as well as to reveal a Māori response that regarded the paintings as irreplaceable ancestral images and consequently priceless. Far from expressing outrage over an unacceptably high price, Māori regarded the purchase as a positive venture on the part of a national institution. Leonard Bell's essay on these two contested paintings, first published in *Art New Zealand* in 1991, is reprinted in this book.

Reproduced here is a representative selection of Goldie's work, ranging from 1886 to 1941 – a career spanning more than fifty years. The text presents an account of Goldie's life and work drawn from documentary sources, followed by a consideration of the artist's posthumous fortunes and the varied and sometimes contradictory later twentieth-century attitudes to his works. Ngahuia Te Awekotuku contributes an essay on tā moko, the depiction of which is central to Goldie's *œuvre,* while David J. Wise analyses Goldie's technique. A selection of historical writings by and about Goldie is followed by a record of the paintings he exhibited during his lifetime.

Goldie is New Zealand's 'Old Master'. Museums and individual owners will continue to treasure his works, while his stature as the country's paramount academic painter of the early twentieth century will undoubtedly be re-evaluated by successive generations. As an *Auckland Star* columnist predicted in 1935: 'It is a hard word to say, but this eminent New Zealand artist will be known long after the present generation is tucked away – and forgotten. ... The others may not be known in 2035 A.D.'[2]

Goldie paintings in the Auckland Art Gallery storeroom, all of which have lost their original frames ('Artist Goldie – is he really all that good?', Auckland Star, *3 November 1973).*

early life

Charles Frederick Goldie was born in Auckland, New Zealand, on 20 October 1870. The second of eight children born to David Goldie and his wife, Maria Partington, he was second-generation colonial on both sides. His father was born in Hobart and by 1870 was a timber merchant in Auckland. Maria Partington was born in Auckland, the daughter of Charles Frederick Partington, builder of the landmark Auckland windmill demolished in 1950. David and Maria named the boy after his maternal grandfather, who had combined amateur artistic pursuits with running a prosperous flour-mill and biscuit factory.[1] The Goldie family would eventually comprise five sons: David Arthur, Charles Frederick, William Herbert, Harry Tinsley and Frank Percy; and three daughters, Alice Eveline (Emmie), Ethel May (Tot) and Violet Elsie (Else).

At the time of Charles's birth the family was living in Albert Street, but later moved into the purpose-built mansion 'Velitoa', 47 Pitt Street. In the 1890s the family built yet another palatial residence, 'Maratea', on the shores of Lake Pupuke at Milford. David Goldie eventually owned three of Auckland's timber mills, supplying much of the last remaining kauri timber to the flourishing building industry. His political career commenced in 1874 with election to the Auckland Provincial Council, and in 1879 he entered the House of Representatives. He was also a City Councillor and commenced his duties as Auckland's Mayor late in 1898, when he instituted a ruthless restructuring of the Auckland City Council.[2] In both local and national politics he was famed for his obsessive concern with economic monitoring. Goldie belonged to the Primitive Methodist sect as well as the Order of the Good Templars, both institutions insisting on total abstinence from alcohol. Such was the strength of his convictions that early in 1901 he preferred to resign as Mayor of Auckland, handing over to the aged Sir John Logan Campbell, rather than propose an alcoholic toast to the visiting Duke and Duchess of Cornwall and York.

The demands of running his business, conducting a political career and supervising the Alexandra Street Sunday School meant that David Goldie had little time to devote to his family. Instead it was the permissive influence of 'Mater', Maria Goldie, that held sway in the elegant Pitt Street town house. According to Eliot Davis, Charles's schoolmate at Auckland Grammar, 'the old gentleman was very religiously minded and was a strong temperance advocate, but not so his family.' Eliot had a crush on Charles's sister Emmie and was a frequent visitor to Pitt Street.

> We had the best fun always on Tuesday and Friday nights, when the old man was down at the Alexander [sic] Street Methodist Hall, either teaching Bible Class or holding a religious service. Sometimes he would come home half an hour earlier than we expected him. That would necessitate a quick change-over from 'Postman's Knock' to reading books or singing at the piano.[3]

More about this cultured home life emerges from a collection of love letters written by a teenaged neighbour of the Goldies, who also frequented Maria Goldie's soirées.[4] Nell Chew, whose father was the minister of the Beresford Street Congregational Church, enjoyed the company of the Goldies and refers to Charles's artistic accomplishments on several occasions. She describes rounders and tennis in the yard adjacent to the Chews' house, and evening concerts and impromptu fancy dress parties at 'Velitoa'.

Late in 1887 Nell wrote that 'Charlie Goldie and I are immense chums. ... He has just turned 17 and is remarkably clever ... and is always sending me flowers and little paintings.'[5] In a later letter, written when Charles was

21 years old, Nell reveals the young man's growing determination to leave Auckland.

> Charles Goldie has distinguished himself more than ever this time. Really, Will, I believe that boy is a genius. Steele, his master, says he certainly is. I think his father is going to send him to Paris next year. He is just 20 [sic]. His father belongs to the Methodist persuasion, and doesn't quite approve of Paris, or even sending one of his children away to devote time altogether to art; but his mother is determined, and as everybody is raving over Charlie, he [David Goldie] is beginning to see that something should be done, especially as Charlie seems to show rather a mania to get away, to say the least, for he says he will simply sell all his pictures and go away on his own hook as soon as he reaches 21. He has been offered good prices for all his paintings already, so that he can sell them if he wants. His father has loads of money, but they say he is awfully close fisted.[6]

Maria apparently confided in her young friends, for Nell writes about Mrs Goldie's discontent ('married for money and position – I have long since come to find that out, and it has not been altogether a happy marriage') and the divided nature of the family.

> Emmie and Tottie know full well that it was not a well chosen match – their father and mother's. Mrs Goldie in Church of England – Mr Goldie, Methodist – strong – and one half of the children go with her & the other half with him, and as you may imagine, it is not a happy state of affairs.[7]

The older boys at least came under the sway of the Primitive Methodists, playing a prominent role in cultural jamborees on behalf of the Alexandra Street Sunday School. Arthur Goldie's model of Bean Rock Lighthouse won first prize when it was exhibited at the Sunday Schools' Industrial Exhibition in November 1886. Together with his younger brother William, Charles exhibited still life paintings 'which would delight the heart of the most æsthetic *habitué* of South Kensington'.[8] One showed 'a group of Maori curios [which] possesses transcendant artistic merit, and would not be out of place in any art gallery in the world'. Charles's particular brainchild formed a category on its own: a 'museum' devoted to 'curios, ornithological and entomological specimens.'

an artist emerges

'Master Goldie' first came to the attention of Auckland's art world in April 1885, when the Auckland Society of Arts awarded the schoolboy second prize and a certificate of merit for a drawing in the category 'Shaded Study from the Round'. Later that same year he won another prize, a letter of commendation, for an unidentified drawing exhibited with student works at the rival New Zealand Art Students' Association. The following year Goldie showed his first attempt at oil painting, a *Study of Still Life,* which received third placing in the Society of Arts' competition. Finally, at the Art Students' second exhibition later in 1886, he received a bronze medal for the 'best study of still life, New Zealand subject'. Depicting 'Maori carvings, mere, baler, matting, and tui-bird', the watercolour is probably the accomplished work reproduced in this book [p.59].

Auckland artist Kennett Watkins was founder and president of the New Zealand Art Students' Association, established in 1883 as an alternative to the Society of Arts. Instead of the loan collections of dubious European works, which accompanied local work at the Society exhibitions, the Art Students mounted two major loan collections of Māori artefacts drawn from private collections.[1] Goldie's medal-winning piece in 1886 was an entry in the category of 'Drawings of Maori Carvings, Mats and Implements': the Art Students' interest in Māori art was primarily as a source for Pākehā artists. Māori visitors to the exhibition were in their turn entranced by Anton Seuffert's scenes of Māori life, intricately inlaid in native timbers. Watkins also served as director of the Auckland Free School of Arts, established by Sir John Logan Campbell in 1878.[2] Although none of Watkins's student registers have survived, two early watercolours by Goldie suggest that he probably studied at this school, which was located in the Auckland Museum in Princes Street. The superb cloak depicted in Goldie's watercolour, a kaitaka with tāniko borders, is still in the collection of Auckland Museum.[3]

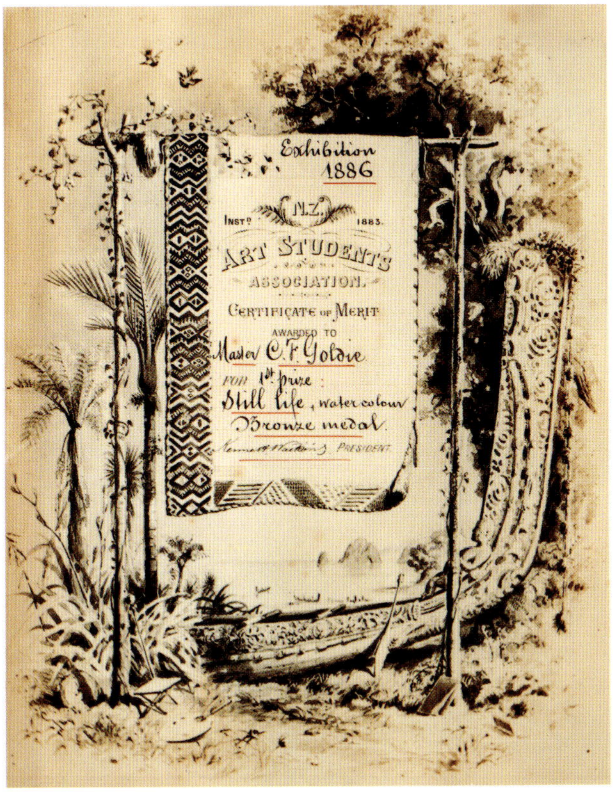

Goldie was involved in a second organisation which rivalled the Auckland Society of Arts. The Auckland Academy of Art was founded in 1889, with L. J. Steele as president and H. P. Sealy as secretary.[4] Like the earlier Art Students, this was another patriotic group intent on promoting New Zealand content in New Zealand art 'before the last kauri tree and ponga fern shall have fallen before the ruthless axe of the settler, and the Maori and his handiwork alike shall have become a thing of the past.'[5] The membership stood at around 100, mostly comprising younger students such as Sealy and his friend Tom Ryan but also including leading citizens such as Sir George Grey and Sir Maurice O'Rorke. The Academy's inaugural exhibition was held in April 1890, the month preceding the Society of Arts' annual showing, in Steele and Watkins's studio on the fourth floor of the Victoria Arcade. 'Perhaps there was a touch of Bohemia in the air which affected people,' remarked one commentator of the lively opening party, so unlike the staid conversaziones of the older Society.[6]

While pride of place was accorded to Steele and Watkins's large history painting, *The Blowing up of the Boyd,*[7] Goldie's still life attracted the critic's attention:

> It represents military helmet, old flintlock holster pistol, spurs, scimitar in brass case, and water bottle. A piece of old tapestry and crimson curtain form the background, while the weapons of war and the fold of the curtain are excellently managed and painted.[8]

Exhibited the following month with the Auckland Society of Arts, *Souvenirs from the Field of Battle* was acknowledged as 'without doubt the best piece of still life work in the Exhibition'.[9] Goldie had hoped to enter the painting for competition, but as a previously exhibited work it was automatically ineligible. Instead the prize for still life went to a Christchurch artist.

Goldie determined on producing a real *tour de force* of still life, making sure its first showing was with the Society of Arts. The painting depicted snapper and mullet displayed on a marble slab, next to a bowl of live goldfish [p.61]. The notoriously cranky critic from the *Star* thought the fish 'wonderfully well painted, the iridescence being especially good' but was less happy with Goldie's fishbowl.

> Of the drawing of a glass bowl of goldfish it is better to say as little as possible. How such a clever young man could half ruin a good picture by such shockingly incompetent perspective is extraordinary indeed. Had it not been for this Mr Goldie must infallibly have taken the prize for still life.[10]

Certificate of merit, New Zealand Art Students' Association, designed by Kennett Watkins (Goldie Scrapbook XI, p.32, Auckland Museum).

Other critics and the admiring public at large were puzzled by the award of the medal for still life to Miss E. G. Culliford, an art student from Christchurch, with Goldie taking no more than an 'honourable mention'. The *Herald* thought Goldie had been disqualified on two grounds: 'that he had already received the highest honour in the same section in which he competed, a couple of years ago; secondly, that a bowl with goldfish could not come under the term, "still life".'[11] Bickering over the prizes was not restricted to Goldie's entry. In the original prize list Miss Culliford gained a bronze for her landscape, but a protest over her depiction of gorse (a non-indigenous foliage) was upheld and her medal revoked.

The fish painting appeared again at the second exhibition of the Academy of Art, held in December 1891 in the Choral Hall in Symonds Street – the same venue used by the Society of Arts. By now secretary of the Academy, Goldie supervised the hanging of the works and decoration of the hall with the usual native foliage. During the year he had painted another still life with a local flavour: *Study of Native Birds*. 'The group of birds comprises pigeon, kaka, wild duck, and landrail, placed on a plain table. The birds are surrounded by sporting accoutrements, gun and bag, and old velvet shooting jacket. The grouping is artistic, and the colouring harmonious and true to nature.'[12] The fish painting had been somewhat modified since its earlier showing:

> It has been considerably improved and retouched generally. The slab on which the fish rest has been re-marbled, and the reflected light on the curtain, which forms the background, has been improved.[13]

Study of Native Birds received the Academy's bronze medal and, together with the fish painting, proved the popular favourite of the exhibition. Among the admirers of Goldie's still life paintings was Sir George Grey, former Governor and Premier, who 'seriously advised Mr David Goldie to allow his son to follow his best as an artist, instead of training him for commercial life'.[14] Goldie was known to sneak away from his clerical work at the paternal timber mill, to spend time in Steele's studio. It may well have been the older painter who prompted Sir George's advice to David Goldie.

Goldie understandably stood aloof from the following year's exhibition of the Society of Arts. He was busy preparing for his overseas education, for which he had settled on Paris. Steele had trained at the Ecole des Beaux-Arts and subsequently worked as an artist in Paris, delighting Goldie with his tales of Bohemian life in the great city. Goldie also painted two outstanding works which appeared at the Academy's third and final exhibition of December 1892. One was an exquisite landscape depicting fern trees in Cemetery Gully, the area beneath the present Grafton Bridge, which received rave reviews for its exceptional detail [p.62]. And for the first time he entered a work in the category of 'Maori Head', a depiction of Kāwhena from Māngere (known also as Johnny Coffin) [p.63].[15] This is Goldie's first recorded Māori portrait and drew the following comment from the *Star*'s jaded reviewer.

> Not knowing the original, one cannot say whether it is a good portrait of the individual or the reverse, but as a picture of a type it is fair. The painter has managed to fix in the eyes something of that expression of conscious mental inferiority which lurks in the eyes of the most intelligent of the lower animals and in semi-civilised man. He, however, has had some trouble to know what to do with his light. The figuring on the mat is a careful piece of work, and the effect is very successful.[16]

The writer evidently did not anticipate Kāwhena numbering among the readers of his column. In the Academy's list of prizes, the result of a democratic ballot among the members, Goldie received a silver medal for both *New Zealand Trees* and *Kawhena*.

Goldie missed the exhibition, receiving his medals *in absentia,* for he had already left Auckland. His first port of call was Sydney, where in late November he attempted to sell his still life paintings through Callan and Sons, prominent art dealers in George Street.

> Mr C. F. Goldie, a young New Zealand artist of considerable promise, who has recently arrived in Sydney, brought with him two remarkably fine paintings of New Zealand still life. One of the pictures has for its subject a collection of New Zealand fish lying on a marble slab; and the subject of the other is a collection of New Zealand birds, with the fowling piece and sportsman's bag. The pictures are very deserving efforts, and the details are supplied with a great amount of delicacy and reality.[17]

Perhaps Goldie was inspecting the possibilities of Sydney as a residence, once he had completed his European education. He would certainly have visited the National Gallery of New South Wales, then Australia's premier art gallery with a collection of oil paintings especially strong in British work, including Ford Madox Brown, Sir Frederick Leighton and J. E. Millais.[18] The most celebrated piece at the time was Sir Edward Poynter's enormous historical canvas *The Visit of the Queen of Sheba to King Solomon* (1890), acquired in 1892.[19] A constant crush of onlookers filled the north end of the British court, admiring and discussing the latest acquisition. One of Sydney's modern French paintings must also have intrigued the young artist, evocative of the Parisian adventure on which he was embarking. This was François Sallé's *Cours d'anatomie à l'Ecole des Beaux-Arts à Paris,* a medal-winning painting from the Salon of 1888. Pondering this depiction of French art students at their anatomy class, Goldie must instinctively have known that a 'continental' education would be essential in order to make a mark resembling anything like that achieved in Sydney by Poynter's grand picture.

the académie julian, paris

The 22-year-old New Zealander enrolled at the cosmopolitan Académie Julian on 3 July 1893.[1] His first address in Paris was the Hotel de l'Univers at 10 Rue Croix-des-Petits-Champs, an accommodation house popular with English-speaking students at the Académie. While H. P. Sealy's later reminiscences claimed that fellow-Aucklanders Tom (Darby) Ryan and Sealy both studied together with Goldie at the Académie, the school's registers show that Ryan's last attendance was on 24 April 1893 and that Sealy overlapped with Goldie by only one week. Sealy, who was living at the Hotel de l'Univers when Goldie arrived, effectively passed the flame to his chum from Auckland, introducing him to the school and to the Parisian lifestyle. Sealy's entertaining account of life at the Académie is reprinted in this book (see pages 178-179). The only other New Zealand students at Julian's during Goldie's time were two from Dunedin, enrolled in a separate studio supervised by Jean-Paul Laurens and Benjamin Constant. Samuel Hales attended between March 1894 and May 1896, and A. H. O'Keeffe from June 1894 to June 1895.[2]

Following in the footsteps of Sealy and Ryan, Goldie enrolled in the studio supervised by the eminent Salon painters William Bouguereau and Gabriel Ferrier. Including occasional absences when he was away travelling and a six-month gap in 1897, Goldie's attendance at the Académie spanned a total of 4½ years, from July 1893 to January 1898. The school established by Rodolphe Julian was essentially a democratic institution where on payment of tuition fees 'women, foreigners, French citizens, fifty year olds and twelve year olds were all equally admitted without entry examination'.[3] While there were smaller rival academies, such as Colarossi's, the Académie Julian was the

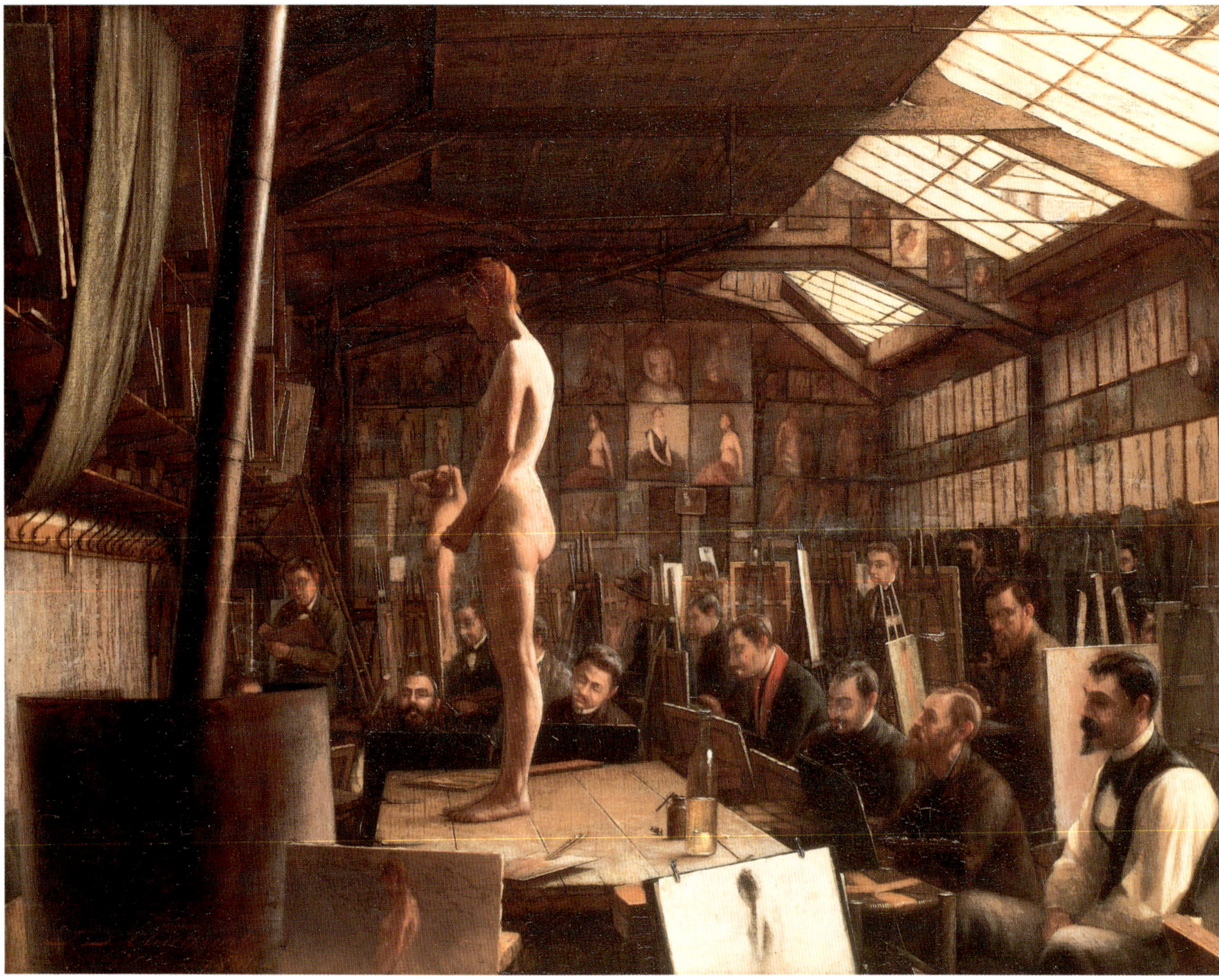

principal private art school of late nineteenth-century Paris. It was a magnet for thousands of élite foreign students, already well-educated but excluded from the official Ecole des Beaux-Arts. The Académie also acted as an important springboard for its more talented French students. For example, Henri Matisse studied at the Académie in 1891 under Bouguereau and Ferrier, who acted as his sponsors when he submitted work to the Ecole des Beaux-Arts.

Bouguereau was Julian's most august professor. Recipient of the Legion of Honour and one of the forty life-members of the Académie des Beaux-Arts of the Institut de France, Bouguereau specialised in soft-core mythological confections which he sold for staggering sums to American millionaires.

> [Bouguereau] had an absolute horror of what we call realism, and always said that reality is charming when it borrows a gleam of poetry from the imagination. And if he had heard it whispered (for no one would have ever dared to say it openly to him) that ugliness is also a part of nature, he would have retorted, with Voltaire, that there are a host of things in nature that Art, that supremely selective discipline, should leave there.[4]

Ferrier, professor on alternate months, was one of the most sought-after muralists of the Belle Epoque. His decorative compositions of seductive women adorned buildings throughout France, including the dining room of the Hôtel du palais d'Orsay (now the restaurant of the Musée d'Orsay). Other masters from whom Goldie claimed to receive tuition (listed by Sealy as Constant, Doucet, Baschet, Schommer and Bramtot) were probably standing

American artist J. D. Chalfant's 1891 depiction of Bouguereau's studio at the Académie Julian (oil on panel, 285 x 368 mm, Fine Arts Museums of San Francisco, gift of Mr and Mrs John D. Rockefeller 3rd).

in for the usual professors.[5] The two known photographs of Goldie at the Académie show him among groups of students posing with Ferrier (c.1896) and Bouguereau (c.1897).

Composition sketches (*esquisses*) were produced weekly, on a topic nominated by the professor, with the winners taking precedence in choosing their places in front of the model. Biblical incidents were favourite topics for the sketches, as exemplified by Goldie's *The Finding of Moses* [p.70] and *The Betrayal of Christ* [p.71]. The really important competitions were the Académie's monthly *concours* of work by the 300-odd students of the combined studios, judged by the entire teaching staff. Goldie is regularly listed as a runner-up, initially in the category of figure drawing and later for painting. His first significant prize at the Académie came in December 1895, when he was jointly awarded a 50-franc prize for figure drawing in the school's monthly competition.[6] Goldie 'upgraded' this 50-franc prize by telling his family back in Auckland that he had won a gold medal against 300 competitors.[7] He finally won his medal in December 1896, coming first-equal (with the French student Georges Boisselier) for a painting of a male torso. Goldie and Boisselier received an additional cash prize of 150 francs.[8] Such prizes were invaluable, for they allowed talented students to cover much of their tuition costs. The full annual fee was 300 francs, allowing morning and afternoon attendance at the Académie. Goldie usually attended for the full day, although there were periods in which he reduced his attendance to morning classes only. Either funds were running low, or he had decided to devote his afternoons to the traditional activity of making copies in the museums.

After purchasing an appropriately sized canvas from Sennelier's art-supply shop on the Quai Voltaire, Goldie would cross the river to the great Musée du Louvre. In addition to a number of paintings by Rembrandt, he copied works by Andrea del Sarto, Fragonard, Tiepolo, Ribera, Goya, Prud'hon [p.72] and Millet.[9] He also made a careful copy of perhaps the most famous French history painting of all, Théodore Géricault's *Raft of the Medusa* [p.73]. Other copies were made in the Musée du Luxembourg, the state gallery of contemporary French art which was then installed in the Orangerie of the Palais du Luxembourg. One of Goldie's larger Parisian copies was of René Xavier Prinet's *Le Bain* of 1888, a work by a younger artist which had recently been added to the Luxembourg [p.67].[10] Most of the paintings displayed there were by eminent practitioners, including his teachers at the Académie Julian. The artistic *cause célèbre* of 1894 was Gustave Caillebotte's enormous bequest of Impressionist paintings to the Luxembourg, initially refused by the state. Goldie remembered this episode as 'The Battle of the Schools', making translations of Bouguereau and colleagues' attacks on the Impressionists in support of his own attack on the modernists of 1930s Auckland.[11] What Goldie preferred not to remember was that by 1897, when he was copying *Le Bain,* the Caillebotte collection had already been accepted into the Luxembourg.

life in paris

In 1894 Goldie moved south of the Seine to Montparnasse, where he found lodgings at 5 Rue Campagne Première. This was in the heart of the artists' quarter, close to the Académie Julian as well as to the boulevard cafés where one could sip an absinthe and watch the Latin Quarter flowing by. While the standard art-student uniform was corduroy trousers and blouse, the denizens of Bohemia vied with each other for originality of attire and demeanour. One mid-1890s fad involved the emulation of seventeenth-century paintings, the aim being to look as if you had just stepped out of a painting by Velazquez or Rembrandt.

Happy the wag who closest approximates the great Spaniard in the 'arrangement' of his beard; or whose nose is long enough to rival the beaks of those solemn old Dutchmen, too dignified to have ever lived outside the vistas of an art gallery![1]

A particularly *fin-de-siècle* highlight of the art student's calendar was the notorious Quat'z'Arts Ball, held each spring at the Moulin Rouge. Open to all bona fide students of the Fine Arts (painting, sculpture, architecture and engraving) at the nominal admission fee of 1.5 francs, the first ball took place in 1893. Although he missed this inaugural ball, which 'took on rather too free-and-easy an aspect for even Paris', Goldie must have enjoyed the carnivalesque event in subsequent years.[2] Another tradition was the annual banquet offered by the pupils to their professors, held in December at the Grand-Véfour at a cost of 15 francs a head.

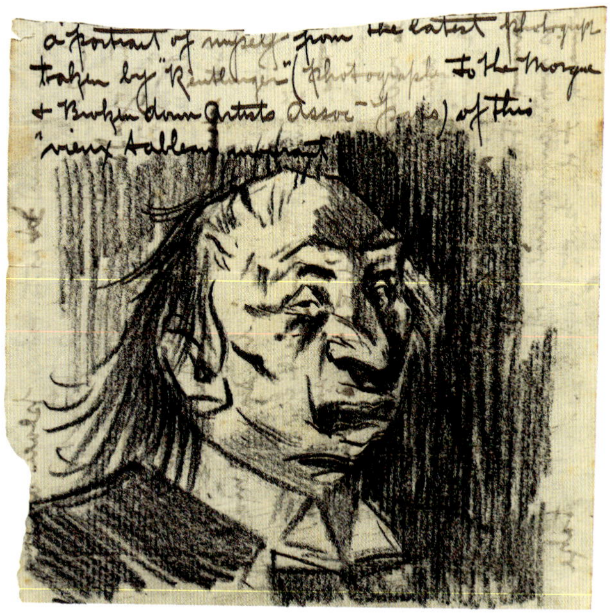

Although he was noted for his 'gossipy letters' to friends, little that Goldie wrote in Paris appears to have survived.[3] All we have are several tantalising manuscript fragments, preserved on the reverse of illustrations excised from letters to his friend Grace Hesketh.[4] Apparently executed while in the grips of a monumental hangover, the drawings are caricatured self-portraits. One is captioned 'a portrait of myself from the latest photograph taken by "Reutlinger" (photographer to the Morgue & broken down Artists Assoc – Paris) of this "vieux tableau mourant".'[5] The tantalisingly incomplete text on the reverse outlines an outlandish picnic, of 'Roti de cheval à la sauce souris' (roast horse with mouse sauce) and 'ragoût de rat aux pommes' (rat stew with apples) washed down with *vin ordinaire*. He refers to outings in the Bois de Boulogne and 'the penny steamboat up the Seine'. Clearly, Goldie was enjoying the leisure offered by Paris.

The one complete portion of text reveals a joking story for fellow-students horrified by the idea of his returning to New Zealand.

> They say 'Oh, you'll never be able to settle down on that desert island.' It is true that they have very peculiar ideas as regards New Zealand & look upon it as a very uncivilised dead & alive country. They suppose that we all live in mud huts in the back woods & that we are all more or less tattooed & in fact are simply nothing but half civilised savages. I think it awfully good fun & rather encourage them in the arguments than correct them. I tell them that I would have been tatooed [sic] only that when my turn came or rather just previous the tatooer of our tribe was called away to arrange a syndicate for the lighting by electricity of our forests so that the king a great sportsman might hunt the 'moa' (they don't know that this creature is extinct by night as well as day).[6]

By his own account, Goldie was also a keen sportsman. He later related how he had helped the Olympic Football Club in Paris beat the visiting Oxford University team by one point.[7]

The only identified friend of Goldie's in Paris is an English student at the Académie, Joseph Kirkpatrick. Kirkpatrick was another achiever at the school, winning a medal and 150-franc prize in 1894 and a frequent runner-up alongside Goldie. He lived in Rue Delambre, close to Goldie, and the two students are shown together in a group photograph of around 1896.[8] This is the probable date of Goldie's portrait of Kirkpatrick, who finished at the Académie in mid-1896. The portrait apparently returned to New Zealand,

'A portrait of myself', Paris, around 1897 (Alexander Turnbull Library, Wellington).

where it was used as an illustration in Sealy's 1901 essay on Goldie.[9] An occasional visitor to Paris was his brother William Goldie, a medical student in Edinburgh during the period Charles spent in Paris. William first visited Paris in August 1893, soon after Charles had arrived, when they made sketching expeditions around Paris and environs.

Charles made an expedition to Italy in April and May 1894, possibly in the company of William. The inscriptions on surviving oil sketches indicate a leisurely progression from the south of France (*Toulon 10/4/94*) [p.64] to the Italian riviera (*Genoa 19/4/94*) [p.64], then on to Pompei and Venice. Charles was back in Paris by mid-June, in time for the final three weeks of studio work. The following year he visited Belgium en route for England, for a Rembrandt copy made in the Royal Gallery at Antwerp is dated *29/6/95* [p.66]. A small landscape sketch inscribed *Anvers Aug 95* indicates that he spent at least a month in Great Britain and returned via Belgium. Other trips took in Holland and Germany. His listing in the 1902 *Cyclopedia of New Zealand* states that, in addition to the Louvre, Goldie had studied and copied in 'nearly all the other famous art galleries in Europe – namely, at Antwerp, Rome, Florence, Venice, Milan, Naples, Amsterdam, the Hague, Rotterdam, Haarlem, Brussels, Bruges, Dusseldorf, and London.'[10]

Even without these travels, Goldie's sojourn in Paris represented a costly undertaking in its own right. An American in Paris in 1897 worked out that an averagely-poor art student needed at least $40 a month, or $480 a year. Rent for a seventh-floor attic or poorly lit studio was estimated at $5 per month; morning coffee, lunch and dinner came to $16.50; other expenditure covered baths, tobacco, club dues, employing models, and $5 a month for 'showing rich friends about the quarter'.[11] Given that the Goldie family was also supporting William's medical studies in Edinburgh, Charles's five years abroad as an art student must have represented a significant drain on their finances. In the early years Goldie prepaid annual tuition fees, while later he paid a month or two at a time. The Académie Julian registers reveal a lengthy absence from Paris – or at least from the school – between April and September 1897. It could be at this time that, having joined William in Edinburgh, he studied under the famed Scottish portraitist Sir James Guthrie.[12]

plans for the future

Goldie made sure he kept Auckland aware of his progress in Paris. The first year he sent drawings of antique statuary for the March 1894 exhibition of the Society of Arts, works which won him yet another medal. One writer was moved to ask why the silver medal had been withheld:

> Young Mr Goldie was a pupil of Mr L. J. Steele and is at present studying at Paris at the Studio Bouguereau, and his pictures must have been passed in Paris before they could be sent here. The local jury have only awarded them their *bronze* medal, because they considered the exhibits do not come up sufficiently to their standard of art to be awarded the silver medal! There is a mistake somewhere, evidently.[1]

The following year he sent back two oils, *Defiance* and *Head of Italian,* demonstrating his progression from statue drawing to painting the live model.

News derived from letters to his family or friends appeared occasionally in the local press. Early in 1897 he indicated his intention to return, which was in turn reported in a local newspaper:

> A private letter from Mr Goldie, of Auckland, studying at Julian's Academy in Paris, states that he obtained third mention in the last

concord, the subject being a portrait, beating the previous year's winner. Mr Goldie returns to Auckland in twelve months and [plans to] establish a school of art on the lines of Julian's Academy.[2]

In other words, Goldie intended to trade on the significant investment of his European education, which for an antipodean artist represented a genuine distinction. While a number of other New Zealand artists studied art in Paris around the turn of the century, few stayed for more than a year or two. Yet Goldie characteristically expected to return to Paris before the turn of the century. He related to Grace Hesketh the wondrous predictions of a Parisian fortune-teller: 'In two years time I am according to prophecy to [be] back in Paris or London for good. And after all, it is possible that I may, provided I don't fall in love with some sweet girl. NO, I must not do that, for I don't think that an artist should marry. Don't you agree with me, Grace?'[3]

the arrival

By mid-1898 Goldie was back in Auckland, sharing a studio with his former master Louis J. Steele. The studio also hosted the teaching institution they called the 'French Academy of Art', the name evoking Julian's famous academy in Paris as well as Steele's Auckland Academy of Art from earlier in the decade. Goldie's Parisian paintings and fleamarket bric-à-brac provided additional continental *chic* to the studio's decorations. Goldie lent nine of his European works to the fine art collection at the Industrial and Mining Exhibition, Auckland's major entertainment over the summer of 1898-99. These included the impressive *Burgomaster* [p.66], copied in the Royal Gallery at Antwerp in 1895, and two other copies after Rembrandt.[1] Goldie would have remembered Lindauer's work from the Art Society and Art Students' Association's exhibitions of the 1880s; here at the Industrial Exhibition he inspected over twenty Māori portraits lent from Henry Partridge's important collection, as well as several Pākehā portraits. At this point there is no suggestion that Goldie intended to compete in the realm of portraiture. He was aiming higher, in the direction of history painting, with a painting of the young Christ in discussion with the Elders already started on a sizeable canvas [p.79]. This painting was to remain in his studio for over a decade, looming eerily in the background of many photographs.

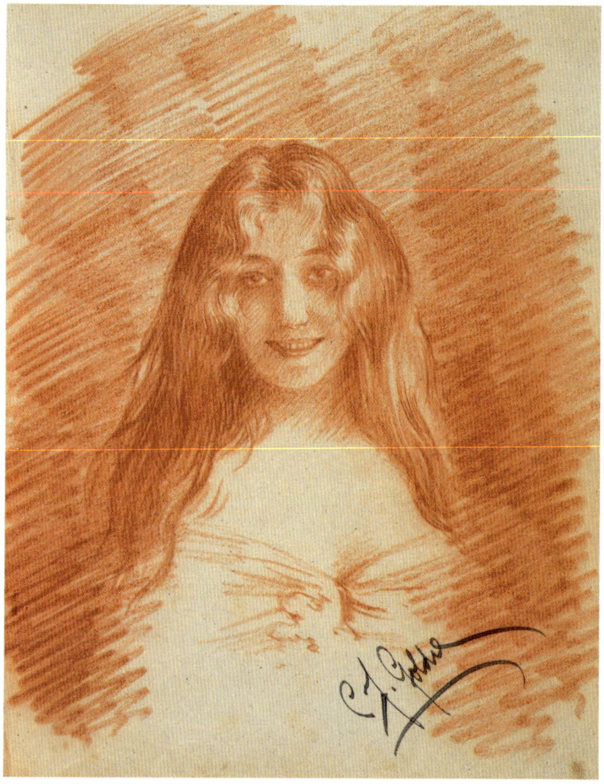

A page from Elsie Goldie's autograph book, around 1900 (conté on paper, 197 x 156 mm, Museum of New Zealand Te Papa Tongarewa, neg. no. B28422).

The principal work in progress at the French Academy was a collaboration between Goldie and Steele. Their creation, destined to become the best-known of all New Zealand 'history' paintings, was *The Arrival of the Maoris in New Zealand* [pp.80-81]. The composition was loosely based on Théodore Géricault's famous *Raft of the Medusa,* which Goldie had recently copied in the Louvre [p.73]. *The Arrival* was finally unveiled at a 'private' exhibition in October 1899, at the studio in Hobson's Buildings, Shortland Street. The *Graphic* hailed the painting as a triumph.

There are many ways in which such a subject might be treated, but we certainly think Messrs Steele and Goldie have chosen the most effective in presenting the starving voyagers from far Hawaiki at the moment when, hopeless and desperate, they catch a glimpse of land through a break in the storm. The canvas, which is a very large one, is full of suggestion. The lowering sky and dark weary waste of the waters over which the weather-

> battered canoe is making its way conveys the idea of utter loneliness, and brings into splendid relief the glint of sunshine which illuminating one corner of the picture shows to the exhausted watchers in the canoe the first, faint indication of land. But it is on the barque itself and those in it that the attention dwells first and last. There is a terrible attraction in these naked emaciated figures huddled in all different postures of agony and despair in the canoe. The artists have made a special study of each of the twenty members of the crew who are visible – a study of wonderful minuteness. The fact that the bodies are, as Maoris would be under the circumstances, almost naked has afforded the fullest opportunity of the painters to delineate the expression not merely of the face but of the entire frame, and they have made the very most of that opportunity. Famine and despair are writ large all over those scarecrows of human beings. Their ribs may be counted, showing through the thin covering of flesh, their limbs are those of skeletons, and there is a world of terrible meaning in the contortions of their bodies. The picture is certainly most gruesome. Its very artistic merit makes it so. Were it less appalling it would be less true, less a triumph for the artists. It is a picture that must command attention.[2]

Other critics also focussed on the details that related the 'appalling' tale:

> The details are put in with painstaking care, the empty gourds betokening the thirst that had set in, the broken paddles, the broken stay, and lashed and mended topside, the dripping battered prows all speaking silently of the extremities to which the explorers has been reduced.[3]

Goldie and Steele produced their epic canvas for competition under Helen Boyd's bequest of £200 for the purchase of an original work, on a New Zealand subject, by a New Zealand artist, for presentation to the Auckland Art Gallery. In November 1899 the painting fulfilled its role as 'sensation of the exhibition' at the Auckland Society of Arts, where it carried a price tag of precisely £200. Its choice by the Boyd trustees was virtually inevitable for, as the *Star* enthused, 'In tragic intensity and supreme suffering, the picture is a wonderful conception, and it possesses a historical and dramatic interest, which seem to make it desirable that the picture should be acquired for the nation – that is, of course, for the colony.'[4] The following year the picture travelled to Christchurch for the Canterbury Jubilee Industrial Exhibition of 1900, where it was again a sensational success with visitors. In 1904 the painting was lent for the Louisiana Purchase Exposition in St Louis, Missouri, where it was displayed in the company of Lindauer paintings lent by Henry Partridge.

The fame of *The Arrival* has been ensured by a more active reproductive cycle than that of any other New Zealand painting. It has been a constant favourite with the illustrated press, first appearing in a *New Zealand Graphic* of 1899 which apologised for the quality of the reproduction by blaming the poor lighting in the Choral Hall. It has also appeared in many books, including Arthur Conan Doyle's 1921 *The Wanderings of a Spiritualist,* where it was titled 'The People of Turi's Canoe, after a Voyage of Great Hardship, at last Sight the Shores of New Zealand'.[5] Other reproductions have occasionally specified a particular migration canoe, such as *The Arrival of the Tainui, 1350 A.D.*, but Goldie and Steele always advised the correct title as *The Arrival of the Maoris in New Zealand.*

The precise nature of the collaboration between Goldie and Steele remains mysterious. Olive Goldie later thought that her husband had done most of the work, an opinion backed up by Charles Henry Gunn who in 1956 remembered being one of thirty pupils at the Academy.[6] Gunn maintained that 'Steele, a tall, thin man, also posed for most of the figures' and that 'no Maoris were used as models, though Maoris often attended the studio for other paintings.' James Cowan alternatively reported that the model for the principal female figure was 'the subject of a now all-but-forgotten novel of which the theme was the reversion to native life of an educated Maori girl.'[7] This novel was Jessie Watson's *Ko Meri*, published in London in 1890, whose half-caste heroine Mary Balmain identifies as one of a doomed race.

Certainly, this one immense painting effectively launched Goldie's career. The critical attention focussed on his star pupil apparently infuriated Steele, who ended his professional association with Goldie. Goldie moved to another studio on the top floor of Hobson's Buildings, taking his students with him. The short-lived glory of the French Academy of Art had ended.

launching a career

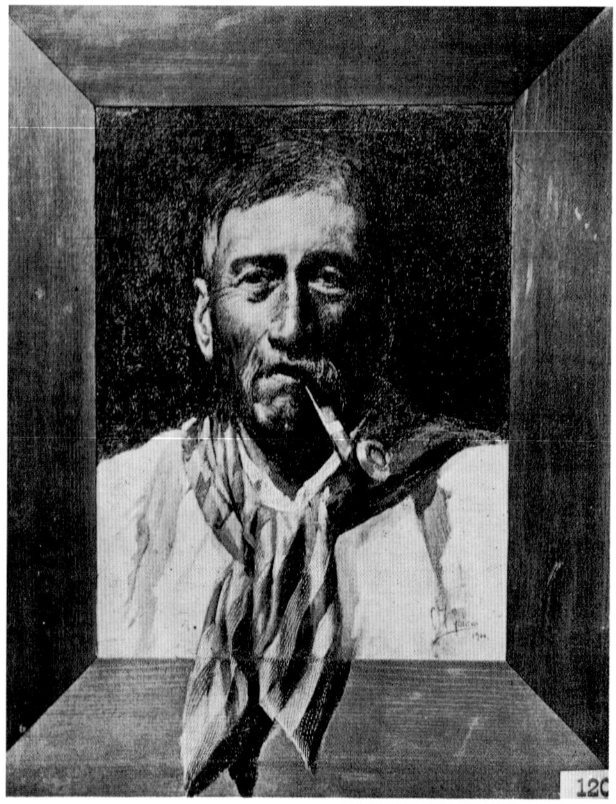

Goldie's career began in earnest in 1900, the year in which he first presented a range of five portraits – Pākehā and Māori – at the Auckland Society of Arts. Goldie's portraits received immediate acclaim, the *Graphic* reporting that: 'Nothing better has been seen here, and it is abundantly evident that in this gentleman we have an artist who in this branch of his profession may reach almost any height.'[1] Singled out for particular praise was the portrait inscribed *A mon ami, Kerry*, exhibited under the title *Portrait of C. L. Kerry, Esq.* [p.84]. Claude Lorraine Kerry was the son of Rubens Kerry, an English artist who had shown with the Royal Academy before emigrating to Auckland with his family. Claude Lorraine fulfilled his appointed destiny by becoming an artist himself, working as an illustrator. A close friend of L. J. Steele, Kerry evidently remained friendly with Goldie after the split with Steele.

Another painting was less a portrait than a genre piece, representing 'an old literary recluse, meditating in a library stocked with musty folios and old records and volumes' [p.78]:

> In one case the artist has broken away from the conventional, and produced a 'genre' picture entitled 'Of making many books there is no end, and much study is a weariness of the flesh'. The picture shows an old man deep in the mysteries of what is presumably an old volume; the book itself is not visible. There is a freshness and daring in the lighting of this picture that will appeal to everyone.[2]

Some have thought the painting could depict the Rev. Dr John Kinder, a retired churchman and bibliophile then living in Remuera. Yet if this were the case, it is odd that H. P. Sealy's essay of 1901 speaks only of 'an old man ... of the bookworm type.'[3]

The best known of the Māori portraits from 1900 is *Tamehana, from Life* [p.83], which was purchased by E. Earle Vaile and given to the Auckland Art Gallery 'as the work of a young Auckland artist, from another Auckland boy and schoolfellow'.[4] Despite Goldie's subtitle *from Life,* and Sealy's contemporary description of Tamehana as 'a well-known Native identity', the model has persistently been misidentified as Wiremu Tāmihana, the great Ngāti Hauā chief who died in 1867.[5] Goldie also painted a companion piece, a view of Tamehana's profile. Together the two paintings form a classic ethnographic

A 1900 reproduction of Tamehana, from Life, *showing the original frame (*New Zealand Illustrated Magazine, *November 1900, courtesy of Auckland Museum Library).*

pairing. A contemporary photograph of *Tamehana, from Life* reveals that Goldie painted a continuation of Tamehana's scarf over the wooden frame, a *trompe l'œil* gesture described by the *Star*: 'the necktie is brought out of the picture and over a portion of the frame, giving an additional touch of realism'.[6] The original frame survived until the 1950s but was later discarded.[7]

Another of the paintings exhibited in 1900 was *Study from Life* [p.85]. Later titled *One of the Old School,* it is a depiction of Ngāti Whātua rangatira Wātene Tautari. Although he looks much younger, Tautari was then in his later sixties. When he died at Ōrākei in 1933, aged 99, his obituary observed 'Tautari's name will be preserved in another way. He was the subject of one of Mr C. F. Goldie's well-known Maori studies which hang in the Canterbury Art Gallery.'[8] Tautari's classic Māori attire – the cloak and tiki – represents his allegiance to the 'Old School', in distinction to Tamehana's European style of dress (albeit with a flamboyant scarf). According to Sealy, Goldie intended Tautari's expression ('eyes turned upwards') to show 'the more serious side of the Maori character'.

As one commentator remarked, Goldie received 'the *grand prix* in popular estimation' for works 'far-and-away superior to anything of the kind ever seen in Auckland':

> The result of his [Parisian] training is now apparent in the very high quality of the work which has so completely astonished many of his old friends. There is a stereoscopic effect about these portraits, that when the heads are seen between the shoulders of a line of spectators, they appear to leave the canvas and to be instinct with life; and the delusion is supported by looking at the subject through a tube which hides the frame.[9]

Another enthusiastic response to Goldie's works came from an anonymous English artist 'at present residing in Auckland'.

> No one with any knowledge of art could walk through this exhibition and fail to pick out the work of the master which makes the show. The work of C. F. Goldie stands out pre-eminently. This is not only apparent in training and technique, but in the higher fields of expression – those qualities which separate the mere copyist and patient labourer on technical rules from the master. Look at the ease in the composition of his big picture, notice the tone, the value of light and shade, the force and vitality which pervades the whole work, and doubt the power behind it. Look at 'Tamehana', the Maori standing out as if he were modelled in clay; think of his knowledge and judgement which alone can give this effect .... Certainly it is the privilege of few exhibitions to show at any time so many powerful works of a single artist.[10]

The author of this letter was the itinerant sculptor Allen Hutchinson, then resident in Mount Roskill. Hutchinson, who was working on a series of relief sculptures of 'typical' Māori heads, had written to Goldie complimenting him on the 'wonderful effect of relief' he had achieved in his paintings.[11]

Goldie's growing reputation was not confined to Auckland. Three paintings were shown in September 1900 with the New Zealand Academy of Fine Arts in Wellington, while in December *The Arrival of the Maoris* played a starring role at the Canterbury Jubilee Industrial Exhibition. Goldie also lent several of his European works to Christchurch, including an accomplished competition study of a male model draped in a toga [p.74].[12] In April 1901 he exhibited *Making many Books* and *One of the Old School* with the Canterbury Society of Arts, each priced at 17 guineas. The Society purchased the latter work for their permanent collection, making it the first Goldie to enter the collection inherited by the Robert McDougall Art Gallery in Christchurch.

Of the ten paintings exhibited with the Auckland Society of Art in 1901, eight were of Māori subjects. Several resulted from a recent painting expedition to Rotorua, where he painted the young Hamiora Haupapa and an older man named Aperahama. A number of the smaller works now had prices listed in the catalogue: *Caught Napping* [p.88], showing Hamiora Haupapa asleep, was priced at 12 guineas; *Kai Paipa* [p.91] at 15 guineas. The larger works, which included his first portrait of Pātara Te Tuhi [p.86] and the portrait of William Swanson [p.94], were unpriced and possibly not intended to be sold.

One critic thought that *Kai Paipa,* 'the portrait of a well-known native woman in Auckland, smoking', would form a suitable companion to *Tamehana,* presented to the Art Gallery the previous year.[13] Another admired the 'sleepy, contemplative mood of the sitter in intense enjoyment of St. Nicotine.'[14] *Kai Paipa* was among the first paintings sold, apparently to the person who also bought the small *Suspicion* [p.90] priced at 10 guineas, for both paintings were later presented to the Russell-Cotes Art Gallery in Bournmouth, England. Colonel W. H. Allen of Honolulu, who purchased two of Allen Hutchinson's Māori portraits in plaster for presentation to the Bishop Museum, was also interested in *Patara Te Tuhi.*[15]

The venerable William Swanson, an 82-year-old family friend of the Goldies, was still serving on the parliamentary Legislative Council. Swanson was one of Auckland's early settlers, pioneering the use of timber dams to transport kauri logs from the Waitākere Ranges. At the time Swanson was

Goldie in his studio, Hobson's Buildings, 1900 (Auckland Art Gallery Toi o Tāmaki, gift of the Goldie family).

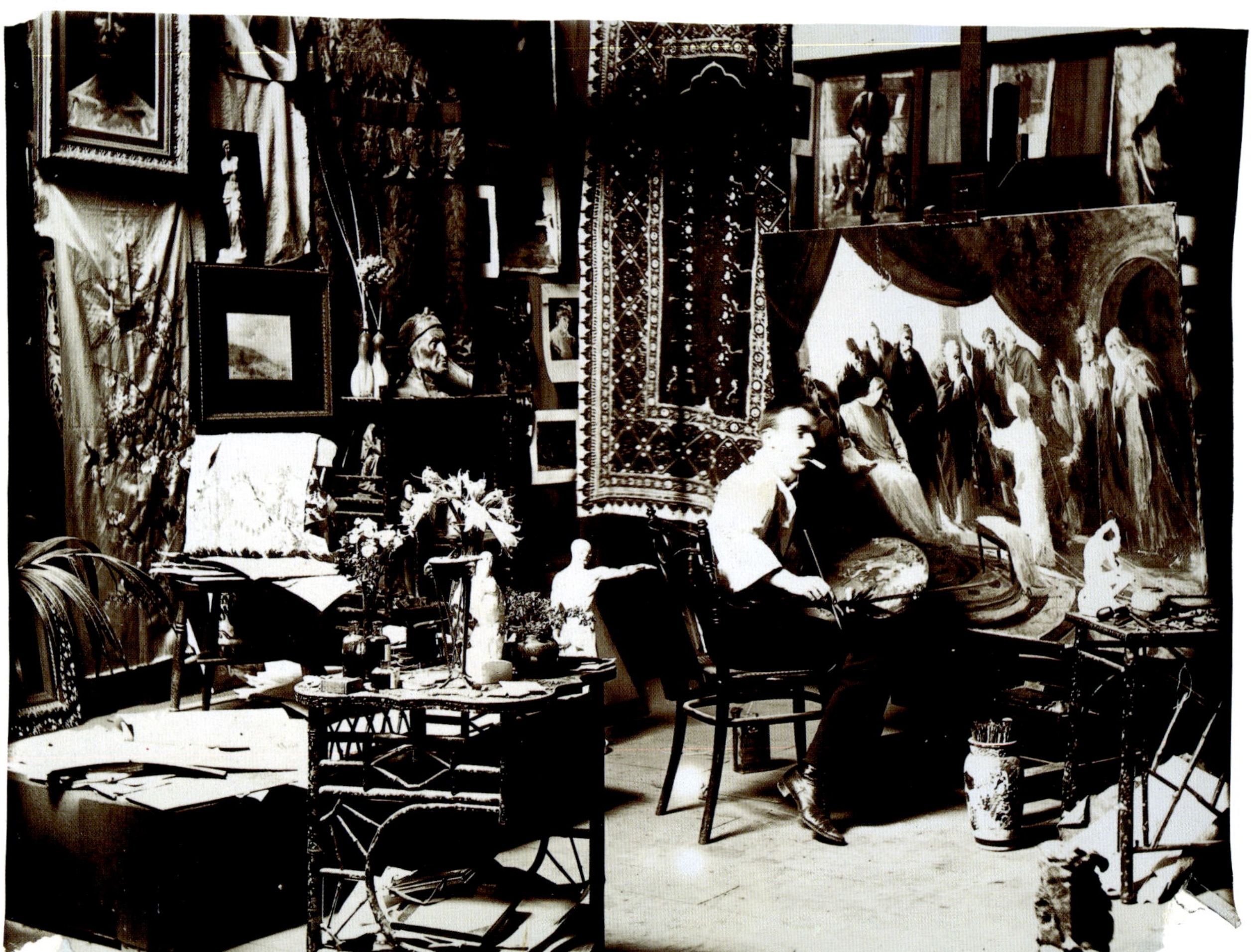

painted, a reporter visiting Goldie's studio thought 'It would be a good idea if a gallery of portraits of our leading "old identities" were painted by our Auckland artists, and secured for the city.'[16] If the work were indeed a commission it is possible that Swanson rejected it, for the painting stayed in Goldie's possession until he presented it to the Auckland Art Gallery in 1920.

The acknowledged star of Auckland's art world, Goldie's renown spread throughout the country. While this was partly the responsibility of the paintings he was exhibiting, which were duly reproduced in the illustrated press, there was an additional facet of self-promotion clearly intended to enhance his reputation as Auckland's leading painter and art teacher. This took the form of portrait photographs, of the artist posed within his opulently furnished studio. The photograph reproduced here was taken with Goldie's own camera and published in the Auckland volume of the *Cyclopedia of New Zealand* (1902) as well as in newspapers and periodicals. A similar photograph was captioned:

> The artist seems to be sacrificing to the goddess Nicotine, even while he works or pretends to work, and from the glimpse thus afforded of his comfortable, even luxurious, quarters, adorned with palms and ferns, and furnished with easy-chairs and rugs, we can well credit the statement that this is the most artistic studio south of the line.[17]

Goldie settled into the duties and privileges that attended his status as leading professional artist. His private pupils took the prizes at the annual exhibitions. He was appointed to the Auckland Art Gallery advisory board established in November 1900, and served on the committee of the Auckland Society of Arts between 1901 and 1903.[18] In Auckland's poisonous art scene, 'where many artists are not on speaking terms', Goldie's apotheosis represented a significant triumph.[19]

'noble relics'

Goldie's contemporaries regarded the 'Māori studies' as something beyond mere portraiture. Critics described them as representing 'types', in the sense of 'specimens' that required collecting before it was too late:

> It is of real importance, apart from picture-making, that the types here so ably delineated should be preserved. The originals are fast disappearing. The type of the old warrior is given in Patara Te Tuhi. The type of Patara will be extinct in a few years.[1]

In deciding to concentrate on the depiction of elderly rangatira with moko, the so-called 'noble relics of a noble race', Goldie was following a path established by Steele's Māori history paintings and portraits of tattooed chiefs. Another important influence was his brother William, who as a medical student in Edinburgh had begun clipping news items of anthropological interest while researching his thesis 'The Medical Customs and Diseases of the Polynesian, Maori and Australian Races'.[2] William returned to New Zealand in 1900 where he continued collecting material on traditional Māori medical practices, which he eventually presented in 1903 as a paper to the Auckland Institute.[3] In 1901, as a response to the census returns, William published an article contradicting the widespread predictions that the Māori were facing extinction.[4] When William died prematurely while visiting Ceylon in 1904, Charles inherited his brother's extensive library and scrapbooks of clippings and continued to collect a wide range of articles on Māori issues written by members of the recently established Polynesian Society, including Elsdon Best and S. Percy Smith, and the prolific journalist and historian James Cowan.

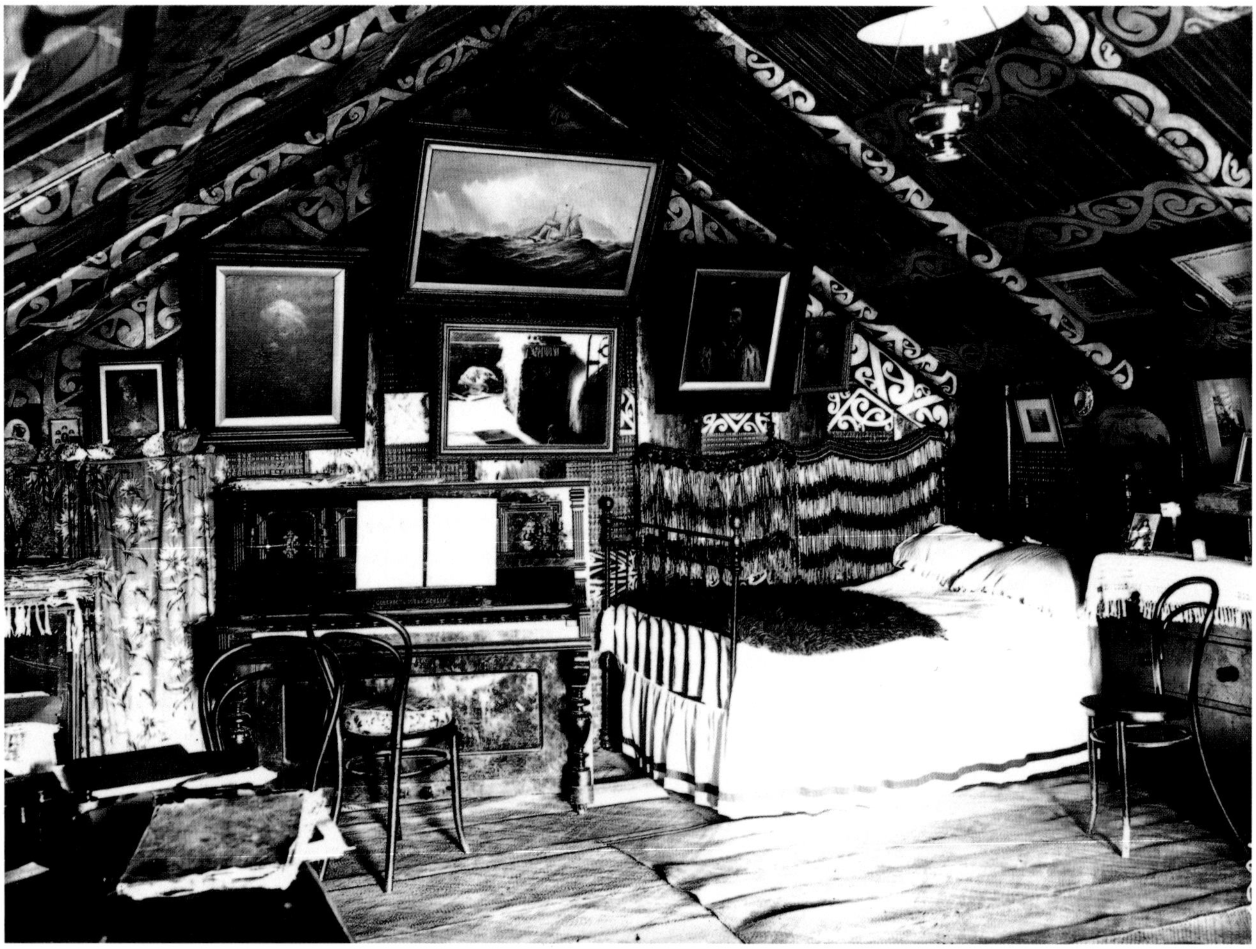

It was through Cowan that Goldie met Pātara Te Tuhi in 1901, and the Ngāti Mahuta chief became a regular model. The following year Goldie painted his first portraits of Ina Te Papatahi of Ngā Puhi [pp.96-97] who posed for him over a number of years. Another important model was Ina's cousin Harata Rewiri Tarapata, the widow of Ngāti Whātua chief Paora Tūhaere. Both Ina and Harata lived at Waipapa, the Māori hostel at Mechanics Bay which was a short walk from Goldie's studio in Hobson Street. A letter from Tarorehua Kaiwaka, addressed to Ina at Waipapa and dated 15 March 1904, suggests that Ina was assisting Goldie in persuading other models to pose. Kaiwaka sends the following message: 'kāore a Te Aho e tae atu, kua purutia e te iwi Māori kia noho' (Te Aho will not be able to attend, because the tribe has instructed him to stay). To Ina he writes: 'Ki a Ina e tai hari atu tēnā reta ki tō Pākehā' (to Ina, take this letter to your Pākehā).[5] The earliest dated portrait of Te Aho-o-te-Rangi Wharepu of Ngāti Mahuta [p.105] is unlikely to be from 1902 as dated; it must be a later replica based on a work painted in 1905.[6]

A trip to Rotorua in 1901 introduced a number of Te Arawa models, including the venerable Perema Te Pāhau [p.102] and Ahinata Te Rangitautini [p.108] both of Tūhourangi and the young Hamiora Haupapa [pp.88-89] of Ngāti Whakaue. Goldie returned to the Rotorua and Taupō region on a regular basis. The crucial go-between was Goldie's old friend Tom (Darby) Ryan, who was operating ferry services at Rotorua and subsequently at Taupō. Married to a daughter of the Ngā Puhi chief Kamariera Te Hau-Tākiri Wharepapa, Ryan lived between the Pākehā and Māori worlds. Assistance may also have been given by Alfred Warbrick, a noted guide and boat-building friend of Ryan's whose mother was of chiefly Tūhourangi descent.

Henry Winkelmann's 1899 photograph of the interior of Thomas (Darby) Ryan's house at Rotorua (Auckland Museum).

Goldie's models usually sat for him in his Auckland studio, draped in a combination of blanket and velvet, or a cloak supplied by the artist. In return they received a daily stipend which was open to negotiation, on top of which Goldie sometimes covered accommodation costs for a model from out of town. By now on first-name terms with Goldie, Te Aho-o-te-Rangi Wharepu sat on at least twenty occasions around 1905, when the artist paid him on a sliding scale according to the time taken. A full day eventually attracted £1, which he occasionally preferred to be paid in shilling coins.[7] Pātara Te Tuhi, writing in 1906, complained of his failing eyesight but nevertheless named his price as eight shillings per sitting.[8] Writing to Goldie from Te Oruoru on 1 July 1907, Kamariera Te Wharepapa outlined the following conditions:

> C F Goldie, I received your letter & very pleased. I will come but I want you to give me more for I will bring my old woman to look after me. Write as soon as you get this letter. I want you to give me 10 or 12 shillings more.[9]

And in a letter later that same year, Kamariera wrote:

> You know I am getting very old. I want a very good place to stop. I won't stop the same place where I stay before. Can you afford to give one more than 10 shillings a day.[10]

The photographs of Kamariera which Goldie took in the studio probably date from an earlier visit during the summer of 1906-07.

Pākehā visitors to the studio included barrister Robert McVeagh, a fluent Māori speaker who may have introduced Goldie to a number of Māori acquaintances. Another visitor was the composer Alfred Hill, who recorded songs from these venerable men and women. Goldie's studio became an important meeting place for 'Māori enthusiasts', as Alfred Hill explained to the Polynesianist Edward Tregear:

> Mr Goldie the artist has taken an interest in my work and has allowed me to chat with some of the old maori 'Models'. This is a haka that I got from the late chief Paul's wife who is also a relative of the great warrior Tamati Whakanena [sic]. She was present at the last stand made by Hone Heke against the British troops 59 years ago. The rythm [sic] of the Haka is intended to imitate the canter of a Horse and was sung by the Ngapuhi tribe after the death of a chief's child.
> Tururu tururu
> Tarara tarara etc
> The old lady speaks little or no English so the translation may be all at sea ... How fascinating the subject is and how one longs to get away amongst the old chiefs with their stories of older days.[11]

Thus, in addition to posing for Auckland's leading artist, Goldie's models were also serving as informants for researchers such as Tregear and Hill who were desperate for the 'real old-time stuff'. Hill thoroughly enjoyed his hours in Goldie's studio, where he conceived the best-selling song 'Waiata Poi'. Hill described how Goldie would improvise meals in the studio to sustain models or friends.

> He used as a rule to go behind a screen and prepare me a marvellous meal ... He seemed to have a restaurant behind that screen. This night there was nothing so he went out to buy something and while he was away, I sat on the sofa and a little mouse came playing on the carpet. I watched for a while and then suddenly the refrain of the poi song came into my mind. When Charlie came back I said 'Charlie, listen to this, I've got a world beater,' and I sang the refrain of the song, words and music. It was not long before I finished the whole song and I dedicated it to Charlie Goldie in memory of all the kind things he'd done for me.[12]

In 1903 Goldie was again the acknowledged star of the Society of Arts exhibition. Of his six offerings, two larger pictures were singled out for special attention: *The Widow* [p.100] and *Darby and Joan* [p.101], the latter listed as 'unfinished'. Added to Goldie's 'wonderful technique', the *Auckland Star's* critic identified 'a power of sentiment':

> An old Maori woman, with one of those strangely aristocratic, semi-Hebraic casts of countenance found alone, we believe, amongst high-born Maoris, is sitting in front of a raupo whare. The pose is characteristically well thought out, and suggests the perfect rest necessary to reminiscence and reflection. In her hands she holds a greenstone Heitiki, at which she is thoughtfully gazing. The whole face suggests in a manner indescribable in words the flood of memories naturally aroused in an aged breast by some familiar heirloom seen and loved in the days of youth, and once worn by one who has long since died. The details of the picture have been attended to with the customary care of this artist. A broken kit and a soiled towel hang to the right, while on the ground at the left are a greenstone mere, a tui feather, some mats and other relics. Through the open doorway one can see faintly the embers of a dying fire. But though each of these details is a careful study in itself, they are so managed and subordinated as in no wise to detract from the central interest of the main figure. The picture is unquestionably a fine one, perhaps the best the artist ever painted, and local effort should be made to secure this, or other of these studies of Maori life, before the generation who can alone afford models has passed away.[13]

The *Herald* commented on 'a glamour of romance woven into the paintings that appeals in a marked manner to the popular fancy'. The introduction of an architectural setting was an innovation for Goldie, echoing similar compositions by Steele. The latter artist's *Tattooing in the Olden Time* of 1894, which Goldie may have seen on his return from Paris, used the porch of a meeting house to stage the composition.[14]

A real publicity coup came in 1903 when the Countess of Ranfurly, departing a year earlier than her husband the Governor, nominated the two paintings she had admired at the Society's exhibition as her farewell present from Auckland. *Darby and Joan* and *The Widow* were purchased by popular subscription at a cost of 100 guineas each and presented to Lady Ranfurly at an enormous garden party attended by Aucklanders of all classes. In her speech, the countess acknowledged 'the two ladies who sat for the pictures', who were present at the gathering and received a round of applause. One paper reported that it was 'no secret that some of the other artists are envious, and were desirous that their landscapes should be inspected'.[15] Leonard Bell's essay 'Their Brilliant Careers', on pages 115-120, outlines the contemporary reception and later adventures of these two remarkable paintings.

The paintings chosen by the countess were quite distinct from the work of Auckland's other artists. Over a boldly brushed ground, which provided the illusion of a painterly surface, Goldie painstakingly created an immaculate, virtually photo-realist effect. He presented the paintings in distinctive kauri frames, toned various shades from bronze to black, which were produced exclusively for Goldie by Auckland framer and art dealer John Leech. In this deployment of a trademark moulding, Goldie is unique among New Zealand artists of the period. Winkelmann's photograph of the 1905 exhibition, the first to be held in the Society of Arts' new purpose-built gallery in Coburg (now Kitchener) Street opposite the main Art Gallery, reveals how these emphatic frames guaranteed visibility for Goldie's works. Not surprisingly, Goldie was the focus of attention for reviewers and caricaturists as well as the starring attraction for the visiting public.

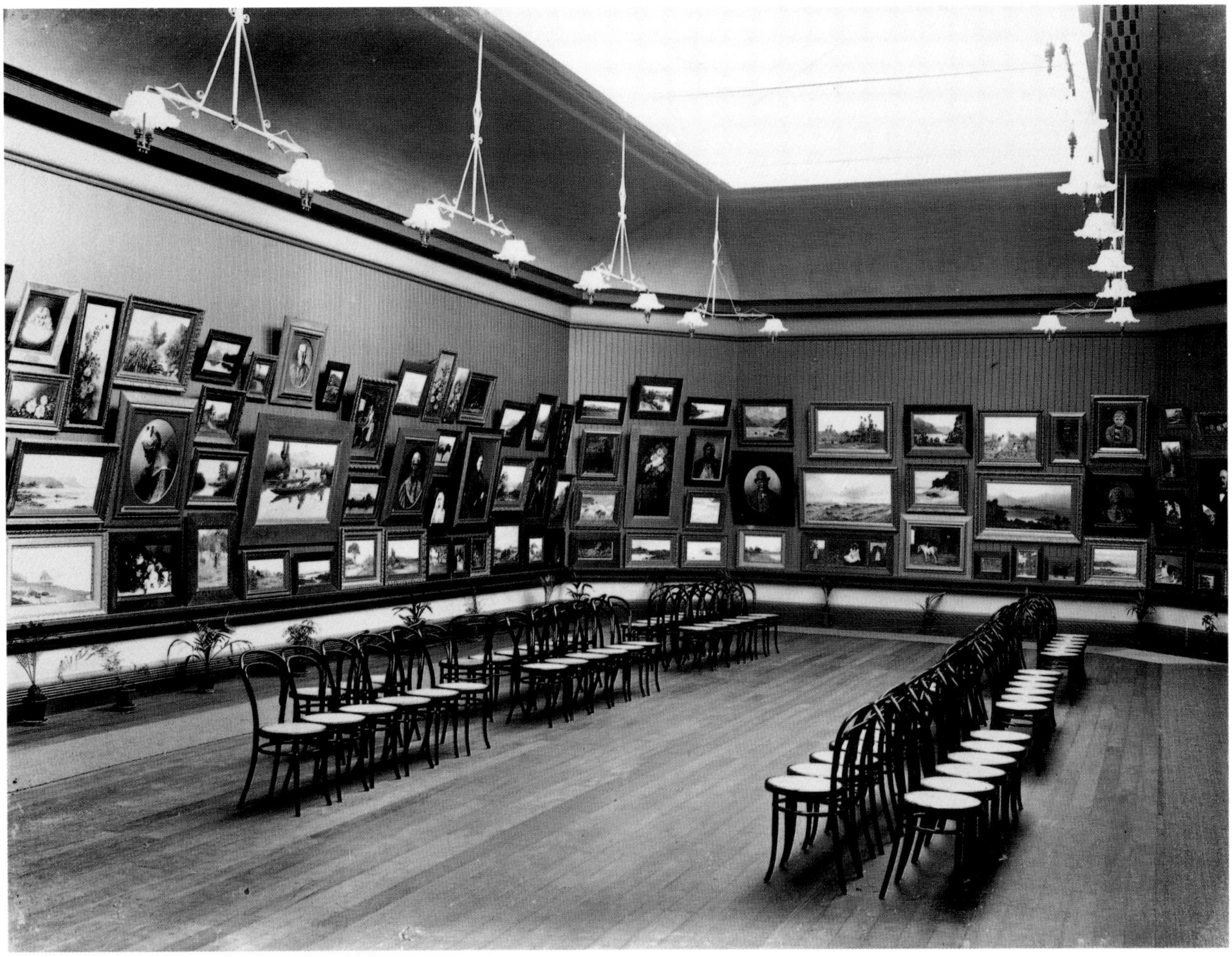

repeat performances

Of the nine paintings Goldie showed at the 1905 exhibition, four were depictions of Te Aho-o-te-Rangi Wharepu: *A Hero of Many Fights* [p.106], *Te Aho, a Noted Waikato Warrior* [p.105], *'All 'e Same t'e Pakeha'* [p.127] and *A Study* [p.104]. Two others, *Perema Te Pahau, the Bone Scraper* [p.102], priced at £31 10s and *Forty Winks,* at £35, were the only pictures priced in the catalogue, while *The memory of what has been and never more will be* [p.107] was exhibited as 'unfinished'. The latter two depicted Ina Te Papatahi. There were an additional two Pākehā portraits, one identified in the catalogue as *T. W. Leys, Esq.* [p.92] and the other simply as *Portrait,* which depicted Mrs Street of Parnell. Before the exhibition even opened, news broke that *'All 'e Same t'e Pakeha'* ('in which the old man is enjoying the joke of wearing the bowler hat of civilisation') had sold for £120, copyright included.[1] *The memory of what has been* later sold for £100, to Lizzie H. Grant, wife of South Canterbury landholder William Grant.[2]

Critics had already noted the reappearance of Ina Te Papatahi in the 1904 exhibition, with one reviewer suggesting that 'the difficulty of securing suitable models is a full excuse for artistic tautology'.[3] The 1905 pictures naturally provoked further comment in this direction, including the following from the *Star*:

Henry Winkelmann's photograph of the 1905 Auckland Society of Arts exhibition (Auckland Museum).

> How long Mr Goldie will be able to secure models is a very serious matter. The difficulty is already acute, for despite what one knows must be his anxiety in this matter, he is now practically confined to two individuals,

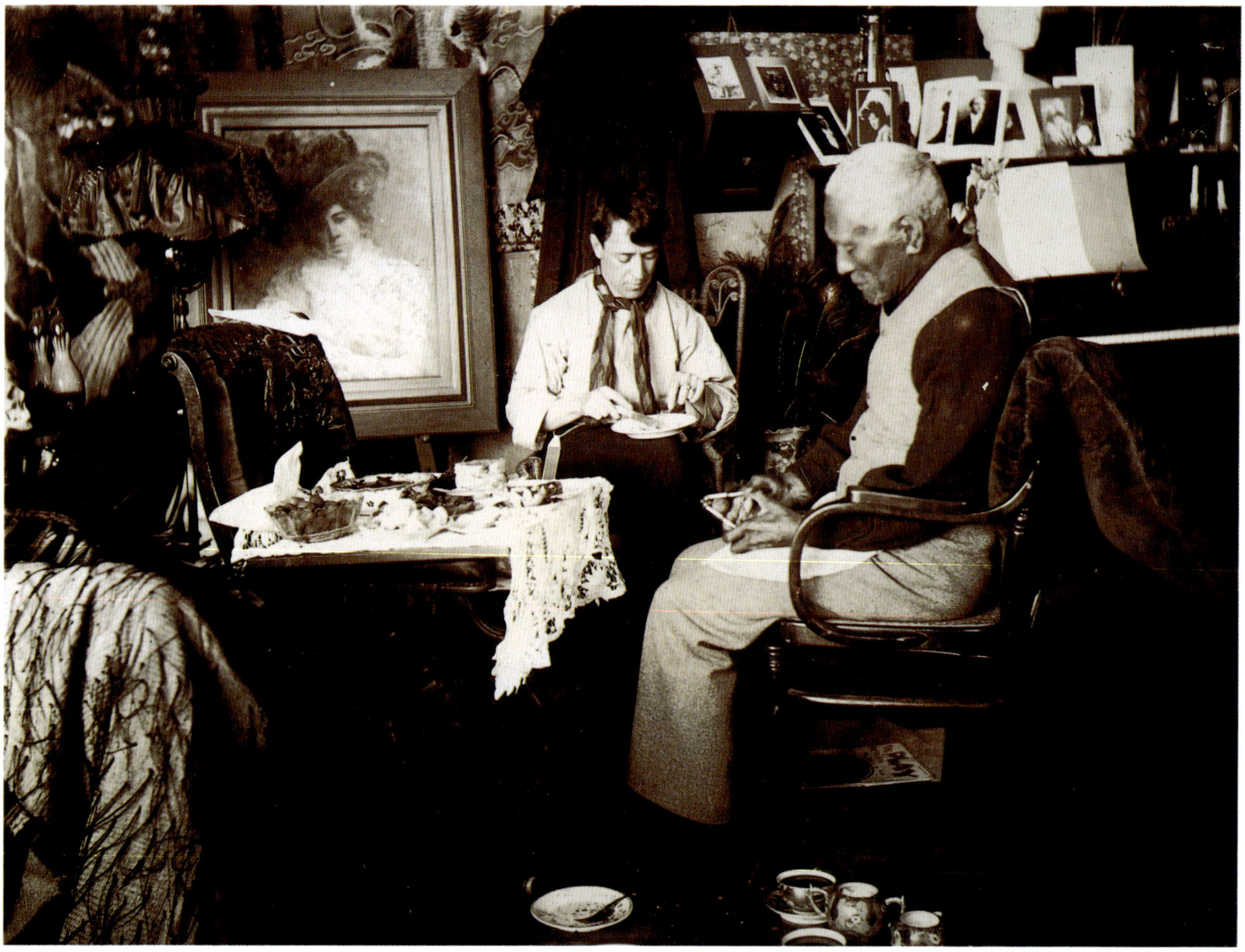

> and in the case of this well-known chieftainess who sat for two paintings this year, as well as two the year before, and two the year before that, this is already leading thoughtless people into criticism that the artist is repeating himself unduly, and issuing paintings so similar as to discount their value and that of previous work. On the surface the similarity of the most popular pictures to previous works is certainly rather striking, but it is but just to point out that this is due almost wholly to the absolute impossibility of obtaining a model, so excellent in feature and natural expression, or even of securing a casual sitting from any old time Maori whatsoever. When the model is the same, and the spirit of sadness which hangs over a dying race is the same, it is impossible for the artist to display much originality. He must be truthful, he must enter into the spirit of the past, and this spirit, therefore, must pervade every picture he paints in that vein.[4]

So far as this writer was concerned, the models' rarity value presented a strong case for the acquisition of Goldie's works for public collections. 'The time is upon us when no models whatever will be available, and it will be a thousand pities if by the purchase of pictures already secured by the artist he is not enabled to go further afield and find subjects which may offer still greater scope for his ambitions, and enable him to produce historical pictures of the finest dark-skinned race the world has ever known.'

It was in 1905 that Augustus Hamilton, Director of the Colonial Museum in Wellington, began his attempt to acquire several of Goldie's works.[5] In September 1905 he obtained Cabinet's approval to negotiate a deal

Goldie with Kamariera Te Wharepapa (Auckland Art Gallery Toi o Tāmaki, gift of the Goldie family).

with Goldie, a move apparently prompted by Henry Partridge's offer of his Lindauer Gallery 'at a fabulous price'.[6] Hamilton visited Goldie's studio, particularly admiring a 'large study' (probably *The Calm Close of Valour's Various Day* [p.128]). Goldie's eventual offer, dated 20 February 1906, revealed that the large work was still incomplete but that he was prepared to let the Government purchase four existing portraits. Goldie accompanied the offer with photographs of the works, now missing, but did not list the titles. If the Museum wanted these originals, with copyright, the price would be 200 guineas apiece; copies ('facsimiles of the originals in every respect') would cost 80 guineas each. Hamilton proposed the acquisition of four 80-guinea works spread over two years and referred the matter to the Hon. James Carroll, the minister in charge of the Museum, who in turn referred it on to Cabinet. Although there is no record in the Museum's archives, it was apparently decided not to pursue Goldie's offer.

The following year saw only three Goldie paintings exhibited at the Auckland Society of Arts. It was reported that the large piece, *The Calm Close of Valour's Various Day* [p.128], was regarded by the artist as his best work yet. This is the painting for which Te Aho-o-te-Rangi had spent many patient hours posing in the studio. 'The technique is simply marvellous,' enthused the *Graphic*, 'and it is not too much to say that in this branch of his craft Mr Goldie is probably one of the greatest masters south of the equator.'[7] The reviewer marvelled over the treatment of the hair, the tattooing, and especially the cloak, 'where every little cord stands out and shows its shadow'. Nevertheless, he concluded by suggesting that earlier works by Goldie, particularly *The Widow* and *The memory of what has been and never more will be,* had provided considerably more appeal:

> The old warrior does not stir in our breasts the immediate surge of pity as did 'The Widow'. The picture does not tell its story to heart and brain so quickly or so well, but it is none the less a painting of which Mr Goldie and the Society may be duly proud, and the possession of which we should like to see in the hands of some colonial collector or municipality.[8]

Later in 1906 Goldie finished the pair to this painting. Titled *Memories,* a depiction of Ina Te Papatahi, the painting was destined to become the favourite Goldie in the Auckland Art Gallery [p.129]. Both works were purchased by prominent Auckland businessman Alfred Nathan early in 1907, at a cost of 175 guineas apiece.[9] They first entered the Auckland Art Gallery in 1933, on loan from Emily Nathan, eventually becoming part of the Gallery's collection on Mrs Nathan's death in 1952. These were the last of the larger-scale Māori depictions produced by Goldie and the only pair that is at all comparable to the 'Ranfurly' paintings. From now on he concentrated on works employing a life-sized bust format, which he complemented with smaller studies.

enlarging the gallery

Several new models made an appearance in Goldie's 1907 offerings at the Society of Arts. Two depicted Kamariera Te Wharepapa, father-in-law to Goldie's friend Tom Ryan. *Te Hau-Takiri Wharepapa, a Chieftain of the Ngapuhi Tribe* is a frontal portrait [p.131], while the accompanying profile portrait bore the title *A Noble Relic of a Noble Race* [p.130]. The two paintings were made over the summer of 1906-07, when Goldie made a series of photographs which show Kamariera and several friends enjoying themselves in the studio. The *Herald* also informed its readers that Goldie had recently made a trip to

Taupō 'catching and transferring to canvas Maori types, which, ethnologically considered alone, are of the greatest importance'.[1] Two paintings which resulted from the Taupō visit depict Te Hei of Ngāti Raukawa, one titled *Touched by the Hand of Time,* and are both inscribed *Taupo, N.Z.* [pp.135-136]. The most unusual work was a smaller depiction of a young Māori, simply titled *A Study* [p.132]:

> Here is a striking contrast to the old chief. The young man is not only ready and able but longing to fight. He has fight in his eye, but it is not the warfare of the old campaigner and strategist, but rather the dash and vigour of the young and headstrong warrior, careless of personal consequences and recking little of the consequences to the common cause.[2]

The man has an alert expression, as if startled, which is in marked contrast to the withdrawn expression in most of Goldie's depictions of older Māori. Critical response to the new portraits was positive, although as usual the *Star* found reason to qualify its praise:

> And having thus paid due and just tribute to his genius, may one lament the weakness of this artist in signing his pictures in the centre of the canvas. It is a very serious artistic blemish, for the signature being, so to say, flung in one's face, in this way, distracts attention from the subject of the picture, and causes a feeling of distinct irritation.[3]

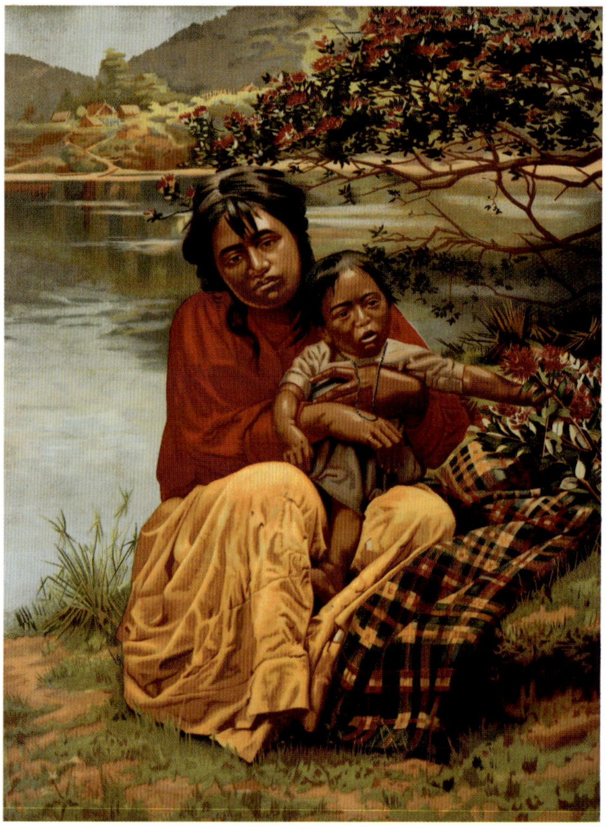

The 1902 chromolithograph Day Dreams: Christmas Time in Maoriland *(540 x 405 mm, Auckland Art Gallery Toi o Tāmaki).*

Goldie's central placement of the signature had to do with his preference for oval mounts which obscured the corners where an artist's signature usually appeared.

In 1908 a second Māori portrait finally entered the Auckland civic collection, when *Patara Te Tuhi* [p.139] was purchased by a 'committee formed to raise a citizens fund for the purchase of pictures by New Zealand artists for the Auckland Art Gallery'.[4] Perhaps it was not coincidental that the President of the Auckland Society of Arts was then E. Earle Vaile, a long-time supporter of Goldie's work who had been responsible for the Art Gallery's acquisition of *Tamehana, from Life* in 1900 [p.83].

The 1908 Auckland Society of Arts exhibition featured a total of nine paintings. Evidence of a further expedition to Rotorua are two depictions of notable figures from Te Arawa: Tikitere Mihi, chief of Ngāti Uenukukōpako at Te Ngae [p.137] and Anaha Te Rāhui, the famous carver of Ngāti Tarāwhai [p.134]. Tikitere's patriarchal beard was shaved later in 1908, when the chief posed for one of the busts commissioned by the Government from the Australian sculptor Nelson Illingworth. It seems that Goldie provided assistance to Illingworth, who was encountering extreme reluctance on the part of prospective models.[5] The subject of his first bust was none other than Pātara Te Tuhi, by now thoroughly accustomed to posing for a Pākehā artist.

Goldie frequently abstained from pricing his works exhibited with the Auckland Society of Arts, probably in order that negotiation could take place with prospective purchasers. It is the out-of-town exhibitions that reveal more of the asking prices. At the 1908 showing of the Canterbury Society of Arts he asked £105 for *Te Hau-Takiri Wharepapa* and £63 for *Touched by the Hand of Time.* On occasions, Goldie used the southern exhibitions to unveil a work not previously seen in Auckland, such as *Fire and Smoke* [p.138] which first appeared in 1908 at the Otago Art Society, priced at £52 10s. In fact,

Fire and Smoke was never seen by an Auckland audience, for it sold from the following year's Canterbury Society of Arts exhibition, at a reduced price of £47 5s. Goldie's are high prices for the time, commensurate with his status as a leading artist. Among the more expensive of the established artists, L. J. Steele usually priced works in the £50 to £75 bracket (the popular racehorse paintings) while up-and-coming stars Sydney Thompson and Horace Moore-Jones occasionally asked £100. The bulk of the work at the society exhibitions came somewhere in the £5-£10 range.

While most of these exhibited works are still extant, there are several major works that are now missing. The most significant of the lost works is *The Last Sleep,* in which Ina Te Papatahi was posed as the deceased at a tangi. It was first shown at the Auckland Society of Arts in 1908, when a published parody by a caricaturist Trevor Lloyd retitled it 'Oh tuck me in my little bed'.[6] The painting was shown early the following year in Christchurch, when the *Press* considered it to be Goldie's finest work:

> Mr Goldie's finest picture, artistically, is undoubtedly 'The Last Sleep', the title of which would have been more appropriately 'The Majesty of Death'. It is that of a Maori chieftainess lying in state, and is very finely painted indeed. The features are thrown up strongly by the note of colour in the green covering in the foreground, and huia feathers, which form a kind of coronet, in the background. Though perhaps the subject may not appeal to the majority, the work in the exhibit is marked by high artistic ability and effect.[7]

The *Lyttelton Times* reviewer instead expressed some discomfort over the subject, describing it as 'a gruesome picture'.[8] *The Last Sleep* remained in Goldie's own collection and can be seen prominently displayed in several photographs of his studio [p.26]. Ina Te Papatahi is said to have expressed alarm over how she had been depicted. This was not to do with Goldie representing her as if dead, but concerned the foreshortening which she thought made her resemble a bulldog.[9]

the other side of fame

Asked in 1908 to name the 'six best New Zealand artists', readers of the *Graphic* delivered a resounding vote for Goldie.

> The votes were spread over thirty-nine different artists, but the plebiscite leaves no doubt as to the six who, in the opinion of our readers, are most deserving of honour. The following are the six who are crowned with 'Graphic' bays, along with the percentage of votes received by them:— C. F. Goldie 90 per cent., C. H. Worsley 70, John Gully 60, C. Bloomfield [sic] 45, W. Wright 35, G. E. Butler 30. Those next in order, receiving from 20 to 25 per cent of the total votes, were:—Kenneth [sic] Watkins, Lindauer, F. Wright, E. W. Payton, L. J. Steele, Miss Bloomfield, and Mrs Walrond.[1]

Goldie's popular fame was undoubtedly linked to the frequency with which his paintings were reproduced in the illustrated press. At the luxury end of the reproductive chain were the chromolithographic prints which have since become collectors' items in their own right. Produced by a range of illustrated journals, these were printed on special art paper and were framed as 'Goldies' for more humble residences. Popular examples included *Day Dreams* in 1902,[2] *A Hot Day* in 1904,[3] *The memory of what has been and never more will be* in 1905,[4] and perennial favourite, *A Good Joke (All 'e same t'e Pakeha),* which first appeared in 1905 [p.48].[5]

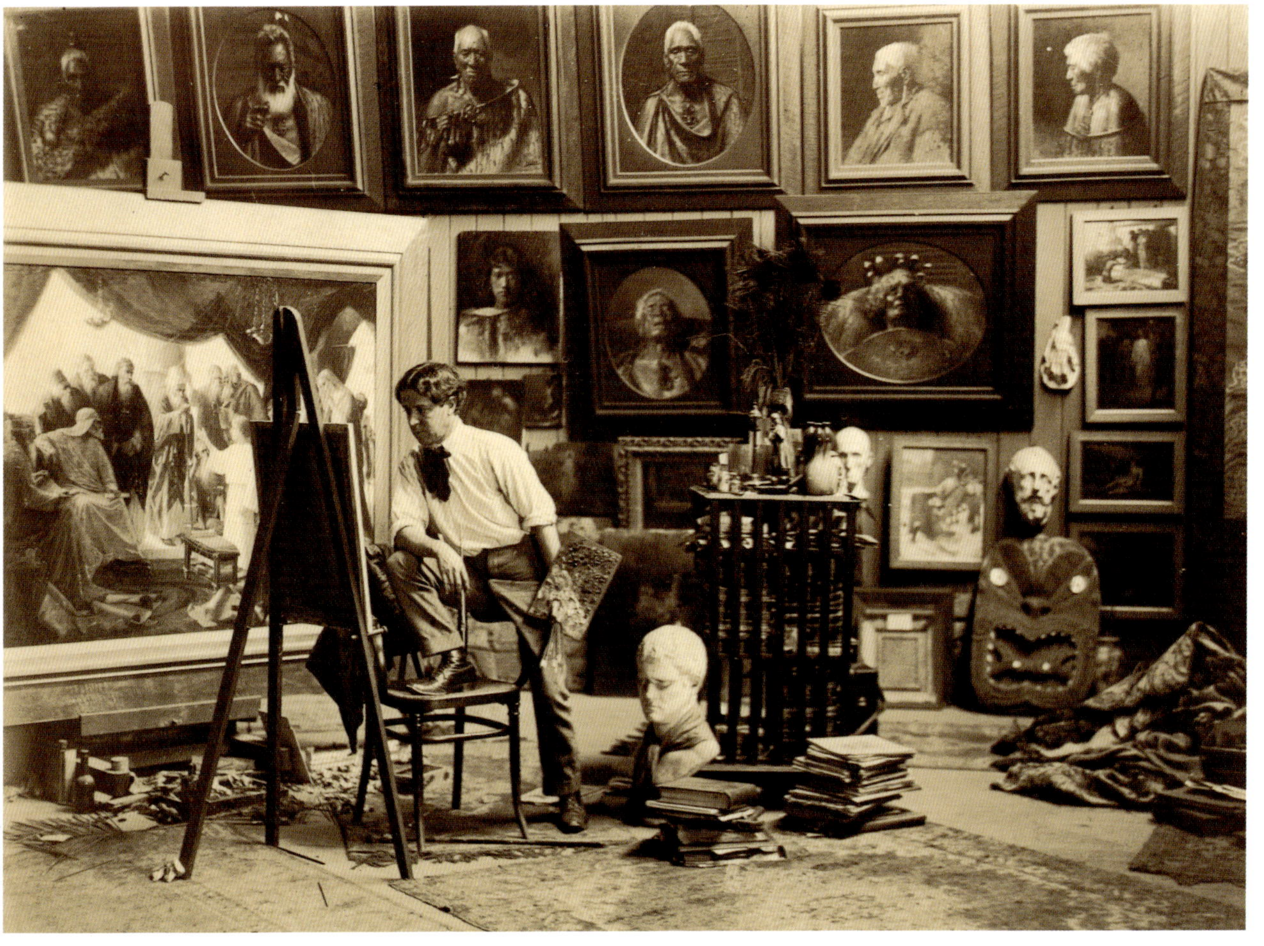

Yet even at the height of his fame, Goldie must have frowned as he clipped some of the less-than-positive remarks by critics who were tiring of an overly minute realism. As early as 1903, the *Triad* diagnosed 'too great a tendency towards still life'[6] and in 1908 the same writer wrote: 'Goldie's "Maori's Head" [possibly *Patara Te Tuhi*, p.139] is good work of its class, but personally I do not like the class. It is too photographic. There is no artistic fancy either in the manipulation or the arrangement. It is simply hard fact and conventionalism.'[7] It may have been the same critic who reviewed the following year's offerings at the Otago Art Society:

> One is tempted to paraphrase Napoleon's famous criticism, and say, 'it is wonderful, but it is not art.' These two little curiosities are the most marvellous imitations of coloured photographs imaginable. The wrinkles on the leathery skin seem modelled, and each individual hair may be almost counted, while the Maori carving is fashioned with remarkable precision. No artist in the world can excel Mr Goldie at the production of ethnographs, and it might well be suggested to the New Zealand Government that, as exchanges with the various museums of the world, this artist's Maori studies would be of great value.[8]

For critics of this ilk, Goldie's works were doubly compromised. Not only were they condemned as hyper-realist productions and therefore out of place in an era of genteel impressionism, but they were dismissed as interesting 'if only from an anthropological point of view'.[9] In 1911, a Wellington commentator wrote 'to my mind these heads, painted with such photographic, meticulous detail, are more suitable for a museum of ethnology and anthropology than for the walls of an art gallery'.[10]

Goldie posing in his studio, around 1908. The Last Sleep, *Goldie's portrayal of Ina Te Papatahi as if dead at a tangi, is prominent among the paintings on the wall behind him (courtesy of the International Art Centre, Parnell, Auckland).*

Later in 1910, a disgruntled Goldie announced his decision to leave the country, apparently with an eye to capitalising on an ethnographic market for his work. In a letter to Augustus Hamilton, director of what was now called the Dominion Museum, he wrote:

> Having decided to return to Europe next year, it is my intention to take with me my collection of Maori portraits, with the object of disposing of them, or of copies of same, to certain Continental Ethnological Societies & Museums.[11]

Hamilton wrote back to assure Goldie of his 'great regret' over the earlier failure to obtain works. Another proposal went before Cabinet on 7 November 1910, where it was again declined. President of the New Zealand Academy of Fine Art, H. Wardell, replied to a similar offer from Goldie. He doubted that the Academy would be able to secure a large work to add to the small ten-guinea painting it had acquired from their 1909 exhibition but nevertheless wished Goldie 'a very satisfactory financial result' from his European venture.[12] Yet without the seeding capital from a group of major sales, Goldie was condemned to remain in Auckland.

continuing the career

Despite the mounting critical hostility, Goldie continued to exhibit new groups of works every year until 1919. Ambitious depictions of 'new' models continued to appear, such as the two portraits of the venerable Aperahama Rairai exhibited with the Auckland Society of Arts in 1909. These were *A Centenarian, Aperahama, aged 104* [p.133], priced at £73, and *Weary with Years* at £63. The *Herald* reviewer was particularly struck by *A Centenarian,* proclaiming: 'There is a terrific realism about this picture, the old chief's expression, his open mouth revealing the fang-like occasional tooth, and the steely glitter of ferocity in the eyes, striking one with dramatic force.' Despite the novelty of a model such as Aperahama, the reviewer focussed yet again on Goldie's lack of 'variety':

> Whilst one could wish that this artist would strike out into a new line for variety's sake, one is compelled to admiration for his gift of detail, and his lifelike reproduction of the Maori type.[1]

Goldie's major work of 1910 was a depiction of Te Aho-o-te-Rangi titled *The Old Lion,* priced at £105 [p.142]. Accompanying this painting at the Society of Arts were *Nikorima and Nicotina* at £45 [p.143] and *Kapi Kapi, aged 102, a Survivor of the Tarawera Eruption* at £15 [p.141]. To Goldie's undoubted chagrin it was the small work, identified as 'a little gem' and 'an extraordinarily cheap picture at the catalogue price', that was chosen for the Auckland Art Gallery.[2] The two larger works remained unsold, appearing later in the year with Wellington's Academy of Fine Arts. *The Old Lion* now had a reduced price tag of £84, while *Nikorima and Nicotina* was offered at £38.

Another larger work, shown for the first time in Wellington in 1910, bore the title *Wharekauri – A Noble Relic of a Noble Race* [p.145]. This painting, under the title *A Noble Relic of a Noble Race, Wharekauri Tahuna, a 'Tohunga' or Priest of the Tuhoe Tribe,* was acquired by the Auckland Art Gallery the following year, when it was shown with the Auckland Society of Arts. Nelson Illingworth had already modelled Te Wharekauri Tahuna of Ngāti Manawa at Galatea in 1908, on the same expedition that he portrayed Tikitere Mihi at Rotorua. Goldie clipped the reference to the old man of over 100, who had taken part in the battle of Te Tumu in 1836, and wrote 'name Wharekauri' beside it in his scrapbook.[3] Goldie then visited Galatea at his earliest convenience, when he made a sequence of photographs of which several remained among his papers. These were the basis for the various subsequent portraits of Te Wharekauri.

The more celebrated piece at the 1911 Auckland Society of Arts exhibition was *The Child Christ in the Temple, questioning with the Doctors, found by His parents,* for which Goldie asked the massive sum of £250 [p.79]. This bizarre painting, so different in character from Goldie's usual productions, was nevertheless received as an important work. J. A. James called it 'The Picture of the Exhibition' and suggested its acquisition for the city.

> This picture, in my opinion, is of such excellent merit that it should undoubtedly have a place in our Art Gallery. The committee have, I believe, a certain sum available each year for the purchase of new pictures. I venture to suggest that the above named work is such a perfect masterpiece that the committee would be well advised to acquire it. It is certainly the piece of the present exhibition, and I trust will not be lost to Auckland. I need not enlarge upon the merits of the picture, but I may add that I am not personally acquainted with the artist.[4]

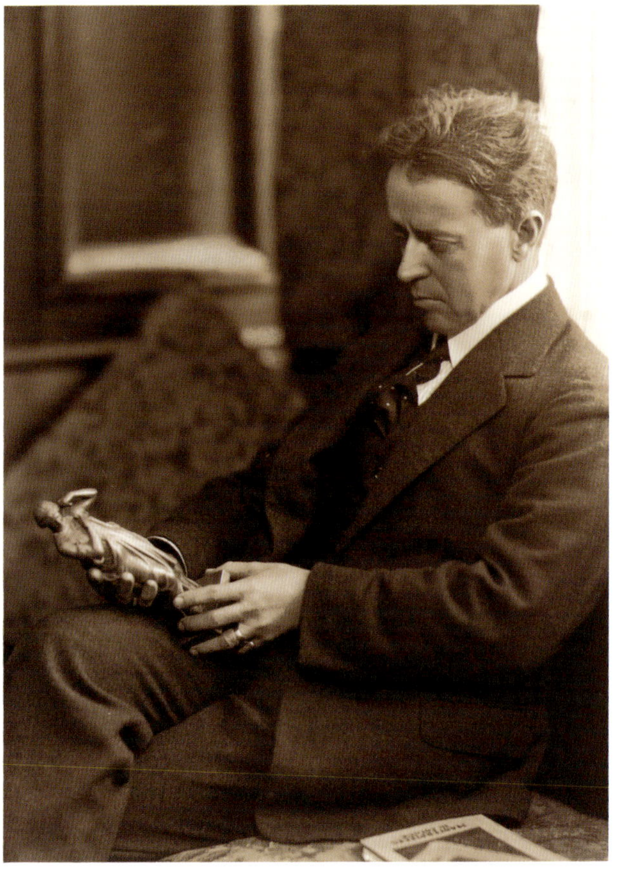

Portrait of Charles F. Goldie (Auckland Art Gallery Toi o Tāmaki, gift of Jack and Joan Cooper, 1995).

The painting entered Auckland's civic collection the following year, as a gift from Goldie's father. At the time of presentation, it was described by the *Graphic* as 'without question the finest figure painting that has ever been done in New Zealand'.[5] David Goldie's motive, apart from supplying an edifyingly religious subject for the walls of his city's art gallery, may have been to provide some financial support for his son.

From now on, apart from an 80-guinea commission in 1913 to paint Sir Maurice O'Rorke, Goldie concentrated completely on his Māori portraits. He showed a total of eight at the 1912 exhibition in Auckland. Notable works were *A Noble Northern Chief, Atama Paparangi* [p.154], priced at £84, and *Night in the Whare* [p.153], an exquisite study of Ina Te Papatahi lighting her pipe which the Auckland Art Gallery bought for £47 10s. The following year he presented a pair of major works, *The Last of the Cannibals* [p.147], priced at £78 15s, and *Memories, the Last of her Tribe,* at £68 15s. The former was a new depiction of Tūmai Tāwhiti, while the latter was described by the *Herald* as a depiction of 'an old Maori woman contemplating with the characteristic abandon of the Maori the disappearance of her tribe'.[6] The two works remained unsold and were sent later in the year to the South Canterbury Art Society's exhibition in Timaru, where *The Last of the Cannibals* was purchased for the society's collection at a price of £84. *Memories* was purchased by James Craigie, Member of Parliament for Timaru. Both canvases are now in the Aigantighe Art Gallery, Timaru. They were among the last of Goldie's larger works, which also included two shown in 1914, *Peeping Patara* [p.155], priced at £73 10s, and *The Last of the Tohungas (or Priests), Wharekauri Tahuna* at £95. The list of exhibited works reveals Goldie moving his paintings around New Zealand's various exhibitions, an indication that he was finding his works increasingly difficult to sell.

Goldie's financial difficulties were eased in April 1913 when David Goldie at last provided a regular income for his 42-year-old son.[7] Goldie also concentrated on producing smaller pictures with an eye to a more modest domestic market. Priced between eight and eighteen guineas, these were considerably easier to sell than the larger works. Many were executed on wooden panels which, unlike the brush-textured canvases, had completely smooth surfaces. Goldie was increasingly producing replicas of earlier paintings, of models who had long since died, or new variations based on earlier photographs and drawings. Like Charles Blomfield, who was still alive and still producing replicas of his Pink and White Terrace paintings, Goldie may have been demoralised by a realisation that he was doing no more than repeating a winning formula.

In an attempt to record the last remaining tattooed men located in the Urewera country, Goldie had begun corresponding with Pene Te Uamairangi Hakiwai, an Anglican minister stationed at Ruatoki. On 23 October 1916 he wrote to Alfred Hill in Sydney, suggesting a joint painting/recording trip the following summer to 'very wild country where the natives are probably less civilized than any Maoris in N.Z. ... There are 3 tattooed men in the district & Hakiwai is arranging with them to sit for me.'

> Ruatoki would be an ideal place for your work as the natives there have had very little contact with Europeans, so that you would have a better chance of getting the 'real stuff'. Ngata is the Maori member for the district & you could probably get him interested. ... I am very pleased to hear that you are still keen on Maori stuff & undoubtedly there is no one who can touch it but yourself. You must not delay getting as much material as possible, such can only be procurable from the old Maori, who in a very short [time] will be a thing of the past. It is surprising how quickly they are dying off.[8]

He told Hill that business was slow. 'Things are very bad here in my line, still I am producing stuff which must sell sooner or later. Am sending to the Dunedin Exhibition this week & as I usually have a certain amount of success there I hope to place a few canvases.'

elopement to sydney

Early in 1920 Goldie finally decided to leave Auckland. He negotiated the loan of his personal collection of over 60 paintings to the Auckland Art Gallery, an agreement formalised on 10 June. Twenty-seven of these were the famed 'Māori studies', while the remainder comprised student works and copies Goldie had made during his European sojourn. When the paintings were placed on display later that year, James Cowan wrote a lengthy essay concerning the subjects of the portraits ('Goldie's Collection. Last of the Rangatiras' is reprinted on pages 187-189). He disposed of other paintings and assorted memorabilia, including two paint-encrusted palettes, by presenting them to friends and business associates. The huge palette he had brought back from Paris, used for painting *The Arrival of the Maoris,* he inscribed *To my friend Bayliss, with best wishes* (Auckland Museum). The painting known as *Joan of Arc,* painted in Paris in 1896, bears the additional inscription *To my friend H. Leech, from C. F. Goldie, 1920* [p.76]. Another Parisian work, *The Betrayal of Christ,* reads *to my friend BARTLETT from C. F. Goldie 1920* [p.71]. This gift-making is the behaviour of someone who intends to be away for some time.

Goldie left Auckland – ostensibly heading for Paris – on 31 October 1920. He disembarked in Sydney where on 18 November, at the age of 50, he married 35-year-old Olive Ethelwyn Cooper, an Australian by birth but a resident of Auckland. Apparently marriage in Sydney circumvented Goldie family disapproval of the relationship between Auckland's famous artist and the milliner from Karangahape Road's Bon Marche Millinery Emporium. The wedding went unmentioned in the Auckland press.

Despite a newspaper announcement early in 1921 that he was planning to travel on to Paris, Goldie and his wife spent just over two years living in Cremorne, on Sydney's North Shore. He was still working as an artist, producing copies of his Māori portraits on which he added *NSW* to his customary signature. Although some paintings may have been sold in Australia, a group was delivered back to Auckland (perhaps even smuggled) by John Barr, Director of the Auckland Art Gallery. On 2 March 1921 Barr wrote to Goldie: 'I forwarded your autograph picture to the proper source early on my arrival and got through the Customs without any difficulty with the pictures for Leech.'[1] Goldie had asked Barr to obtain some of his favourite small brushes from an art supply store in Auckland. Apart from the sale of these paintings and the allowance from his father, it is uncertain how the Goldies survived. Olive may have resumed operations as a milliner in Sydney, where she had worked before being recruited by the Bon Marche.

His old friend Alfred Hill lived nearby in Mosman, and Charles undoubtedly spent time visiting the Art Gallery, a short ferry ride across the harbour. Arthur Streeton had recently returned from a period in England, placing his celebrated *Golden Summer* on loan to the Sydney gallery. Tom Roberts had also returned to work in Australia and in mid-1921 Sidney Long likewise returned after eleven years in England. The returning artists characteristically praised Australian art, favourably comparing the local tradition with 'decadent' European tendencies. Long's feelings were reported under the heading 'Sanity in Art':

> Art has reached such a crazy state in England, with post-impressionists, cubists, the new schools springing up every day, that the sane men feel they really ought to fight against this tendency towards anarchy in art.[2]

In November 1921 Goldie received a visit from his friend Robert McVeagh, who was in Sydney on the outset of a world trip. McVeagh's journal entry for Tuesday 22 November records a visit with Goldie to the Art Gallery, where the works they admired included 'The Visit of the Queen of Sheba to King Solomon', 'Wedded' and 'The Sea hath its Pearls'. McVeagh's journal records two further afternoons spent in the artist's company, when Goldie seized the opportunity to write his will.

By January 1923 Goldie was back in Auckland. It seems that he had been seriously ill, for the *Observer* reported in August 1923 that his health was improving:

> The art circle in Auckland and those interested generally in art matters will be pleased to hear that Charlie Goldie is regaining his health and has commenced painting again. It is indeed good news, for his famous 'Maori Head' studies have been a feature of New Zealand's distinctive art, in fact, he was looked upon as the Dominion's premier artist. It is understood that he has resumed work upon some big canvases, of New Zealand life, the appearance of which, at the next art exhibition, will be eagerly awaited.[3]

If these 'big canvases' really were begun, they were never completed. Ill-health plagued him throughout the 1920s, when he produced almost no paintings. Gossip maintained the problem to be alcoholism; symptoms such as memory loss and delusion suggest that lead poisoning may have played a part in his health problems. By smoking cigarettes while he worked, Goldie may have ingested lead from paint residues on his fingers. His illness could also have resulted from a cocktail of factors, including long-term exposure to solvent fumes as well as the fondness for alcohol and tobacco he acquired as a student in Paris.

the menace of modernism

Goldie's paintings soon became one of the attractions of twentieth-century Auckland. A German writer in 1912 dismissed New Zealand's art galleries, 'where soiled canvas hangs like washing on a clothes line'.[1] An exception was the work of Goldie, 'whose Maori heads surprise one by the accurately detailed treatment of the subject and the reality of the colouring'. In 1920, when the loan collection went on display, Goldie became the definitive star of the Auckland Gallery. Percy Kahn, a famous pianist visiting in 1924, expressed his opinion that 'Goldie's Maori studies in the Auckland Art Gallery are the most wonderful and interesting exhibits in the whole building.'[2] 'Where Charles Goldie is Supreme' ran the headline of an account of the Art Gallery in 1935 by Iris Wilkinson (better known by her penname Robin Hyde).[3] According to Wilkinson, the single most popular picture in the gallery was *The Arrival of the Maoris in New Zealand.*

Goldie jealously guarded the copyright on his paintings, frequently adding 'copyright reserved' to reproductions and exhibition catalogues to indicate that no further reproduction was permitted. Writing from Sydney in December 1921, he stressed to director John Barr that there should be no copying of the loan collection, photographic or otherwise:

> I trust that the collection has not suffered in any way from heat, dampness etc during the last year & that every care is being taken to prevent deterioration of any kind & that *no copying or photographs of the collection either as a whole or in detail have been made. This is most important* & I would be pleased if you could impress this point on the guardians in charge of the Gallery.[4]

R. Love of Edwards' Studio made the first photographs which allowed the reproduction of Goldie's works, while another photographer who undertook work specifically for the Auckland Art Gallery was Henry Winkelmann. Winkelmann made a new photograph of *The Arrival of the Maoris* in 1914, which served as the basis for many subsequent reproductions. Love and Winkelmann were superseded by *Auckland Weekly News* photographer, A. N. Breckon. It was Breckon who in the 1930s photographed important paintings as John Leech was framing them. These images accompanied newspaper stories in the *Herald* and *Weekly News,* but also allowed Goldie to use Breckon's photographs as a type of 'limited-edition' print he could frame for presentation to friends and family. Discussing a proposed tourist souvenir publication with Cowan, Goldie said he wanted the publishers to emulate the sepia quality of Breckon's photographs. (For this correspondence, see pages 183-187.)

The real danger to Goldie's prestige lay not so much in the feared copying or reproduction of his works, as in the gradual conquest of the art establishment by modernism. When A. J. C. (Archie) Fisher arrived from England to take over the directorship of Elam School of Art in 1924, he created a furore by denouncing the contents of Auckland Art Gallery. 'On my first visit to your art gallery,' he told the ladies at the Lyceum Club, 'I felt I would like to pull the rubbish down and get it away, with the exception of about four pictures, which I would not destroy.'[5] Fisher expressed surprise over the vehement reaction that followed his indictment: one anonymous phone call warned he would soon be run out of town. He later explained that he did not intend Goldie's work to be destroyed:

> Respecting the Goldie pictures, Mr Fisher said that he recognised that they had archeological and historic value, but considered that they would be most suitably placed in a little gallery adjoining the museum of Maori art.[6]

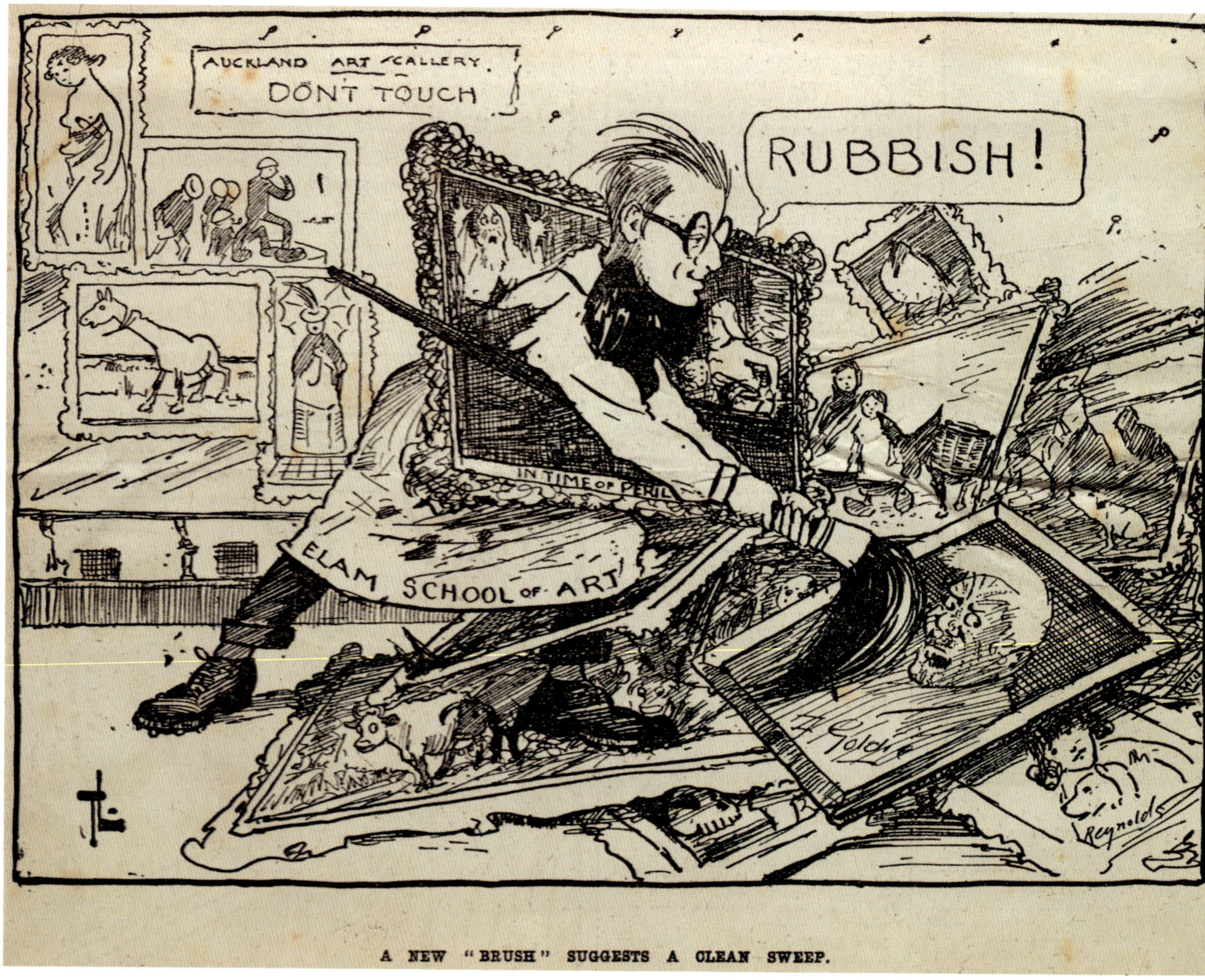

Herald cartoonist Trevor Lloyd depicted Archie Fisher stripping the walls of the Art Gallery, with a Goldie on top of the rejected pile.[7]

The choice of works for public presentation in a civic art gallery is inevitably a major focus of any city's art politics. The 1930s was a period of change in the Auckland Art Gallery, when the style of hanging in much of the gallery shifted from a traditional massed display towards a single line of spaced-out pictures. The catalyst for change was provided by incoming loan exhibitions, which temporarily dislodged the permanent collection. The first of these was in 1934, a large show of British art organised by the Empire Art Loan Collections Society. Goldie denounced the British show in the *Herald,* under the sub-heading 'Decadence in Art'.[8] Fellow traditionalist Evelyn Vaile meanwhile fretted over the changes that would inevitably follow: 'The modernists are sure to try to rearrange the gallery according to their own ideas, and if they are allowed to very few, if any, good pictures will go up again.' Vaile spoke admiringly of the letters on art which Goldie had contributed to the *Herald,* crediting him with 'trying to save us from the modernists'.

> In Auckland the trouble with the modernists started about twenty-five years ago through Edward Fristrom and nobody thought it mattered; but from that time on art has steadily gone from bad to worse. It is not a question of what any of us like in art, the whole question is, what is art?[9]

It seemed to both Goldie and Vaile that the Art Gallery was infested with 'art freaks', hovering with intent to waylay unsuspecting visitors. These may have been enthusiastic amateurs, the predecessors of today's museum guides. Such

*'A new "brush" suggests a clean sweep', Trevor Lloyd's cartoon of Archie Fisher sweeping out the rubbish from the Auckland Art Gallery (*New Zealand Herald*, 1 November 1924).*

guides were pessimistically foretold by Goldie himself: 'It seems to me that the time is not far distant when it will be necessary for visitors to be conducted through art galleries by interpreters.'[10] The most elaborate of Goldie's diatribes against modernism is reprinted in this volume. It was published 'by arrangement' – the *Herald*'s subtle indication of a paid advertisement from the Auckland art world's equivalent of Colonel Blimp.

Early in 1937 the Gallery was preparing for another large temporary exhibition, this time comprising European and Australian paintings from the Sydney Art Gallery. Goldie's loan collection had to come down again. On New Year's Eve 1936, while removing the Goldies so he could prepare the walls for painting, odd-job man R. J. James lost his balance while on a ladder. The result was a head-sized hole in one of the Rembrandt copies. In a 1938 letter to *Herald,* which he subsequently amplified into a full-scale address to the Mayor and Councillors of Auckland, Goldie deplored this constant shuffling of the Art Gallery's collection to accommodate itinerant exhibitions: 'The safest and most sensible place for all pictures is on the walls of the gallery, even should it be necessary to "sky" many of them as is done in the Louvre.'[11] Evelyn Vaile wrote concerning the annoyance of tourists and locals alike when Goldie's Māori portraits disappeared from display, only to be replaced by a collection of posters:

> It is no good the city owning good works of art and having them shut away where they cannot be seen by the public. I have often thought how very disappointing it must be to visitors when the Maori portraits are not on view. As to that wretched little thin line of exhibits round the walls, the only time it is ideal is when the works are painted on modern lines, then the less shown the better.[12]

In reply to Goldie, John Barr defended the new selective hanging of 'a single line of pictures only'.[13] Nevertheless, except when the area was used for itinerant shows, part of the gallery continued to offer a massed display of Goldie's loan collection [p.38].

For someone who had become an Old Master in his own lifetime, an appreciation of modernist trends in art and gallery display could scarcely be expected. Goldie felt aggrieved, not just because his valuable loan collection was sustaining damage, but because he felt removed from the changes under way in Auckland's art institutions. The exclusion must have been particularly galling, given the international renown he had recently achieved from a new body of work which he was marketing on the international stage.

the late career

Although local newspapers continued to trumpet news of his successes, Goldie's later career evolved independently of Auckland's art world. Just as Sir George Grey and Lady Ranfurly had provided vice-regal boosts to Goldie's earlier career, it was the high-powered patronage of a later Governor-General which gave Goldie the confidence to embark on the final chapter in his career. Opening the annual exhibition of Wellington's Academy of Fine Arts in 1933, Lord Bledisloe paid homage to Goldie, who he said 'was only just in time to catch those grand old tattooed faces that are seen no more. He has conspicuously done his share of painting living history, the figures of a heroic and poetic past.'[1] While on a visit to Auckland late in 1933, Bledisloe and his wife visited Goldie at his residence, 94 Upland Road.[2] Their intention was to commission a painting relevant to the Waitangi estate which Bledisloe had purchased and would present to the nation early the following year. Bledisloe suggested that, using a famous early photograph, Goldie should paint a portrait of Tamati Wāka Nene – one of the protagonists of the 1840 signing of the Treaty of Waitangi [p.164]. Aucklanders caught a brief glimpse of the painting late in January 1934, shortly before Waitangi Day, when John Leech exhibited it after framing. The plaque read 'Presented by the artist to His Excellency Lord Bledisloe, and by him to the Waitangi National Trust.'[3]

Now in his mid-sixties, Goldie embarked on a distinctive body of work marked by a warmer palette and considerably thinner application of paint. Mostly depicting models he had originally painted decades earlier, the works were inevitably based on earlier paintings as well as on sketches and photographs. Titles usually echoed earlier examples, though there were new departures as well. Goldie called a 1933 painting of Hera Puna *As Rembrandt would have painted the Maori,* evoking the hero of his student years, while a 1938 portrait of Te Aho-o-te-Rangi bore the tendentious title *His thought: 'The Treaty of Waitangi, was it worthwhile?'*.[4] These works were adaptations, rather than simple copies of his earlier paintings. He would begin by making a drawing of the composition, which he carefully transferred to a prepared canvas by means of a pencilled grid. Although his collection of photographs was an important source, he never worked over a photosensitised base as asserted by later critics. The 'photographic' naturalism of Goldie's technique, instilled during his student years at the Académie Julian, stood him in excellent stead now that his work usually represented pure improvisation unmediated by a human model.

At Lord Bledisloe's prompting, Goldie sent three paintings to London for the 1934 exhibition of the Royal Academy of Arts. *Memories: Te Arani, Thoughts of a Tohunga: Wharekauri Tahuna* [p.162] and *An Aristocrat: Atama Paparangi.* All three were selected, 'very well hung and much commented on' among the 1600 paintings on display.[5] Other New Zealand contributors were Cecil F. Kelly from Christchurch and Mary E. R. Tripe of Wellington. The following year Goldie sent one of these canvases to Paris for the Salon of the conservative Société des Artistes Français, under the title *Les Pensées d'un prêtre: Wharekauri Tahuna.* In the midst of over 2000 paintings his work drew critical attention and several requests for photographs and information on tattooing, accolades which Goldie translated for local consumption. Writing to Cowan in August, Goldie reported that he had won a diploma or medal at that year's Salon, he did not know which. The grandiose certificate of *Mention Honorable* finally arrived from Paris the following year.[6]

Goldie exhibited with the Royal Academy again in 1935 and with the Paris Salon on a further three occasions (1936, 1938 and 1939), events duly noted by Auckland newspapers and clipped by Goldie for his albums. *Sleep, 'tis a Gentle Thing,* a depiction of Hōri Pōkai [p.163], appeared at the Royal Academy of 1935 and in Paris the following year. *In Dreamland* [p.167] went to Paris in 1938, where it was chosen as one of the catalogue reproductions. The following year, his two final contributions to the Salon were a portrait of Atama Paparangi titled *In Doubt* [p.169] and *Thoughts of a Tohunga* [p.166]. While the publicity about these successes abroad must have gratified the status-conscious artist, he was perplexed by the Royal Academy's rejection of his works after 1935 as well as frustrated in his expectations of a medal or sale from the Salon. He told his nephew in London that he wished to contribute only to 'important Continental Exhibitions, where awards are made'.[7] Nevertheless, his considerable public profile undoubtedly helped secure two important awards in 1935: King George V's Silver Jubilee Medal and the Order of the British Empire. This latter award occasioned the visit of a *Herald* photographer to Goldie's residence in Upland Road, when the artist posed in front of an improvised backdrop. A cropped version of this photograph appeared several times, including in Goldie's obituary. The full frame of the portrait reveals paint-spattered work trousers below the facade of pinstriped jacket, and the unsettling absence of a left hand.

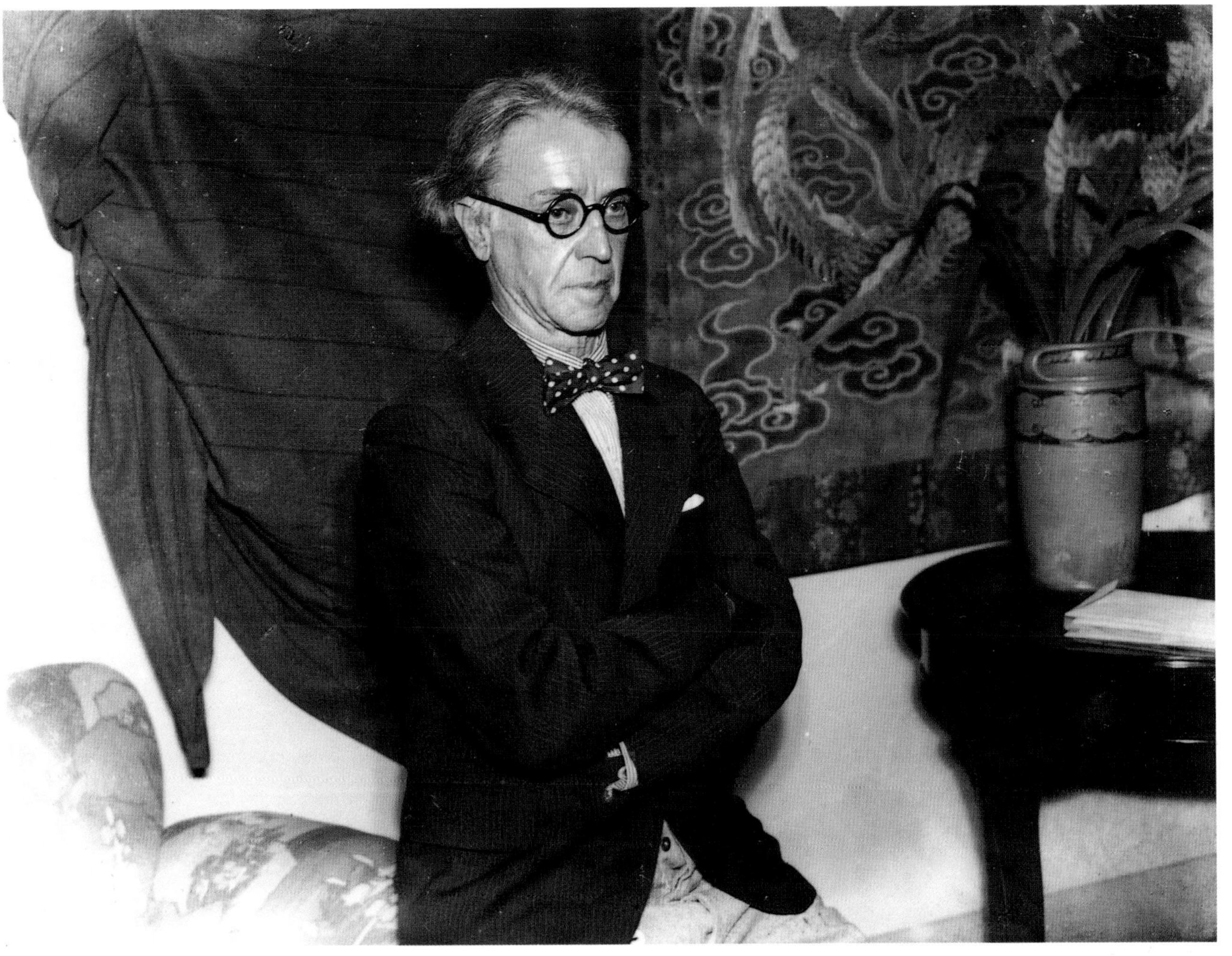

Charles F. Goldie, June 1935. Taken on the occasion of his appointment as O.B.E., a cropped version of this photograph appeared in the Herald *on several occasions (*New Zealand Herald *photograph, courtesy of Auckland Museum).*

Goldie used high prices to maintain the prestige of his works. Two of his 1934 oils for the Royal Academy were particularly steep: *Thoughts of a Tohunga* was £420 and *An Aristocrat* £393 12s 6d.[8] In the event, he sold *An Aristocrat* to Lady Bledisloe for the nominal sum of 100 guineas before it left New Zealand, while *Thoughts of a Tohunga* was later given to his nephew Terry Bond in London.[9] The third painting exhibited in 1934, *Memories,* sold to an 'English lady' for the sum of 250 guineas. These were the publicly celebrated pieces, but Goldie was also creating works for sale to wealthy tourists through his Auckland dealer, John Leech. In 1935 he informed Cowan of one such sale at £350 and others at 150 and 250 guineas, this at a time of economic depression when the Auckland Society of Arts held an exhibition at which every work cost just one guinea.[10] Since John Leech's sales records of the 1930s are missing, the precise extent and value of Goldie's later *œuvre* can never be established with precision. What is clear, however, is that prices were never cheap and that the trade in 'Goldies' must have considerably eased the Depression of the 1930s for both artist and dealer.

In 1935 Goldie corresponded with James Cowan over plans for a souvenir book of sepia reproductions, which he thought could be titled *'Noble Relics of a Noble Race', Rangitiras of Ao-tea-roa.* Unhappy with the standard of the proof reproductions, and evidently suspicious of mass-reproductive technology, Goldie eventually aborted the project. Perhaps he had realised that the true source of his wealth lay in the original oil paintings and the mystique that surrounded them. Surprisingly, in view of his difficult relationship with the Auckland Art Gallery, Goldie donated two of his late paintings in December 1939. *A Hundred Years have Passed* [p.170] and *Reverie: Pipi Haerehuka* [p.171], both dated 1939, were a gift in memory of his beloved Mater, Maria Goldie, who had died the previous year. With a value nominated by the artist at 250 guineas apiece, they were gratefully accepted and hung in the Gallery.

Goldie's health seems to have been particularly precarious around 1936. In a telegram to James Cowan dated 18 March 1936, Olive Goldie wrote: 'Goldie ill publication book off'; five months later Goldie wrote: 'Since my wife (not sister) telegraphed you some months ago my health has not improved, owing to continuous worry.'[11] A great many of the late paintings bear the date 1939, as though a group of works in progress thoughout the decade were definitively 'finished' in a burst of energy. This may have been at Olive's urging, for she now had power of attorney over Goldie's business affairs and needed a stock of paintings to maintain an income through John Leech. The artist stopped painting altogether around 1941, spending his final years at the house he and Olive had acquired at 152 Upland Road:

> He could often be seen standing on the street outside his home. Sometimes he would be deep in thought, oblivious even to heavy rain, at other times he shouted to passers-by, warning of the dangers of progress and such things as gas AND electricity in the same house.[12]

Much of his time indoors Goldie spent leafing through his sizeable library, including the volumes of newspaper clippings documenting his career as New Zealand's most famous artist. Evidence of this favourite occupation are the thousands of signatures, *C. F. Goldie,* written in various inks and with differing degrees of tremor, which he compulsively inscribed throughout the books. When Goldie's library was dispersed in 1949, rumour maintained that the multiple signatures were supposed by the elderly artist to demonstrate his sanity. Effectively, they indicated the reverse.[13]

Charles Frederick Goldie, O.B.E., died at his home on 11 July 1947, aged 76, and was buried the following day at Purewa Cemetery. According to his death certificate he had suffered for years from a duodenal ulcer, and for seven days a cerebral thrombosis. He left Olive well provided for. There was the Remuera house valued at £4500, a healthy bank balance, a lifetime income from the family trust, and a collection of paintings (including those on loan to the Art Gallery) valued by John Leech at £5570. Despite the inroads of modernism, Goldie's popular reputation as New Zealand's premier artist was still secure. Terry Bond and Lord Bledisloe both lent paintings to the British Overseas Dominions Exhibition held in London in 1937, while two important early oils from the Auckland Art Gallery were included in the 1940 National Centennial Exhibition of New Zealand Art. Perhaps the ultimate recognition had come in 1941 with the installation of two Goldie paintings, male and female portraits, as 'real Maori souvenirs' on the New Zealand Navy's destroyer H.M.S. *Maori.*[14]

goldie's posthumous fortunes

Late in 1947, only several months after her husband's death, Olive Goldie notified the City Council that she was withdrawing the collection of paintings which had been on loan to the Art Gallery since 1920. Dr E. B. Gunson, a past president of the Auckland Society of Arts, informed *Herald* readers that the entire collection had earlier been offered for sale 'for a comparatively low sum, to be precise £4000, at a time when the artist would have welcomed the sale' but that the offer had been rejected.[1] John Barr, director of the art gallery since the original loan was negotiated in 1920, disclaimed any knowledge of such an offer. From Ōtāhuhu, Juan Les Pins suggested: 'If now they could be bought for the nation and displayed in the ethnological section of the War

Memorial Museum, in the sub-section dealing with the Maori race, they would be fulfilling a far more useful function than they have done in the past, masquerading under the cloak of art.'[2]

After first exploring the possibilities of selling the collection, Olive Goldie presented twenty Māori portraits to the Auckland Museum in 1951. She retained a further nine Māori paintings (including *The Last Sleep*, or *The Majesty of Death,* the depiction of Ina Te Papatahi as if dead at a tangi) as well as the 29 works from Goldie's student years. Olive's action was undoubtedly motivated by the Gallery's lack of enthusiasm for Goldie's work, expressed in the frequent dismantling and storage of the 'permanent collection'. The irony is that, in her choice of a permanent home for Goldie's collection, Olive Goldie unwittingly assisted the modernist establishment in finally effecting Goldie's demotion from 'artist' to 'ethnologist'. For with the collection placed on regular display in the Museum's Māori Hall [p.39], the Art Gallery evidently felt it could dispense with its Goldie display.

Increasingly, the paintings were portrayed by leading commentators as an embarrassing legacy of colonial times. In 1951 John Bell, a visiting Scottish artist and teacher, opened a provocative critique of the Auckland Art Gallery by denouncing the remaining Goldies, singling out the favourite work of all.

> Goldie is your conjurer, the illusionist who brought rabbits out of the hat. For the woolliest tricks of illusion see the tartan blanket wrapped around 'Memories'. What does this laborious technique achieve which the clicking shutter in colour photography does not? As art in Auckland progresses, Goldie and Co. may depart to their spiritual home – the Old Colonists Museum. Meanwhile 'The Arrival of the Maoris in New Zealand' delights adventure-loving adolescent minds of all ages.[3]

The Old Colonists Museum was a compendium of colonial relics (including many of the current treasures of the Auckland Art Gallery) which was then situated upstairs within the Art Gallery.

Newspaper articles suggest that, in response to curatorial suppression, there was insistent public demand for the reinstatement of Goldie's works. Late in 1954 a 'rather dowdy old room' was dedicated to a permanent display of Goldie and Lindauer. 'We get a lot of requests to see the Goldies,' director Eric Westbrook plaintively told the reporter, 'and until we can make a more satisfactory permanent display of them I hope this arrangement will meet the need.'[4] For this exhibition, fifty works by Goldie and Lindauer were placed in narrow white frames and shown against whitewashed walls. An article the following year, about the gallery's picture restorer L. Charles Lloyd and his attempts to collect information on Goldie's techniques by tracking down former pupils of the artist, refers ominously to 'the damage to certain Goldie oils now in his care'.[5]

It was the arrival of incoming art gallery director Peter Tomory in 1956 that truly planted the modernist cat among the colonial pigeons. Tomory infuriated locals by pronouncing: 'Lindauer was no Gauguin. His work is of social and historical importance but it is not great art. ... Goldie, on the other hand, is a second-rate Lindauer. Not only did he do a great deal of his work from photographs, but [he] lacked all Lindauer's sincerity.'[6] Auckland's Goldie-lovers were not prepared to accept this assault lightly. Among the disputees was 'Art Lover' of Ponsonby:

> In spite of the opinion expressed by Mr Peter Tomory, director of the Art Gallery, it is my opinion, shared by thousands of others, that Goldie was the greatest painter of Maori pictures. One only has to study some of his work. The face and hands of the Maori not only live, but Goldie is such a master one can also distinguish the fabric in his paintings. For

instance, a rug definitely shows it is woollen, the Maori woman's skirt is velvet, and so on. Is Mr Tomory a painter himself? If so, could he produce anything as good as a Goldie?[7]

Many others wrote in Goldie's defence. The opinion of 'Burnt Umber' was that 'If Mr Tomory hopes to wean the New Zealand man-in-the-street off Goldie he needs to offer something rather more palatable than the bewildering smudges and anatomical distortions that seem to dominate the walls of recent exhibitions.'[8] Another observed that 'no such criticism will affect the honest appreciation and deep admiration of thousands of New Zealanders for what they feel or know to be true and faithful portraits of old Maori characters reacting to the impact of the pakeha. Tread softly, Mr Tomory.'[9]

By 1960 the dowdy upstairs room had been stripped of the Goldies and Lindauers to form a club room for the newly formed Gallery Associates (later the Friends of the Gallery). Seven Lindauers (out of 70 in the Partridge Collection) were relegated to the vestibule, while Goldie's work was hung on an adjacent staircase. Inevitably, letters of complaint appeared in the newspapers. As one writer pointed out: 'These pictures are among the gallery's treasures and should be properly shown much more often.'[10] Another, responding to a suggestion from Eric Lee-Johnson that the Goldies and Lindauers might realise their 'ethnological value' through a transfer to the Museum, wrote: 'If the Goldies and Lindauers leave the Art Gallery it will be an even drearier place than it is now.'[11] Auckland's quandary over the Lindauers and Goldies perplexed commentators in other centres, where there were fewer examples of their work. Under the heading 'Goldie Portraits Proudly Displayed in Wellington', Eric Ramsden of the *Evening Post* informed

Interior of Auckland Art Gallery, November 1946, showing the Goldie loan collection. Compare the width of the frames with those displayed at Auckland Museum several years later (photograph courtesy of New Zealand Herald).

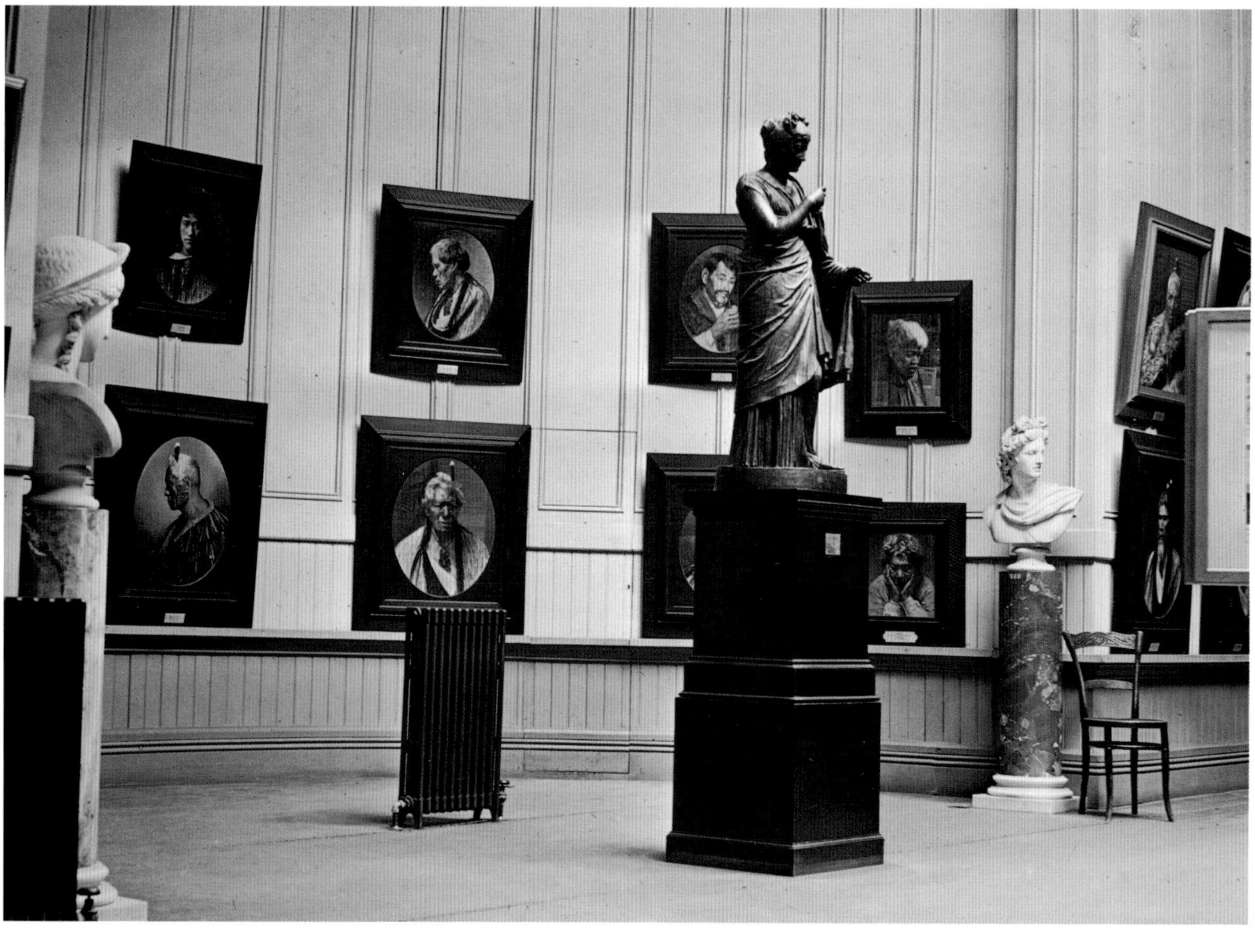

Auckland Museum in March 1952, showing some of the twenty paintings donated by Olive Goldie in 1951. The carved panels are the work of Anaha Te Rāhui, whose portrait by Goldie is fourth from the right (photograph courtesy of New Zealand Herald*).*

readers that, although they were minor works, all three Goldies in the National Art Gallery were prominently hung. 'Goldie will live on when his detractors are forgotten. ... If Auckland has no desire to show its Goldie collection, then surely Wellington will gladly do so. Is it just that overseas visitors who, with deliberation, seek out the work of one of the few masters this country has produced, should be denied the pleasure of seeing it?'[12]

Another controversy erupted in 1963, when the Auckland City Council received a petition that 'Goldies and Lindauers "tucked away in storage" at the Auckland Art Gallery be displayed'. The petition was initiated by a Birkdale woman, disgusted at finding only one Goldie hanging in the stairway when she visited the Gallery with her six grandchildren: 'This is New Zealand and we should have our New Zealand things out.'[13] As if to underline the distinction between public appreciation and art world denigration, a publishing firm issued a successful calendar illustrating Lindauer's portraits. While this may have earned some money for the Gallery, the calendar reproductions undoubtedly led to the disappointment of visitors who quite naturally expected to encounter a Lindauer display in the Gallery. And Goldie, who reputedly loathed the very name of Lindauer, had to accept a latter-day partnership in the public mind, as a component of 'Goldie and Lindauer'.

The decades of curatorial suppression failed to dampen the public's adoration for Goldie. What has changed instead is the attitude of the art establishment, now increasingly prepared to accept work that was created outside the modernist tradition. The 'academy' may finally accept what has long been asserted by visitors and ordinary New Zealanders alike: that Goldie is the country's leading academic painter.

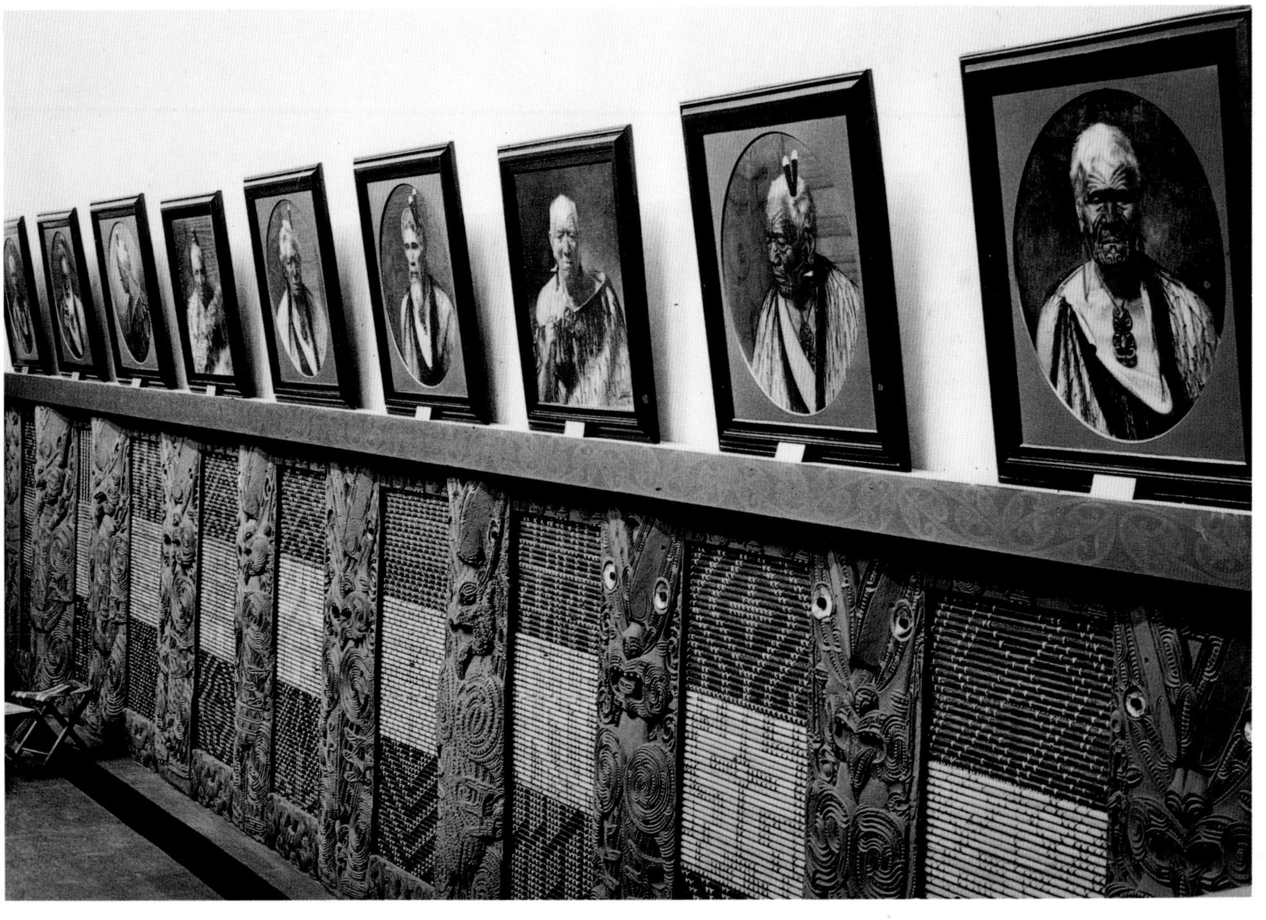

breaking the records

To a significant extent, late-twentieth-century public awareness of Goldie hinges on a spiral of record-breaking prices achieved by his work in the marketplace. The highest price Goldie ever asked for one of his paintings was £420 for *Thoughts of a Tohunga* [p.162] at the Royal Academy in 1934. Despite the 350-guinea sale he reported to Cowan in 1936, Goldie's prices usually hovered around 150–180 guineas. At a time when the Auckland Society of Arts organised an exhibition at which no picture cost more than one guinea, Goldie's stratospheric prices were truly remarkable.[1] At some stage Olive Goldie assumed power of attorney over Charles's business affairs, dealing directly with Gilbert Meadows of John Leech Ltd. A 'gentleman's agreement' drawn up by Olive's lawyers in 1945 reveals that Meadows's commission was 15%, on top of Goldie's price, and that he was then holding nineteen pictures. The price bracket at this stage, reported by John Barr to a Californian collector, ranged from £98 to £240.[2] Clearly the market in Goldies eased the economic depression of the 1930s and the uncertainty of the war period.

Goldie's death opened a new era. Suddenly realising that the 'stable' of Goldies was finite, Auckland businessmen began investing in the paintings which appeared in the window of John Leech Ltd at 50 Shortland Street, now run by Allan (Bunny) Swinton. Auction prices began their upward swing, beginning with £450 for a portrait of Te Aho-o-te-Rangi Wharepu at a Parnell auction in 1948.[3] In 1951 the Dunedin Public Art Gallery bought a major early painting, *The memory of what has been and never more will be* [p.107], from a Timaru auction for the sum of 800 guineas.[4] The following year the same gallery bought *In Doubt* [p.169] for £550, bringing Dunedin's Goldie collection to three. These proved to be canny purchases, for prices were set to rise. 'What is the special appeal of a painting by Charles Frederick Goldie?', journalists wondered aloud. 'Why is there gold in the Goldies?' asked a headline in 1969, after a 1904 painting changed hands at $5200. The mystery was only heightened by the contempt of the art establishment: 'The professional artists and critics, almost to a man, scarcely acknowledge Goldie to be an artist at all.'[5]

Gil Docking, Director of the Auckland City Art Gallery, explained the popularity of Goldie's work as 'a manifestation of what in Australia is called "out-backery".'

> It is a trend to see anything depicting early colonial days in a romantic light. He [Docking] calls its New Zealand manifestation 'Maoriana'... 'These people probably think it is a good investment and it probably is, because the prices have never gone down'... 'There is no doubt Goldie exerts a curious appeal over people. I don't praise it and I don't condemn it. I simply observe it.'[6]

The auction records of the 1960s record an astonishing fact: that any authentic painting by Goldie, regardless of whether it dated from the earlier years or from the later period, *any* painting by Goldie was proving to be a brilliant investment. In 1972, when Goldie prices had reached $7000 ('the high four-figure bracket' as it was called), the *Woman's Weekly* reported art critic Hamish Keith's opinion on the inflationary spiral: 'Mr Keith feels the Goldie market has reached its peak, and certainly doesn't think the prices will swing any higher – if anything, they'll drop.' Meanwhile, Peter Webb (then auctioneer for John Cordy Ltd) was predicting that Goldies would hit the $10,000 mark before long. Sir Henry Kelliher was convinced his Goldie collection would soon double in value. In Sir Henry's words, a painting by Goldie was a 'gilt-edged investment'.[7]

Consistently record-breaking prices continued to ensure variants on the eye-catching headline 'Record Price For Goldie': $16,000 in 1975, $18,000 in 1976, and $28,000 in 1977. In 1984 Peter Webb, who prophesied the five-figure break-through of the 1970s, was predicting that Goldie would soon break the $100,000 barrier. This duly came to pass in 1988, when the *Herald*'s headline simply announced 'Top Goldie'.[8] What was truly remarkable here is that the painting which had just sold for $110,000 was precisely the same painting that created the $18,000 record in 1976 as well as the $28,000 record in 1977. Dealer Grahame Chote boasted that it was the fourth time in twelve years that his gallery had owned the work. The painting of Te Aho-o-te-Rangi was like a comet sweeping through the market-place at regular intervals, leaving a trail of profit.

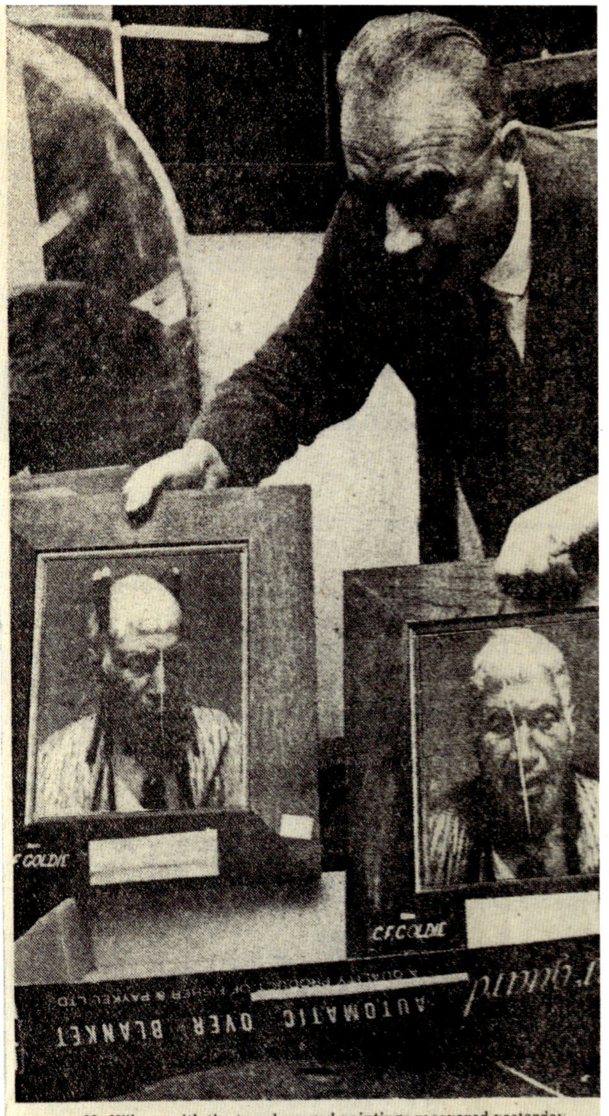

Mr Wiberg with the two damaged paintings recovered yesterday.

Goldie Harm 'Malicious'

Two valuable paintings lost from the offices of George Walker, Ltd, auctioneers, in Queen St last week are believed to have been maliciously scratched with a sharp instrument.

A member of the firm's | "When I asked him for his

*Mr Wiberg with the stolen and vandalised paintings (*New Zealand Herald *29 July 1969).*

theft, vandalism and forgery

Reports of stolen Goldie paintings have only reinforced the mystique surrounding their value. In mid-1969 a thief broke into Auckland auctioneers George Walker Ltd, making off with two Goldies but ignoring two others also hanging in the manager's office.[1] Both paintings depicted Ngāti Awa chieftainess Wiripine Ninia and were valued at $3500 each. Several days later the paintings – each of which had been slashed vertically – were located in an old electric-blanket carton on the firm's cartdock.[2] The portraits were restored and sold several months later, with no culprit or explanation of the event ever discovered.

Perhaps the most sensational theft occurred on 7 September 1973, when two small Goldie paintings were stolen from a display in the National Art Gallery, Wellington. 'Golly! They're gone!' read one of the headlines, quoting the security guard who discovered them missing. 'I broke out in a sweat . . .I thought hell's bells what do I do now?'[3] One was *Te Hei* from 1909, measuring 7¾ x 5¾ inches; the other was a 1919 depiction of Pipi Haerehuka titled *Pipi Puzzled,* measuring 10½ x 8½ inches. Each was valued at $6000. The *Dominion*'s editorial thundered: 'The theft of the Goldies is undoubtedly more than a crime: it is a violation of the trust of the people of New Zealand into whose hands such items have been placed.'[4] There were rival opinions, such as the handwritten legend 'They've gone missing! Isn't it marvellous!' on a flier advertising the theft.[5] An attempt to claim the reward led police to the Wairakei Hotel near Taupō, where a Wanganui man was intercepted with the stolen paintings in his possession. They then returned to the Gallery 'in good condition except for damage caused by being cut from their frames'.[6]

While these two missing paintings were in the news, someone stole a larger work from a 15-foot-high vantage point in the hall of Auckland Grammar School.[7] A gift to the school from Goldie's classmate Eliot R. Davis, this painting soon returned from what was described as an 'unscheduled trip to Rotorua'.[8] An even more nightmarish plight for any institution is the theft of a painting which is merely on loan. A few days before Christmas 1981, a small portrait valued at $10,000, on loan from a private collector, was noticed missing from a storage area in the Dowse Art Museum in Lower Hutt.[9] The following day, under the headline 'Stolen Goldie slipped back at secret rendezvous', the public was informed that a clandestine meeting between police and 'an unknown party' had succeeded in recovering the painting, less than 48 hours after its theft had first been reported. Although lacking its frame, *The Scribe* was reportedly no worse for the experience.

Intentional vandalism is a perpetual worry for museums, although there are few recorded instances of Goldie's work suffering in this way. In 1944, the *Herald* reported on the work of a knife-wielding vandal in Christchurch's Art Gallery.[10] The portrait of Ina Te Papatahi had sustained a small knife-scratch on the face, minor damage compared to the metre-wide slash across a large figure painting by the English artist G. Sheridan Knowles. Sometimes damage can be inflicted unintentionally, but still be perceived as vandalism. In 1985, only days after the closing of the Auckland Art Gallery's blockbuster Monet exhibition, a small, finger-sized hole was found in *The Arrival of the Maoris in New Zealand*. First reported in the *Auckland Star*, the news was soon relayed throughout New Zealand's network of regional newspapers.[11] The value of *The Arrival* was reported to be 'at least $100,000', at a time when the record for a New Zealand painting at auction was $50,000 for a Colin McCahon. The strongest public reaction was a letter from Ian Gordon of Avondale to the editor of the *Auckland Star*, reported under the headline 'A curse on you': 'May the person responsible be cursed by the tohunga and all things evil.'[12] As this incident demonstrates, the New Zealand public's love affair with Goldie and the fate of his works is perpetuated by the media's own innate passion for his name.

In terms of media interest, theft and vandalism are eclipsed only by the topic of art forgery. Goldie forgeries are distinct from the variously skilful copies of Goldie's works which enjoy a wide circulation. Pupils of Goldie such as Veronica Cummings made copies of their master's work, while early colour reproductions spawned many subsequent oil copies, some of which have been mistaken for originals. In 1938 Thomas H. Smith of Wanganui, searching for Māori artefacts in a Sydney curio shop, found what he believed to be an original Goldie worth at least £200. From Sydney he announced his intention of presenting it to the Wanganui Museum or the Sarjeant Gallery, Wanganui.[13] Once Smith was back in Wellington, a newspaper photographed the painting and solicited the artist's opinion. Goldie proclaimed it 'probably not even a copy, but a copy of a copy, and a bad one at that' of *A Hot Day* from the Christchurch collection, which had been a colour print in 1904.[14]

The nature of forgery dictates that its practitioners remain anonymous. The single current exception is Karl Feodor Sim, New Zealand's only convicted art forger, who changed his name by deed poll to Carl Feodor Goldie and now quite legitimately signs his productions *C. F. Goldie*. Until he was raided in August 1984, Sim had spent more than a decade happily concocting works by a range of artists including Goldie, Frances Hodgkins and Rita Angus – the common denominator being that all were key players in the art market and therefore attractive to gullible bargain-hunters. A primary motive for most forgers is to fool the 'experts' and Sim claims considerable success on this score, asserting authorship of a group of Petrus van der Velden drawings purchased for $5500 by the National Art Gallery.[15] Eventually the flood of historical art originating from Sim's Foxton wine bar and antique shop led to a seven-week trial in mid-1985, held in the High Court at Wellington. His sentence was a $1000 fine and 200 hours' community service: 'Much of that was spent painting the Foxton council offices and toilet, at their insistence

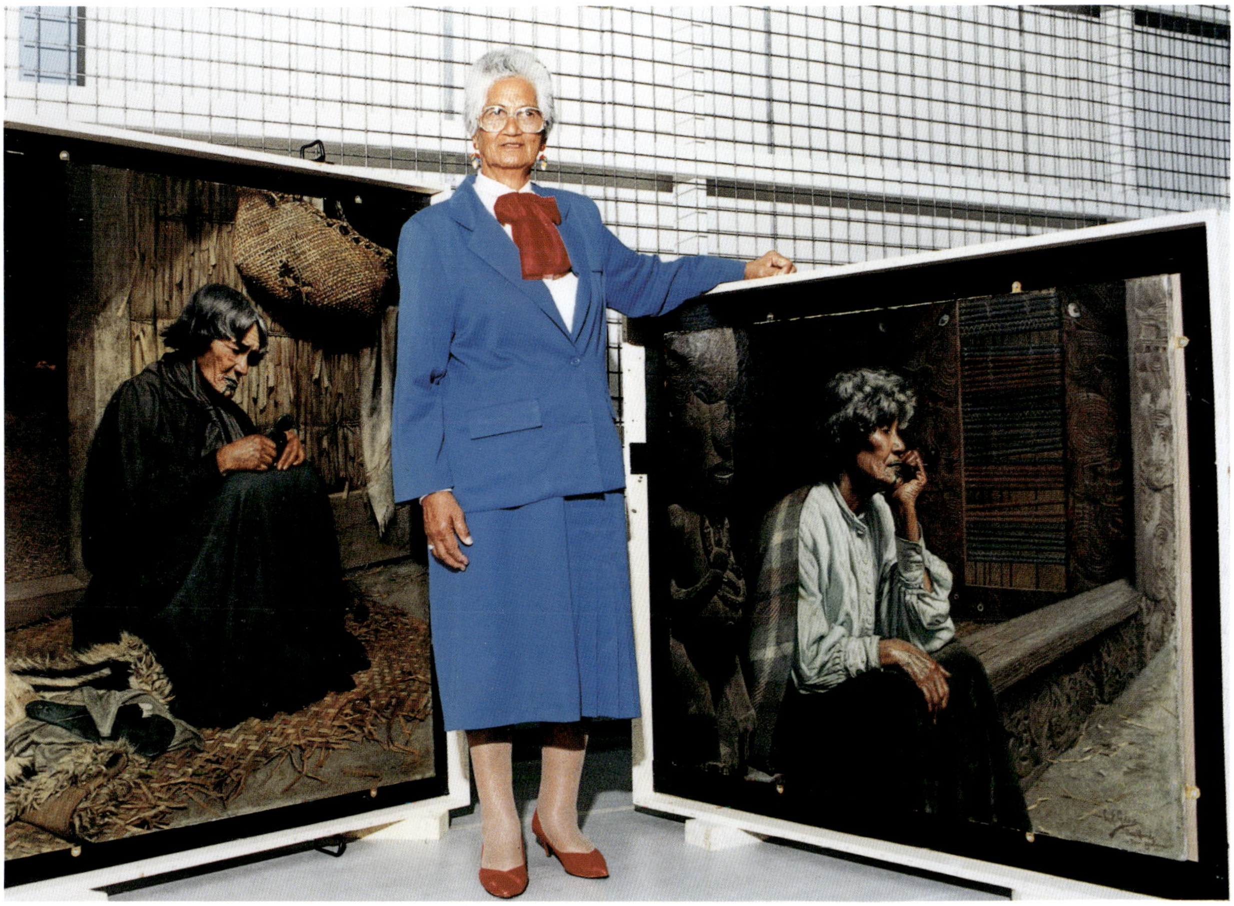

Mrs Ellen Hulme, a fifth-generation descendant of the Ngā Puhi chief Patuone, greeting her relatives Ina Te Papatahi and Harata Rewiri Tarapata at the National Art Gallery, December 1990 (photograph by Martin Hunter, courtesy of New Zealand Herald*).*

signing his new name in pride of place on the ceiling.'[16] The pictures used as court exhibits quickly sold, indicating that the other C. F. Goldie had established his own market. Subsequent work has verged on surrealism, including portraits of Frances Hodgkins and Colin McCahon signed by Goldie. 'One of his last pictures was a portrait of Sir Rob Muldoon in the style of Goldie. It is now hanging in a National Party office.'[17]

Karl Sim's Goldie drawings are of relatively poor quality and easily recognised, at least retrospectively. Yet Sim is undoubtedly correct in announcing that there are 'more forgeries out there'. Although he is referring to his own work, there also exist suspicious paintings and drawings by more accomplished hands than Sim's. There are very good prospects of further headlines concerning Goldie forgeries.

the 'ranfurly' controversy

The mother of all Goldie controversies erupted in late 1990, when the public learned that the National Art Gallery had purchased for $900,000 (or over $1 million, including GST) the two Goldie paintings presented to the Countess of Ranfurly in 1903.[1] The furious public debate focussed largely on the purported value of the works, which had been turned down by a previous administration at the Gallery when the English owner offered them to the New Zealand government in 1989 at their long-standing insurance value of $300,000. The owner, the great-granddaughter of the Countess of Ranfurly, eventually sold them at half that amount to two prominent New Zealand art dealers, who sold them on to the National Art Gallery at a massive personal profit.[2] One justification offered by the Gallery was that, as an institution founded in 1936, it had never had an opportunity to acquire 'classic' Goldie works from his best period. Yet what was never admitted, or rather had been forgotten over the subsequent decades, was that its older sisters (the Colonial Museum, Dominion Museum and Academy of Fine Arts) had considered and refused works offered by the artist in 1906 and 1910.

Although many of the participants in this debate questioned Goldie's stature as an artist, the inevitable result of this controversy was the enhancement of the artist's profile in the public imagination. Many commentators compared the prices paid for the paintings with auction results for much lesser works, obscuring the fact that the two paintings occupied a unique place in Goldie's production. In an essay first published in *Art New Zealand* and reprinted on pages 115-120, Leonard Bell pointed out that the paintings were in their own time recognised as superlative productions by a young man then thought to be New Zealand's greatest artist. Neither the Countess who received the gift, nor the Aucklanders who made it, had any doubt over this issue. And as Rosemary McLeod pointed out, 'Past art brawls were always based on knowledgeable institutions clashing with an ignorant public: the smart against the uneducated. In this case, there's a novel twist: the public loves Goldie and is expected to enjoy these portraits.'[3]

The 'Ranfurly' paintings, undeniably two of Goldie's more significant works, fully deserve their place in the Museum of New Zealand Te Papa Tongarewa. Not only are they superlative works of Pākehā art from the late colonial period, but by virtue of their subject matter they function as taonga Māori. Although one Pākehā critic described the works as 'coon humour', Māori were unanimously supportive of the purchase. Bruce Gregory, Member of Parliament for Northern Māori, denounced the debate over their value: 'Artwork depicting ancestors had a worth beyond monetary value to Māori'.[4] Once they were on display in the Museum, the visitors' book resounded with enthusiastic praise interspersed with occasional criticism. *Ka nui ō mahi! Tino ātaahua ngā taonga... You can't place a price on History – and they belong here... ohooho ana te mana, te wehi, ka tū honohono te hā o te wairua o rātou mā kua wehe ki te Pō... Truly, Goldie is the Rembrandt of New Zealand... What an appalling waste of my taxes... Ka pai ngā taonga a ō tātou tīpuna... Welcome home, Goldies.*

goldie in the māori world

Māori enthusiasm for Goldie's works is intrinsically linked to their nature as portraits. As depictions of named individuals, the paintings command respect and evoke pride, especially among descendants and relatives of those depicted. In 1926, Australian writer A. G. Stephens hailed Goldie as one of Australasia's leading portrait painters, his 'men and chiefs alive in the likeness of their living'.

> A Maori descendant of the warrior Te Aho, for example, might stand in front of Mr Goldie's pictures and feel his blood leap as he traced his own lineaments and even his own character in the painted portrait.[1]

Pākehā writers have repeatedly evoked Māori reverence for depicted ancestors. Concluding a 1941 essay on 'The Art of C. F. Goldie', James Cowan wrote: 'He has gained high and well-merited honour at the Royal Academy and the Paris Salon. Greater still is the worship, expressed in tears and murmured song, which Goldie's portraits arouse in the loving heart of the Maori.' Writing at the time of Goldie's death in 1947, Herbert Wadham maintained that: 'Old Maoris wept to see such faithful rendering of their dying chiefs and

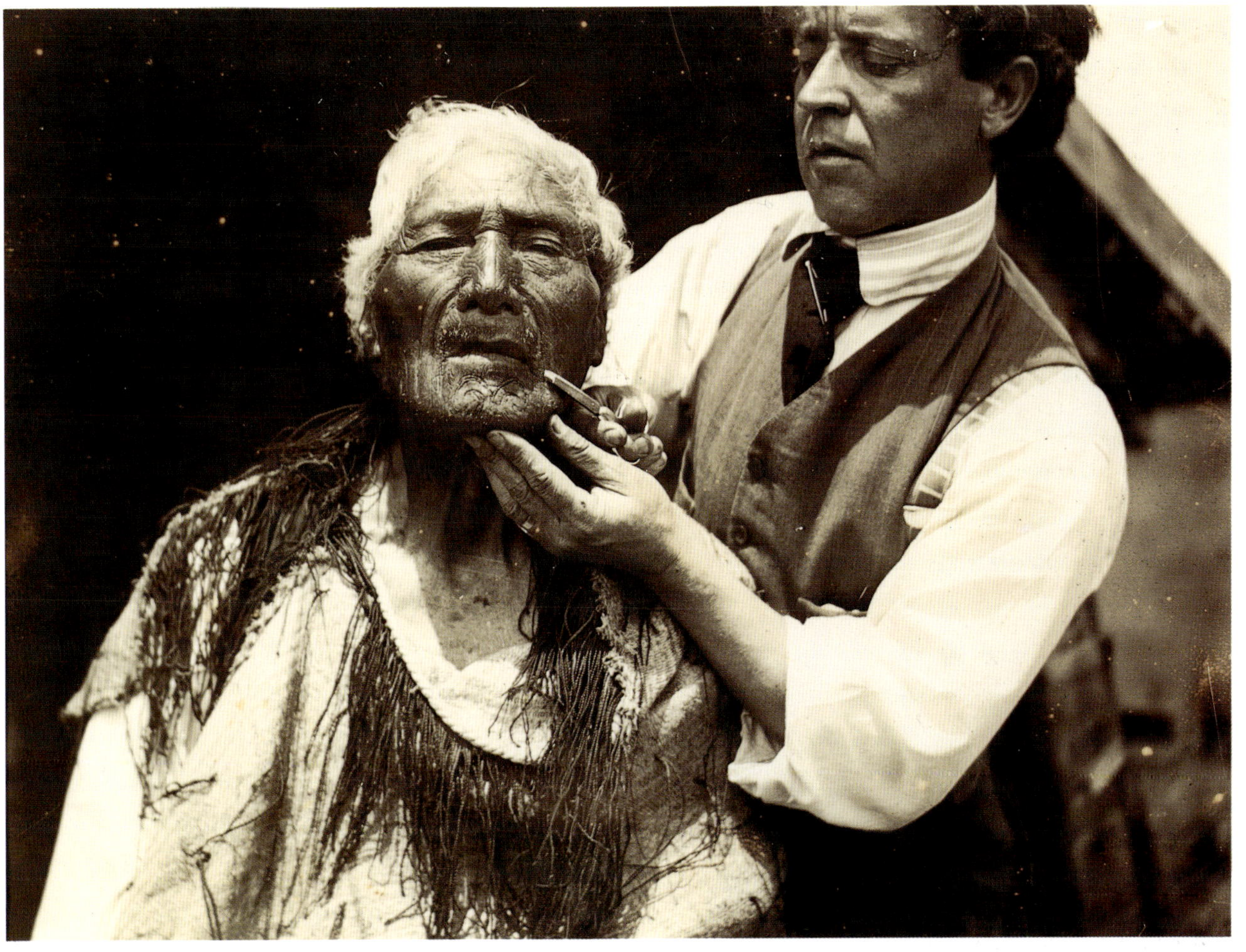

failing culture.' Subsequent commentators continue to speak on behalf of Māori, either hailing his evocation of the 'soul' of the Māori, or condemning the 'racist' agenda epitomised in his nostalgic portrayal of the 'old-time' Māori.

Māori visitors to the Auckland Art Gallery have never shared the general Pākehā enthusiasm for *The Arrival of the Maoris*. As early as 1902, there was a report that 'Maoris who view the picture in the Art Gallery are indignant at the manner in which it is represented that the natives arrived in New Zealand'.[2] In 1934, George Graham wrote concerning 'faults' in the Goldie-Steele *Arrival* and an alternative depiction by Kennett Watkins:

> I have often accompanied elderly Maoris to view these pictures. Far from being appreciative, they always regard them with dubious feelings and disdain. To them they are mere creations of the pakeha mind and not consistent with the traditional records of the matters represented.[3]

Interestingly, the elders were equally uncomfortable with Watkins's more 'correct' version of the arrival which had been on display since 1912. James Cowan joined the debate, agreeing with Graham's criticism of the anachronistic canoe carvings.[4] But it was the emaciated condition of the voyagers that dismayed Māori visitors, who refused to believe that their forefathers arrived in Aotearoa in such severe straits.

Goldie trimming the beard of Atama Paparangi, around 1911 (Auckland Art Gallery Toi o Tāmaki).

Pākehā ethnologists were also unhappy with the painting. Writing in a journal for museum professionals in 1974, David Simmons explained:

> Ethnologically ... the picture is a disaster. The crew are shown as Polynesians with no tattoo, wearing tapa cloth, but they are sailing a mixed-up double Maori canoe of the eighteenth century using a sail form which probably never existed. So we have a presumably fourteenth century Maori arriving in New Zealand in a canoe with an eighteenth-century carving and a notional construction.[5]

Māori have continued to voice their displeasure over the painting. *The Arrival* was 'insulting to the Māori people and their ancestors' mastery of the sea', announced Ōtorohanga kaumatua and historian Tahana Pango Wahanui in 1980, when the picture went back on display after restoration.[6] According to Wahanui, Goldie and Steele's image had caused 'a degeneration of cultural understanding'. The Māori response to this work, contrasting so markedly with the acclaim by Pākehā, provides a clear indication that paintings can never be ideologically innocent portrayals of pure 'history'.[7]

Māori responses to Goldie's portraits present quite another story altogether. Goldie's Māori portraits initially required the close collaboration of his models, with whom the painter entered into a business agreement. Although it may not have been their primary motivation for working with the Pākehā artist, the models were happy to accept payment for posing and on occasion expressed delight over the finished works. Unlike Lindauer, from whom Māori clients would commission portraits for their own purposes, Goldie was producing highly priced commodities for a Pākehā market. Nevertheless, an appreciative letter from Atama Paparangi at Hokianga, dated August 1914, records his pleasure on receiving the framed photographic print and states that his tribe was equally delighted. There is a photograph from this period showing Goldie trimming Paparangi's beard, a contentious image which nevertheless reveals something of the trust operating between Goldie and his models [see previous page].[8]

Writing in the 1930s, Te Heuheu Tūkino, paramount chief of Ngāti Tūwharetoa, described Goldie as 'Ko te tangata tino mōhio tēnei o te ao, ki te whakaahua (peita) i te kara o te Māori', world-renowned, particularly for his paintings of Māori people. Te Heuheu considered Goldie's works as 'he tohu mō ngā Māori i roto i te whakatupuranga', icons for Māori of future generations. The implication is that some Māori were less than happy with Goldie's portrait work, most probably disquieted by news reports of portraits being exhibited and subsequently sold overseas. Te Heuheu's letter expresses the opinion that Māori could only benefit from inclusion in the Paris Salon and is evidence that Goldie enjoyed support from the very highest echelons of Māoridom. The texts by Atama Paparangi and Te Heuheu Tūkino appear on page 181.

On the other hand, the failure of the Colonial and later the Dominion Museum to acquire works by Goldie indicates lukewarm support from other Māori highly placed in Government: James Carroll and Āpirana Ngata. Sir James Carroll was the minister in charge of the museum when the cabinet of Seddon's government considered Goldie's offer in 1906. When the second offer was considered in 1910, Carroll was still a cabinet member alongside Ngata. Carroll may well have been supportive of Hamilton's proposed acquisition, as he probably was of the 1908 commission to Australian sculptor Nelson Illingworth for a series of Māori busts. It may have been Goldie's relatively high asking prices, especially the price of 200 guineas for an 'original', which determined the eventual outcome.

Māori could also be forthright critics of portraits which fell short of expectations, as was the case with Illingworth. Regarding his initial work with

Pātara Te Tuhi, the *Herald* commented: 'It was only a rough cast, and the natives formed a poor opinion of "Iringiwata" as a sculptor, nor had they any scruples about making their opinion known.'[9]

Māori have always been keen purchasers of books which include Māori portraits and were among the subscribers to Alister Taylor's limited-edition volumes of the late 1970s. The first volume's 1600 copies, distributed by Masterton bookseller David Hedley in 1977, were priced at $200 each and had sold out four months *before* the publication date. At the time of the second volume in 1979, the *Herald* reported on Hedley's earlier visit to Auckland:

> Hedley made the distribution to these buyers from a city motel. It was, he says, an interesting exercise. One of his first callers drove up in a Jaguar, received his book and 'didn't even look at it.' The next buyer was a Maori from Otara. He arrived with his family in an old car and with much excitement they leafed through the book, admiring Goldie's works, delighted to find an ancestor among the portraits.[10]

The reporter then noted that the 1977 book, only a year after its publication at $200, had increased in value to $600. What we are encouraged to infer from this story is that the man in the Jaguar was probably attracted by the investment potential of the book, whereas the Māori family was truly interested in the portraits themselves.

Writing within Taylor's book, on 'The Maori and C. F. Goldie', Michael King points out that Goldie's work 'preserves the European fantasies about Maori people held during the artist's lifetime':

> Some of the more romantic, especially those that include native costume, imply noble savages. Others contain strong doses of sentimentality and jingoism in their suggestion of a formerly self-reliant race now confused (*Pipi Puzzled*), brooding over spiritual defeat (*Thoughts of a Tohunga*) and facing extinction (*One of the Old School*). There is also considerable condescension in the suggestions of an inability to master language (*All 'e same t'e Pakeha*) and a people one step removed from heathenish practices (tattooing itself and titles like *The Last of the Cannibals*).[11]

In contrast with these culturally biased elements, King identifies the positive side of Goldie's project as the preservation of 'a formerly coherent system of Polynesian art'. That is, its role in documenting tā moko, or facial tattooing.

There is general agreement that no other painter – or photographer – depicted the effect of chisel-carved moko as effectively as Goldie. Theo Schoon, a Dutch colonial immigrant who became interested in moko during the 1950s, realised that Pākehā portraits of Māori were a storehouse of information on the unique art of tā moko.

> From a European artist's point of view, Goldie and Lindauer are little more than 'calendar' artists of little or no consequence. But the fact that they became recording artists in New Zealand, who understood that meticulous care was one of the essentials, they became important artists in their own right, beyond the European – or old world yardsticks of values.[12]

Schoon's comment helps to explain the wider Māori interest in Goldie's portraits, which goes beyond the reverence for their ancestors on the part of descendants. The paintings are of especially intense interest to many Māori concerned with tā moko and its current revival. The fact that Goldie's models are from a range of tribal areas means that the corpus of paintings presents students of tā moko with a rich source of images, within which the styles of individual practitioners should be identifiable. The only tohunga tā moko named in the Goldie literature is Huitara, who tattooed Atama Paparangi of Hokianga.[13]

trouble with reproductions

The most problematic area for Māori has always been that of reproduction, linked to the fact that actual ownership of the paintings was almost exclusively in Pākehā hands. As Michael King explains:

> Fear of commercialisation is perhaps the most intense manifestation of this anxiety [over inappropriate use of images]. And it is justified. People have seen paintings of their relatives by Lindauer and Goldie fetch huge prices for owners who neither know nor care about the subjects of the portraits. Family photographs have appeared on posters and in advertisements. Others have been used on postcards or (worse) on food wrappings, biscuit tins and walls in hotel diningrooms – obscene gestures in Maori terms.[1]

It is the inappropriate context of many Goldie reproductions which continues to infuriate many Māori. Descendants report feeling ill when faced with auction advertisements featuring their ancestor's image, often alongside an estimated price.

Goldie's models clearly consented to the paintings they saw the artist produce, which they knew would be offered for sale. What is less certain is whether the models knew of Goldie's intention to produce replicas for sale, an activity revealed by his 1906 offer to the Colonial Museum. Goldie permitted the production of high-quality chromolithographs: the best type of colour reproduction possible at the time. These were widely distributed at Christmas time by the illustrated journals, such as the *Auckland Weekly News* and the *New Zealand Graphic,* and were framed for display in both Māori and Pākehā households. This was during the lifetime of his models, including Ina Te Papatahi, Pātara Te Tuhi and Te Aho-o-te-Rangi Wharepu, whose consent for high-quality reproductions of this type can be construed by their continuing to model for him. Around 1905, Te Aho-o-te-Rangi wrote the following note to Goldie:

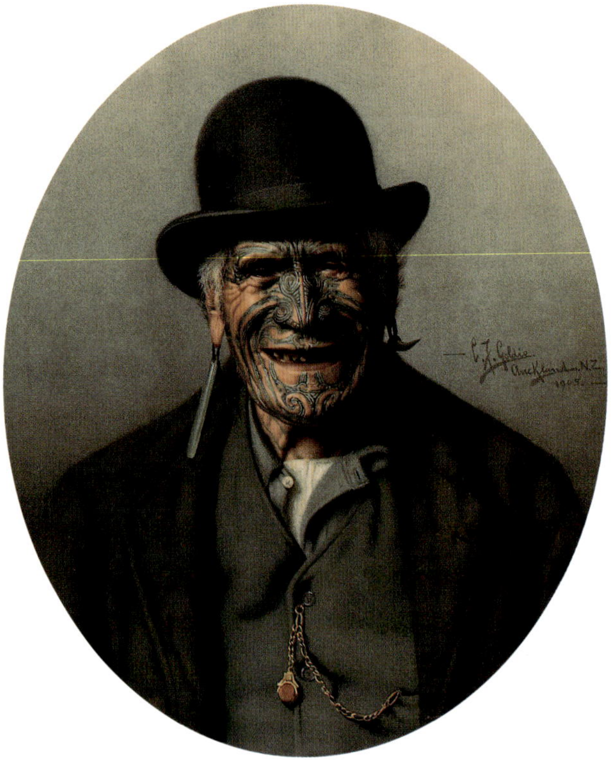

> Ki a Hāre, ka pai te whakakata ka ngahau tāua, ka kino te riri ka wehi au. Nā Te Aho. (Charlie, it's good to laugh and amuse ourselves; anger is bad, it frightens me. Te Aho.)[2]

The first part of this text probably provided the title *A Good Joke,* which appeared on reproductions of *'All 'e same t'e Pakeha'*. The second part is ambiguous, suggesting either that Goldie and Te Aho-o-te-Rangi had been quarrelling, or that Te Aho-o-te-Rangi had encountered anger from other quarters.

It is possible that this anger related to the several reproductions of Goldie's 1905 paintings of Te Aho-o-te-Rangi which appeared within the pages of the *Auckland Weekly News* and *New Zealand Graphic.* Newspapers, disposable and used for profane activities, were considered inappropriate vehicles for portraits. On the other hand, the contemporary chromolithographs were eagerly collected by Māori, placed in meeting houses and displayed at tangi. Goldie himself remembered seeing two copies of *A Hot Day* hanging over the coffin when he attended the tangi of Pātara Te Tuhi in 1910.[3]

The reproduction of Māori portraits continues to be a fraught issue, while the 1998 expiry of Goldie's copyright promises to complicate matters even further. In 1994, descendants of Te Aho-o-te-Rangi were alarmed by

The 1910 chromolithograph A Good Joke *(391 x 322 mm, Alexander Turnbull Library, Wellington).*

widely distributed advertisements offering the image of their ancestor on a 'limited-edition' ceramic plate, from the international firm Bradford Exchange. The appearance of an ancestral portrait on a receptacle for food was offensive in Māori terms. Although the plate reproduced a 1905 painting in a private collection, anger was understandably directed towards the Auckland Museum which houses an almost identical painting. The plate ('limited to an edition of 45 firing days') was advertised as the first in a series of 'Masterpieces of Charles Goldie' and later advertisements significantly appended the statement 'not intended for food'. Apparently, lack of interest terminated the planned series.

A recent court case, reported in the *New Zealand Herald,* presents a story of cross-cultural conflict concerning the inappropriate presentation of Goldie paintings, or rather reproductions of his paintings.

Goldie fan jailed for hotel attack

ROTORUA — An Opotiki man who thought it disrespectful that Goldie paintings were hanging in a hotel was sentenced to six months' prison yesterday for breaking a pool cue over the head of a publican.

Peter Griffith Helmbright, aged 44, unemployed, was appearing before Justice Morris in the High Court at Rotorua.

He had pleaded guilty to wounding with intent in an Opotiki hotel on December 30.

His counsel, Mr Simon Lance, said Helmbright had strong feelings for Goldie paintings in the Opotiki hotel and thought it disrespectful that they were hanging in a place where alcohol was consumed.

He and a friend took the paintings.

Police later came to Helmbright's house and found him in a drunken slumber. They detained his wife and took her to the police station. When Helmbright awoke his children told him what had happened. He became angry and went first to the police station and then next door to the hotel.

He blamed the publican for what happened, picked up the nearest object – a pool cue – and hit the publican over the head.

Justice Morris said Helmbright received some leniency for being remoreseful and for his early guilty plea.

'But it is a tragedy that a person with such good references has fallen from grace.' – NZPA[4]

Other Goldie reproductions have been more smoothly repatriated from drinking establishments. A news story in 1987, headed 'Chief back on marae', recounted how the picture of Pōkai, usually displayed in the Tikitiki pub near Ruatoria, was shifting to the meeting house named Pōkai at Tikapa Marae.[5] Mōrehu Te Maro explained: 'We wanted the painting back because we are all descendants of Pōkai. His painting does not belong in a pub.' Yet Goldie's Pōkai, whose depiction is held by Mr Te Maro and Mr Peke in the accompanying photograph, is not the Ngāti Porou ancestor of Tikapa Marae. The Hōri Pōkai painted by Goldie was from Thames, the son of Tuari Netana of Ngāti Maru.

Other, more serious cases of mistaken identity have followed in the wake of forged Goldies. At least one forgery has been formally welcomed on to an ancestral marae. In another case, a housewife of Wainuiomata and her family spent $4000 on two drawings they thought depicted their grandmother. This was before police took possession of the drawings in preparation for Karl Sim's trial.[6] Descendants frequently express dismay over poor-quality photomechanical reproductions or hand-painted copies of their ancestor's image offered for sale in tourist shops. Still other descendants have themselves made enquiries to Auckland Art Gallery Toi o Tāmaki regarding how they might obtain a 'forgery' of their ancestor.

smoothing the pillow

At the time Goldie was painting, despite evidence that the drastic decline of the nineteenth century had been halted, the prevailing Pākehā view held that the Māori race was facing extinction. Over and over again, reviewers of Goldie's paintings cited this 'fact' as one of the prime justifications of his work. 'The Maoris were dying out, and the artists of the present day should not miss the opportunity of personally studying them and their magnificent history,' affirmed the *Auckland Star* in 1905.[1] Three decades later, when Goldie was awarded the Order of the British Empire in the Birthday Honours of 1935, the *Star* evoked the old image of the dying race:

> It is a hard word to say, but this eminent New Zealand artist will be long known after the present generation is tucked away – and forgotten. His great pictures of Maori men and women will be 'Old Masters' – and connoisseurs will fight for them in Christie's and elsewhere, perhaps when none of the race he perpetuates are here.[2]

At the turn of the century there were two rival schools of thought concerning the 'end' of the Māori. One was virtually genocidal, proclaiming the literal end of the Māori as a separate race; the other was assimilationist, proposing future New Zealanders of predominantly mixed racial heritage. Both were discourses on the 'end' of Māori culture as such and were calmly debated by Pākehā society.

Addressing the Wellington Philosophical Society in 1884, president Walter Buller proclaimed the 'fact that the Maori race was dying out very rapidly' and predicted that in 25 years only a 'remnant' would remain:

> That the race was doomed he had no doubt whatever in his own mind. What had happened in other parts of the world must inevitably happen, and indeed is happening, here. The aboriginal race must in time give place to a more highly organised, or, at any rate a more civilised one. This seems to be one of the inscrutable laws of Nature. ... He had often reflected on an observation of the late Dr Featherston on their first meeting just 28 years ago:– 'The Maoris (said he) are dying out, and nothing can save them. Our plain duty, as good, compassionate colonists, is to smooth down their dying pillow. Then history will have nothing to reproach us with.'[3]

Buller's confident predictions of a speedy extinction are representative of a dominant view within colonial thought, expressed by politicians, educators and churchmen. Archdeacon Walsh's paper 'The Passing of the Maori' was read before the Auckland Institute in 1907, to an audience containing the eminent Māori doctors Māui Pōmare and Te Rangihīroa.[4] William Baucke, writing from Te Kuiti in 1905, was one of the few who focussed on the moral implications of such a discourse: 'It is immoral ... to suggest that, to be rid of [the Māori] and the eternal perplexities he creates, his remnants be collected into a huge gasometer and gently asphyxiated, and be done with the trouble!'[5]

An opposing view considered that racial amalgamation promised a very different future for the Māori. The young Āpirana Ngata, writing in 1897, deplored the mixing of the races: 'Must we languish and die by the hearths of our *pakeha* lovers and husbands, that the mongrel race of the future may boast a long descent from the Gods of the Pacific, that there may be added to the all conquering all devouring Anglo-Saxon, a fresh strain of blood. . .?'[6] Yet the census returns, which in the nineteenth century had appeared to spell extinction, and by 1901 confirmed Māori regeneration, also revealed the burgeoning mixed-race population (5539, or 12.84% out of a total Māori population of 43,143). Goldie's brother, Dr William Goldie, commented on the 1901 census returns in an essay titled 'The Destiny of the Maori Race'. William contradicted the genocidal predictions of Buller and company, seeing a fusion of the races as both inevitable and desirable. He predicted that 'the Maori half-castes, and eventually the mixed race, will be superior to either of the parent stocks.' While William Goldie's assimilationist text inevitably partakes of a colonial paternalism, like Baucke he is concerned with undermining the appalling predictions of extinction.

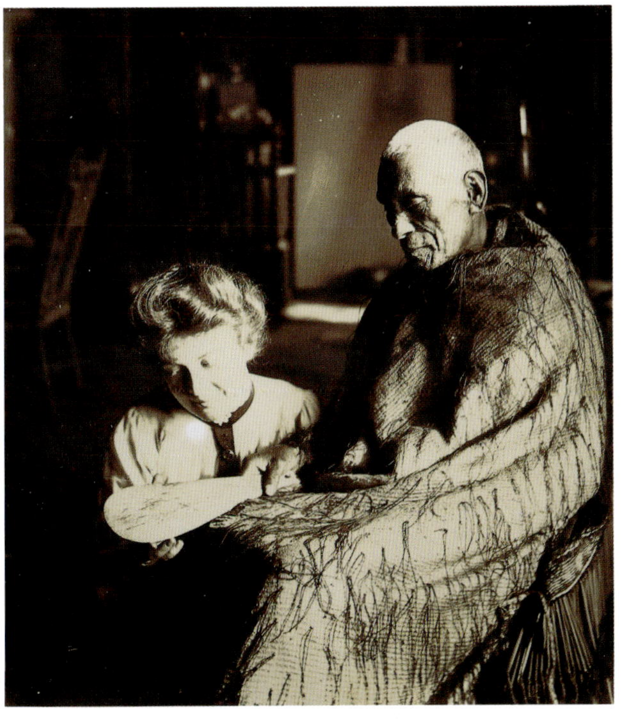

Essays concerning the fate of the Māori race appeared in publications in which Goldie's paintings were reproduced. For example, in the same 1903 issue of the *Illustrated Magazine* as an illustration of Goldie's *The Widow,* the feminist writer Edith Searle Grossman asked: 'Is it necessary to change the Maoris altogether, to stamp out the genius of the race?'

> The modern Maoris are a degraded people because, although we have not actively oppressed them, we have never taught them to respect themselves, but have crushed them by our superiority. There are two alternatives before us. We may absorb the higher members of the race into our own, and let the rest decay, or we may keep them as a separate but friendly race in our midst, emerging from their old savagery, but on their own natural lines of development.[7]

Charles Goldie must have read contributions such as Grossman's, but his own views on this debate are unknown. It is likely that he knew that the Māori was facing change rather than extinction. Nevertheless, his primary focus was on the elderly survivors of the pre-colonial era, that 'classic past' which so obsessed the ethnologists of this period. The widespread notion that Goldie believed he was painting the last members of a dying race is therefore understandable, given his models' dejected demeanour and accompanying titles such as *The Last of Her Tribe* and *A Noble Relic of a Noble Race.*

Goldie's focus on elderly models necessarily excluded any sense of the dynamism of contemporary Māori culture, attracting criticism from recent commentators. As Ken Gorbey remarked in 1974:

> In an age of the Young Maori Party, in an age when Te Puea was, in kibbutz-like conditions of toil and hardship, re-establishing the Kingmen's marae at Turangawaewae, Goldie chose to pick his subjects from among the old, and often among the dead, and further chose to present these subjects as stereotypes, relics, remnants.[8]

It should be noted, however, that Goldie's *œuvre* does contain depictions of young and middle-aged Māori. While a number date from the early years of his career, before he commenced his concentration on the 'Noble Relics', they recur at regular intervals. Examples include *Hinemoa, the Belle of the Kainga* [p.151] of 1913, depicting a model of mixed Pākehā-Māori parentage, and such late works as *The Heir Apparent* of 1939 [p.174]. Another late work, *Ancestors and Descendants* [p.173], juxtaposes ancient carvings with a young mother and child.

Kamariera Te Wharepapa with a visitor to Goldie's studio, possibly the actress Grace Palotta (Auckland Art Gallery Toi o Tāmaki, gift of the Goldie family).

pākehā 'history'

The Arrival of the Maoris in New Zealand is New Zealand's most famous 'history painting'. Its popularity for a Pākehā audience has been related to the nineteenth-century predilection for shipwreck imagery, as well as to the comforting message that the tangata whenua or original owners of New Zealand were themselves immigrants.[1] Yet *The Arrival* can additionally be seen to embody in visual terms the genocidal discourse of the period, graphically presenting a dying race hurtling forward on a broken vessel. An instinctive understanding of the subtext of the image could help to explain its popularity among Pākehā, as well as the revulsion felt by Māori.

A similar relationship with contemporary history haunts many of Goldie's works and is revealed both in his titles and by the 'dying race' descriptions of contemporary commentators. Consider the following description of *The memory of what has been and never more will be*:

> Mr Goldie's pictures of Maoris are always more than mere ethnological studies. Each and every one of them has a story to tell. This is most conspicuous in 'The Memory of What Has Been and Never More Will Be'... The old woman is as if under the narcotic influence of tobacco – she holds a pipe in her hands, is looking towards the ground, but there is that in her half-closed rheumy eyes that suggests communion with the past, and its long procession of the departed. Surviving her companions of the 'Never More Will Be', she seems to see again all that was, and to live not in the future, nor for the future, but in the long ago.

Ina's nostalgic dreams of the 'Never More Will Be' take place in a decadent present, made explicit by the decaying building seen in the background [p.107]. In a sense, therefore, the cracked carvings and disintegrating mats in Goldie's works of this period can be regarded as a politicised form of still life painting. Rather than the mythic pre-colonial past, preferred by L. J. Steele, Goldie is painting the colonial present tense.

Many commentators expressed the opinion that the narrow focus of Goldie's work meant that it lacked true historical qualities. Society of Arts president A. E. T. Devore, opening the 1905 exhibition, proposed that artists should take up 'such subjects as the British taking possession of New Zealand, the massacre of the *Boyd,* the arrival of the first emigrant ship... Such pictures as those he had suggested would be of great historical and educational value.'[2] Another critic in 1905 gave Goldie the following advice:

> Before leaving this exceedingly clever artist's work I cannot refrain from expressing the hope that instead of confining himself almost exclusively to Maori heads he will paint some historical picture, some striking episode in the history of the colony, such, for instance, as the storming of the Gate Pah, and then forward the same to England for exhibition in the Royal Academy. With a strong subject dealt with by such a master hand a picture as suggested would create an immense amount of attention, for there is not a shadow of doubt it would be received and well hung. In any case, it would prove a splendid addition to our own Art Gallery.[3]

The same Wellington critic who thought Goldies 'more suitable for a museum of ethnology and anthropology than for the walls of an art gallery' proceeded to ask 'why does not this artist, who has, apparently, so many Maori models at his disposal, set to work on a big canvas of some great historical incident, say, in the Waikato war?'[4]

Yet there were others who thought that Goldie's work *did* qualify as history painting. In a 1933 essay titled 'Painting history', James Cowan followed Bledisloe's lead in attributing historical significance to Goldie's work:

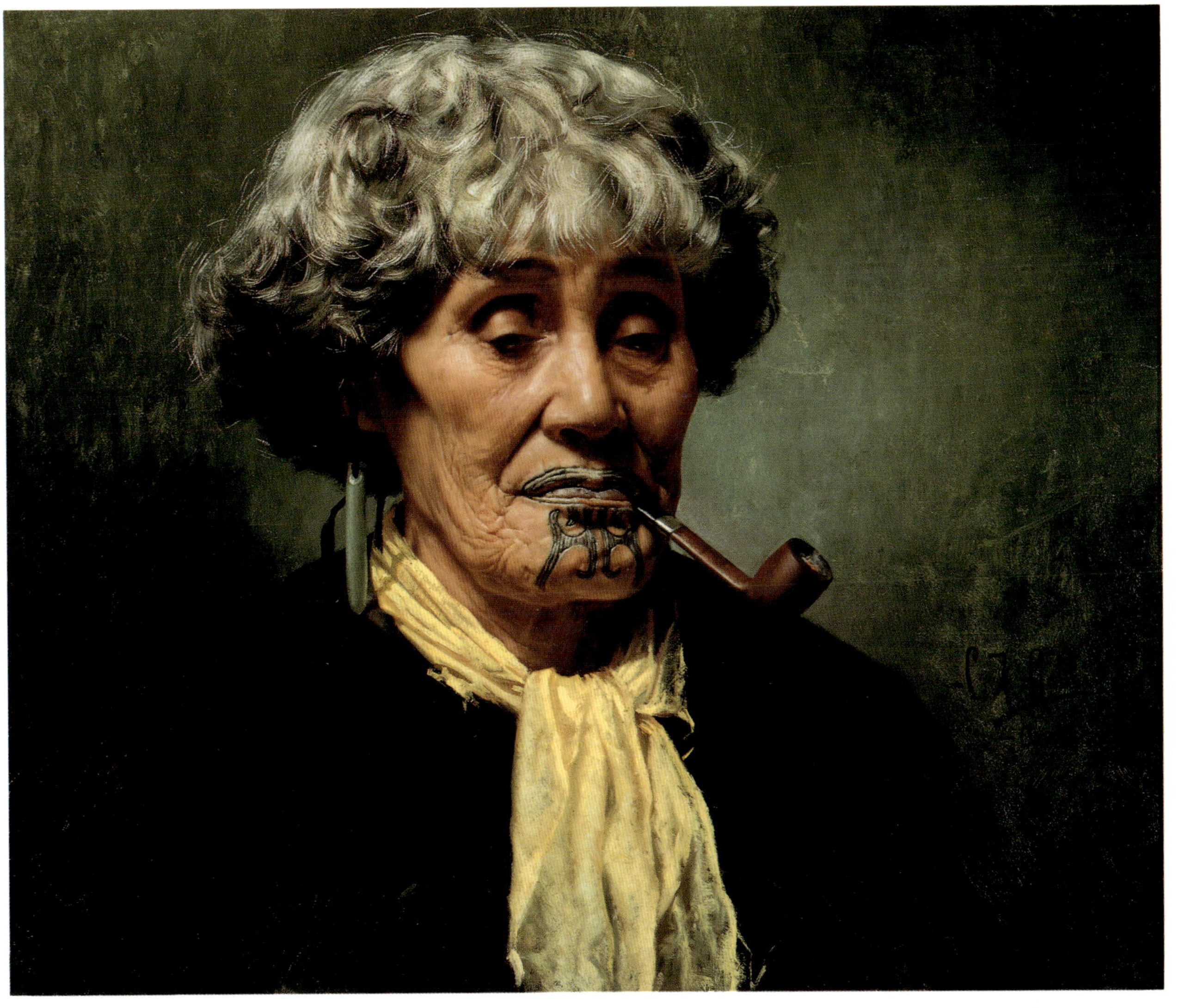

A 1902 painting of Ina Te Papatahi (oil on canvas, 510 x 610 mm, Robert McDougall Art Gallery, Christchurch, gift of the family of James Jamieson, 1932).

'Mr Goldie was only just in time to catch those grand old tattooed faces that are seen no more. He has conspicuously done his share of painting living history, the figures of a heroic and poetic past.'[5] Contemporary commentaries often stressed the role that Goldie's models played in a distant past, usually the pre-colonial era of tribal warfare with its attendant cannibalism, or the more recent colonial wars. James Cowan specialised in this type of commentary, as seen in his account of the pictures Goldie placed on loan to the Auckland Art Gallery in 1920 (see pages 187-189).

Certain portraits have more unusual historical rationales, such as *Aue! Aue!*, a depiction of Rahapa Hinetapu wearing a traditional cloak and gazing upwards.[6] This painting relates to a day in April 1922 when an aeroplane called *High Jinks* provided the astonished residents of Rotorua with their first glimpse of an aircraft. It then proceeded to make a crash landing adjacent to hot pools.[7] Rahapa's cry of astonishment, supposedly over seeing her first aircraft, could equally be alarm over its fateful flight path. Other paintings, ostensibly presenting figures from a distant past, nevertheless have contemporary relevance. The inverted commas in Goldie's title of the 1910 depiction of Te Wharekauri Tahuna, *'Tohunga' or Priest of the Tuhoe Tribe*, relate to the controversial suppression of traditional medical practices formalised in the Tohunga Suppression Act of 1907. Early this century, 'tohunga' was a particularly loaded word.

Goldie's 'ethnographs', the paintings of models decked in cloaks and greenstone, are of course the very works that critics thought should be housed in museums rather than art galleries. But what are we to make of the considerable number of models who are attired in contemporary dress, including Ina Te Papatahi (*Darby and Joan*), Harata Rewiri Tarapata (*The Widow*), Pātara Te Tuhi (*A Hot Day*) and Te Aho-o-te-Rangi Wharepu (*'All 'e Same t'e Pakeha'*)? To what extent does Goldie's depiction of contemporary Māori fashion, of what may have been the clothing that his models really wore, qualify as contemporary history painting? Edith Searle Grossman, visiting Auckland in 1902, had a keen eye for the particularities of Māori fashion:

> A party came toiling up Constitution Hill, the women with velveteen blouses of scarlet and crimson and green, but shabby black skirts. I once met a pleasant-faced matron who had on a man's calico shirt instead of a blouse. Another was wheeling her baby up Princes Street in an elegant basket perambulator. She had a gorgeous blue 'kerchief tied over her head, its ends fluttering in the breeze, a red apron, a mauve skirt, and a man's jacket of nondescript style and hue. Particoloured shawls are much affected, and skirts are generally of an impartial width all round.[8]

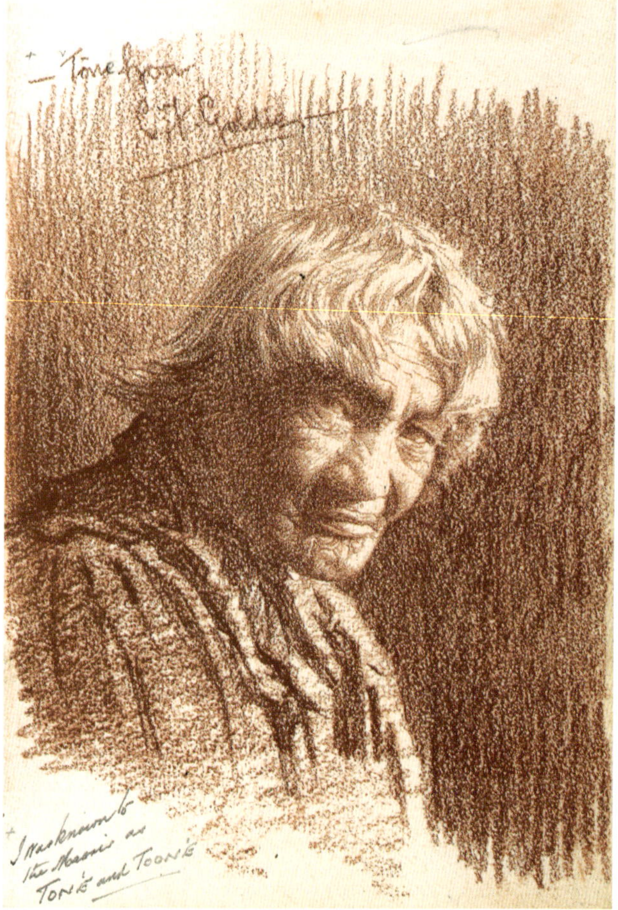

'Tone hoa', Goldie's drawing of Harata Rewiri Tarapata in T. E. Donne's autograph book (conté on paper, 230 x 150 mm, private collection). Donne, who was in charge of the Department of Tourist and Health Resorts, has explained 'I was known to the Maoris as TONÉ and TOONÉ.'

This is precisely the attire of Ina with her velvet blouses and headscarfs, while Harata (in *Meditation*) is sporting a 'particoloured' shawl. Perhaps it is noteworthy that Ina and Harata both lived at Waipapa, the Māori hostel at the foot of Constitution Hill.

The juxtaposition of these colourful garments, remarked on by contemporary critics, suggests the possibility that Goldie may have supplied the clothing as props, just as he did the traditional Māori adornments. One reproduction of 1958, of a painting of Sophia Gray, states: 'The scarf Sofia [sic] is wearing was lent to her by the artist.'[9] Photographs showing Goldie and McVeagh wearing a striped scarf in the studio suggest that Goldie may have procured a supply of such garments. On the other hand, there is every likelihood that in *'All 'e Same t'e Pakeha'* Goldie presents Te Aho-o-te-Rangi Wharepu in his usual clothing of a non-matching jacket and waistcoat, which he would otherwise have removed in order to don a cloak. The 1901 photograph of Goldie and Pātara Te Tuhi in the studio reveals Pātara's shirt, jacket and hat propped on the stack of frames to the left of Goldie, while his trousers and boots protrude below the cloak [p.viii].

A further historical dimension within Goldie's works involves the depiction of Māori women smoking, a pastime which has led to the alarming levels of smoking-related disease among Māori women today. At the turn of the century, smoking in 'polite' Pākehā society denoted masculine behaviour and was reserved for the sexually segregated smoking room or smoking compartment in a train. As vigorous smokers, Māori women blurred this boundary. Their willingness to be depicted in active enjoyment of smoking tobacco provided Goldie's pictures with a cross-cultural *frisson*, showing a pastime that would (in the form of cigarettes) only slowly become acceptable for Pākehā women. A group of his works were given the title *'No Koora te Cigaretti'* [p.149], the translation of which is provided by a 1913 reviewer:

> Of several smaller pictures No.6 ('No Good the Cigarette') is the best. The old lady would evidently prefer a well-seasoned briar to the trifling

> cigarette with which she has apparently to content herself, and the expression of tolerant disgust on her wrinkled face is perfect.[10]

A painting such as *Kapai te Torori, Kiri Matao* goes even further in celebrating what was then known as 'native tobacco', a home-grown product with a notorious stench.[11] Goldie himself was an enthusiastic smoker, although he probably drew the line at tōrori.

And then there are the missing paintings, presumably destroyed by the artist, as well as others which were projected but never realised. Terry Bond remembered seeing one such ambitious work depicting a Māori war party 'digging up the tattooed heads of chiefs they had killed earlier', which he claimed was on a scale similar to *The Arrival of the Maoris.*[12] Goldie's intention of producing work along the lines of Steele's historicising pieces is suggested by an undated list from Edward Tregear, giving incidents from Māori mythology and appropriate page references to his 1904 publication *The Maori Race.* Late in life, Goldie produced small paintings which present a type of history painting in miniature, in which he liberates himself from the portrait genre altogether. A beautiful example is *The Story of the Arawa Canoe,* painted on a mahogany panel from a Cuban cigar box [p.176]. An elderly woman sits beside a young boy, both watching a toy canoe as she recounts the story of the great migration canoe that brought their tribe to Aotearoa. Another shows the elderly Rahapa Hinetapu peeling potatoes alongside a small child [p.176].

goldie's legacy

Despite the extraordinary volume of written material that pertains to Charles F. Goldie and his work, the personality of the artist remains elusive. Hardly any correspondence of a personal nature remains among the papers Olive Goldie deposited in the Auckland Museum, suggesting that Goldie or his widow decided to leave no more than an official account of his career. Among other correspondence there must have been numerous letters from James Cowan, whose widow told Eric Ramsden about his close friendship with the artist:

> The two were lifetime friends and Jim told me many tales of Goldie's eccentric ways. His widow is just as eccentric and I wonder what will become of all his most valuable finished & unfinished work! He thought that New Zealanders were artistically absolutely uneducated and held them all in vast contempt.[1]

Also missing are letters from other close European friends, such as the actor W. S. Percy of the Pollard Opera Company, who commissioned a portrait from Goldie [p.56]. Evidently, the peripatetic theatrical world not only provided Goldie with cosmopolitan company, but also financial support. Another travelling actor of the Edwardian era, Cecil Ward, purchased one of Goldie's first portraits of Ina Te Papatahi [p.97].[2]

Just as Goldie was guilty of romanticising his Māori subjects, so Goldie's own relationship with the Māori was romanticised in its turn. According to his nephew, Terry Bond, Goldie 'took the trouble to learn the Maori language and speak it fluently.'[3] Yet apart from a handful of invoices and negotiating letters from models, and the letters from Atama Paparangi and Te Heuheu Tūkino (see page 181), there is little Māori-language material among the artist's papers. He did own the 1892 edition of Williams's dictionary and occasionally ventured into Māori-language titles. Nevertheless, in light of such an ungrammatical effort as *Ka Ra Te Wera* (instead of *Ka Wera Te Ra*) the claim of proficiency in the language seems untenable. While the thousands of newspaper clippings he collected confirm that Goldie was extremely well informed on Māori events and concerns, his relationship to the Māori world was essentially that of an observer rather than a participant. Apart from a carved paddle presented to him by Anaha Te Rāhui (and later purchased by the Auckland Museum), Goldie's sizeable collection of Māori artefacts was largely acquired through auction sales. A receipt dated February 1908 records the purchase of an 'antique carved Maori block from Pah' (10 shillings) and a 'rare carved bowl for serving flesh' (£1 15s).[4] The 'block' could be the spectacular kōruru, or gable mask from a meeting house, prominent in a photograph of around 1908 [p.26].

During the early years he worked in collaboration with his models, either in the studio or out in the field, but with the passage of time Goldie must have realised that his specialisation was leading towards a dead end. The photographs he had taken, simply as an aid to painting rather than as independent works of art, became a vital source once he was no longer able to find suitable models. Most of the later works, featuring subjects who had died decades earlier, were inevitably based on earlier photographs and drawings. Except for several poor-quality images in his scrapbooks, very few of Goldie's photographs of his models have survived. Perhaps the bulk of these photographs, along with his preparatory drawings for the paintings, were destroyed in an attempt to preserve the mystique of the paintings.

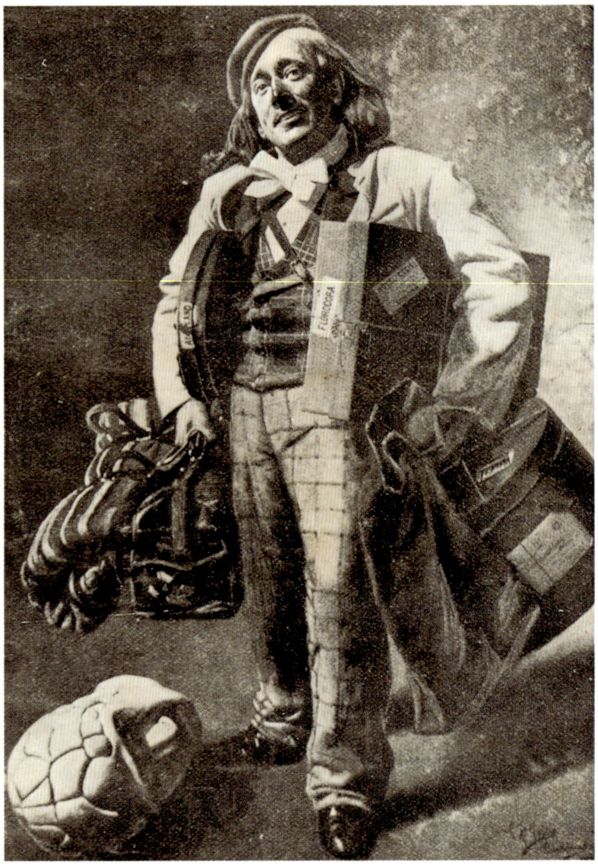

Goldie's 1903 portrait of the actor W. S. Percy in the role of the phrenologist 'Tweedlepunch' in Floradora *(from a contemporary newsclipping, private collection).*

A number of writers have claimed that Goldie employed an epidiascope and sensitised canvas, although no evidence supports this. As David J. Wise has ascertained, the early work is painted over a charcoal drawing applied directly to a prepared canvas, while the later paintings are usually transferred from drawings. Many contemporary critics dismissed his work on the basis that it resembled colour photography – this at a time when colour photography had still to evolve. Yet there was usually the recognition, whether grudging or not, that Goldie's craftsmanship was superior to the norm. One Christchurch reviewer put the negative criticism into its proper context when describing Goldie's works at the 1916 exhibition of the Canterbury Society of Arts:

> ... Maori heads, all exhibiting that smooth and careful technique which moves lovers of the impressionistic school to talk cuttingly about 'coloured photographs'. The jibe is one that should not have much sting in colonial art circles, since it implies accurate drawing and modelling and sufficient technical ability to paint minutely without producing unnatural effect. Mr Goldie knows his subject, and paints with sympathy and consummate care.[5]

The level of Goldie's realism accounts in large degree for the popularity of his work, typically inducing in viewers a desire to touch the painting. A reviewer in 1902 described the illusionism of the heitiki in *Caught Napping,* 'standing off so much as to cause visitors to go up and test the smoothness of the canvas' [p.88].[6] Similar remarks apply to the fabrics painted by Goldie, as well as the models' skin, 'painted in such a manner that the fingers are tempted to tweak it to test its reality.'[7]

Goldie's name is persistently coupled with that of Gottfried Lindauer, yet there are clear distinctions between the work of each artist – not least in the realm of technical prowess. Lindauer, an immigrant, was working firmly within the genre of portraiture, undertaking commissions from both Māori and Pākehā. Goldie, a native New Zealander of the succeeding generation, formulated in his Māori subjects something beyond straightforward portraiture. Although a work such as *Darby and Joan* is in one sense a portrait of Ina Te Papatahi, it is also invested with a heavy dose of *fin-de-siècle* nostalgia which connects it with European orientalism. There was considerable contemporary uncertainty over the precise category in which Goldie was working. Writing about the 1903 'Ranfurly' paintings, the *Triad* confused the repose of the subjects with 'too great a tendency towards still life'.

> It is true, of course, that the Maori is much more stately and slow in movement, and more lifeless in repose, than the European, yet there is a certain monotony in the pictures of Maori life, supreme though they are in the style of subject.[8]

Writing to James Cowan, Goldie made a distinction between 'subject' portraits and 'straight' portraits. The latter were usually frontal and carrying the model's name as a title; while the 'subject' portraits presented three-quarter or profile views and were more likely to bear tendentious titles such as *A Noble Relic of a Noble Race.*

Within Polynesia, the only work truly akin to Goldie's was produced by the Dutch-born artist Herbert Vos in Hawai'i. Vos's portraits of native Hawai'ians, such as *Kolomona: Hawaiian Troubadour* of 1898 in the Honolulu Academy of Arts, are uncannily similar to the earliest Māori portraits Goldie produced on his return from Paris.[9] American art has a tradition of 'Last of the Tribe' imagery, especially in photography, and an orientalising strain among painters of Goldie's generation who studied in Europe. Eanger Irving Couse was one turn-of-the-century specialist in American Indian themes, who had earlier studied under Bouguereau at the Académie Julian.

In Australia there is no artist to parallel Goldie. Aborigines exist on the extreme margins of early twentieth-century art, appearing in historicising reconstructions of important colonial events but very rarely as individual portraits. The dominant tradition at the turn of the century was landscape painting, the so-called Heidelberg School, intent on celebrating white settler identification with the land. Australia's grim colonial history meant that there was no equivalent to the New Zealanders' identification of their country as 'Maoriland'. Although Goldie is a New Zealand exponent of the European orientalising tradition, in the colonial context his work is perceived as a form of naturalism. As a journalist noted in 1903, at the time of the presentation to Lady Ranfurly: 'Mr Goldie ... is a distinct product of Maoriland. He has wisely followed the bent of his talent, instead of risking his chances in the pursuit of exotic genres.'[10]

In 1976, near the end of his life, Goldie's nephew Terry Bond thought that it was not yet possible to assess Goldie's importance: 'I don't think Goldie's value can be adequately assessed by this generation or the next.'[11] He may be right, but a retrospective exhibition in 1997 – the first ever, marking fifty years from the artist's death – will allow that assessment to be based on the works themselves. Undeniably, Goldie holds a unique position among New Zealand artists. His paintings are held in aristocratic collections and major museums as well as in many unassuming homes. They are revered by Māori, hotly contested by investors and generally acclaimed by most New Zealanders. The very fact that he has been both celebrated and demonised, loved by a wide public while simultaneously reviled by the cultural establishment, is in itself an accolade to the achievements of Charles F. Goldie.[12]

a note on goldie's titles

Goldie usually wrote the titles of his paintings on labels he fixed to the back of the frames. Sometimes this was simply the model's name and tribe; more often it took on a 'poetic' bent. Titles such as *A Noble Relic of a Noble Race*, regardless of how distasteful they are to a modern audience, especially a Māori audience, are nevertheless the titles assigned by the artist, familiar to his earliest audience and cited by the reviewers. Where possible, titles are based on Goldie's handwritten versions. Where these have been lost, as on most publicly owned works, exhibition catalogues and reviews have provided the original titles for the paintings.

Following Goldie's title comes the name and tribal affiliations of the model. In several cases, modern spelling diverges from that used by Goldie.

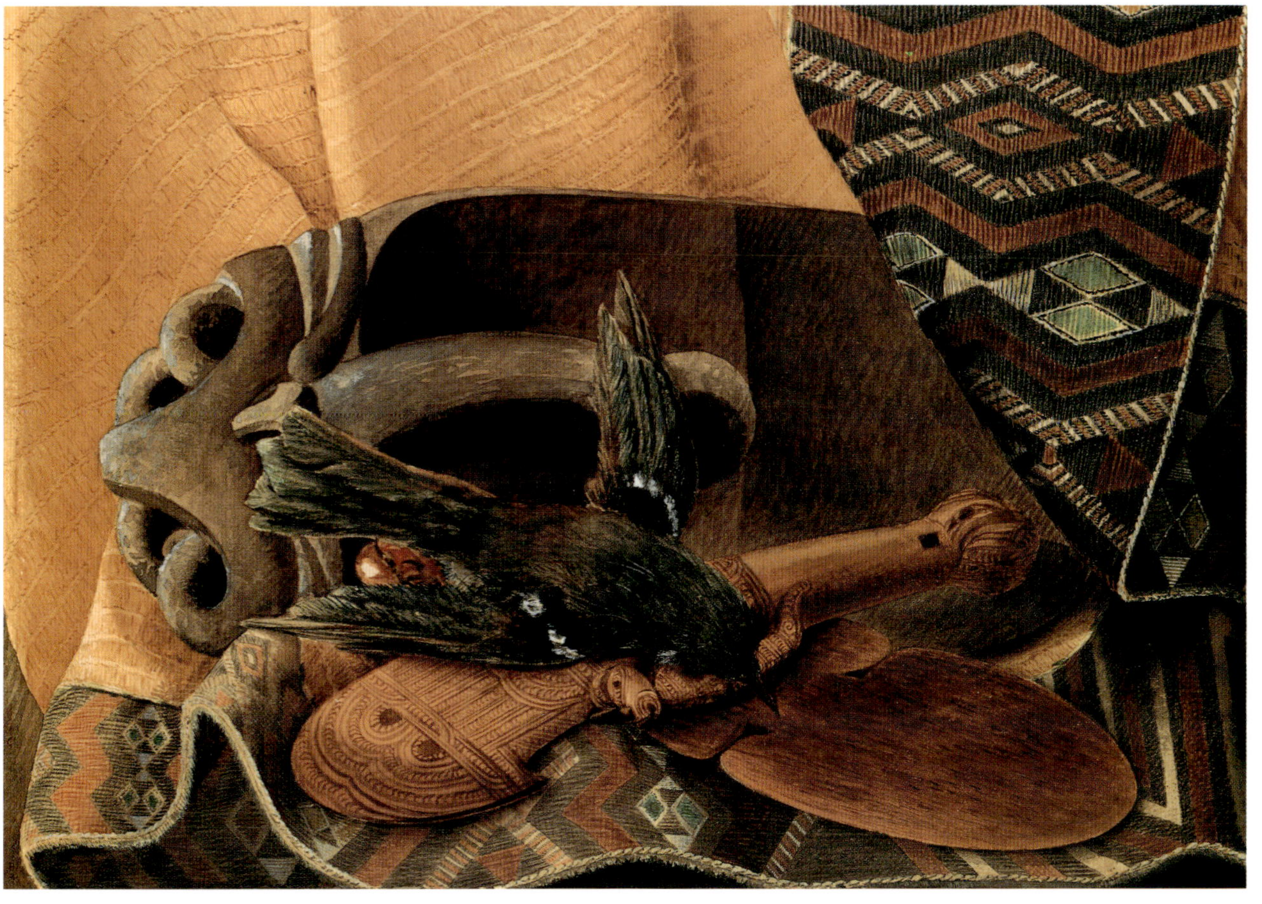

Still Life 1886
watercolour, 264 x 370 mm
private collection

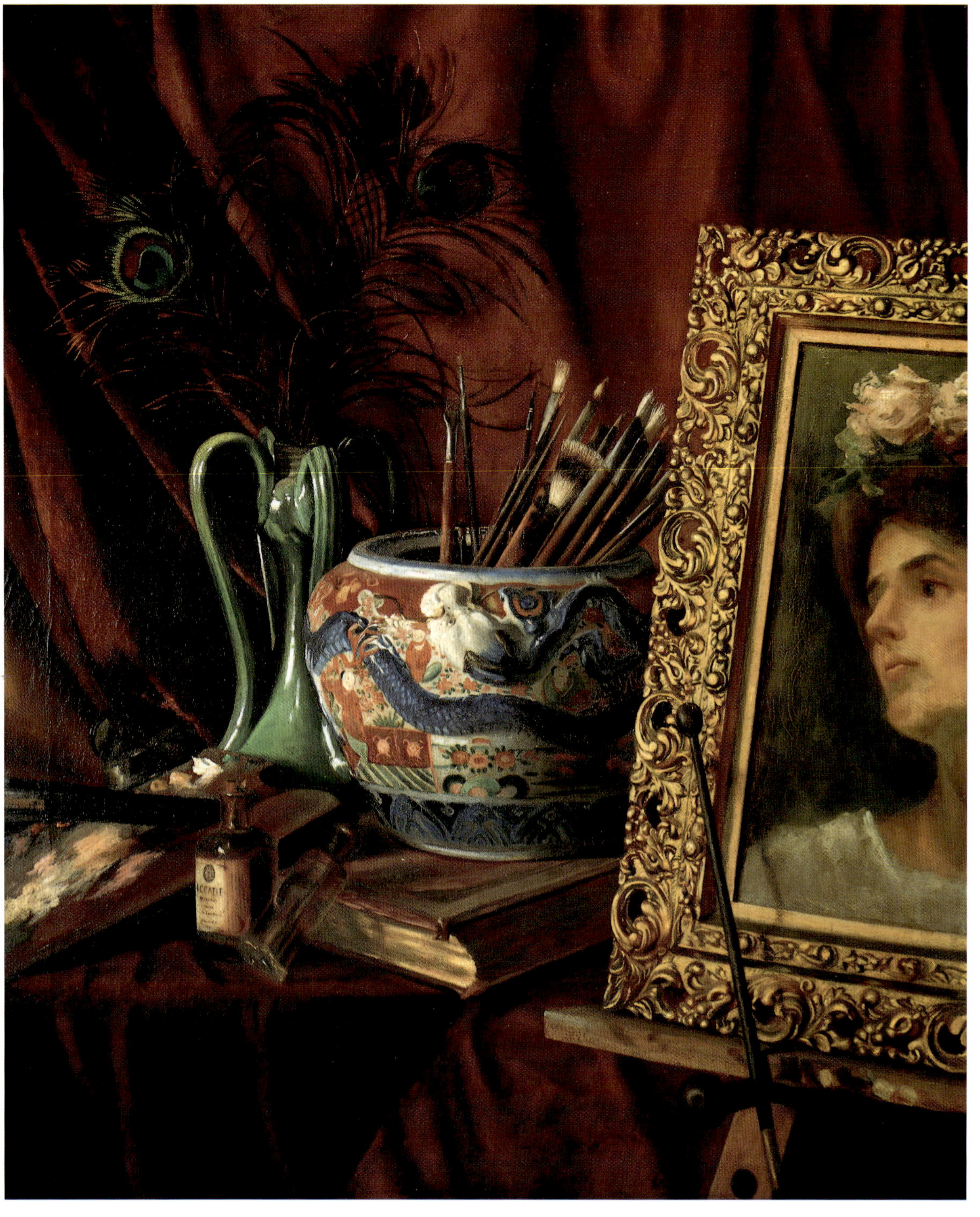

Study of Still Life c.1890
oil on canvas, 890 x 730 mm
private collection

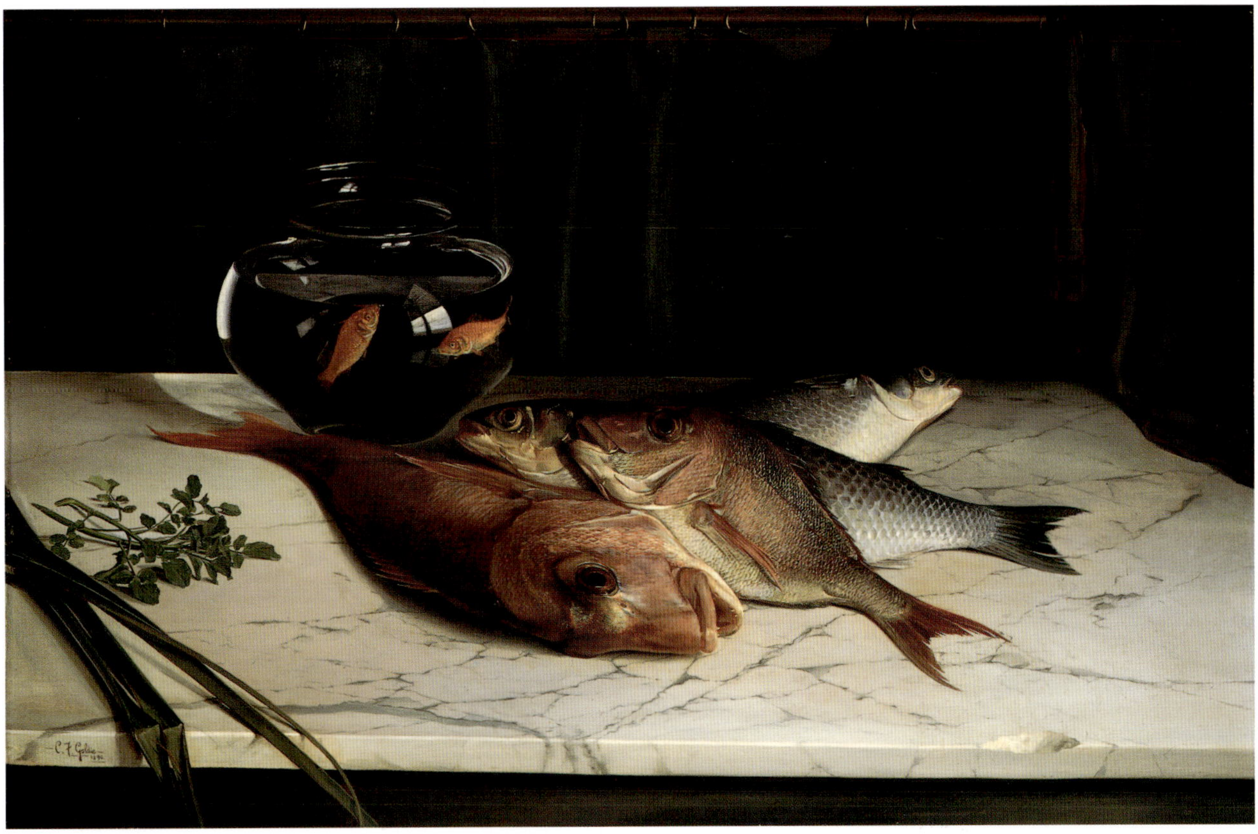

Still Life 1890
oil on canvas, 610 x 945 mm
private collection

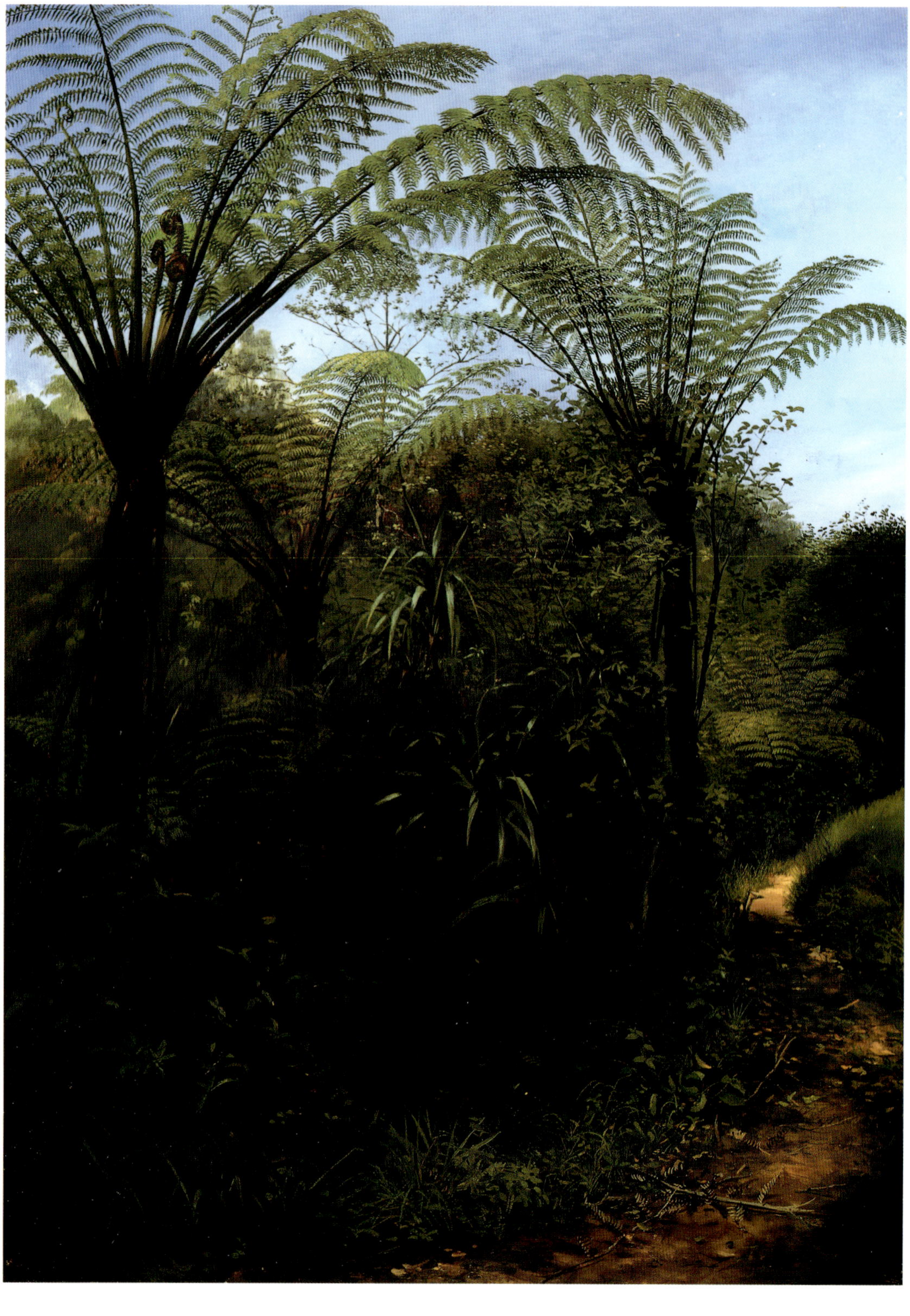

Study of New Zealand Trees 1892
oil on canvas, 605 x 450 mm
private collection

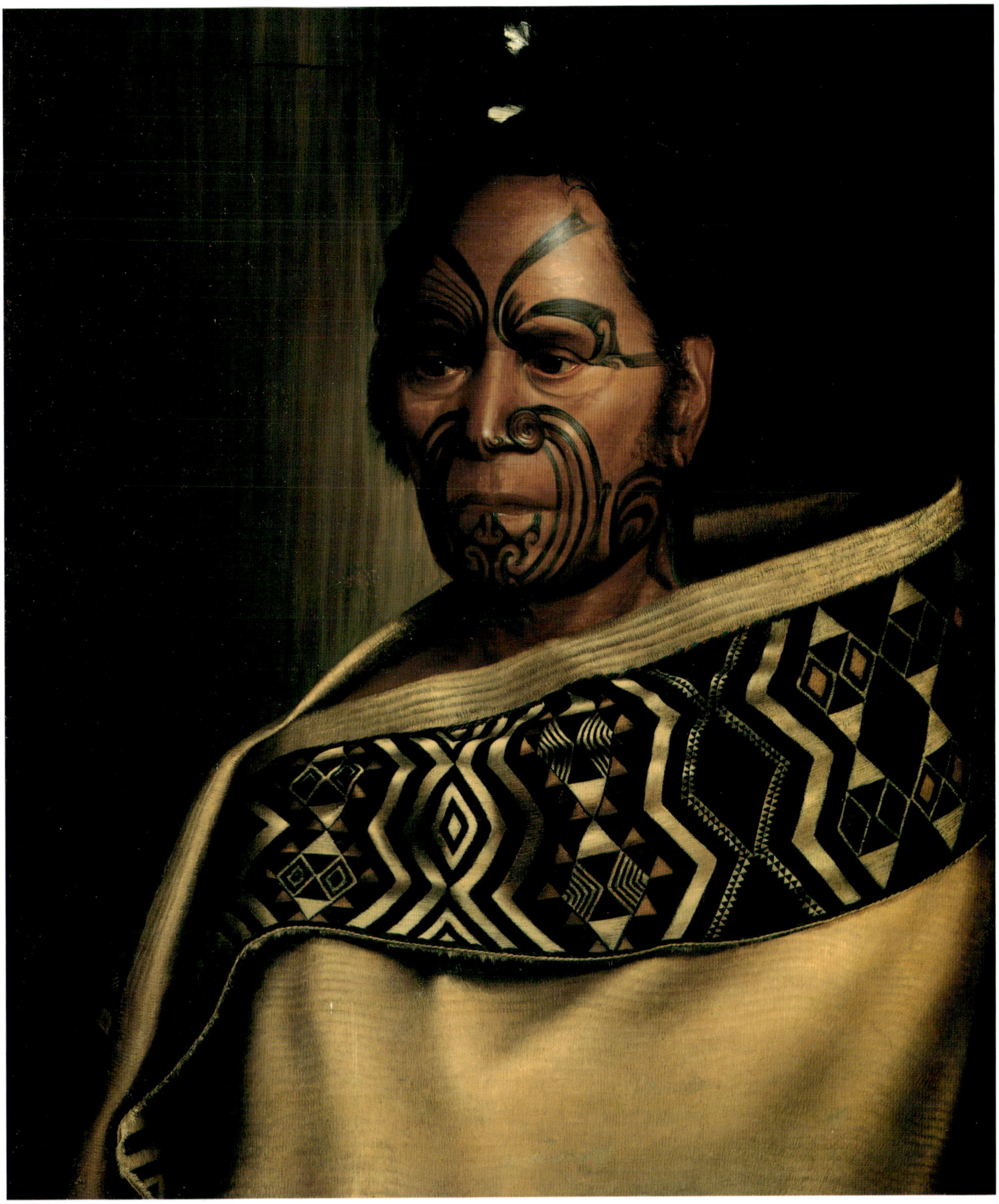

Kawhena 1892
Kāwhena, Ngāti Mahuta
oil on canvas, 773 x 670 mm
private collection

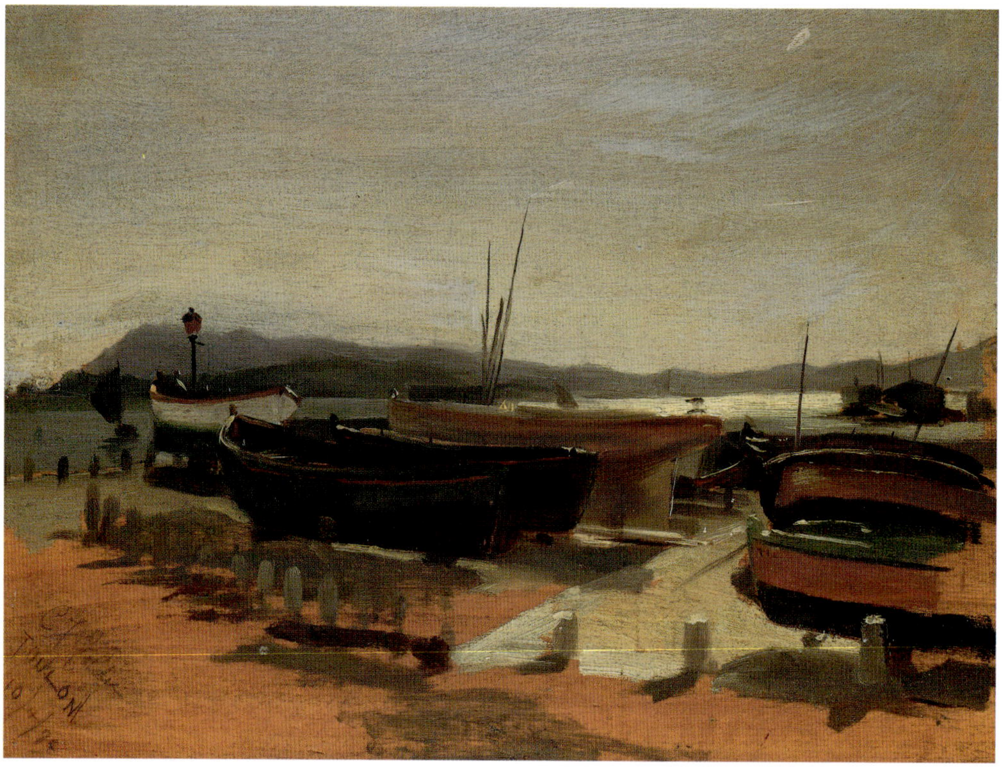

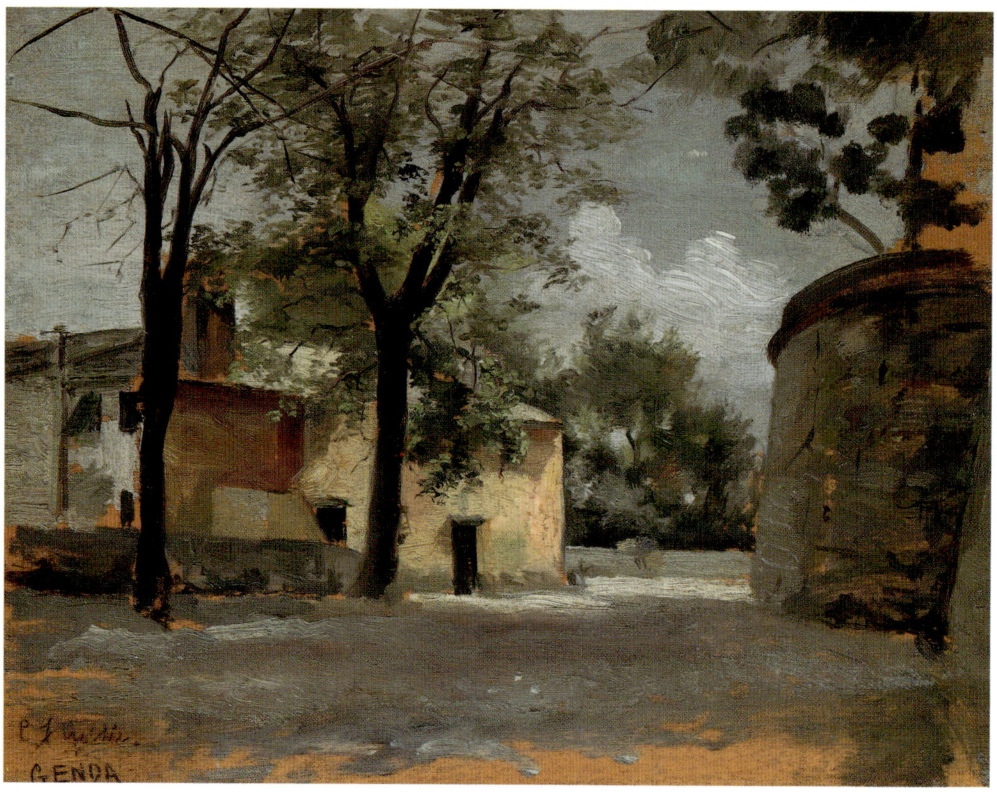

[above]
Toulon 10 April 1894
oil on panel, 256 x 349 mm
private collection

[below]
Genoa 19 April 1894
oil on panel, 264 x 343 mm
private collection

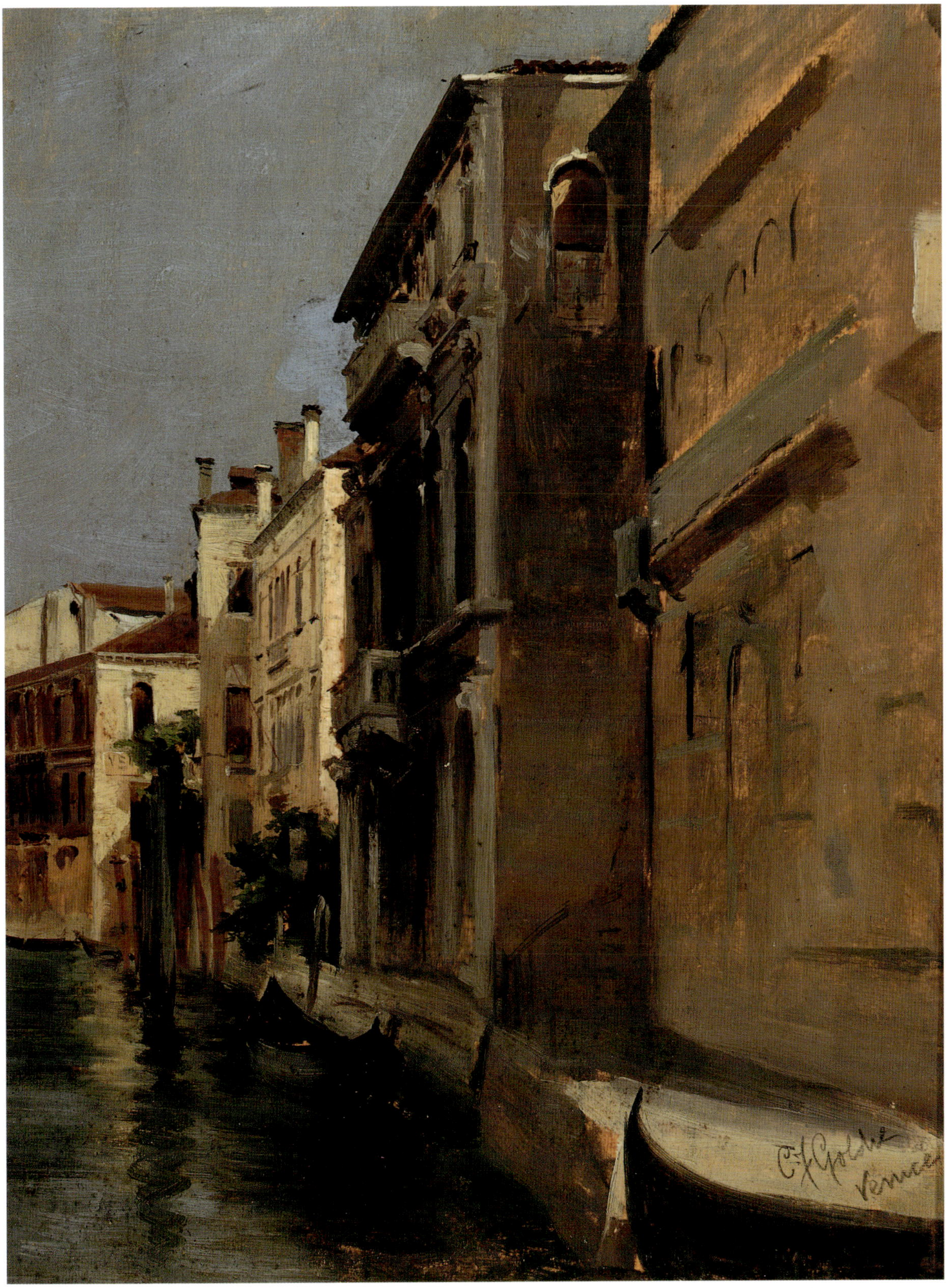

Venice 1894
oil on canvas, 320 x 245 mm
private collection

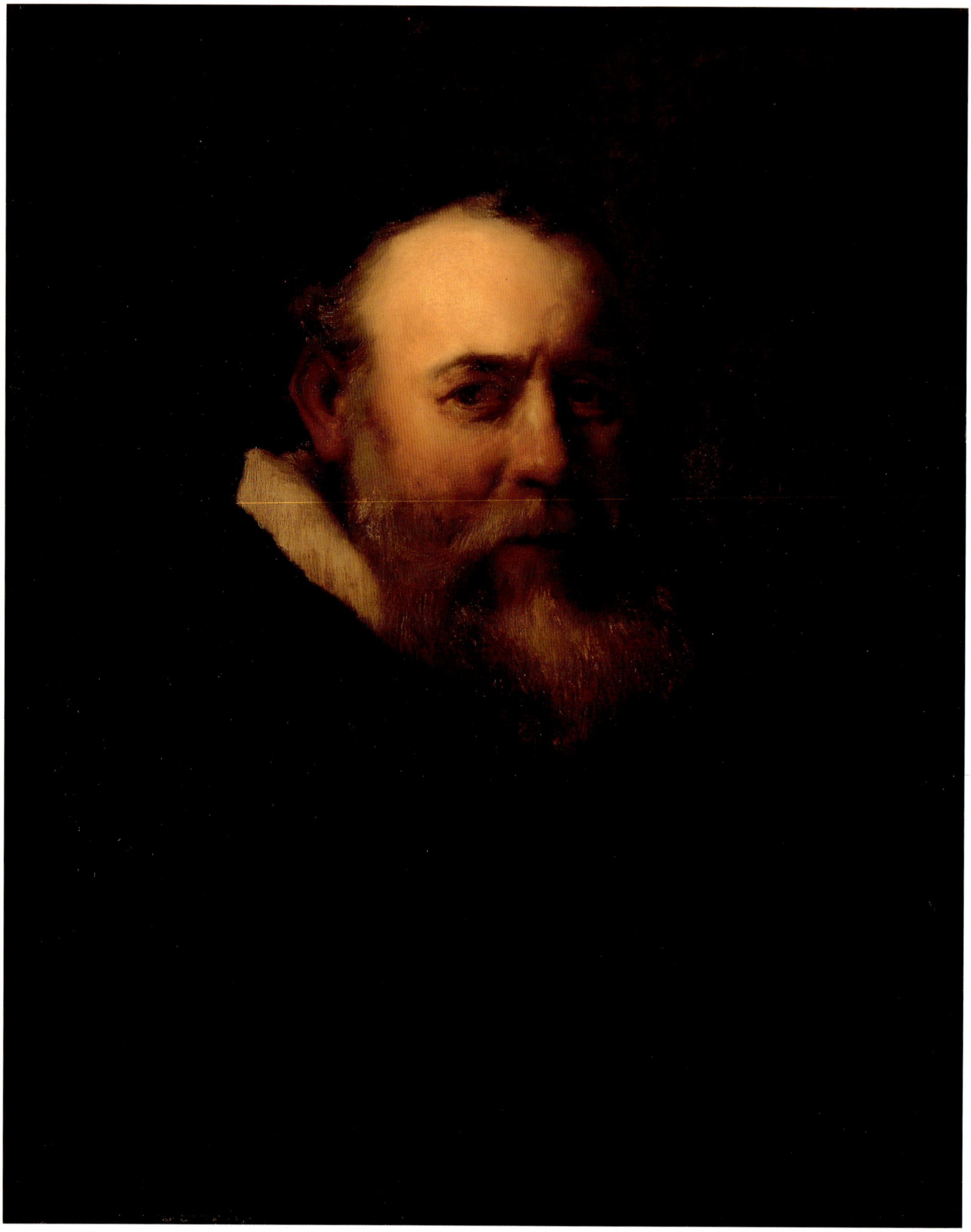

Portrait of a Burgomaster, after Rembrandt, Royal Gallery, Antwerp 1895
oil on canvas, 612 x 500 mm
private collection

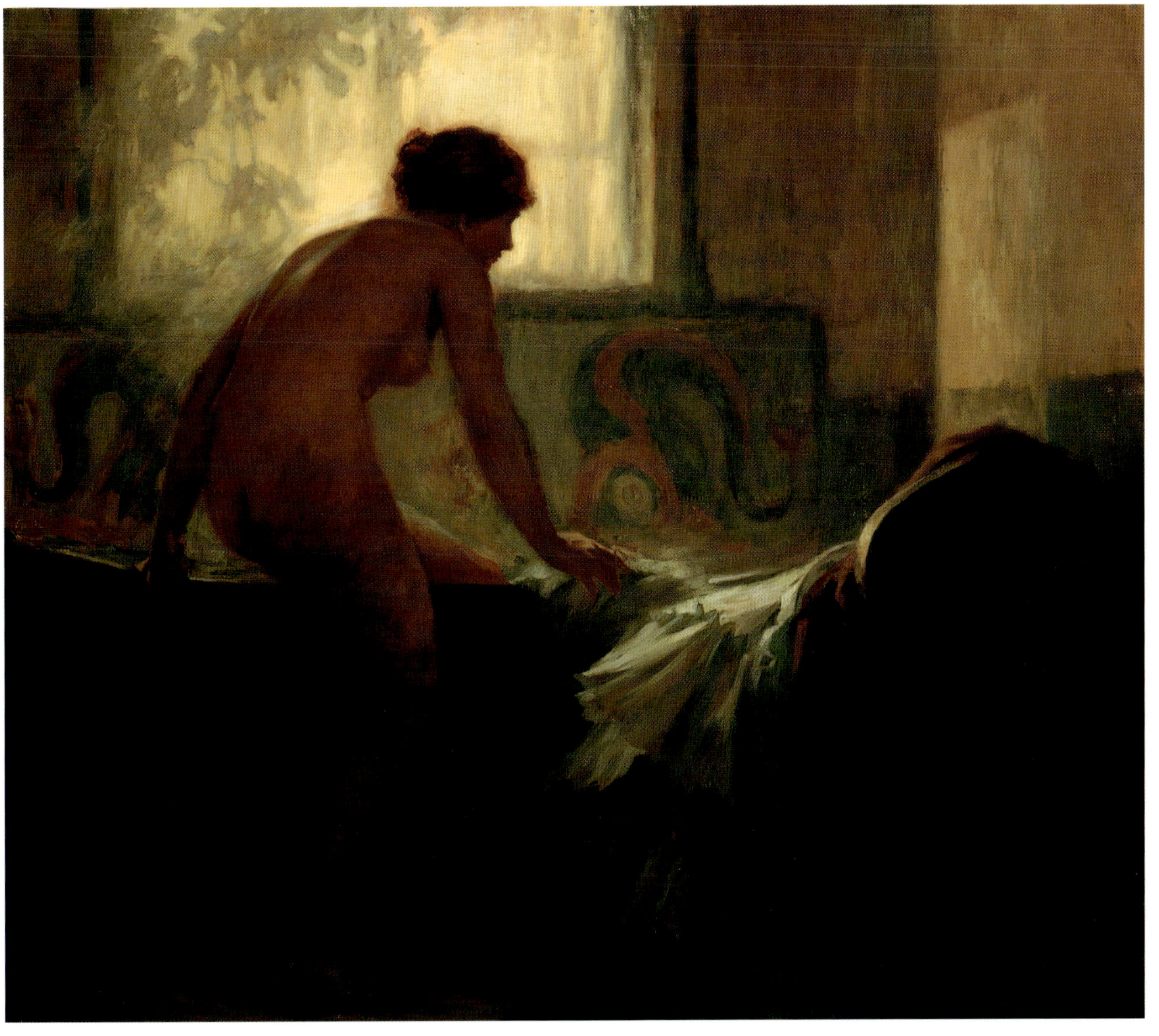

La Femme au Bain, after Prinet,
Luxembourg Gallery, Paris 1898
oil on canvas, 745 x 840 mm
Auckland Art Gallery Toi o Tāmaki

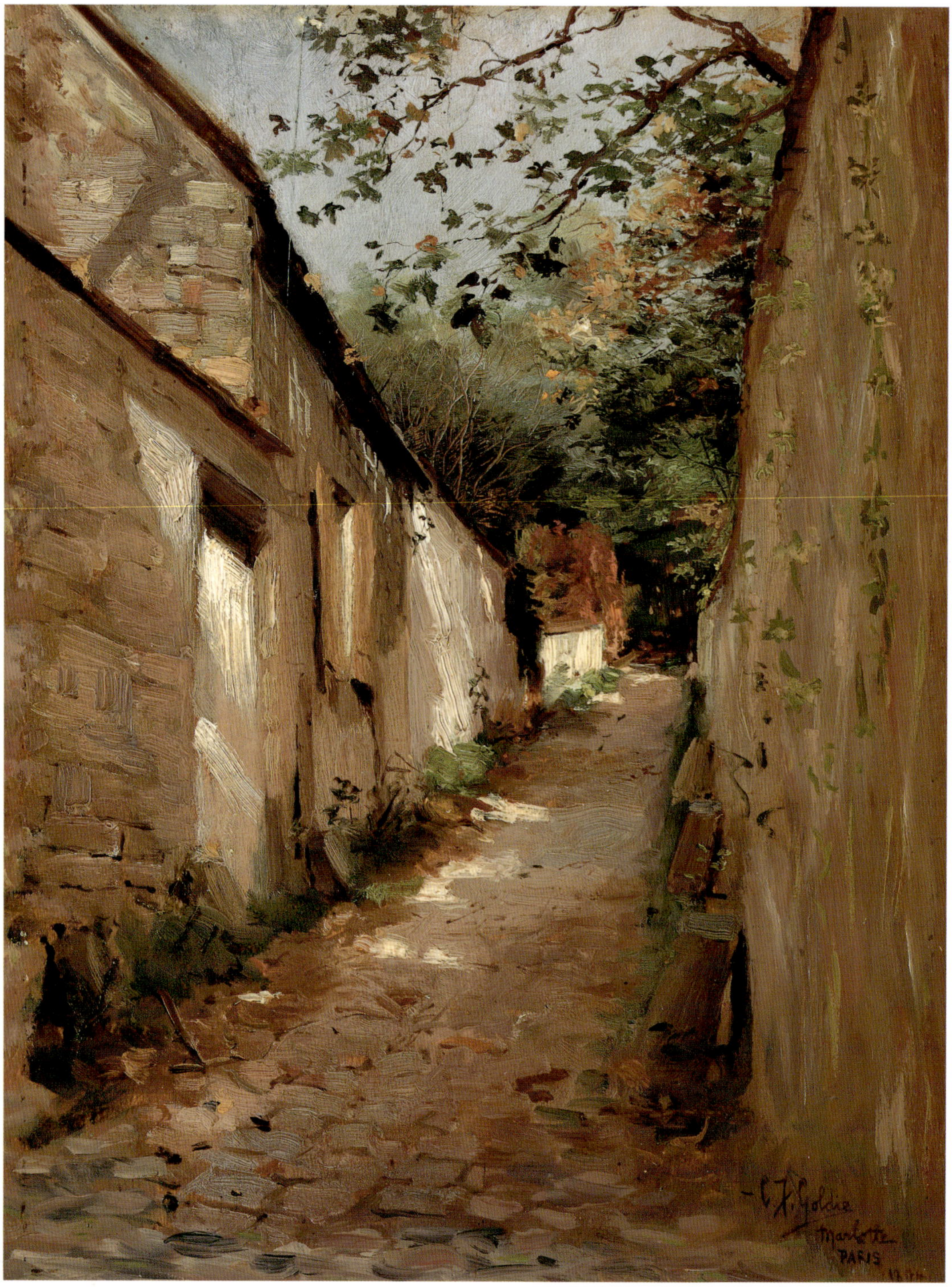

Marlotte, Paris 1894
oil on panel, 345 x 265 mm
private collection

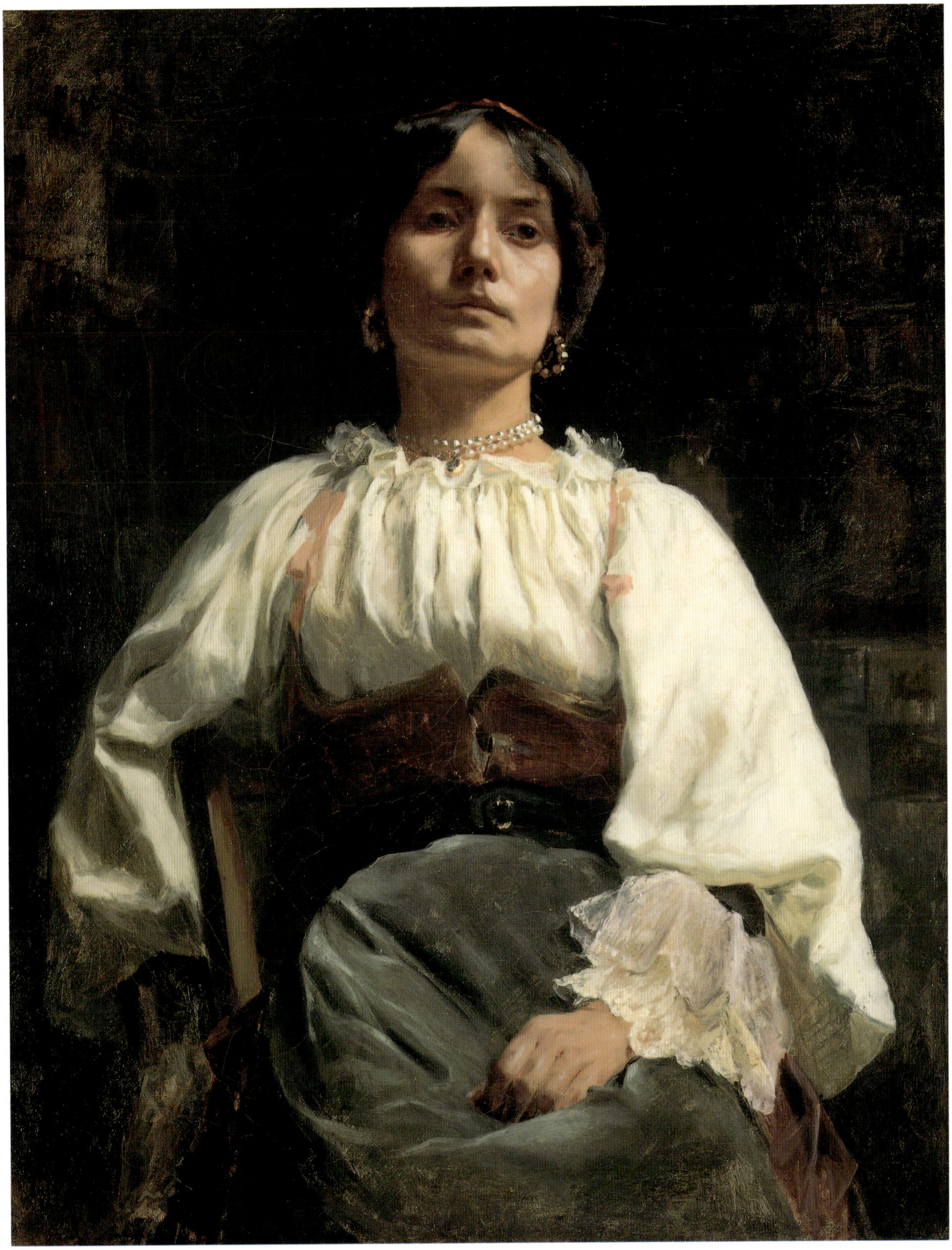

Competition time study (5 1/2 days), Julian's Academy, Paris c.1896
oil on canvas, 905 x 720 mm
private collection

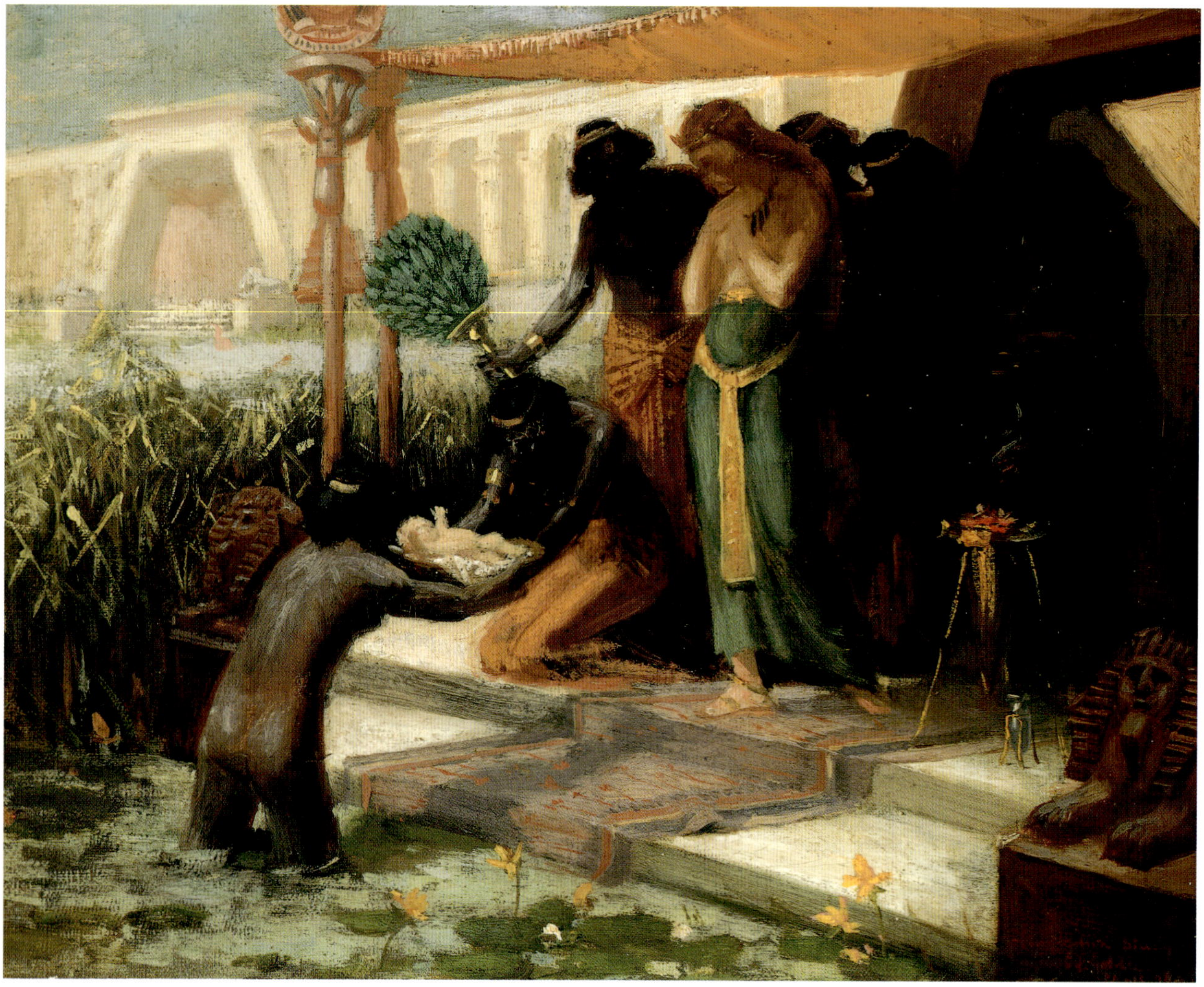

The Finding of Moses, study in composition 1896
oil on canvas, 320 x 410 mm
private collection

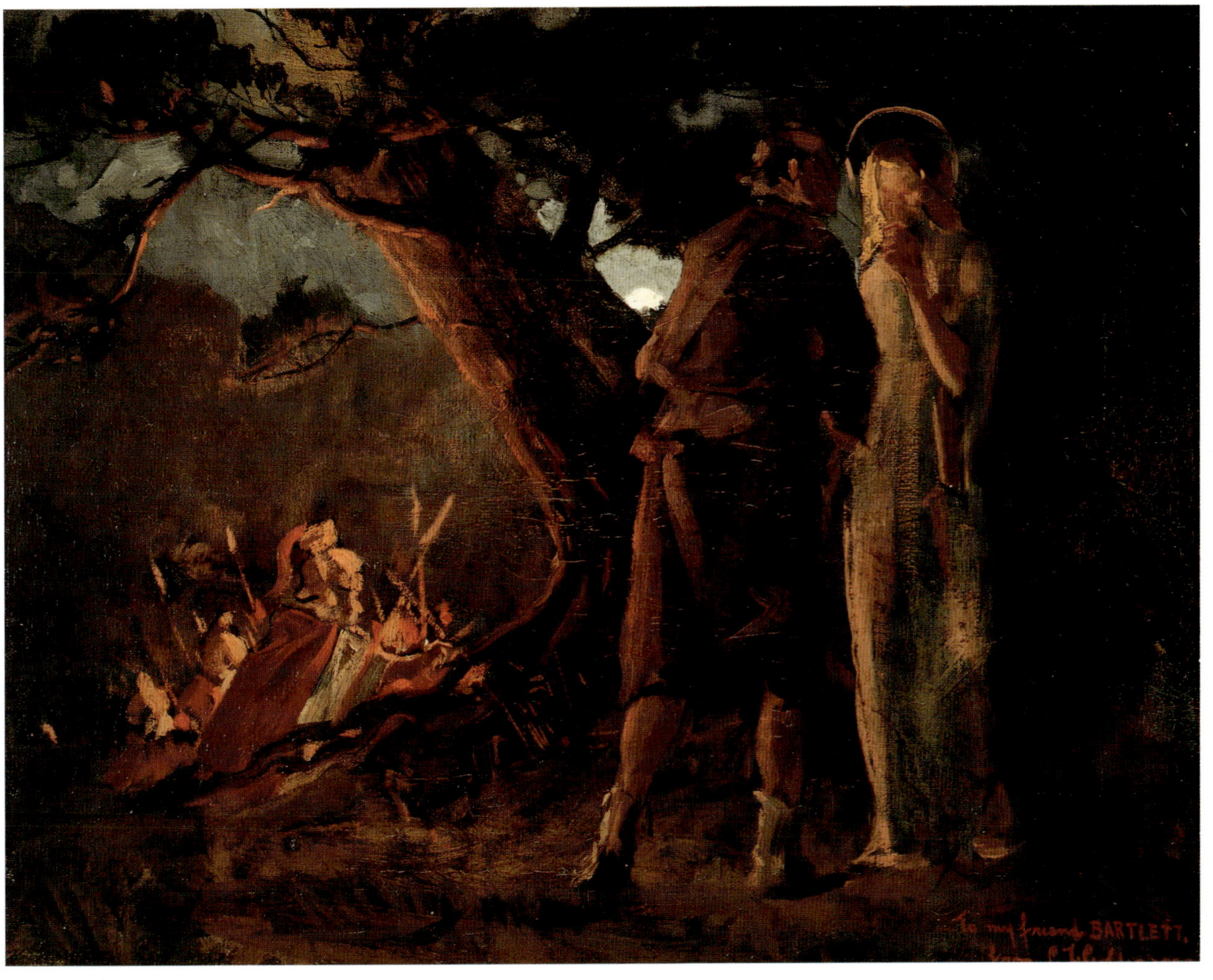

The Betrayal of Christ, study in composition c.1896
oil on canvas, 325 x 405 mm
private collection

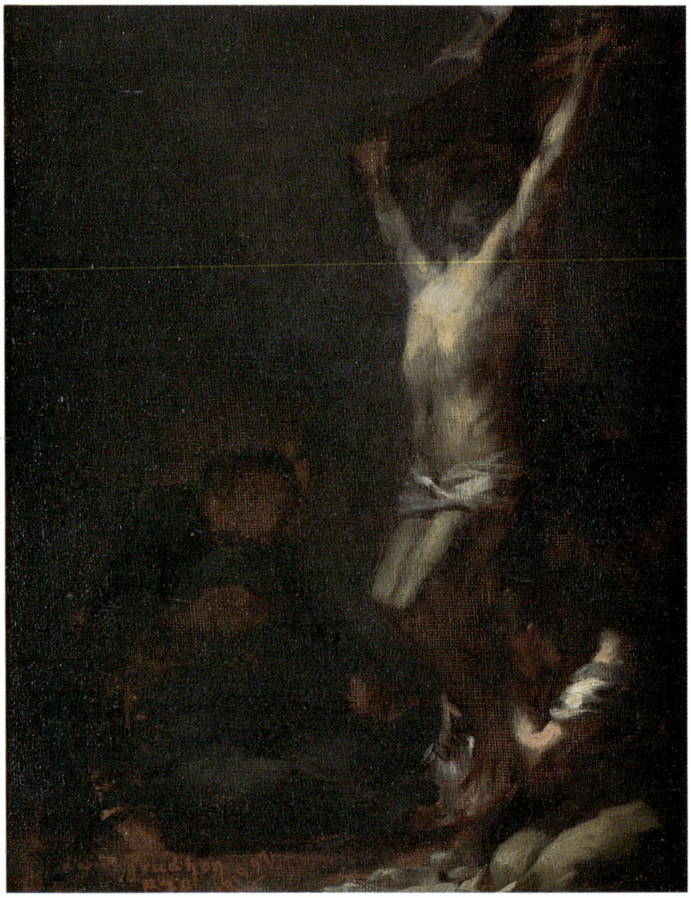

The Crucifixion, after Prud'hon, Louvre Gallery, Paris 1897
oil on canvas, 240 x 190 mm
private collection

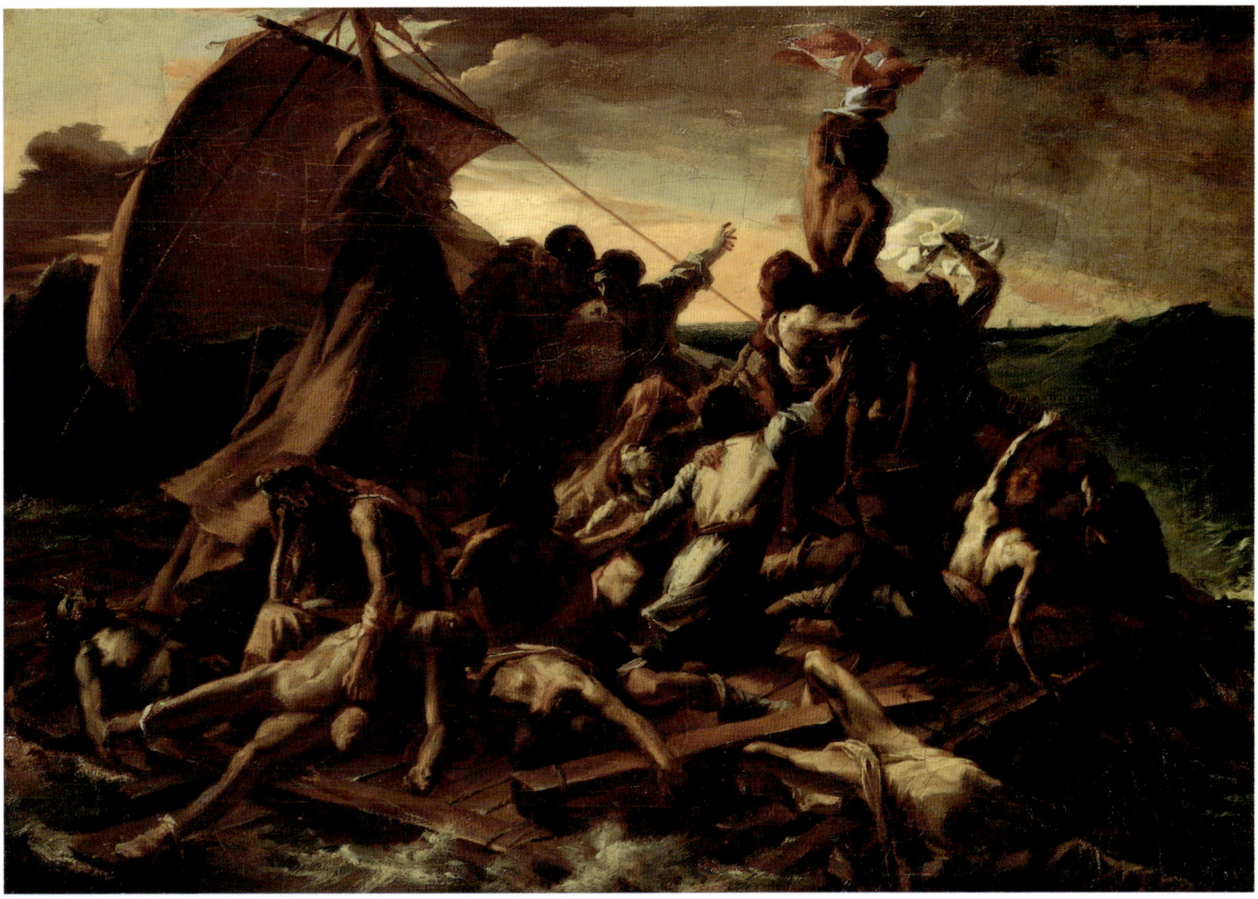

The Raft of the Medusa, after Géricault, Louvre Gallery, Paris 1897
oil on canvas, 490 x 708 mm
private collection

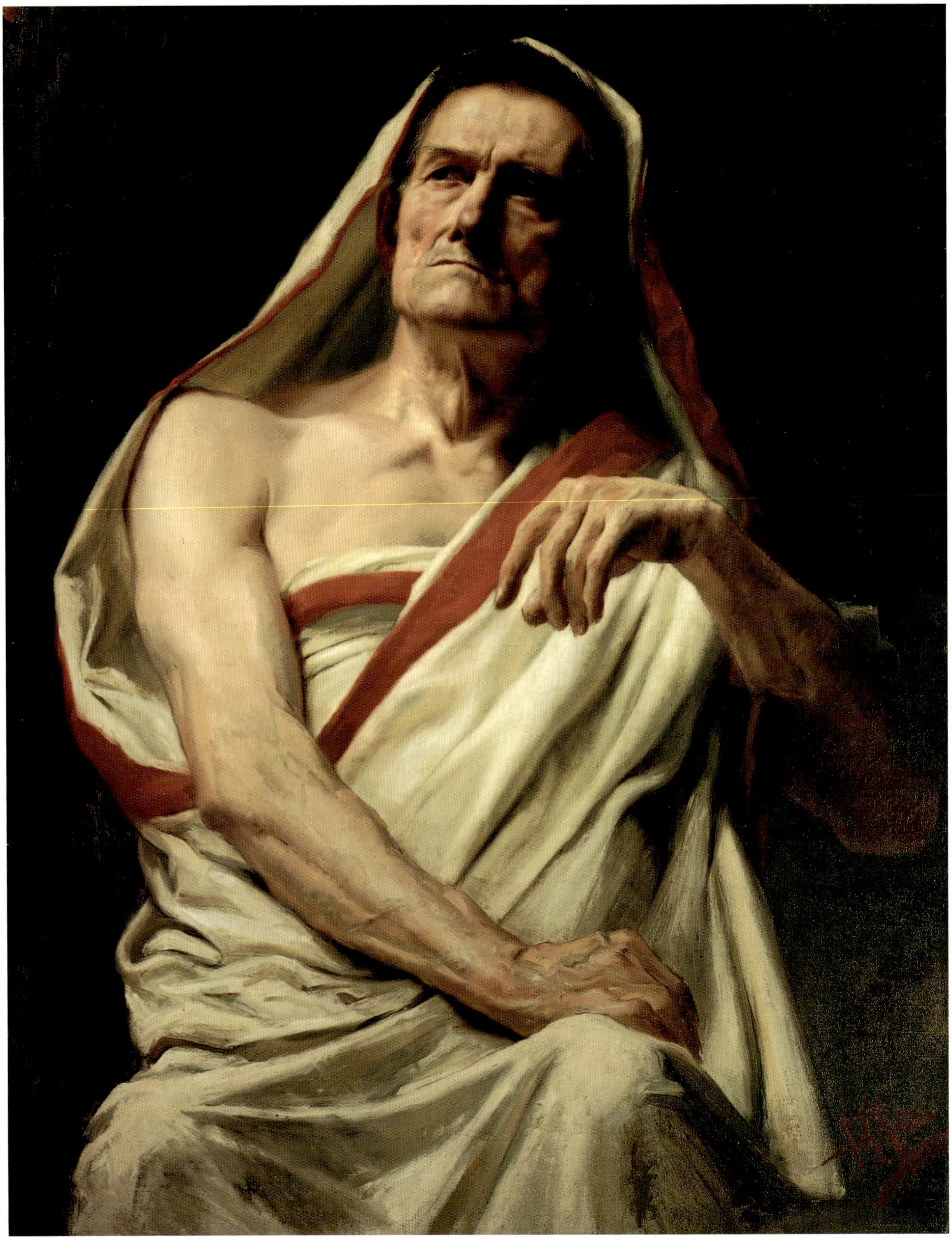

Competition time study (5 1/2 days),
Julian's Academy, Paris (The Senator) 1897
oil on canvas, 920 x 730 mm
private collection

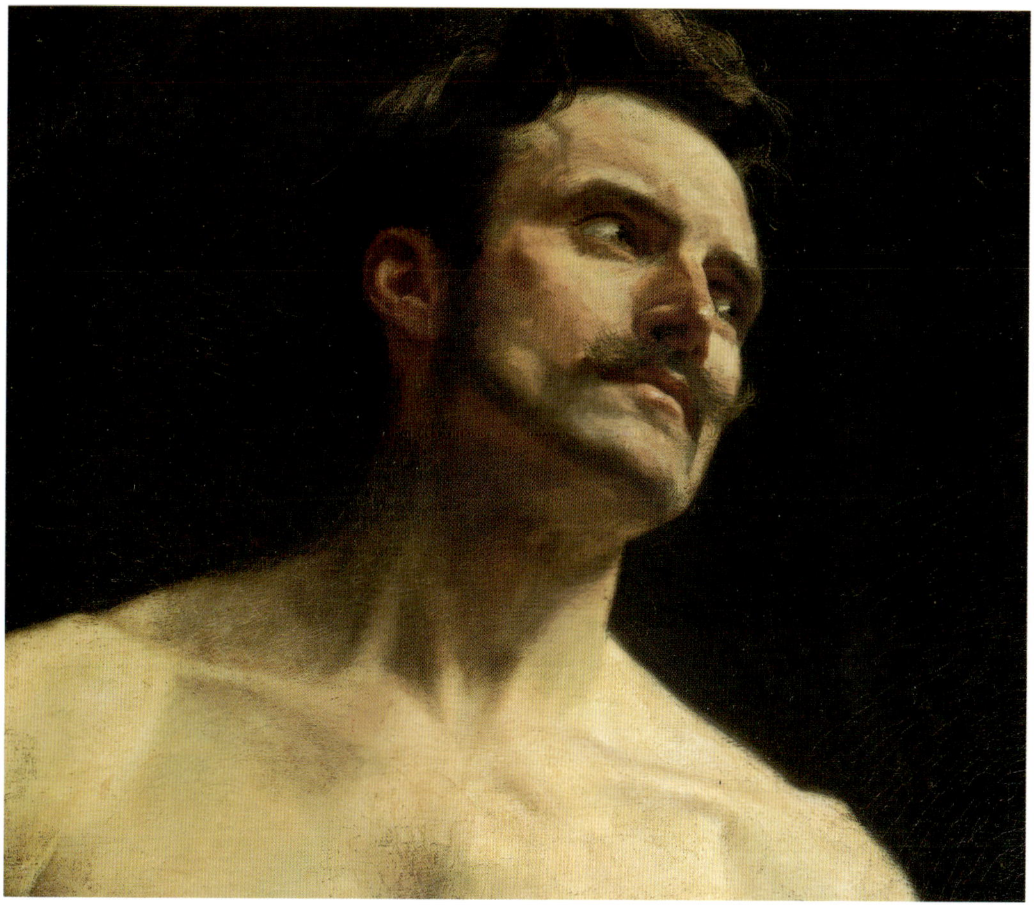

Male torso, Julian's Academy, Paris 1897
oil on canvas, 375 x 440 mm
private collection

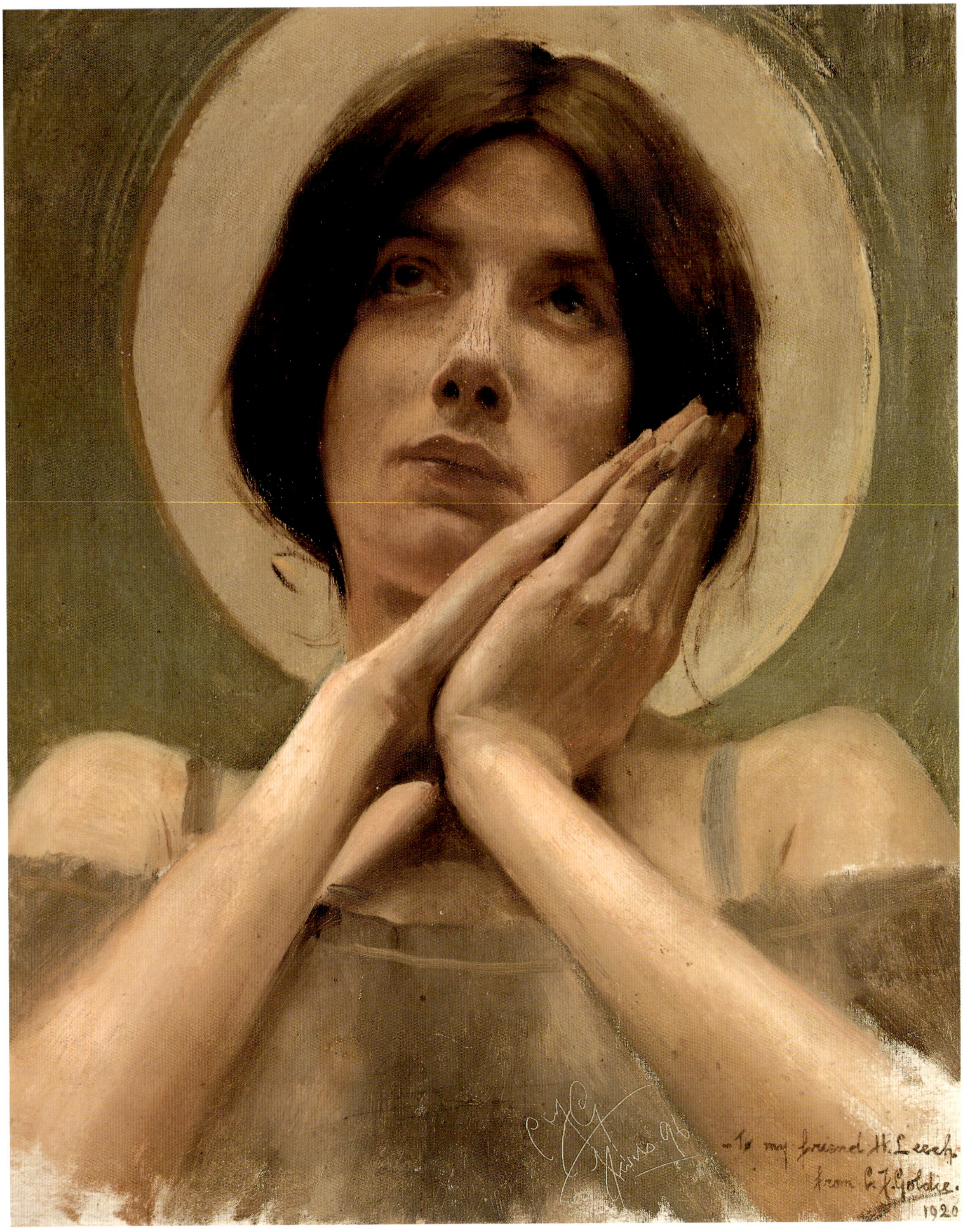

Joan of Arc, Paris 1896
oil on canvas, 463 x 385 mm
private collection

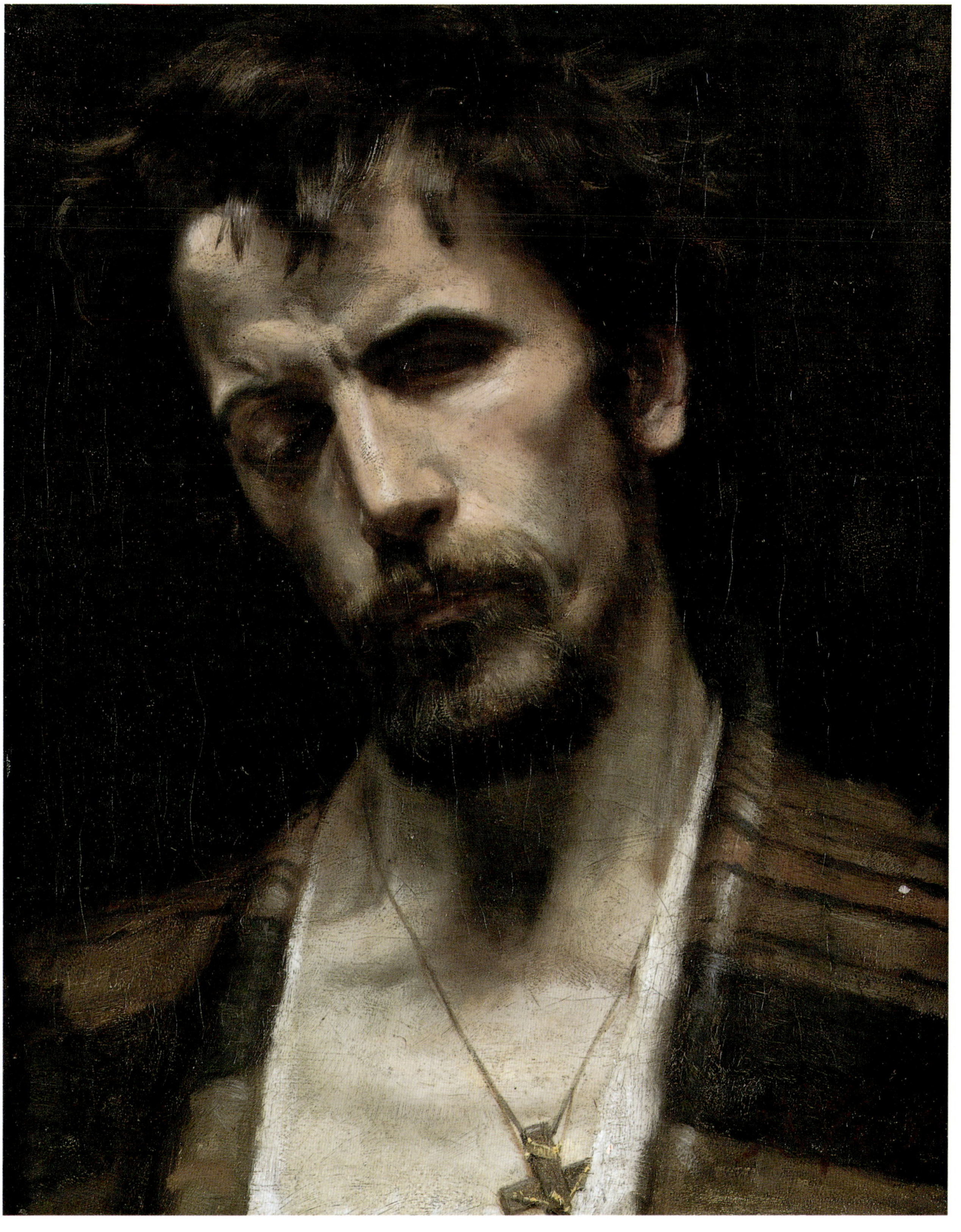

The blind model, Julian's Academy, Paris 1897
oil on canvas, 420 x 340 mm
private collection

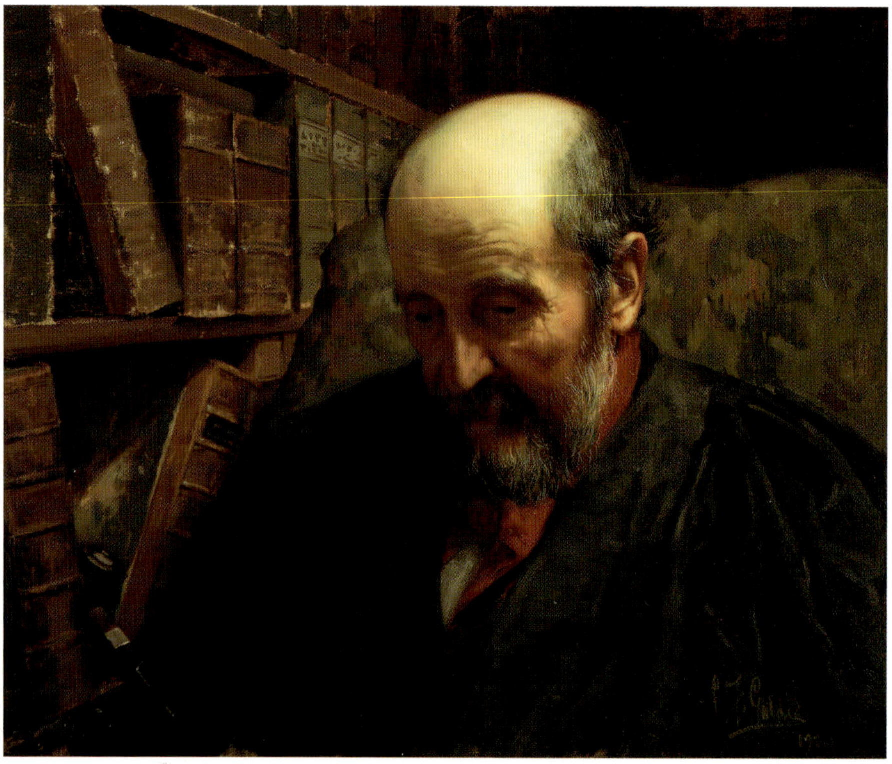

Of making many Books there is no end,
and much Study is a weariness to the Flesh 1900
oil on canvas, 510 x 610 mm
Sarjeant Art Gallery, Wanganui, gift of
the Wanganui Society of Arts and Crafts, 1901

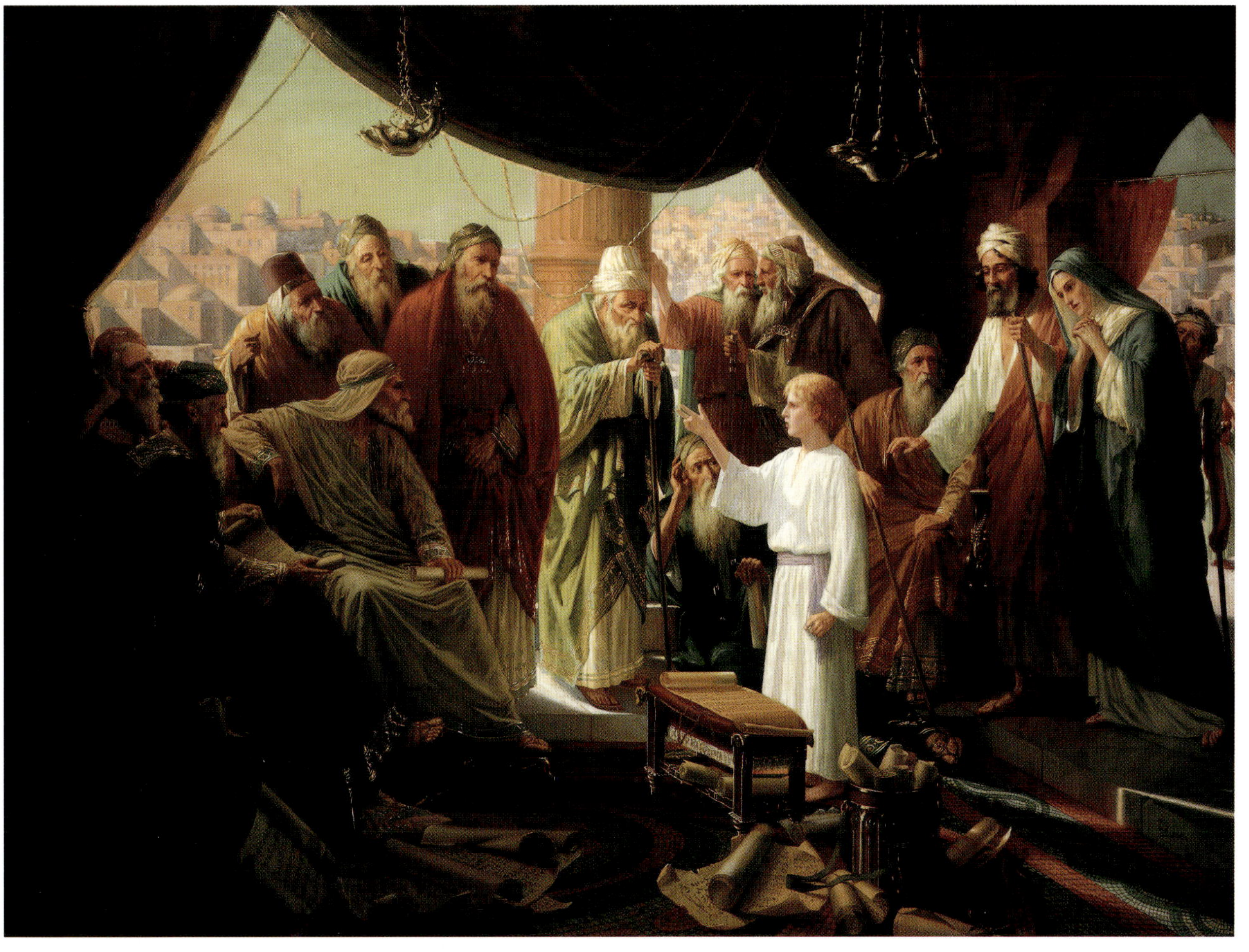

The Child Christ in the Temple, questioning with the Doctors, found by His parents 1898–1911
oil on canvas, 1298 x 1735 mm
Auckland Art Gallery Toi o Tāmaki, gift of David Goldie, 1912

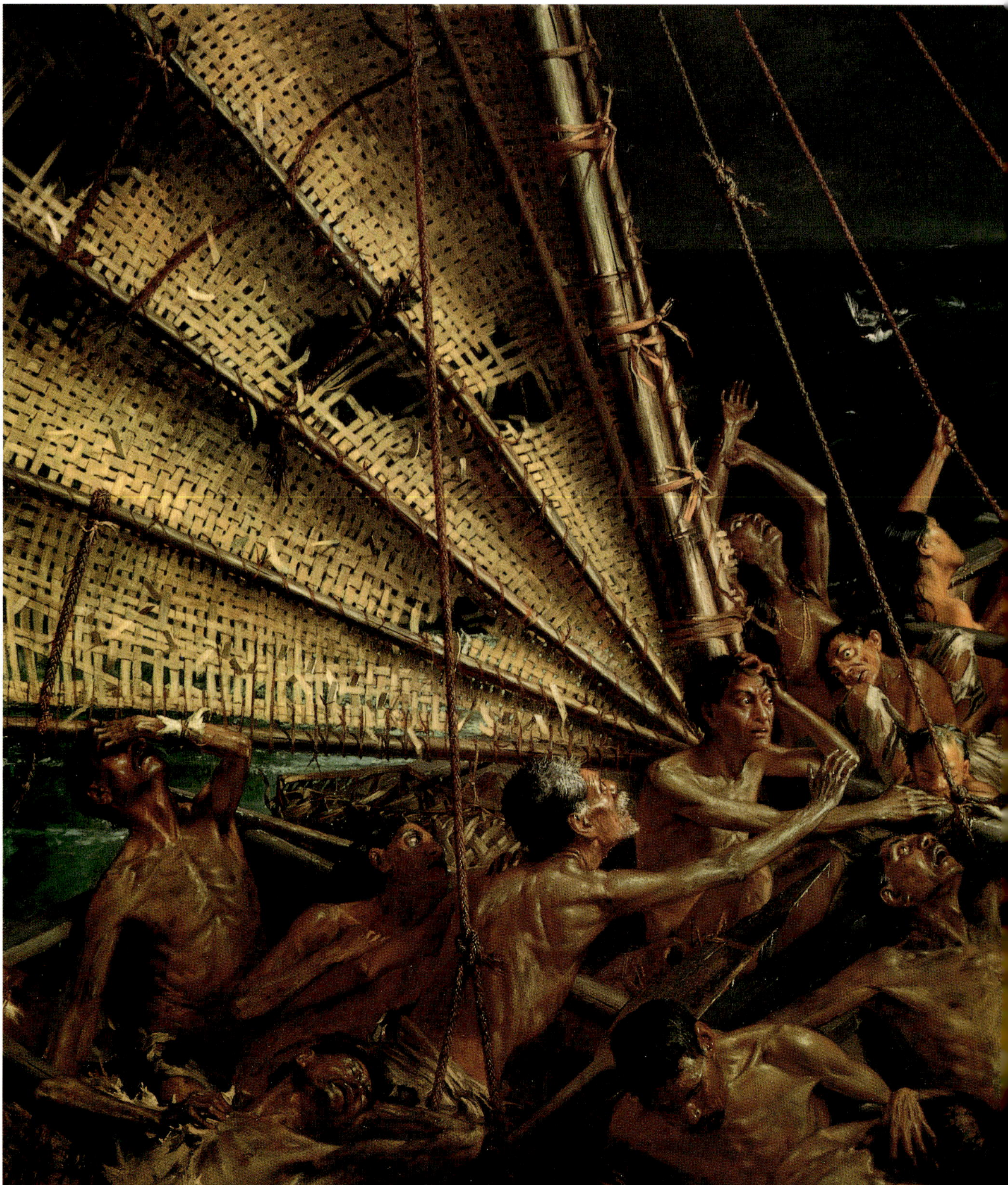

The Arrival of the Maoris in New Zealand 1898 (collaboration with L. J. Steele)
oil on canvas, 1380 x 2450 mm
Auckland Art Gallery Toi o Tāmaki,
bequest of Helen Boyd, 1899

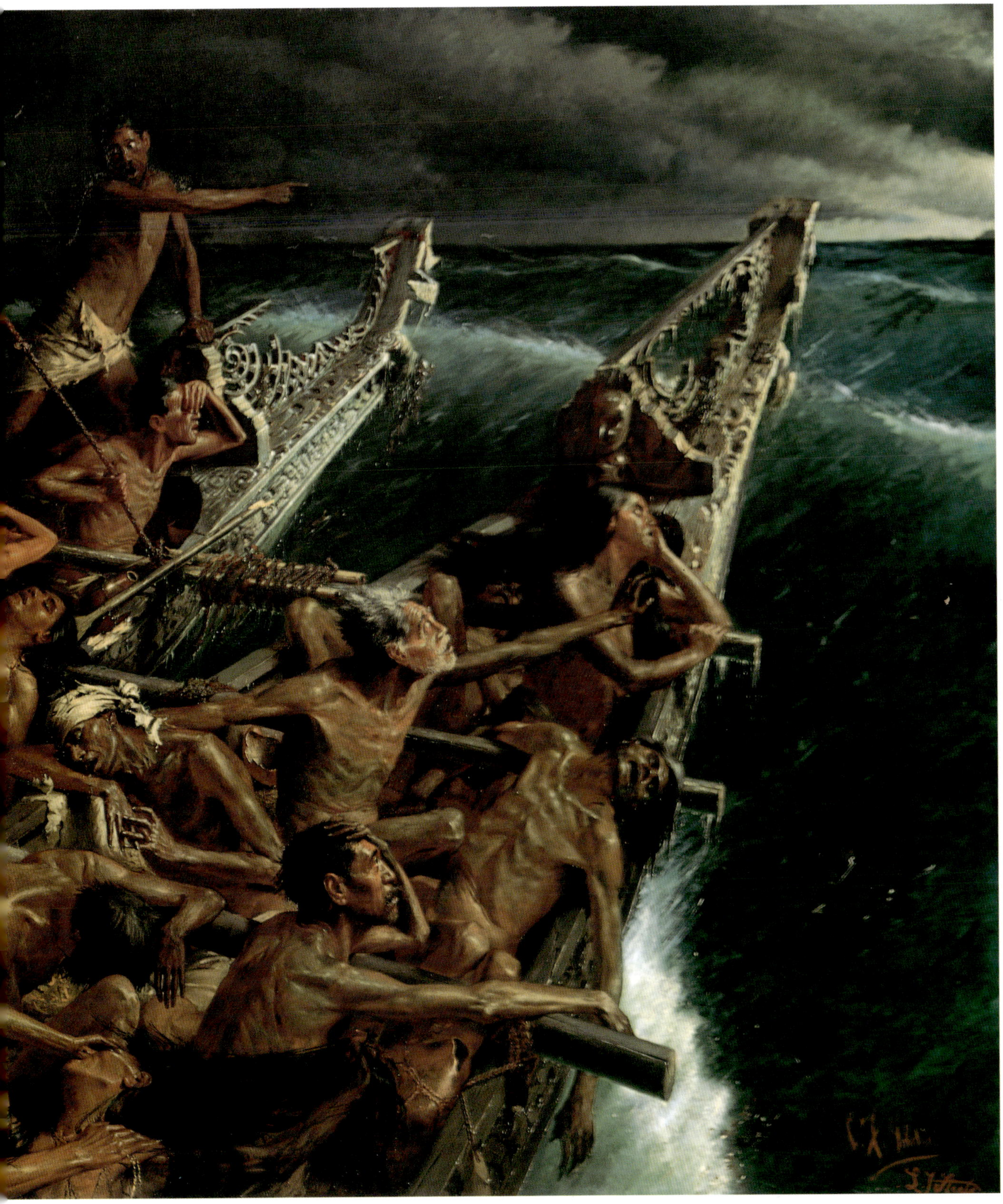

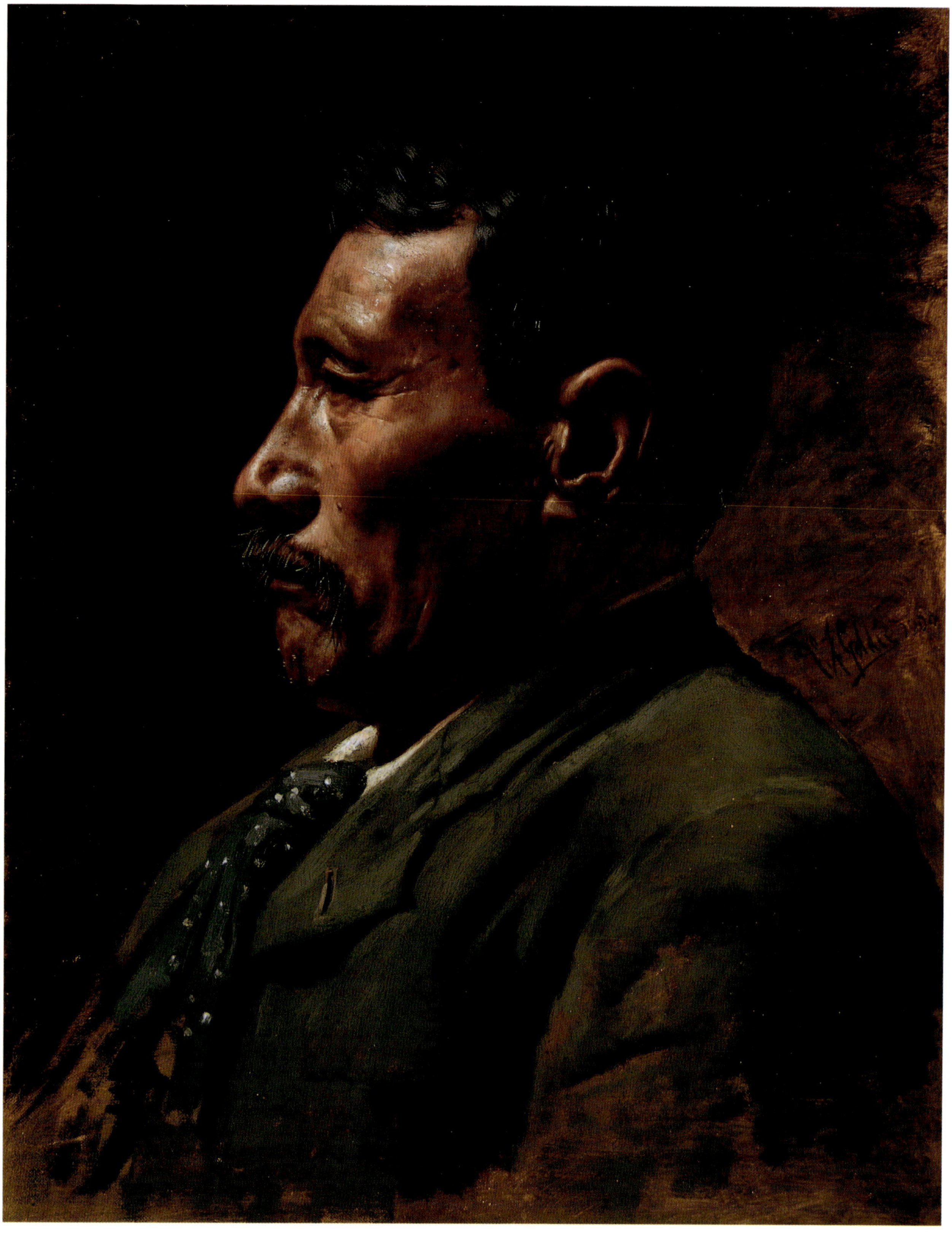

Tamehana 1900
oil on canvas, 505 x 407 mm
private collection

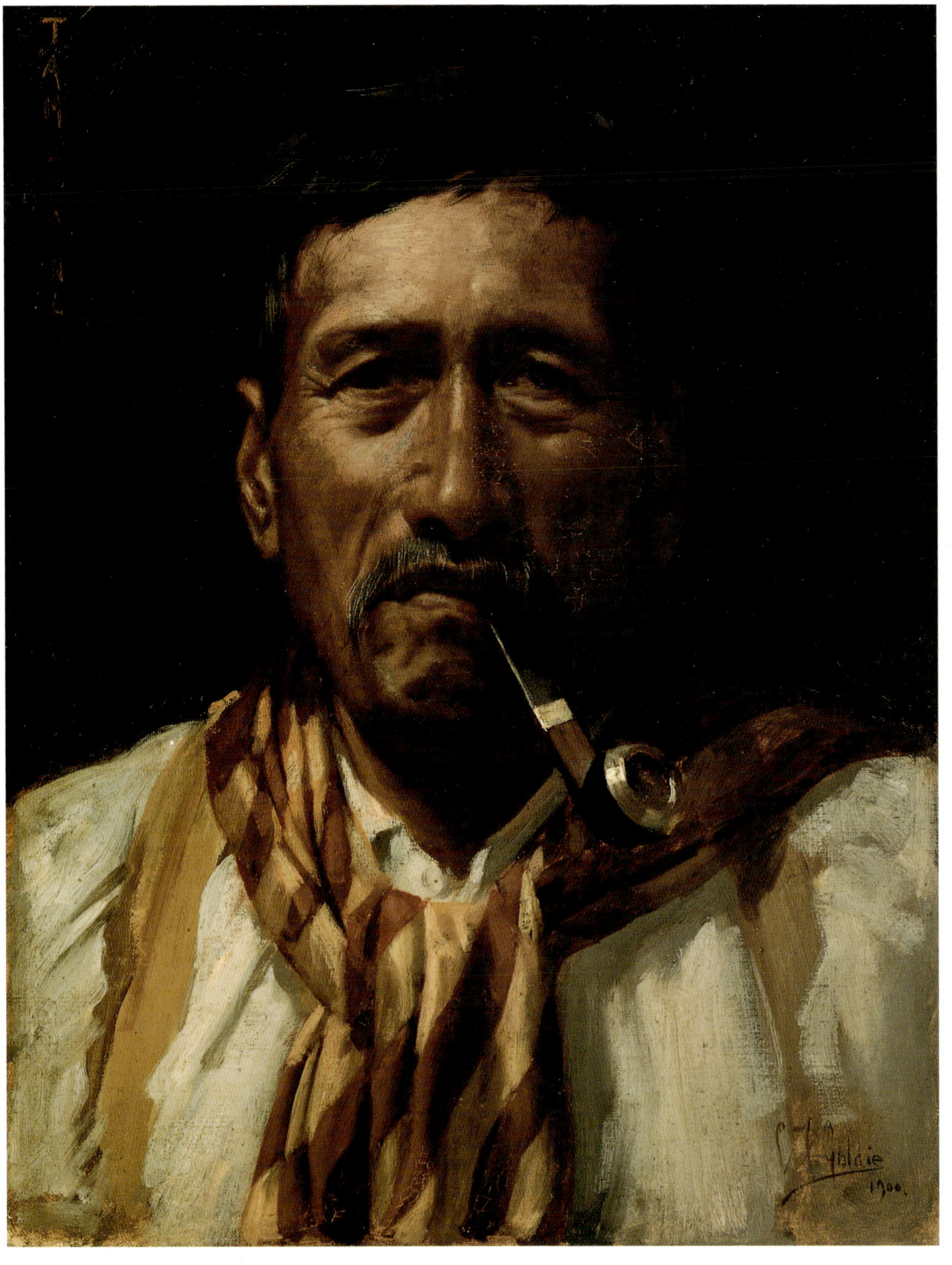

Tamehana, from Life 1900
oil on canvas, 460 x 355 mm
Auckland Art Gallery Toi o Tāmaki,
gift of E. Earle Vaile, 1900

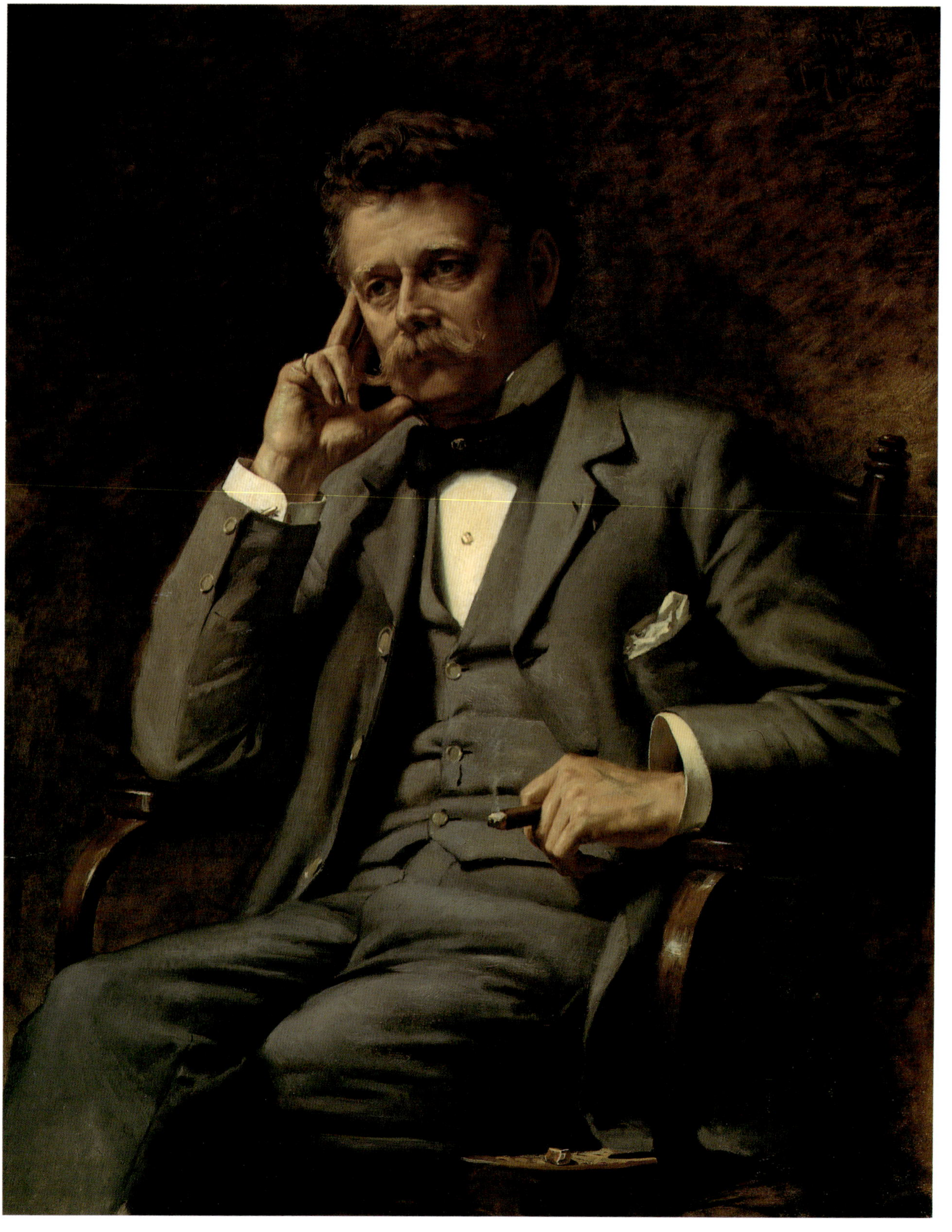

Portrait of Claude Lorraine Kerry 1900
oil on canvas, 1010 x 800 mm
private collection

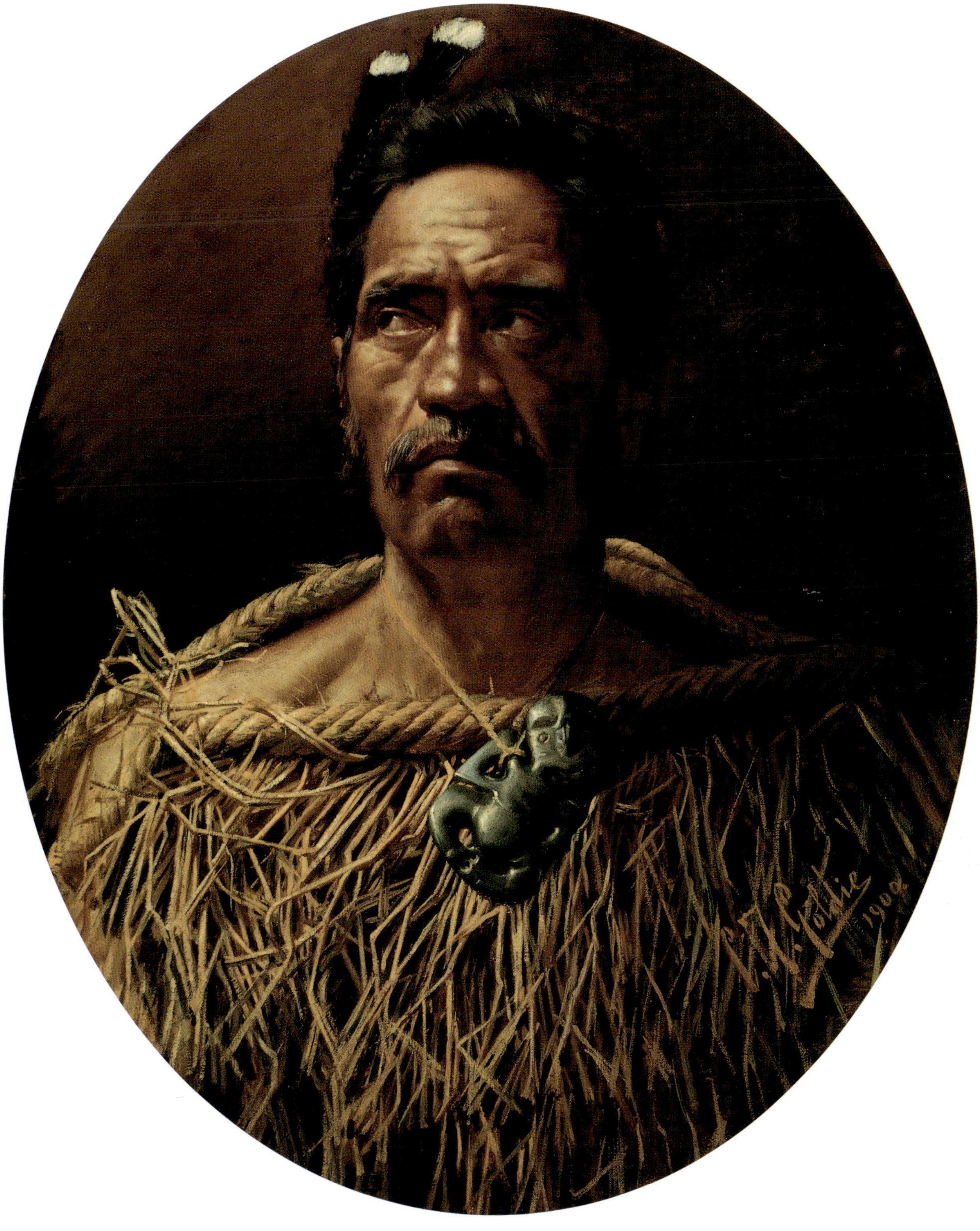

Study from Life, or *One of the Old School* 1900
Wātene Tautari, Ngāti Whātua
oil on canvas, 680 x 585 mm
Robert McDougall Art Gallery, Christchurch

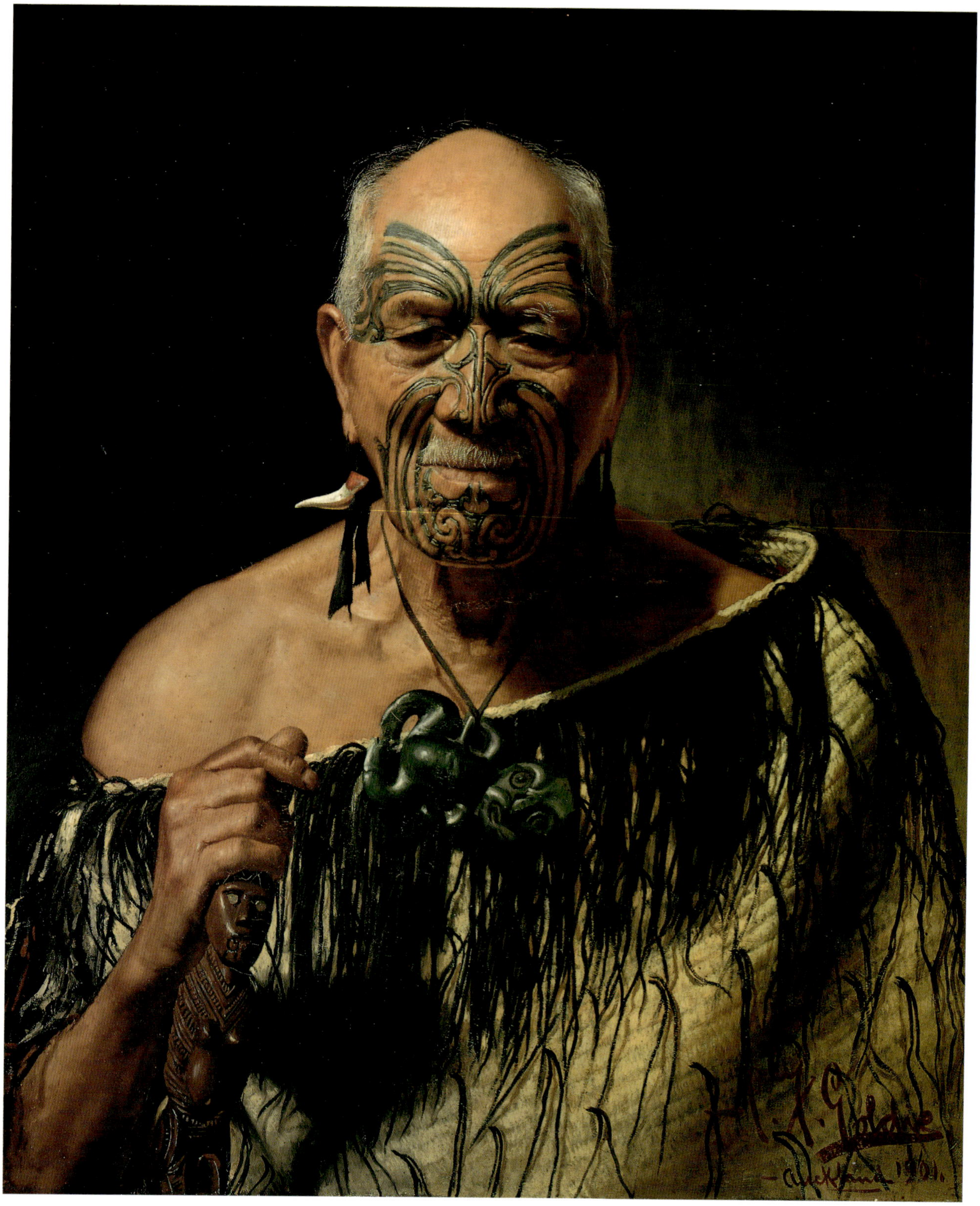

Patara Te Tuhi, an Old Warrior 1901
Pātara Te Tuhi, Ngāti Mahuta
oil on canvas, 765 x 635 mm
Auckland Museum, gift of Olive Goldie, 1951

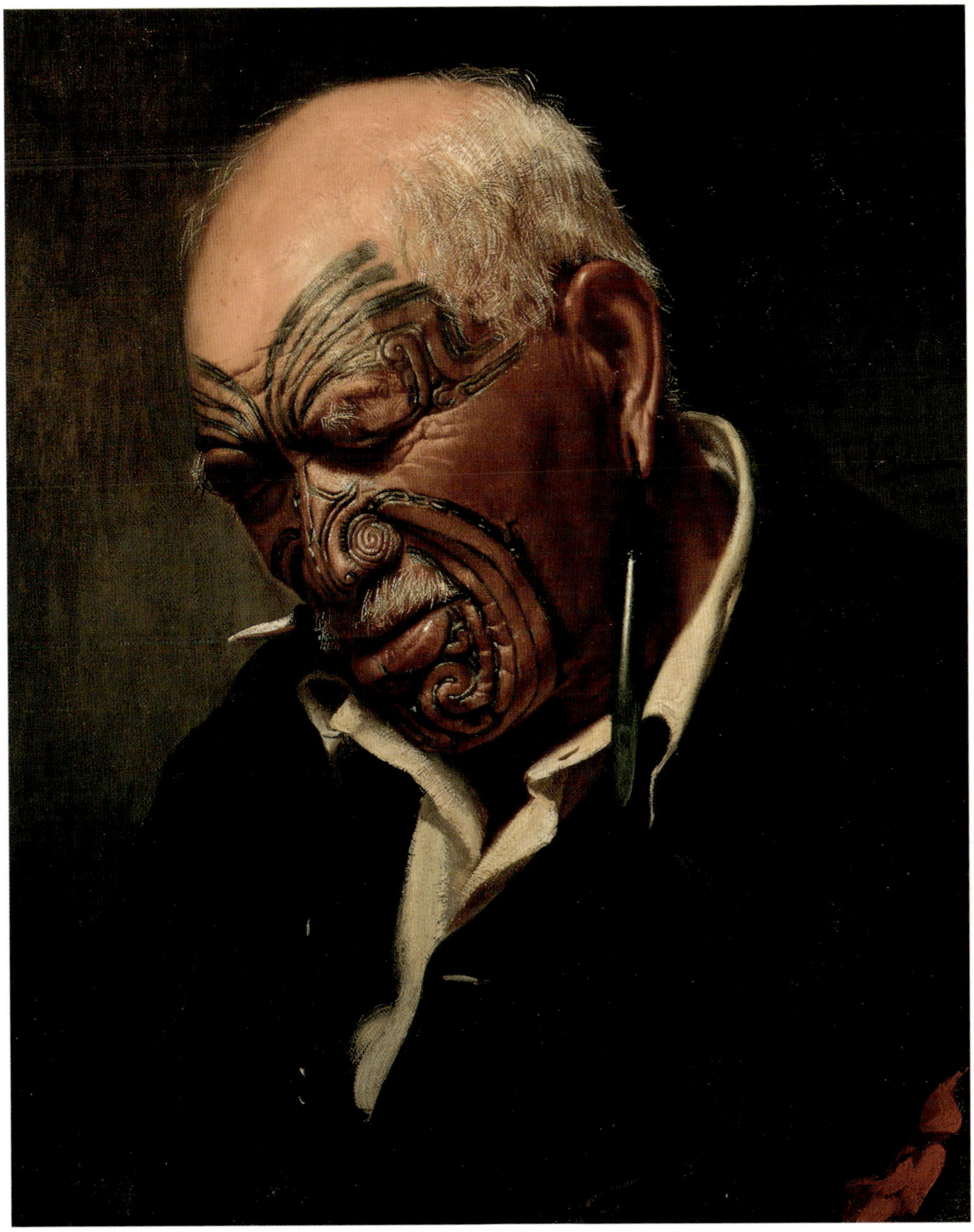

A Hot Day 1901
Pātara Te Tuhi, Ngāti Mahuta
oil on canvas, 437 x 359 mm
Robert McDougall Art Gallery, Christchurch

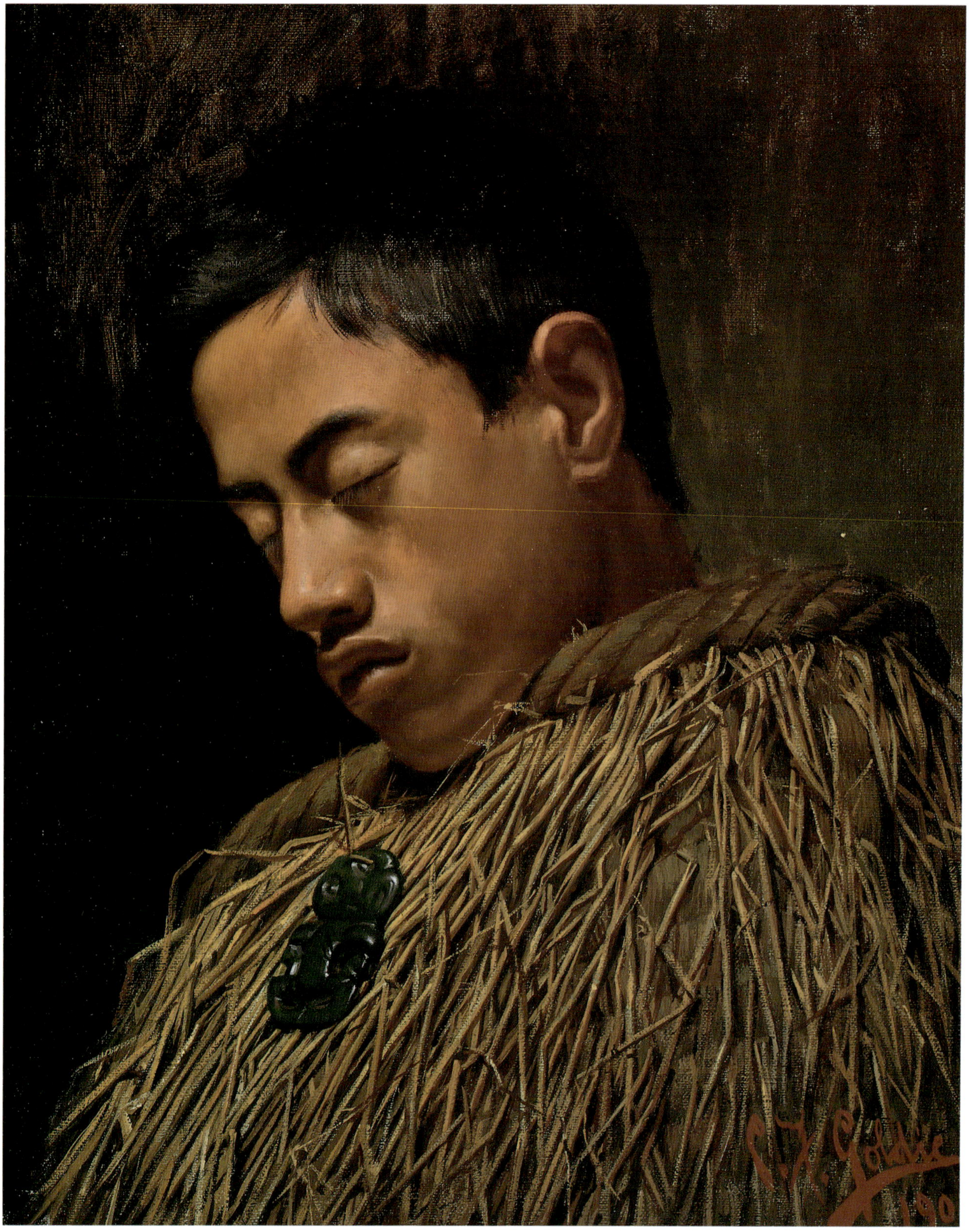

Caught Napping 1901
Hamiora Haupapa, Ngāti Whakaue
oil on canvas, 430 x 355 mm
private collection

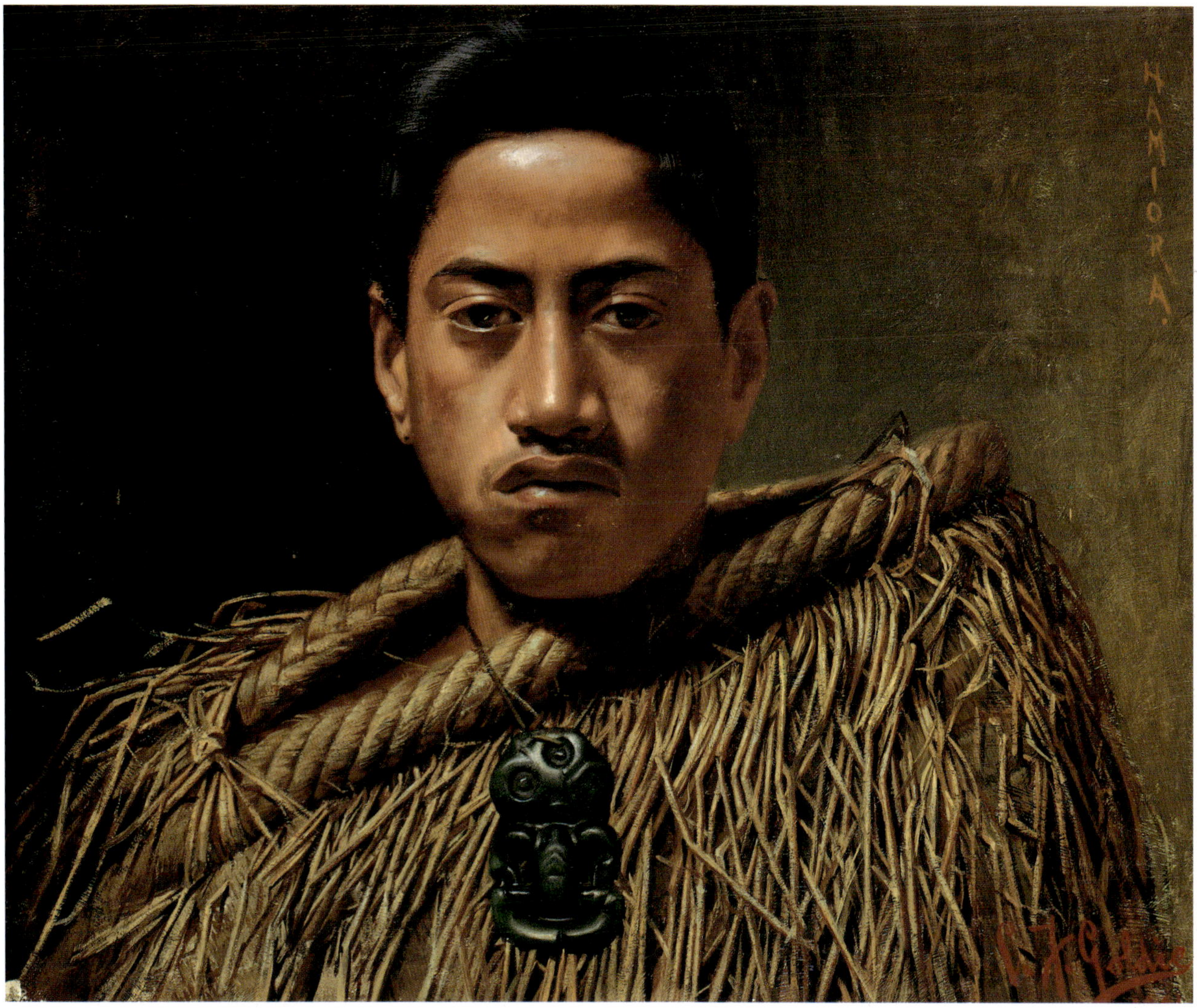

Hamiora 1901
Hamiora Haupapa, Ngāti Whakaue
oil on canvas, 456 x 560 mm
Bishop Suter Art Gallery, Nelson,
gift of the Nelson Suter Art Society, 1904

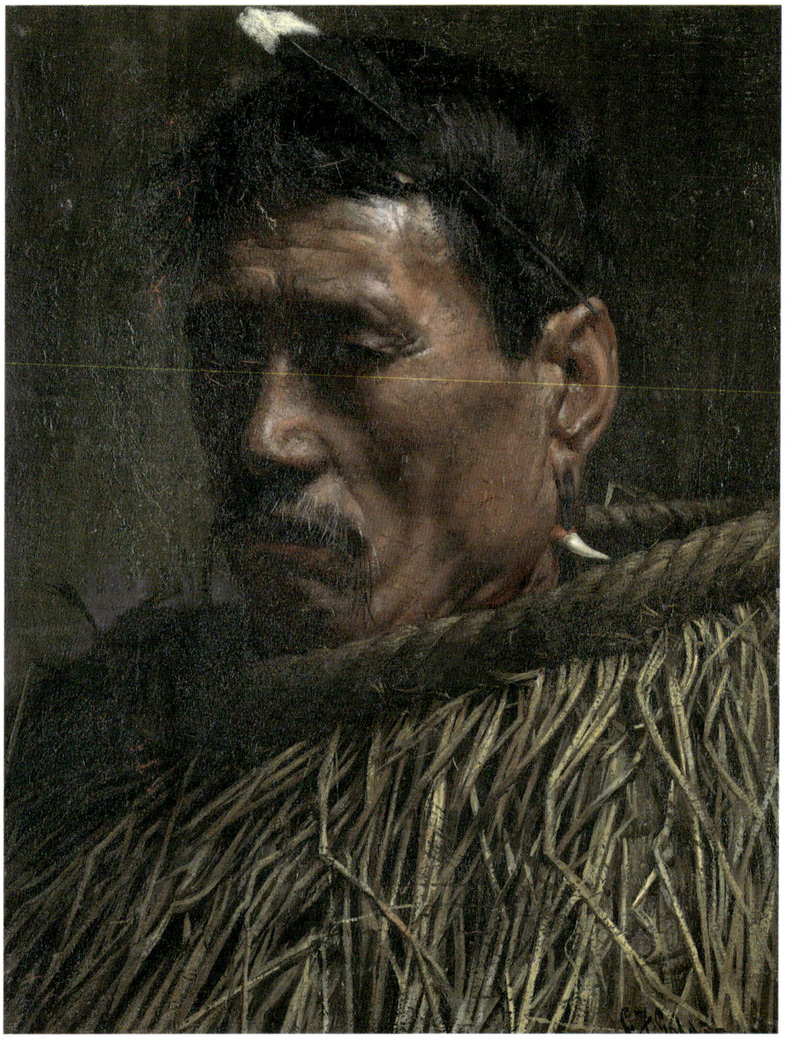

Suspicion 1901

oil on panel, 280 x 216 mm

Russell-Cotes Art Gallery and Museum,

Bournemouth, England

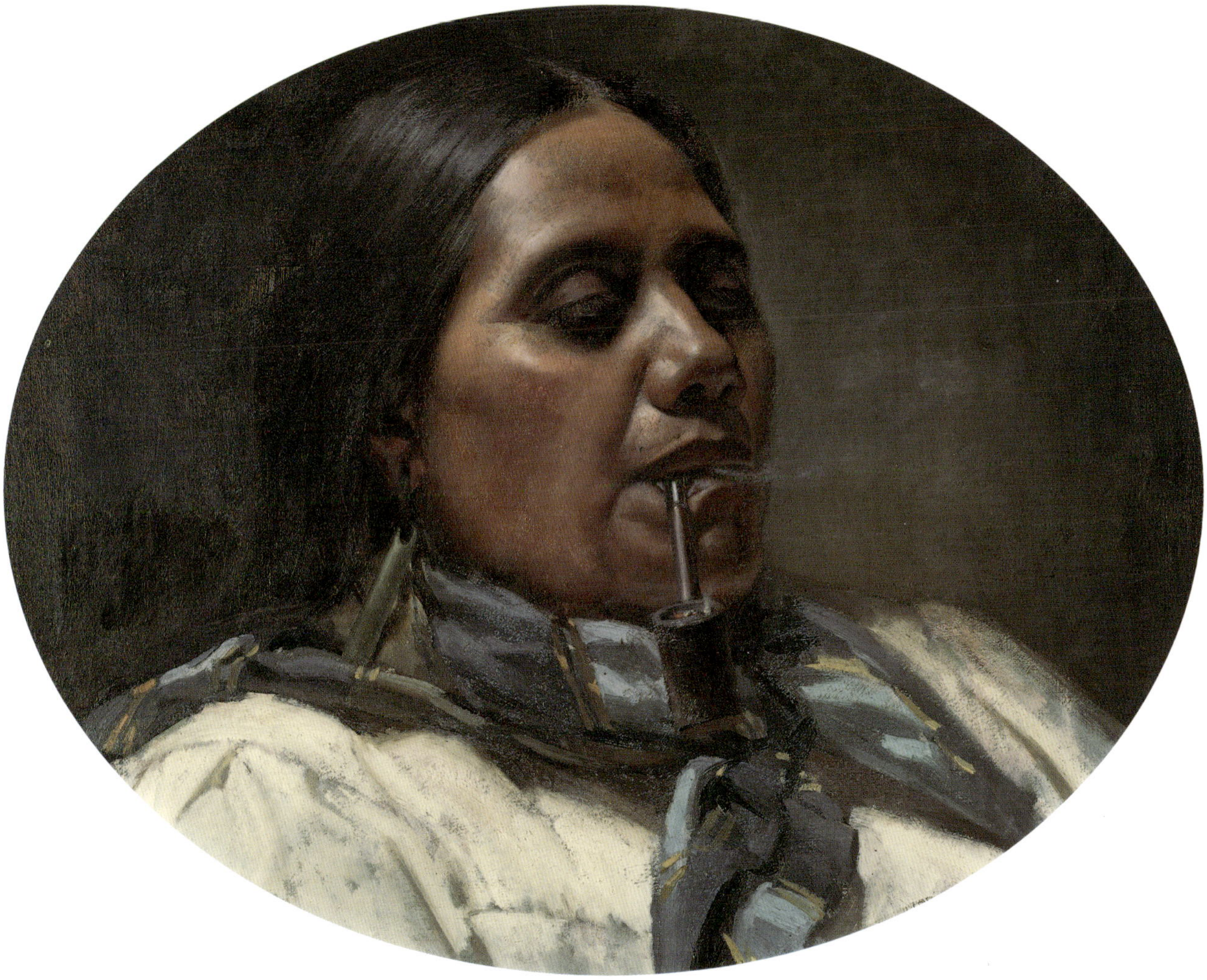

Kai Paipa 1901
oil on canvas, 390 x 482 mm
Russell-Cotes Art Gallery and Museum,
Bournemouth, England

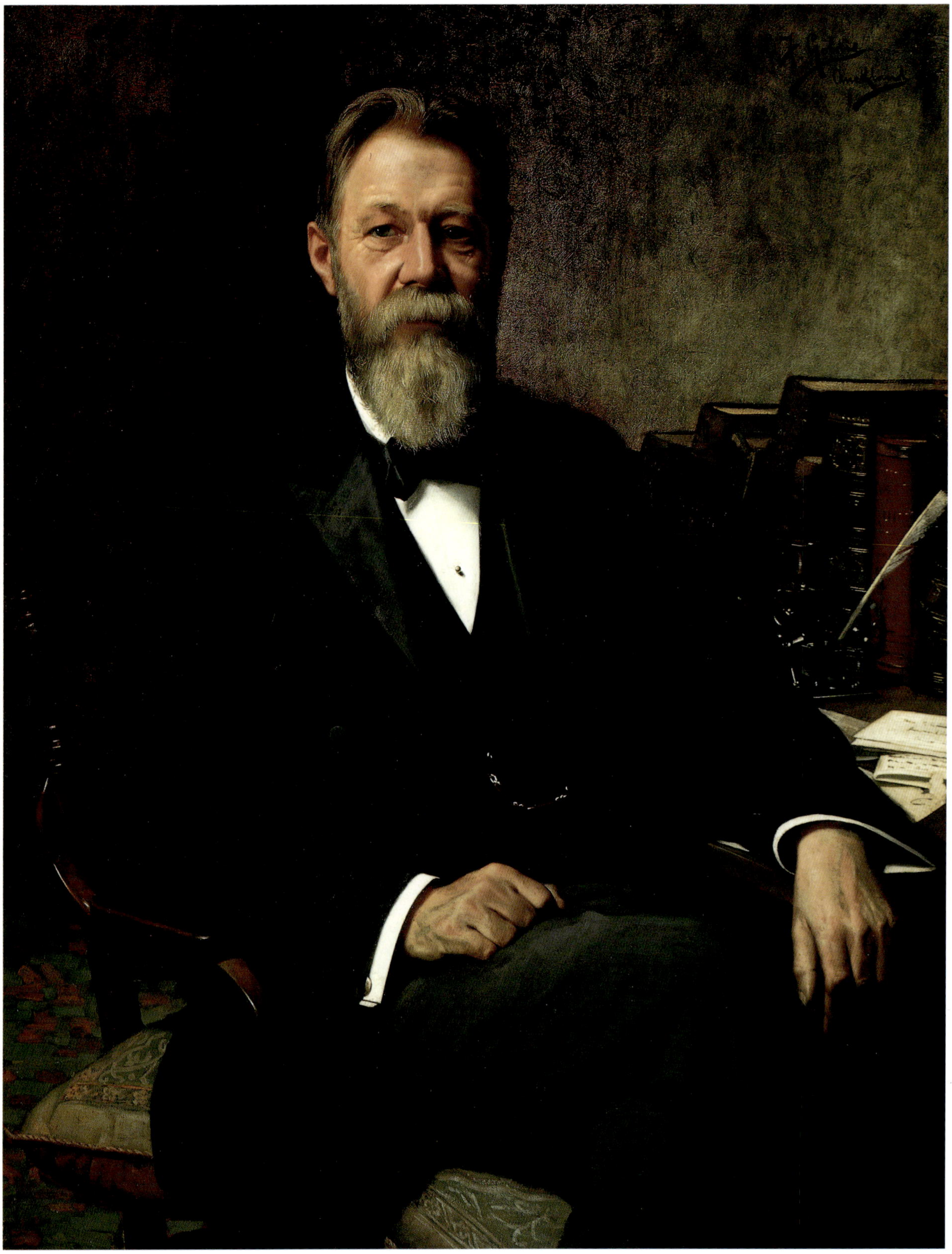

Portrait of Thomson Wilson Leys 1904
oil on canvas, 1170 x 913 mm
Auckland Art Gallery Toi o Tāmaki,
bequest of Dr T. W. Leys, 1925

Portrait of the artist's mother, Maria Goldie c.1900
oil on canvas, 920 x 730 mm
private collection

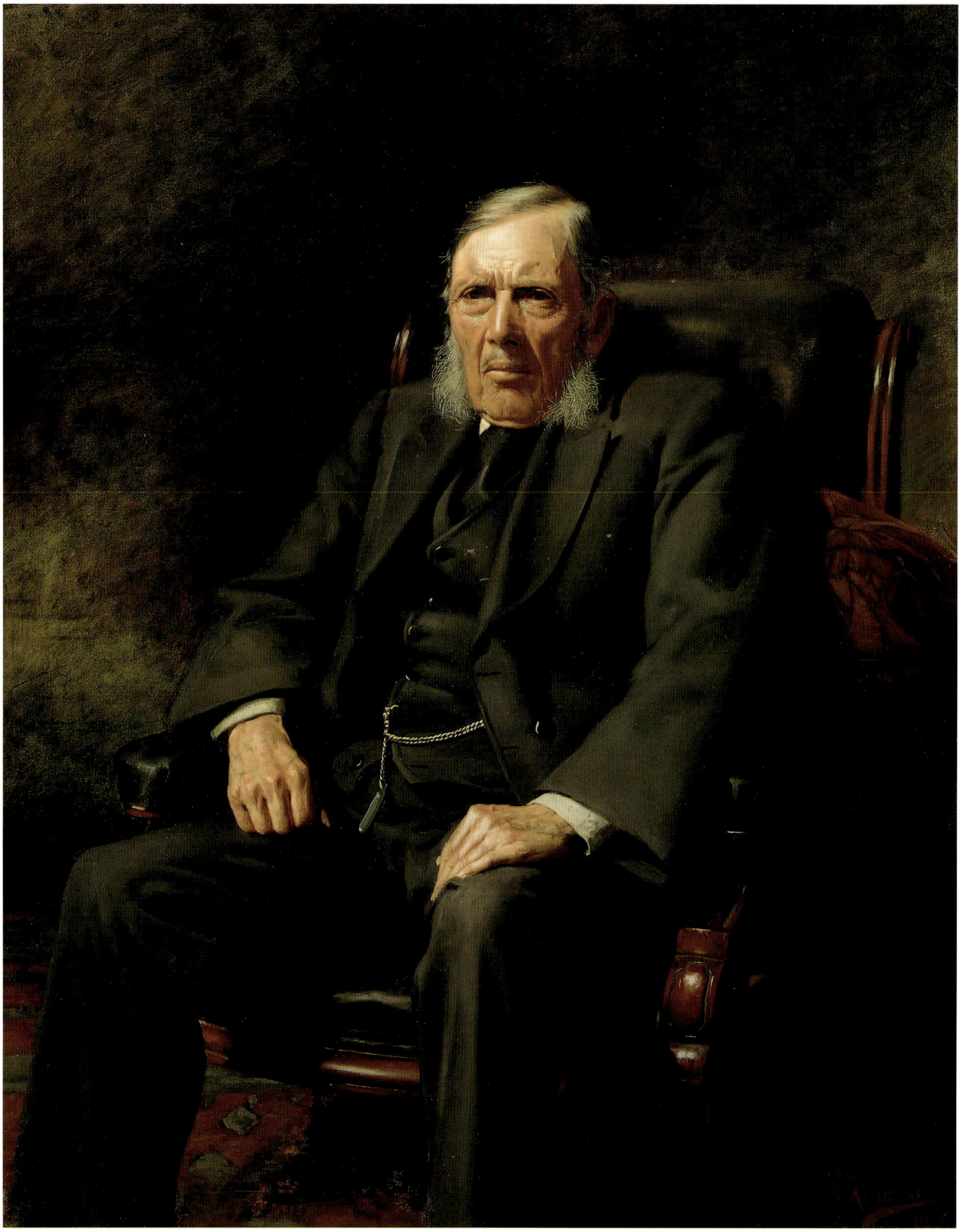

Portrait of the Hon. William Swanson, M.L.C. 1901
oil on canvas, 1275 x 1020 mm
Auckland Art Gallery Toi o Tāmaki,
gift of Charles F. Goldie, 1920

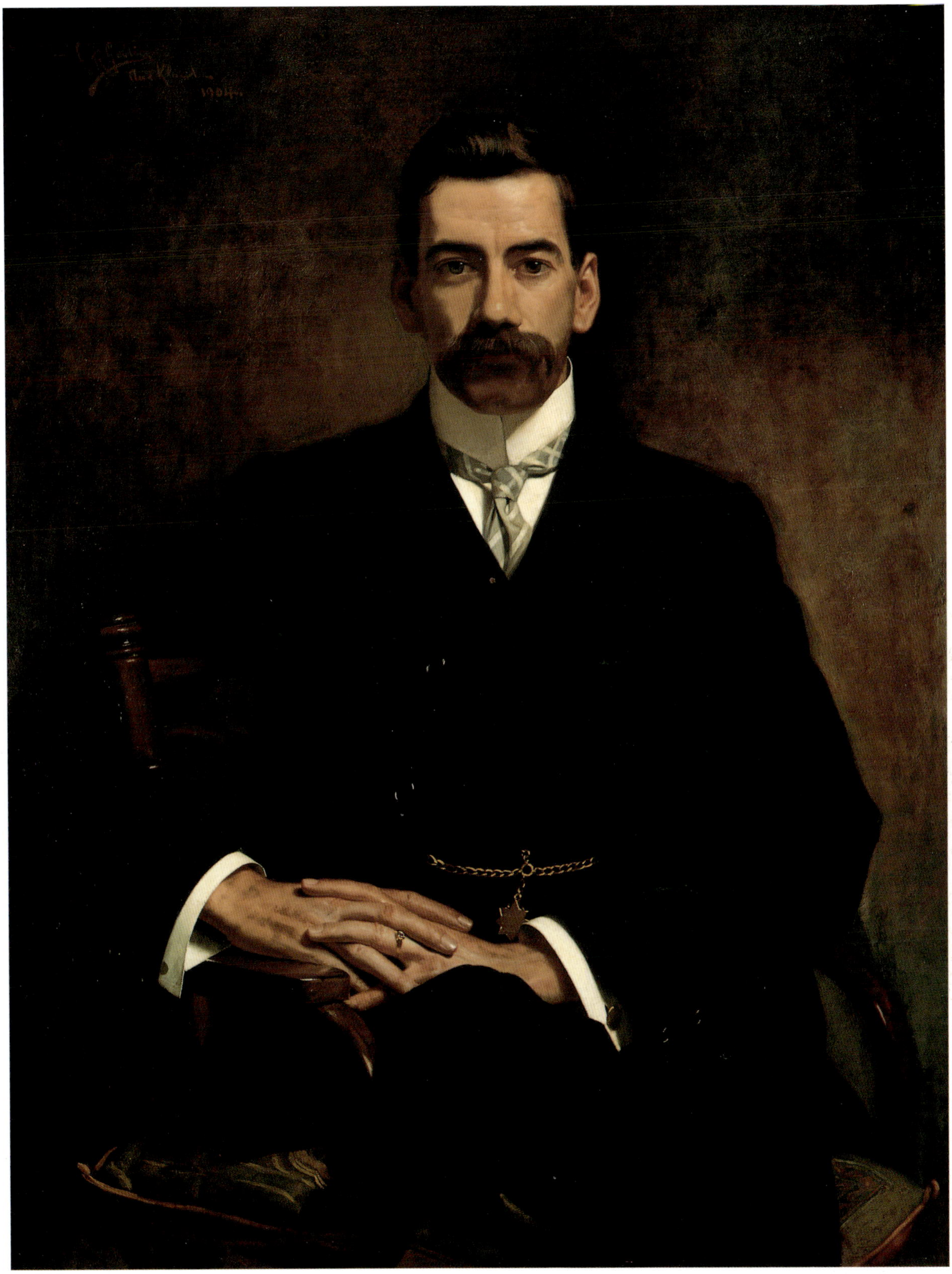

Portrait of J. R. Hooper 1904
oil on canvas, 1120 x 865 mm
private collection

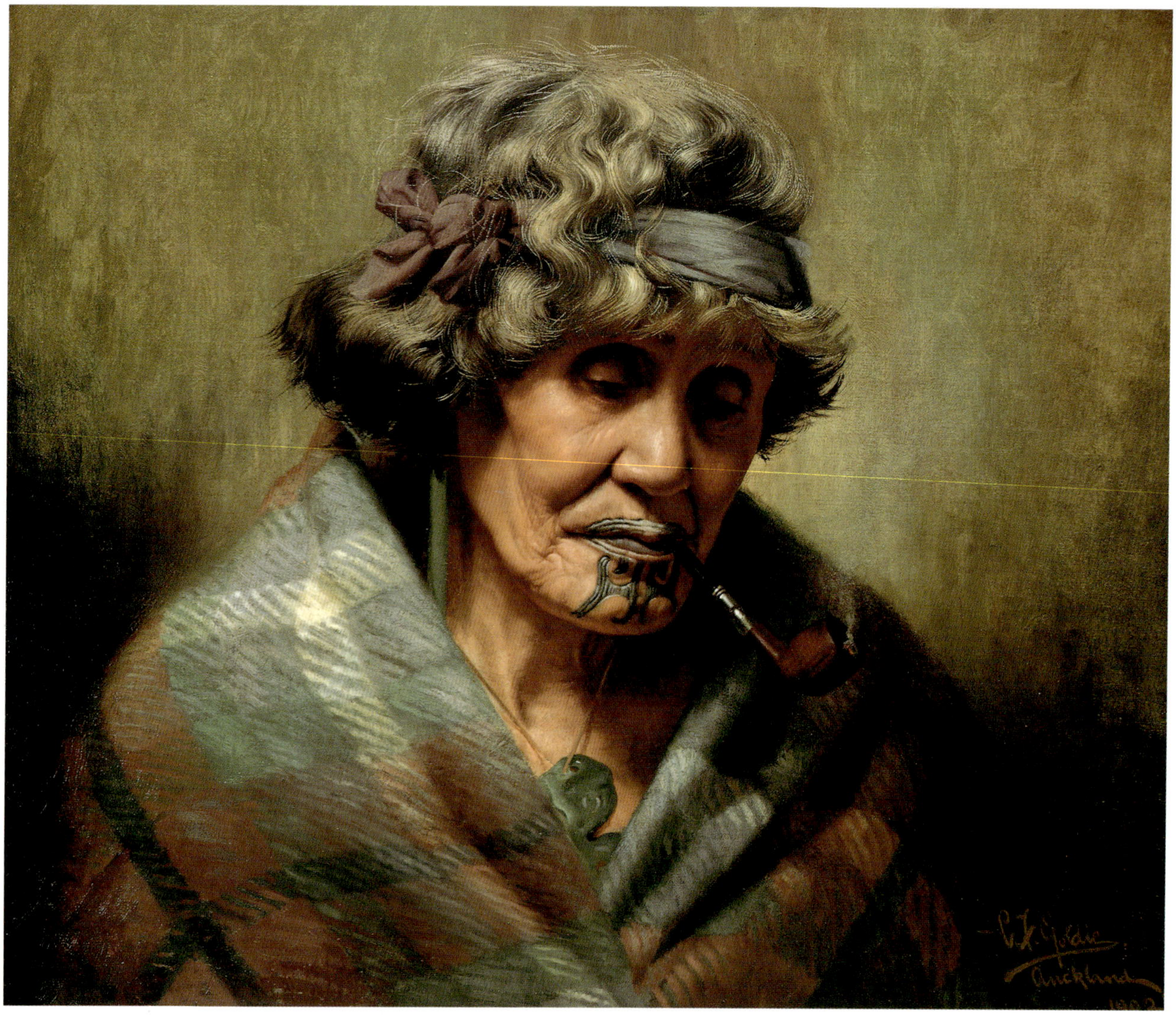

Ena Te Papatahi 1902
Ina Te Papatahi, Ngā Puhi
oil on canvas, 510 x 612 mm
private collection

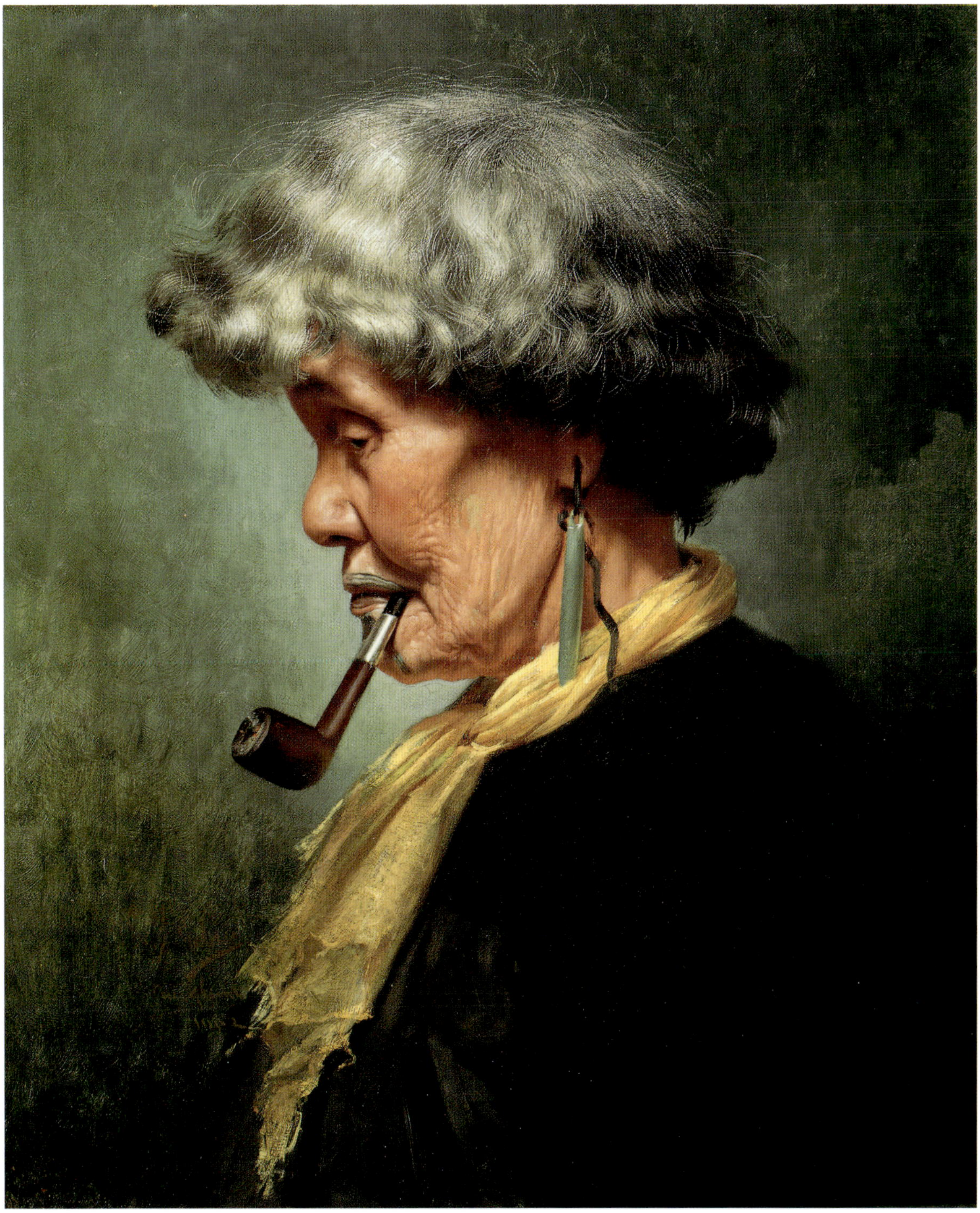

Ena Te Papatahi, a Chieftainess of the Ngapuhi Tribe 1902
Ina Te Papatahi, Ngā Puhi
oil on canvas, 600 x 505 mm
private collection

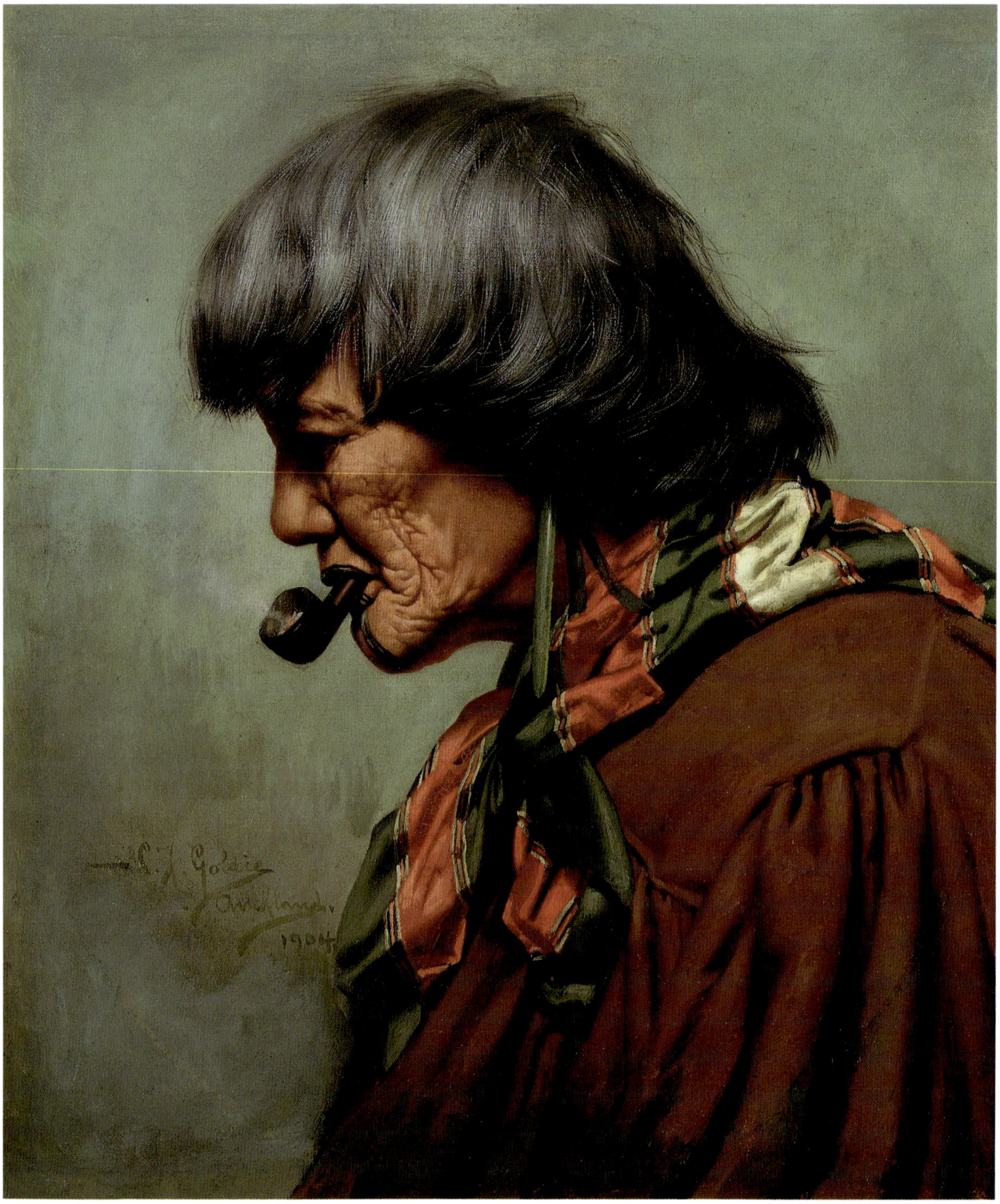

Meditation 1904
Harata Rewiri Tarapata, Ngā Puhi
oil on canvas, 545 x 479 mm
private collection

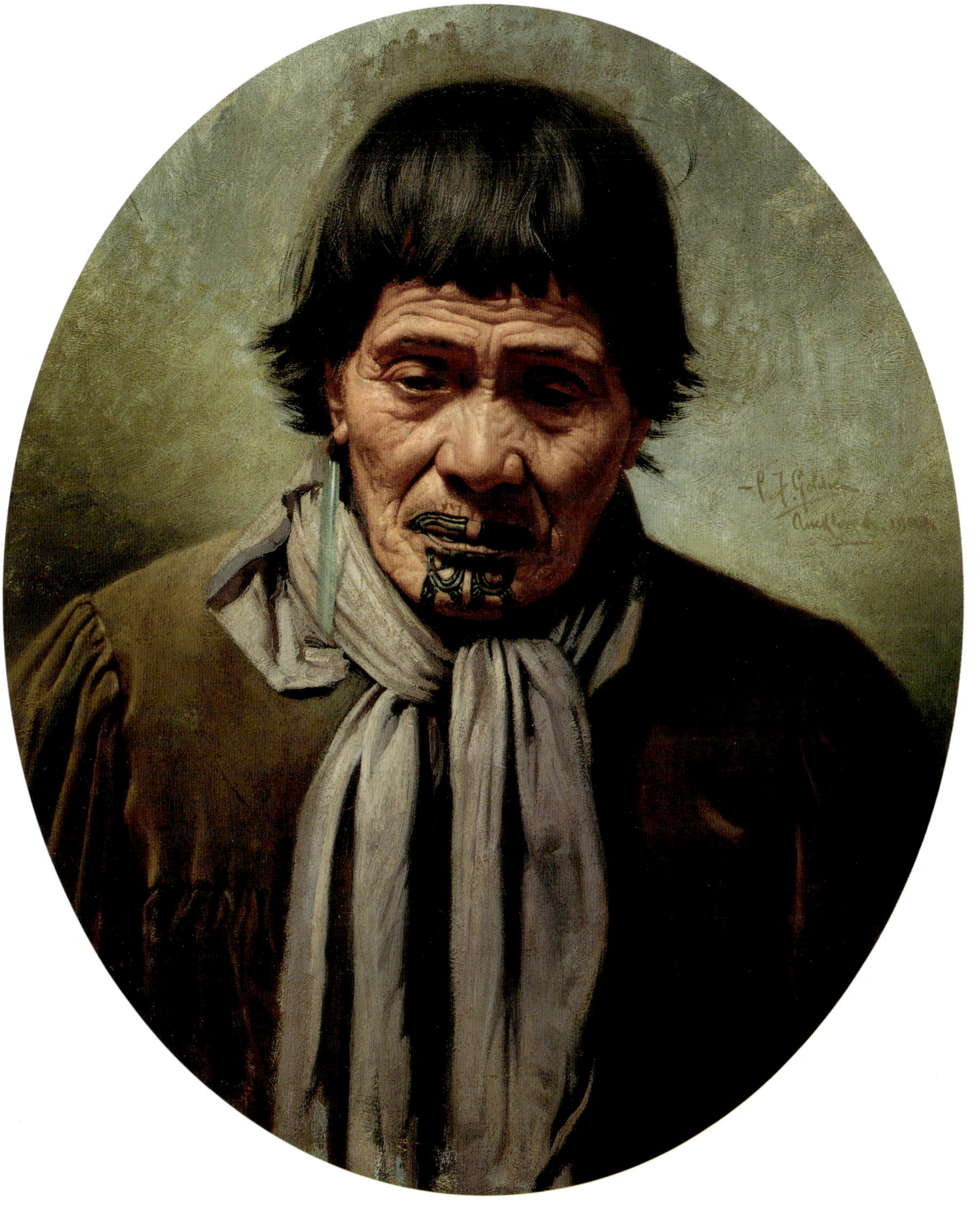

Memories 1903
Harata Rewiri Tarapata, Ngā Puhi
oil on canvas, 585 x 490 mm
collection of Roger Bhatnager, Auckland

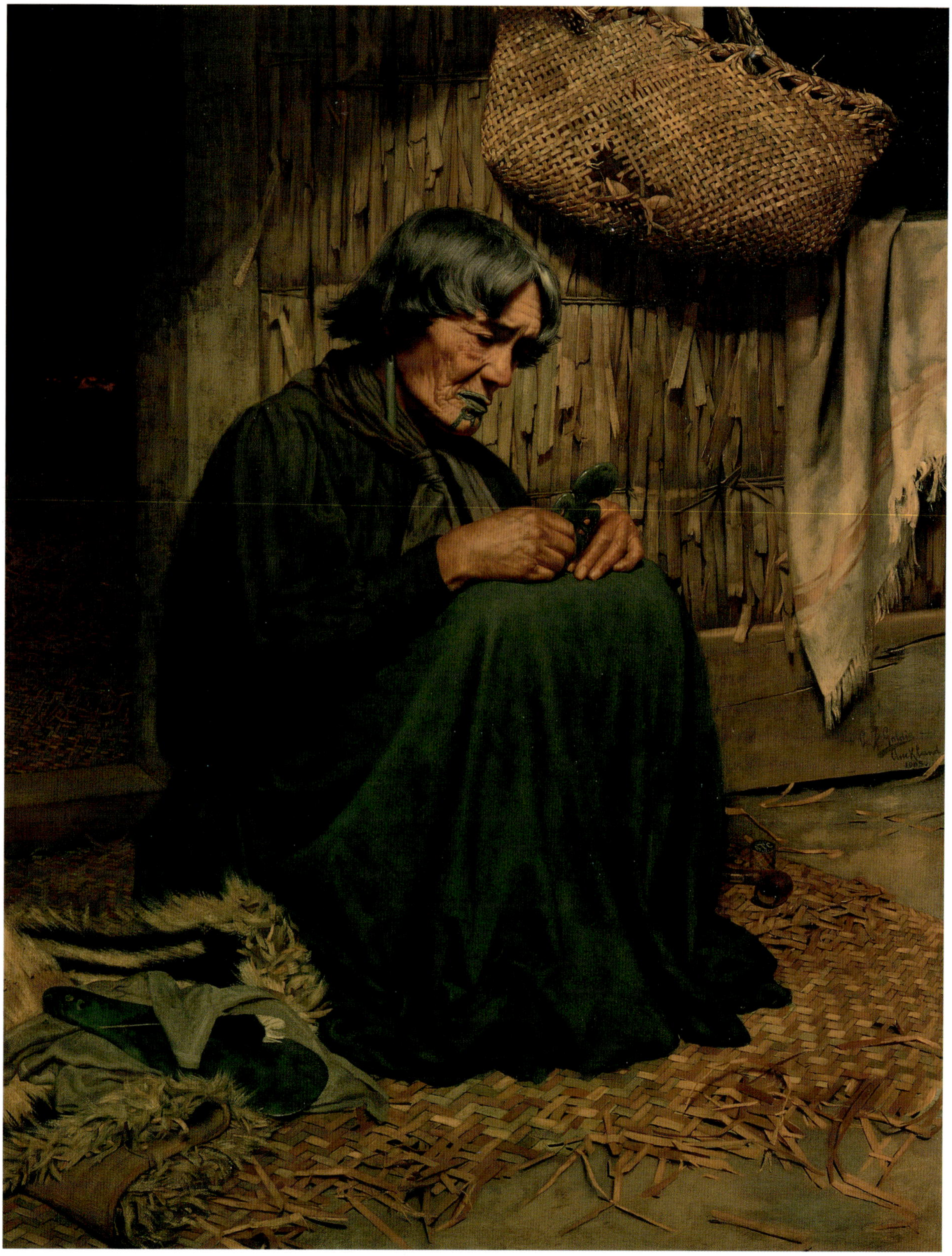

The Widow 1903
Harata Rewiri Tarapata, Ngā Puhi
oil on canvas, 1297 x 1052 mm
Museum of New Zealand Te Papa Tongarewa
(neg. no. B41998)

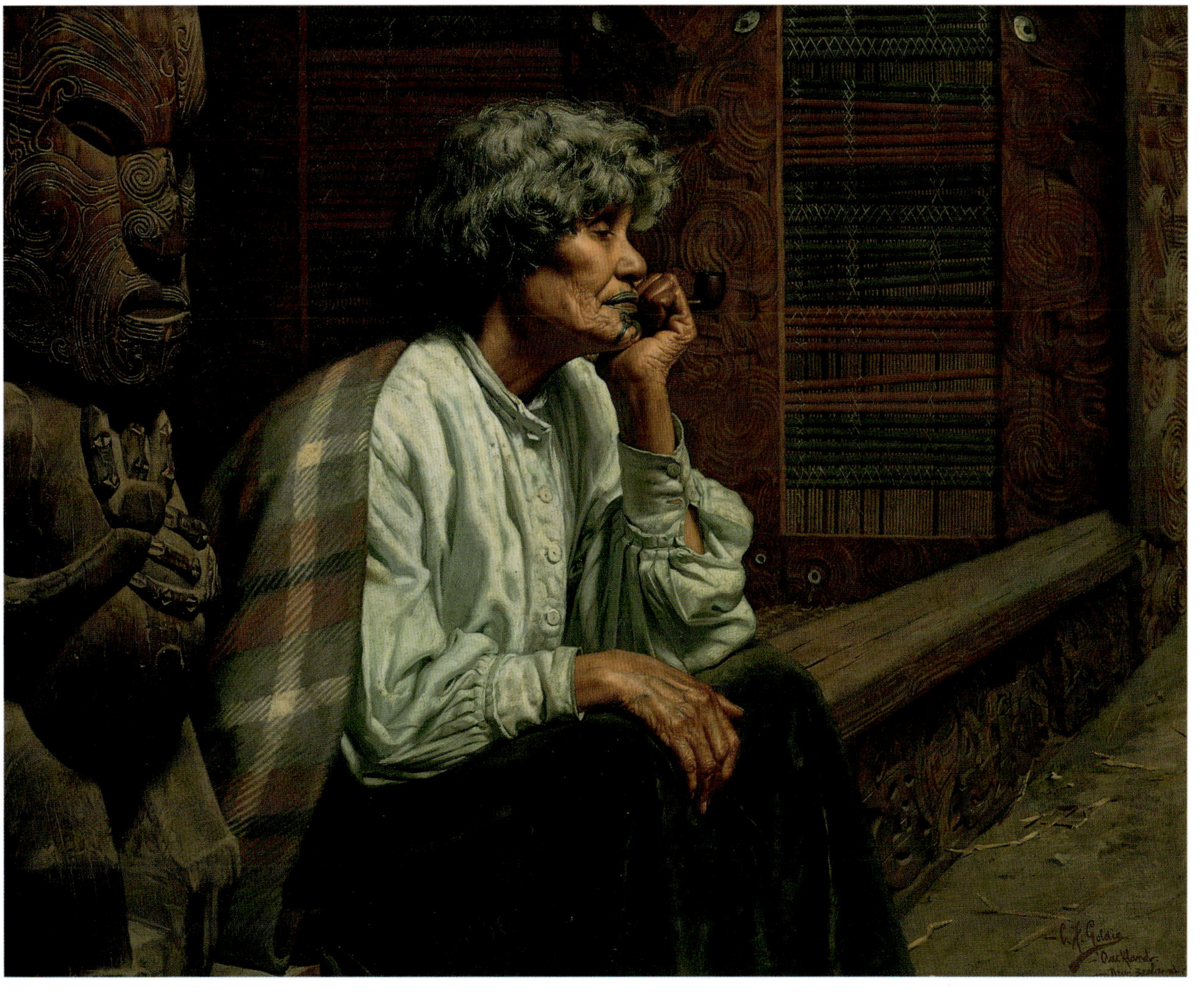

Darby and Joan 1903
Ina Te Papatahi, Ngā Puhi

oil on canvas, 999 x 1250 mm
Museum of New Zealand Te Papa Tongarewa
(neg. no. B41997)

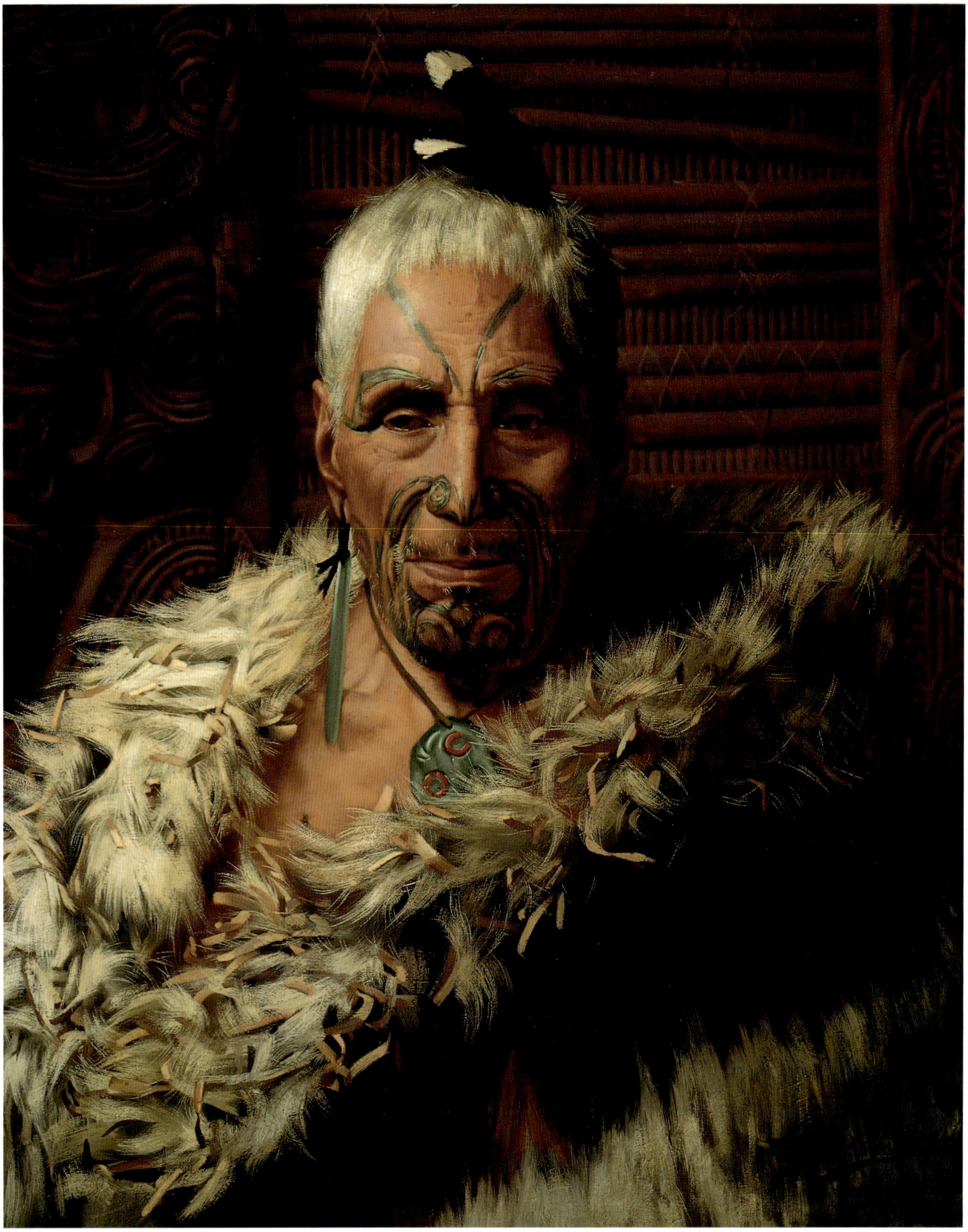

Perema Te Pahau, the Bone Scraper 1904
Perema Te Pāhau, Tūhourangi, Ngāti Wahiao
oil on canvas, 765 x 640 mm
Auckland Museum, gift of Olive Goldie, 1951

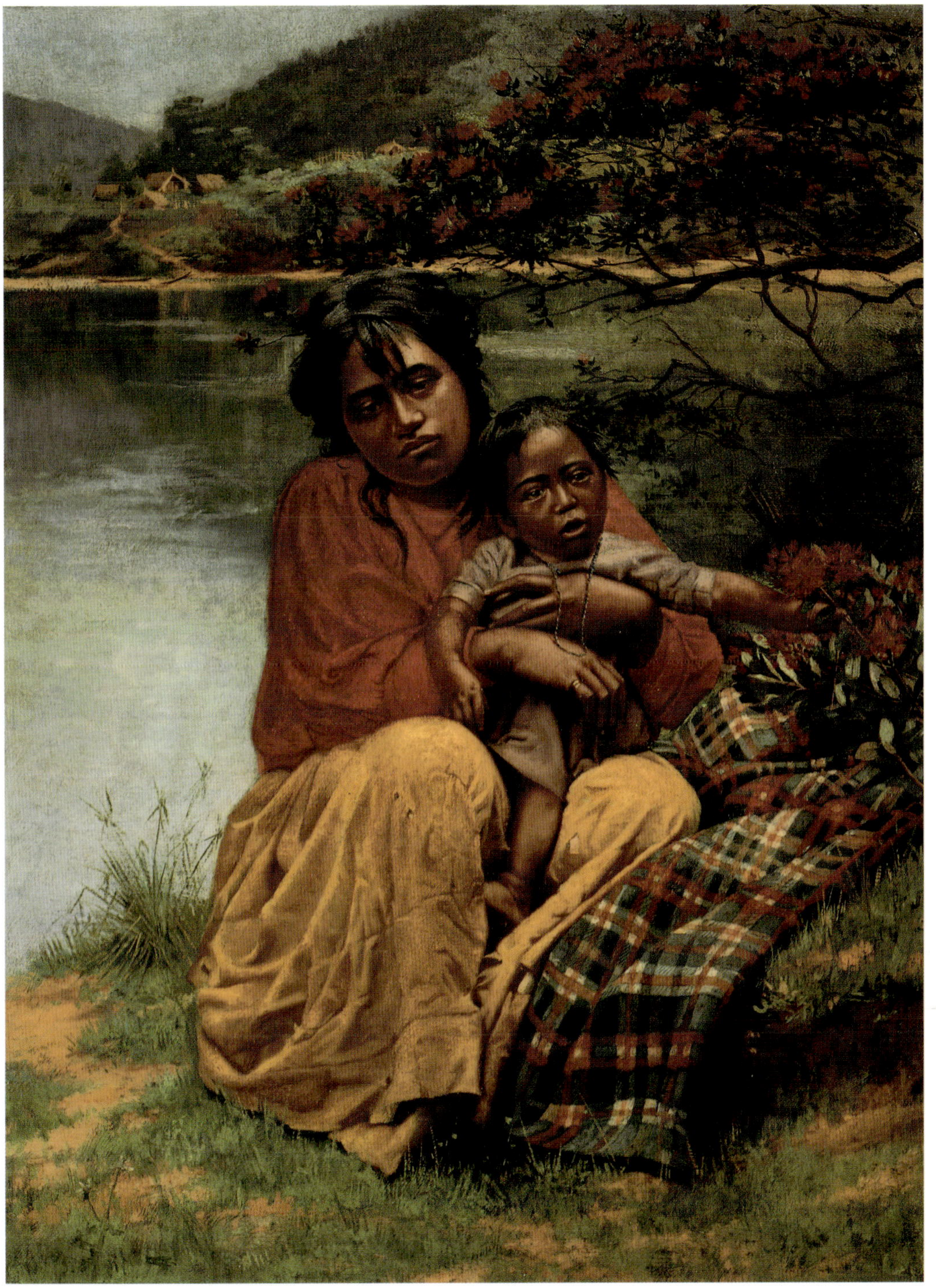

Day Dreams: Christmas Time in Maoriland 1902
Nataria Mitchell, Ngāti Whakaue
oil on canvas, 555 x 415 mm
Auckland Art Gallery Toi o Tāmaki,
gift in memory of Frank Anthony Eden, 1988

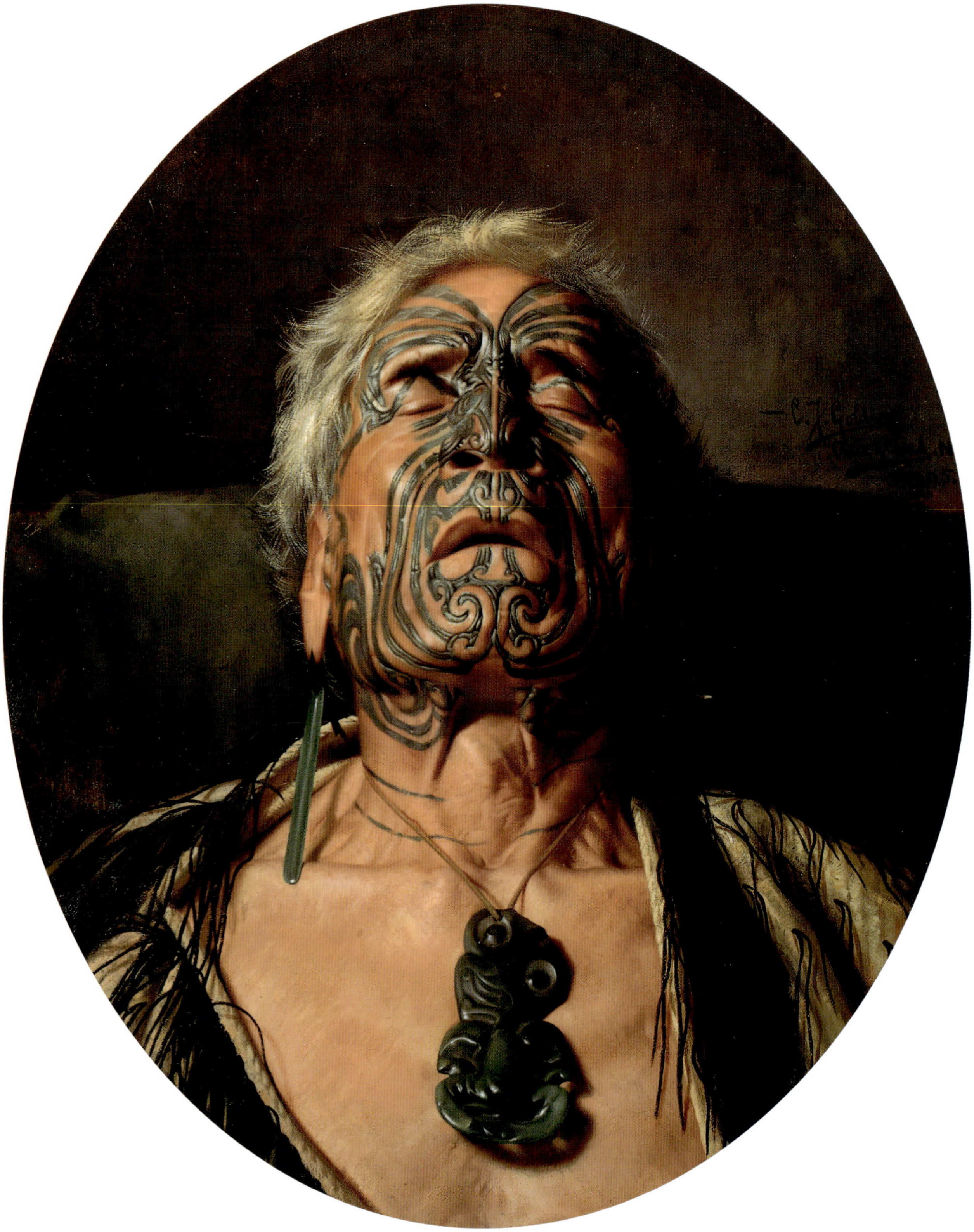

A Study 1905
Te Aho-o-te-Rangi Wharepu, Ngāti Mahuta
oil on canvas, 635 x 540 mm
Auckland Museum, gift of Olive Goldie, 1951

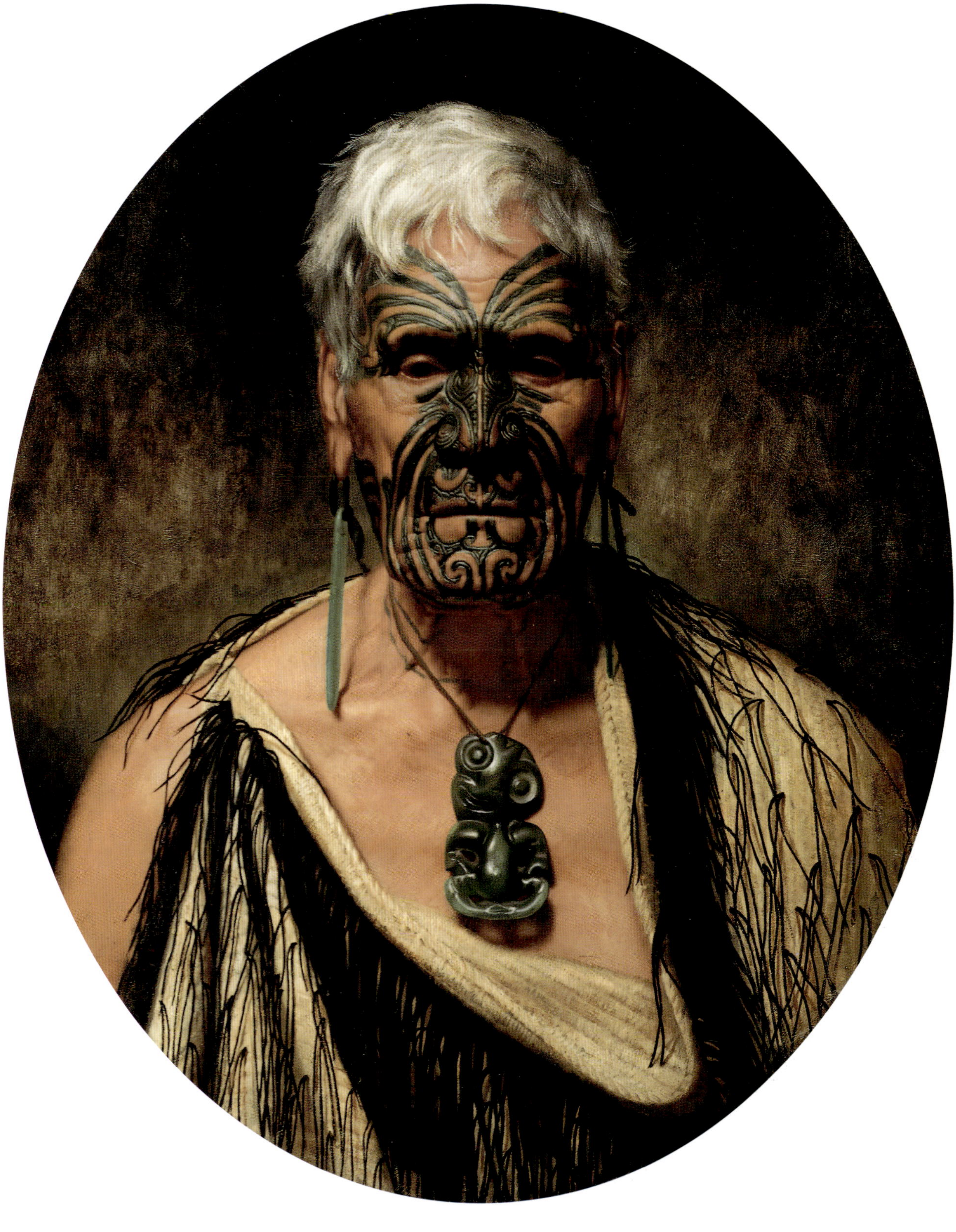

Te Aho, a Noted Waikato Warrior dated 1902
Te Aho-o-te-Rangi Wharepu, Ngāti Mahuta
oil on canvas, 635 x 540 mm
Auckland Museum, gift of Olive Goldie, 1951

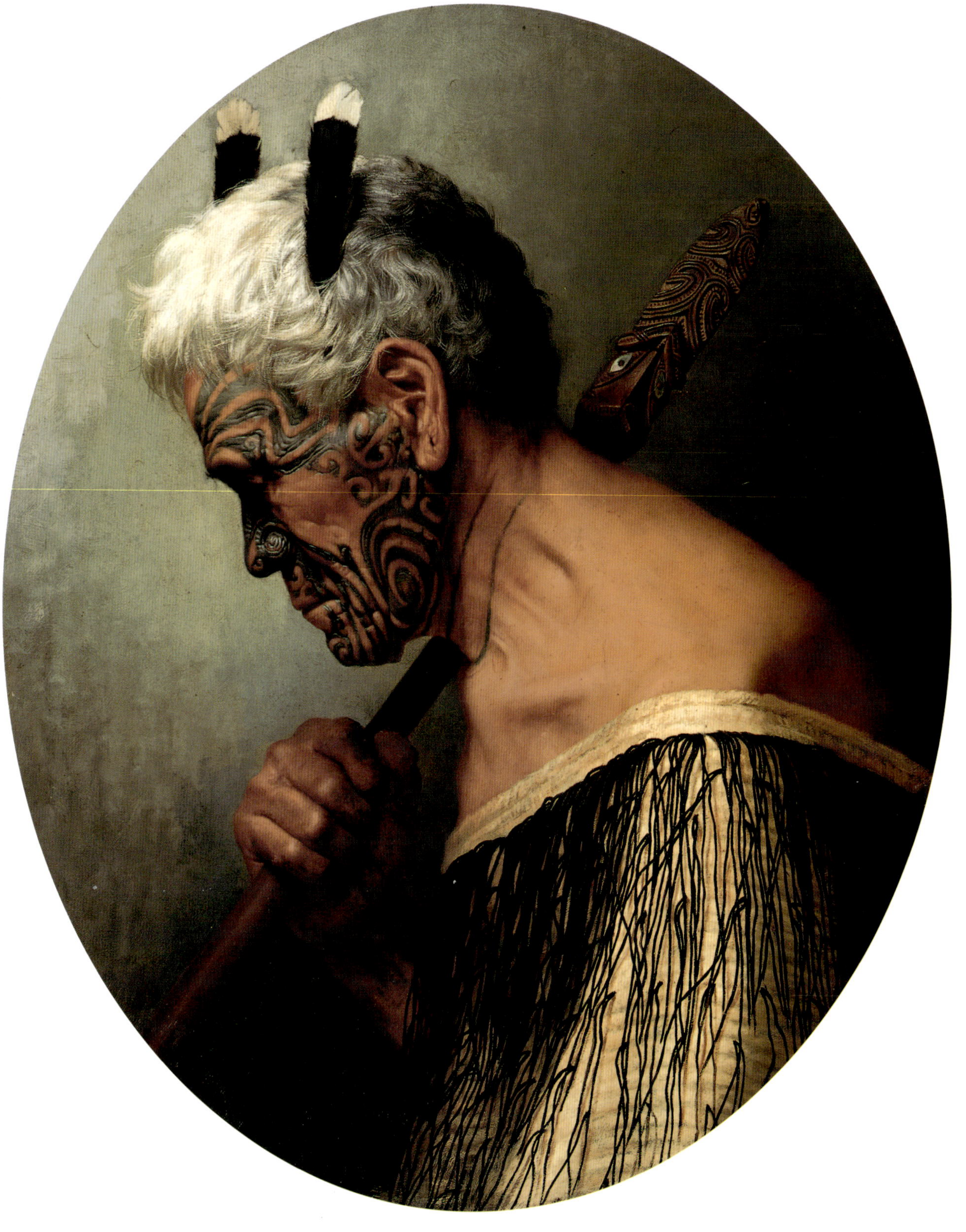

A Hero of Many Fights 1905
Te Aho-o-te-Rangi Wharepu, Ngāti Mahuta
oil on canvas, 765 x 640 mm
Auckland Museum, gift of Olive Goldie, 1951

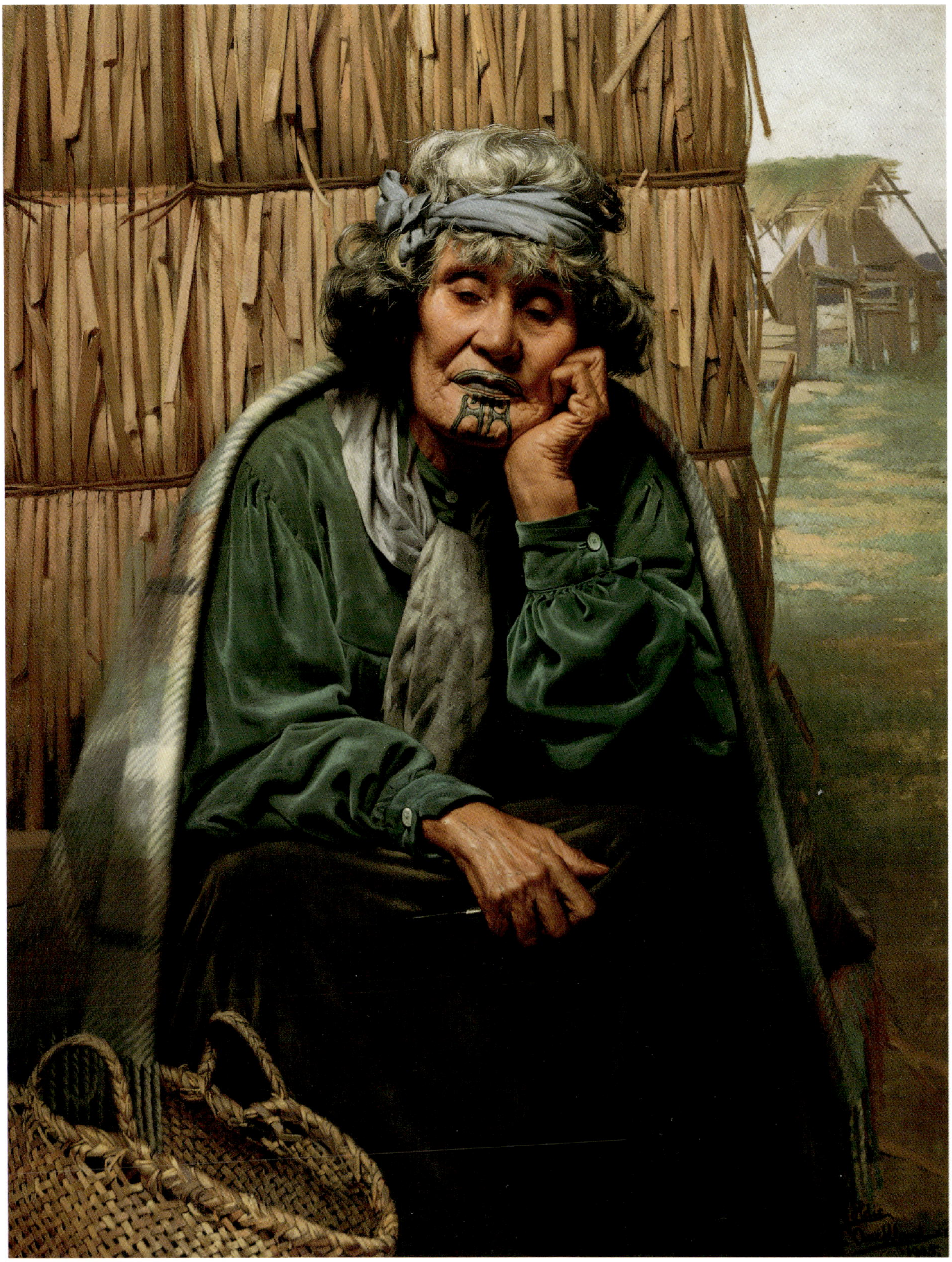

The memory of what has been and never more will be 1905
Ina Te Papatahi, Ngā Puhi
oil on canvas, 1150 x 900 mm
Dunedin Public Art Gallery

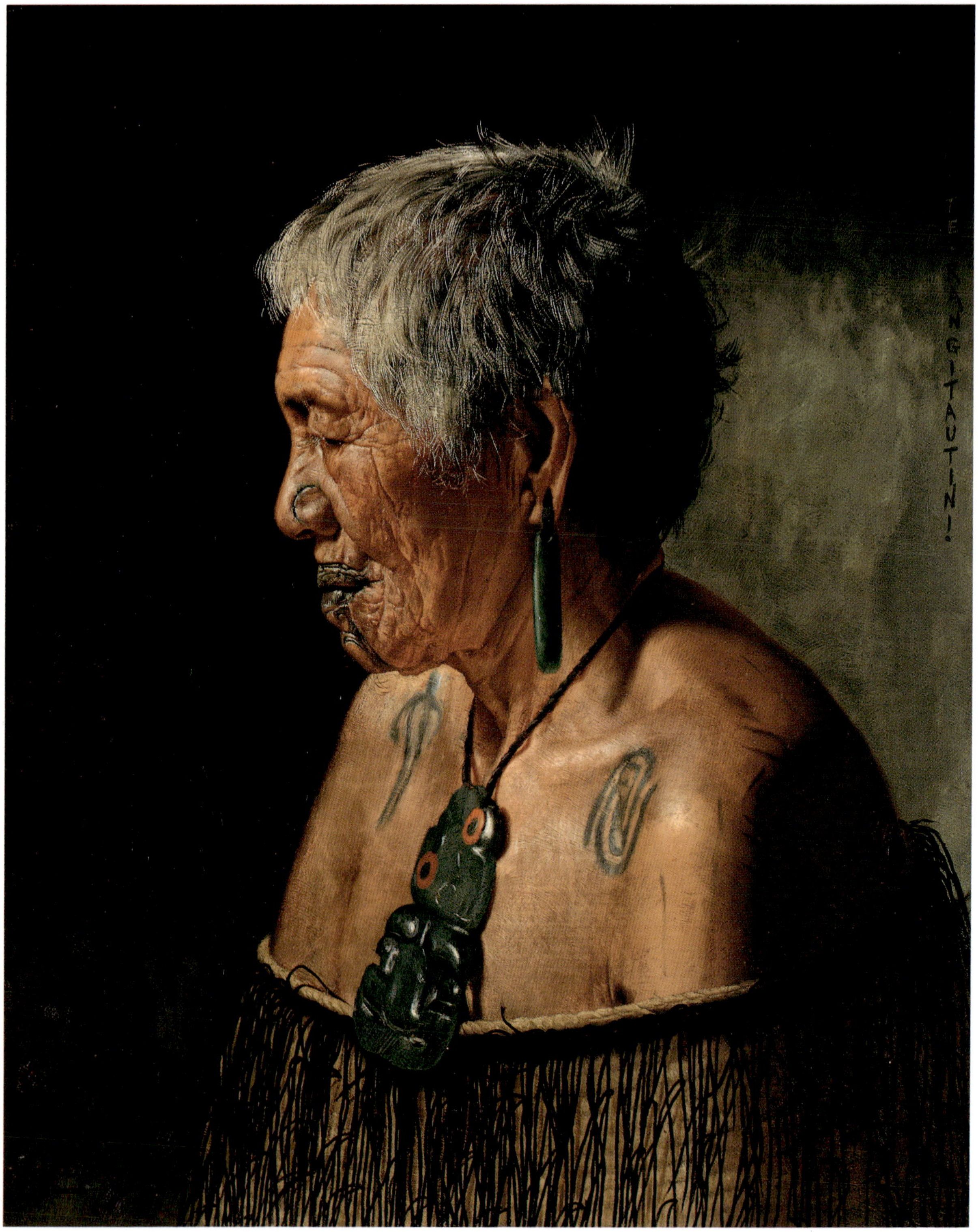

Ahinata Te Rangitautini, Tuhourangi Tribe 1903
Ahinata Te Rangitautini (Kapekape), Tūhourangi
oil on canvas, 615 x 512 mm
private collection

NGAHUIA TE AWEKOTUKU

tā moko: māori tattoo

> You may lose your most valuable property through misfortune in various ways ... your house, your weaponry, your spouse, and other treasures. You may be robbed of all that you cherish. But of your moko, you cannot be deprived, except by death. It will be your ornament and your companion until your final day.
>
> Netana Whakaari of Waimana, 1921

Mataora was the husband of Niwareka, who came from the underworld. He abused her and she fled back to her people. Remorseful and distressed, Mataora set out looking for her. He dressed in his finest garments and enhanced his already handsome face with colour; he wanted her forgiveness, he missed her and so he followed her trail.

She was with her father, Uetonga, when Mataora arrived, desperate, exhausted, dishevelled, the pigment running with the sweat from his face, smeared and unsightly. Everyone laughed at him. Their skins were incised with rich patterns; their adornment was forever. And though he was embarrassed and angry, Mataora was humble, too. He begged forgiveness of Niwareka and her family; he begged knowledge of her father. They relented, teaching him the art of tā moko, while Niwareka learned that of tāniko, weaving with coloured fibres. And so two important art traditions, tāniko and tā moko, were brought back to the world of light and celebrated by humankind for their magic and their beauty.

Tā moko is the Māori form of a tradition[1] that extends throughout the islands of Polynesia; tattoo chisels have been found in the earliest excavations in Aotearoa, and the Eastern Pacific. This archaic material includes wider combs, suggesting a relationship to the implements of Samoa and the possibility of more geometric designs and blocks of solid colour; it may also be argued that the tā moko recorded so graphically by Goldie and documented by Robley was developed with the introduction of metal. The works of Parkinson, de l'Horne and other eighteenth-century artists, present the tā moko as a series of flat incisions into which pigment was inserted as the chisel cut, rather than the sculpted and highly textured scarification procedure assumed in later decades and which Goldie so meticulously detailed.

Tā moko is related to the tatu of Eastern Polynesia, and the uninterrupted, superlative tatau of Samoa. Though the patterns taken by the skin vary dramatically from one island group to another, the technique of rhythmically tapping a bone chisel lashed to a small wooden haft remains the same. At least two artmakers – one, the tohunga or accomplished expert, the other an apprentice/assistant – were engaged in the operation, as each section of skin being worked on required manual stretching, so the chisel pierced a taut surface. Graphic representations of the tā moko process, notably by Steele and Lindauer, present an artist working on his own, yet this was most unlikely – tohunga tā moko worked with a number of helpers, as the process required a lot of careful attention.

Robley also noted the use of shark's teeth, and the manipulation of a single slashing instrument which opened the skin for the application of pigment; a tool like this exists in the British Museum collection, and is currently the focus of some debate.

The conventional toolkit of the original tohunga tā moko comprised a series of hafted chisels (uhi) made in varying widths from albatross bone. While the narrowest (2 mm) were honed to a flat edge and thus served as 'cutters', the wider blades had a serrated, comblike edge which penetrated the flesh and inserted pigment at the same time. The larger type was known as 'uhi matarau' – the chisel of a hundred faces. Set in handles of kauri, tōtara or maire wood, often elaborately ornamented, they were struck by a mallet of mahoe which also varied according to the blade size and type. As well as the chisels and mallets, the kit contained a small pot – usually of wood, sometimes pumice, always carved – of pigment, or awe kāpara. The ingredients of this pigment differed from one tribal region to another, but it always included a mix of soot and oil or water. Differences arose in the material burned to make the soot – the āwheto caterpillar, kauri gum, or vegetable matter. The darkest and the most permanent substance was the most desirable. Containers holding decades of lovingly concocted pigment were highly prized and closely guarded heirlooms. Also remarkable for their beauty were the kōrere, or broth and water feeders, finely carved funnel-shaped objects designed to distract the patient from the pain while giving some liquid food safely by minimising all contact between the traumatised skin and the food itself. These too were precious objects, greatly admired.

Healing concluded the process. Clear, clean, spring water – wai māori – is still regarded as the most effective healing agent, but Robley's collection included a karaka leaf – dry, flat and beige one hundred and thirty years later, but still visibly a karaka leaf of the kind which continues to be used on wounds, cuts and skin infections in the Māori world today. It is particularly soothing on traumatised and infected skin.

Ritual was an essential component of tā moko, to safeguard both the operator and the patient. Most basic of all was the tapu of hygiene – no one involved in the process handled food, and any necessary sustenance was provided by helpers at the appropriate time. The patient had to refrain from intimate contact until the healing was complete, and was earnestly warned against looking at her or his reflection – originally in water, more recently, in mirrors. This was sound psychology and common sense.

Despite the current belief that only male artists practised as tohunga tā moko, Māori oral history as revealed by mōteatea or chant poems, Dumont d'Urville's account and events of more recent decades dispute this. King notes that two women were practising between the First and Second World Wars in the Waikato district, and people in the Rotorua/Bay of Plenty area recall two women also adept at the art.

With the introduction of metal, and more specifically iron, the technology changed, and it is believed that the patterning and design reflected this. Much finer work was produced; a specialist in one branch of Polynesian tattoo suggests that the grooved shape of sailmaking needles reworked into a tattoo blade could easily cicatrise the skin and effect the raised skin art so intimately associated with the nineteenth-century images of Māori mau moko.

Different parts of the body were ornamented in the different sexes. Women were usually adorned on their lips and chin, taking this around the time of their first menstruation; until the late nineteenth century, the central forehead, nostrils and upper lip were also marked. The thighs, hips, lower

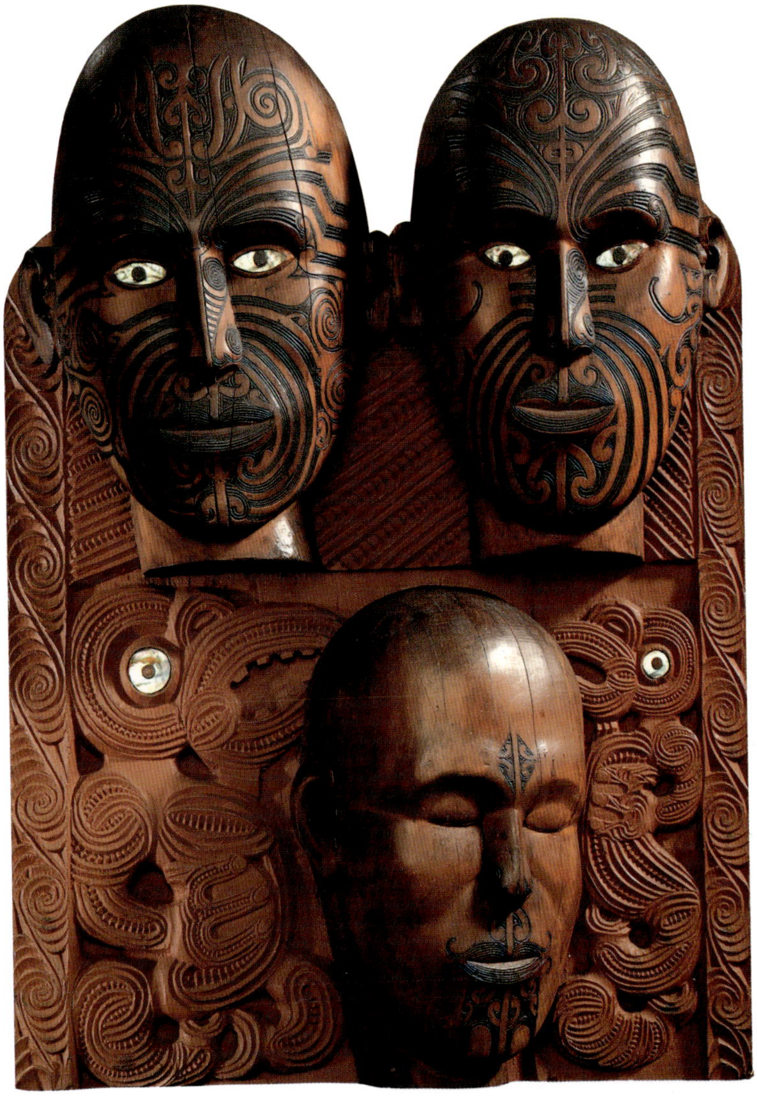

abdomen, neck, breasts and arms were tattooed and the tara whakairo, or *mons veneris*, was also marked. Such instances, in contrast to the kauae moko or chin tattoo, were local variations; full-facial or half-facial work on women, while recorded in both oral and Pākehā accounts, were rare indeed.

The full-facial moko of the Māori male, balanced by the complex patterning between lower back and knees, were designed and presented to inspire fear, excite admiration and arouse erotic interest. All of this occurred when such moko were first encountered by the eighteenth-century voyagers.

> . . . it is impossible to avoid admiring the immence Elegance and Justness of the figures in which it is form'd, which in the face is always different spirals, upon the body generaly different figures resembling something the foliages of old Chasing upon gold or silver; all these finishd with a masterly taste and execution, for of a hundred which at first sight you would judge to be exactly the same, on a close examination no two will prove alike.
>
> Joseph Banks, 1769

Panel of tattooed faces carved by Tene Waitere of Ngāti Tarāwhai, Rotorua, in 1894, as an example of the different forms of tā moko. Noted for the oblique aspect of the female portrait, this work was commissioned by the Colonial Museum (Museum of New Zealand Te Papa Tongarewa, neg. no. B18702).

One can imagine the impact of Māori mau moko in the streets of Sydney, New South Wales, or in the port cities of Britain. They were applauded and objectified; followed around and pestered. They included adventurous crewmen on brigs from that part of the world; or visitors, like Hongi Hika, to the court of St James; and young noblemen sponsored by missionaries or colonists, like Tītore and Te Pēhi. The latter obliged his Liverpool hosts by drawing his own moko, and those of his family members, many times over – the English were fascinated. Such drawings were regarded as signatures, and the inscription of moko designs on early land settlement papers and the Waitangi Treaty indicates that they were thus perceived as seals of honour.

With the arrival of whalers, runaway convicts, explorers, remittance men, flax traders and eventually missionaries and land 'speculators' came irrevocable change – in technology, indigenous economies and religion, and many other elements of Māori cultural practice and belief. Warfare was transformed by firearms, and their acquisition was inevitable. Subsequently, a particularly gruesome and vicious commerce emerged. Decapitation, and the preservation of tattooed heads, were an integral part of mourning and memorial traditions in the ancient Māori world – the visage of a beloved spouse, relative or exalted chief was kept close and cherished, brought out to converse with and admire, dressed and elevated to inspire and motivate. Even those of old enemies were accorded respect.

The morbid fascination of Pākehā collectors changed this, and between 1811 and 1831 (when it was outlawed by order of the Government of New South Wales), a grisly traffic conveyed scores of tattooed heads, many supposedly 'done to order' or posthumously incised, to foreign shores. A large number have since come home, primarily through the incomparable efforts of the late Māui Pōmare; nevertheless their presence as ethnological specimens in the American Museum of Natural History, the British Museum and other institutions remains a contentious and bitter reality. Work continues for their repatriation and appropriate demise; most ironically, their tragic beauty and haunting artistry inform us, their descendants, of technique and pattern, of excellence in design and precision of symmetry. *E Koro mā, moe mai koutou; māringiringi noa ngā roimata o te iwi, moe mai.*

By 1840 and the signing of the Treaty of Waitangi, Christian missionaries had established stations throughout the islands and the demonising of tā moko as a pagan and unspeakable perversion was well under way. The decline began, although tā moko was resurrected vigorously and effectively during the Land Wars of the 1860s. Charismatic Tāwhiao Matutaera Te Wherowhero, paramount chief and Second Māori King, personified resistance to Pākehā invasion; his face was exquisitely adorned and he encouraged the art's revival. This was, alas, shortlived – with the illegal and unjustified confiscation of millions of acres, the pestilence of northern hemisphere diseases, and the burgeoning encroachment by Pākehā, Māori vitality waned and the tattooed face seemed to fade away. According to Cowan, the last traditional full-face operation occurred in 1865, and by the century's turning these venerable faces were few indeed.

For this reason, despite their gravely inappropriate titles and often highly disturbing arrangement or aspect, the portraits by Goldie are immensely important – as images of our own koroua and kuia, and as a record of a profoundly troubled period in our people's history. Despite being the graphic perception of a single white man, these portraits for just about every Māori person, and certainly for all of the descendants, resonate with an integrity, a sense of spirit, that draws tears and makes the heart ache. Because by 1930, the fully inscribed face of the chiefly Māori male of te ao tawhito, the ancient world, had passed into the realms of Hinenui i te Pō, the Goddess of Death.

Kauae moko – the treatment of women's chins – persisted until the 1950s, with some innovation. While such persistence may be due to conservatism, it is also likely that Māori women in the rural areas were seldom engaged in activity beyond the marae or home. They did not mix with Pākehā often, and they rarely worked for wages. Their world was relatively confined and contact with Pākehā judgment or approbation was minimal. However, it is interesting to note that kauae moko was worn with great pride by tourist

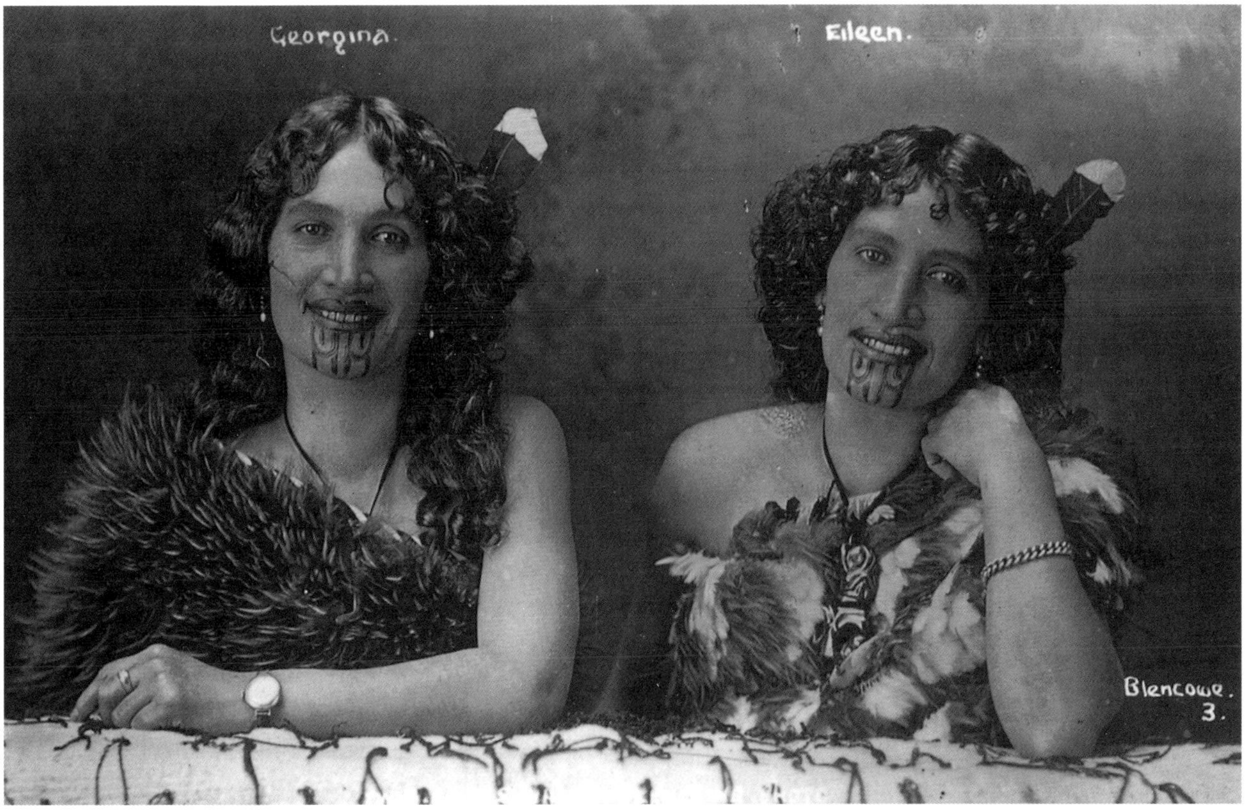

guides in Whakarewarewa, Rotorua, until the 1960s. Working with metal and bone, at least eight tohunga tā moko from throughout the North Island were practising before the First World War. At this time needle tattooing was introduced, and its practitioners included women from Waikato and Rotorua. It produced a markedly flatter finish but was nevertheless regarded with huge awe and admiration – as a child growing up in the early 1950s, I remember well the mixed feelings of amazement, fear and curiosity the Kuia mau moko stirred in me. My two favourites were Kuia Maraea, whose chin felt and looked gouged - I know hers was done by uhi matarau, probably Taiwera's of Tūhoe; and Kuia Makarita, whose patterning was wide and smooth, but very blue. Kuia Hera, who brought me up, affected her moko on her arm – her name in subtle Times Roman capitals, sadly faded, always intrigued me.

> Kei muri i te awe kāpara
> he tangata kē.
> māna e noho te ao nei;
> he mā
>
> After the tattooed face,
> someone with unmarked skin
> may claim this world
> (Māori saying)

Perhaps that seemed so for a while; but no more! Generations of young Māori in boarding schools and state schools, in offices and army barracks and gaols and ships at sea, mark their skins. It has always been the most natural thing to do, printing colour into the body's surface with a compass point or pins tied to a matchstick or fine needles or even a sharp lead pencil. Despite the active loathing of teachers, and the confused reactions of parents, most of us did it. And our own children continue this manifestation of the heritage of mem-

The 'Twin Guides', Georgina and Eileen of Whakarewarewa, Rotorua, who worked in the thermal valley in the 1920s and '30s (private collection).

ory. Many argue it is programmed in the genes. Proudly framed portraits of very recent forebears adorn the walls of meeting houses and private homes, their tattooed faces considered and revered. They lived and worked and loved, producing today's Māori, not so very long ago – four or five, or for a few from one to three, generations. The mere pounamu of a majestic blue-chinned dance leader still sings in the hands of her great-granddaughter; the engraved face of a notable nineteenth century orator shadows the eloquent gestures of his grandson as he wields his ornate walking staff. The past is recent, and the past is today – which is why Māori are wearing it now. On our bodies – and increasingly, on our faces too.

As a fine art form, with formally trained exponents who sustained the original tradition, tā moko endured almost two decades of decline; the last kauae moko, by the needle technique, were done in the 1950s. Almost twenty years later, thanks to the courage and commitment of individual women and the visionary talent of two professional tattoo artists, Merv O'Connor and Roger Ingerton, the kauae moko was seen, blue-black, crisp and beautiful, on the marae once again, just as the last of the Kuia mau moko were passing on. Those involved in this first wave of revival were active in women's rituals and performance, famous as composers and chanters, weavers and oral historians. Motivated by an assertion of identity, they reclaimed the art form and reinforced their mana whenua in highly visual, indelible terms. Soon after this, the first male, a colourful and passionate orator, began work on his face.

One hundred and fifty years after the Treaty, tā moko was being actively reclaimed, albeit with electric machines; patterns reappeared on faces, buttocks, thighs, backs, arms – all over the Māori body. Much of the finest and most inventive work is being done in gaols, and as part of the contemporary pantribal culture of rural and urban gangs; the tattooed face, or 'mask', intentionally achieves the same impact – ferocious, menacing, aggressive, yet often aesthetically elegant and attractive, too.

As in ancient times, the artists travel, moving as required from one community to another. Currently only a handful are practising. They include Te Wharemānuka Lardelli, a graduate of Ilam School of Fine Arts, and Te Rangikaihoro Nicholas, a protégé of the late tohunga whakairo Hone Taiapa; both are training apprentices, and acknowledge the wise guidance and generosity of Pākehā practitioners, including the famous Danish Celt Jorgen Kristiansen, who gave informal workshops in Aotearoa over the summer of 1990-91. While they work with electric machines, both men are also committed to reintroducing the uhi technique, and Te Wharemānuka manipulates both steel needles and uhi and mallet with a confident and exacting grace. In at least two rural communities, this latter practice is preferred. With the quietly disciplined research and well-informed reconstruction and manufacture of chisels and associated equipment, they maintain a conscious privacy, but their work is unmistakable.

Tā moko today is much more than a fashion statement, a passing fad for Māori. It is about who we are, and whom we come from. It is about where we are going, and how we choose to get there. And it is about for always, forever.

Charles F. Goldie may have assumed he was doing future generations a great service by recording 'the Māori as he was'; by picturing, for posterity, the vanishing times of a noble race. He misjudged his sitters. He misjudged their descendants. He assumed too much. The world has moved on, indeed.

> And their time is done.
> But their blood moves in our hearts.
> Their voices rise in our throats.
> Their song glows in the pigmented surface
> Of our skins. In this time. Now.
> Pai Mārire.

LEONARD BELL

two paintings by C. F. Goldie: their brilliant careers

Paintings are never basically what one thinks of them as being.
David Markson, *Wittgenstein's Mistress*[1]

The National Art Gallery's purchase of Goldie's *Darby and Joan* and *The Widow* in 1990 triggered off a controversy not just about the price, but also about the cultural and artistic values of the works. It is not my concern to focus on either the circumstances of the purchase or the price paid compared with actual market value. That ground has been well thrashed over. What remains intriguing is the extraordinary range of response to the paintings, the seemingly mutually exclusive assessments of their meanings, values and places in contemporary New Zealand culture. At times one may well wonder whether the protagonists in the argument are talking about the same paintings. For instance, they have been described as examples of 'coon humour',[2] images that demeaned their Māori subjects, held them up to ridicule and continue to do so. They have been characterised too as typifying Goldie's output of Māori pictures, which 'often look like a lot of old people sitting around in the sun waiting for pension day. One Goldie in any collection is enough.'[3] In contrast, Margaret Austin, former Labour Government Minister of Arts and Culture, who pressed for their purchase, described the paintings as 'part of the soul of this nation ... There was no question that they captured the moment in history when they were painted';[4] that moment being when the 'sense of immense pressures felt by Māori' at the turn of the century led to 'fears for their possible extinction'.[5] Hamish Keith, Chairman of the National Art Gallery Council, ascribed 'historical significance' to the paintings 'far beyond anything in the national collection'.[6] Their purchase, for him, was a 'real contribution to our cultural heritage'.[7] Jenny Harper, Director of the Gallery, attributed 'enormous cultural significance'[8] to them, noting that they were 'widely considered the best and most important in [Goldie's] career'.[9] For some Māori their meaning and value have been different again. Mrs Ellen Hulme, a descendant of the paintings' models, Ina Te Papatahi for *Darby and Joan* and Harata Tarapata for *The Widow*, became 'very emotional' at a 'welcome' to the works at the National Art Gallery: 'I took one look at them and knew they were part of me.'[10]

Given the diverse responses and evaluations now, an examination of the circumstances of the production and original uses of the paintings and their meanings then may well be a useful counterbalance, particularly to some of the flights of rhetoric their re-presentations have recently evoked. *Darby and Joan* and *The Widow* were first exhibited at the annual Auckland Society of

Arts show in 1903; the exhibition being opened by the Governor-General of the colony of New Zealand, the Earl of Ranfurly. Reviewers responded enthusiastically to these and the other three Goldie Māori paintings. They were described as 'the best' and 'the most striking in the gallery'[11] – for their 'wonderful technique' and 'power of sentiment',[12] and for their 'splendid academic qualities', the 'beautiful reality ... in the hands and faces almost Pre-Raphaelite in their fidelity'.[13] Of the pair now in the National Art Gallery it was claimed: 'No two finer paintings have been executed in the colony ... and they may be said to show the present high-water mark of art in New Zealand.'[14] The two paintings, then, are not obscure or secondary works, which have been elevated to fulfil roles now out of keeping with their original status.

Goldie's own status in the colonial art world was very high too. In the early 1900s, the Paris-trained painter (born 1870) was widely regarded as 'the first figure painter in New Zealand',[15] one whose work would be lauded 'even in the great art centres of the world';[16] an estimation that brought with it considerable financial rewards: 'Goldie is probably the most successful painter of the Maori in a commercial sense', it was reported at the time.[17] The hundred guineas apiece for *Darby and Joan* and *The Widow* was big money on the local art market in 1903.

The two paintings were first exhibited at the same time as there was public discussion in Auckland about a suitable gift for the Countess of Ranfurly, wife of the Governor-General, whose term of office was coming to an end. The Ranfurlys' tenure in New Zealand (1897-1903) was regarded as outstandingly successful and popular.[18] The Ranfurly Home for Veterans of the Boer War and the Ranfurly Shield for rugby (instituted in 1902) were among their legacies. The Countess was described as 'most charming ... a New Zealander at heart', who 'endeared herself to all classes'.[19] She had a keen interest in art and patronised local artists. Wilhelm Dittmer was to dedicate his prestigious illustrated book on Māori mythology, *Te Tohunga* (London, 1907) to her. *Darby and Joan* and *The Widow* were considered the most appropriate gift, and because of the Countess's preference they were 'chosen as being typical of Maori life',[20] for which she was reported to have had 'a great attraction'.[21] The works were bought by public subscription by the citizens of Auckland and presented to the Countess at a farewell ceremony in late June 1903.

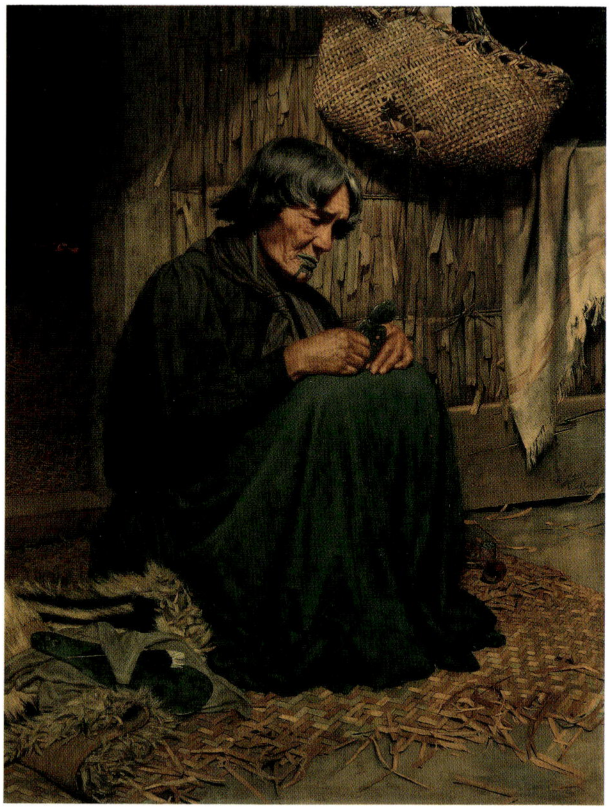

The Widow.

Before leaving Auckland the paintings were publicly exhibited again in the window of the British and Continental Room (not a fine art milieu) in the Strand Arcade off Queen Street.[22] They were also extensively reproduced – *Darby and Joan*, for instance, in the *New Zealand Graphic*, 27 June 1903, and on a double page supplement of the *Auckland Star*, 23 June 1903. The latter was 'printed on fine art paper ... for framing so that everyone in the colony may procure a copy of the splendid work of art and thus possess A BEAUTIFUL PICTURE AND A PERPETUAL SOUVENIR OF THE GRACIOUS LADY WHO NOW OWNS THE ORIGINAL' [capitalised in the *Star*]. So the images had a circulation and life far outside the Arts Society environment. They must have been among the best-known and acclaimed fine art representations of Māori in the late colonial era. Highly esteemed paintings, then, by a highly esteemed artist were gifted to an equally highly esteemed dignitary of the colonial order.

The Goldies returned with the Ranfurlys to their estate at Dungannon in Ulster, Ireland, England's first colony. They were installed, after a short period in the dining room,[23] in the 'New Zealand room' with a display of oceanic artefacts. They could have functioned in various ways there – as part of the household decor, as items in a collection of Antipodean curiosities, as mementoes of the Ranfurlys' time in New Zealand, or as signs of fondness for their Māori subjects. Lady Ranfurly, it was reported, 'used to say they [Māori] reminded her, in their care-free way of living and their evident desire to please, of her Irish tenants.'[24] What now appears as a kind of patronising 'benevolence' towards colonised peoples suggests another way of seeing the paintings – as representations with a fundamental ideological correlative; as symbols of imperial and colonialist power and control. The 'natives', passive and compliant, were 'captured' on canvas, possessed.

Lest this reading seem either tenuous or too extreme, consider the primary features of the paintings and the connotations or significations of these in their contexts of initial use. Both paintings represent old Māori women. However, though the models were known and identifiable, these works were not originally presented or used as portraits of specific individuals. They were anecdotal or narrative pieces, as their titles indicate. Each painting told or implied a story (or, so it emerges, a number of stories) – a fundamental feature of Goldie's Māori representations generally that was recognised in the early 1900s.[25] The paintings were no more portraits of Ina Te Papatahi and Harata Tarapata in 1903 than Pre-Raphaelite narrative paintings, in which identifiable friends, relatives and acquaintances of the artists modelled for the characters, were portraits of those individuals.

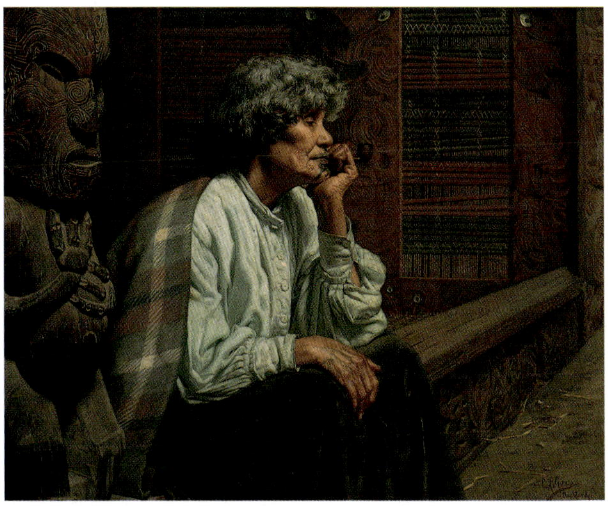

In respect of the titles, the narrative or anecdotal implications of *The Widow* are self-evident. That painting images an appropriate grief, sense of loss and despondency. The meanings and references of the title *Darby and Joan* may not be commonly known today, but the term, the coupling of those names in 1903, would have required no explanation. The name has its origins in the third stanza of an English song, titled 'The Joys of Love Never Forgot', recorded in the *Gentleman's Magazine* in 1735:

> Old Darby with Joan by his side,
> You've often regarded with wonder;
> He's dropsical, she's sore-eyed,
> Yet they are never happy asunder.[26]

Versions of this song continued through the nineteenth century, and the figures of Darby and Joan popularly signified any old couple, long-time partners, touchingly still closely attached to one another. There was also a well-known pair of china or pottery figurines of such a couple called a Darby and Joan piece. In Goldie's painting the old woman is obviously Joan. Darby presumably is the carving, the ancestor figure, beside her – an identification made by a contemporary reviewer, who described the couple as 'picturesque' and Joan as 'the ancient crone'.[27] At best this sort of response and the very titling of a representation of a Māori woman and carving were culturally insensitive (to use current terminology). In terms of Māori-European relations in the early twentieth century, they could have taken on a patronising, even facetious quality, that served to diminish or place the Māori subject in an inferior, objectified position vis-à-vis the viewers and users of the image, who in 1903 were predominantly, probably exclusively, European. The painting was, after all, made for Europeans.

Darby and Joan.

How the figures were depicted was not neutral either. These images were not 'windows on the world'; unmediated 'snapshots' of actual scenes simply observed by Goldie. He worked from models posed by him in the studio and/or from photographs, the figures in which may have been directed how to look, what pose to assume by the photographers. As was usually the case in Goldie's works, the paintings are characterised by a meticulous attention to detail in the rendering of dress, artefacts, physiognomy and moko – a realism of surface appearances, that might provide useful ethnological information. But this sort of realism and the fact that the models were identifiable should not obscure the essential point that Goldie's depictions of Māori were carefully calculated constructs, each element of which carried social and emotional connotations. Consider the poses, expressions, gestures of the figures; their body language. They are either slumped, sagging or weighted downwards; their expressions far-away, daydreaming or dejected, miserable. In *Darby and Joan* the chin resting on the hand brings to mind that traditional sign of melancholy in European culture and visual representation.

The two figures belong to a type commonly found in Goldie's Māori representations. He depicted Māori in a very limited number of ways, using and reusing a small number of models (or photographs or earlier paintings of them after their deaths). In contrast to Lindauer, who produced portraits of a large number of Māori, Goldie was not attempting to produce a pictorial record of leading personalities in Māoridom, past and present. His favourite mode of presentation of his subjects, exemplified by the Ranfurlys' pair – mostly elderly, eyes averted, with passivity, sadness or resignation, sleepiness or dreaminess in mood prevailing – correlated with the notion, popular among

'The "New Zealand room" at Dungannon, Lord Ranfurly's home in Ireland' (New Zealand Graphic, *2 December 1905, private collection).*

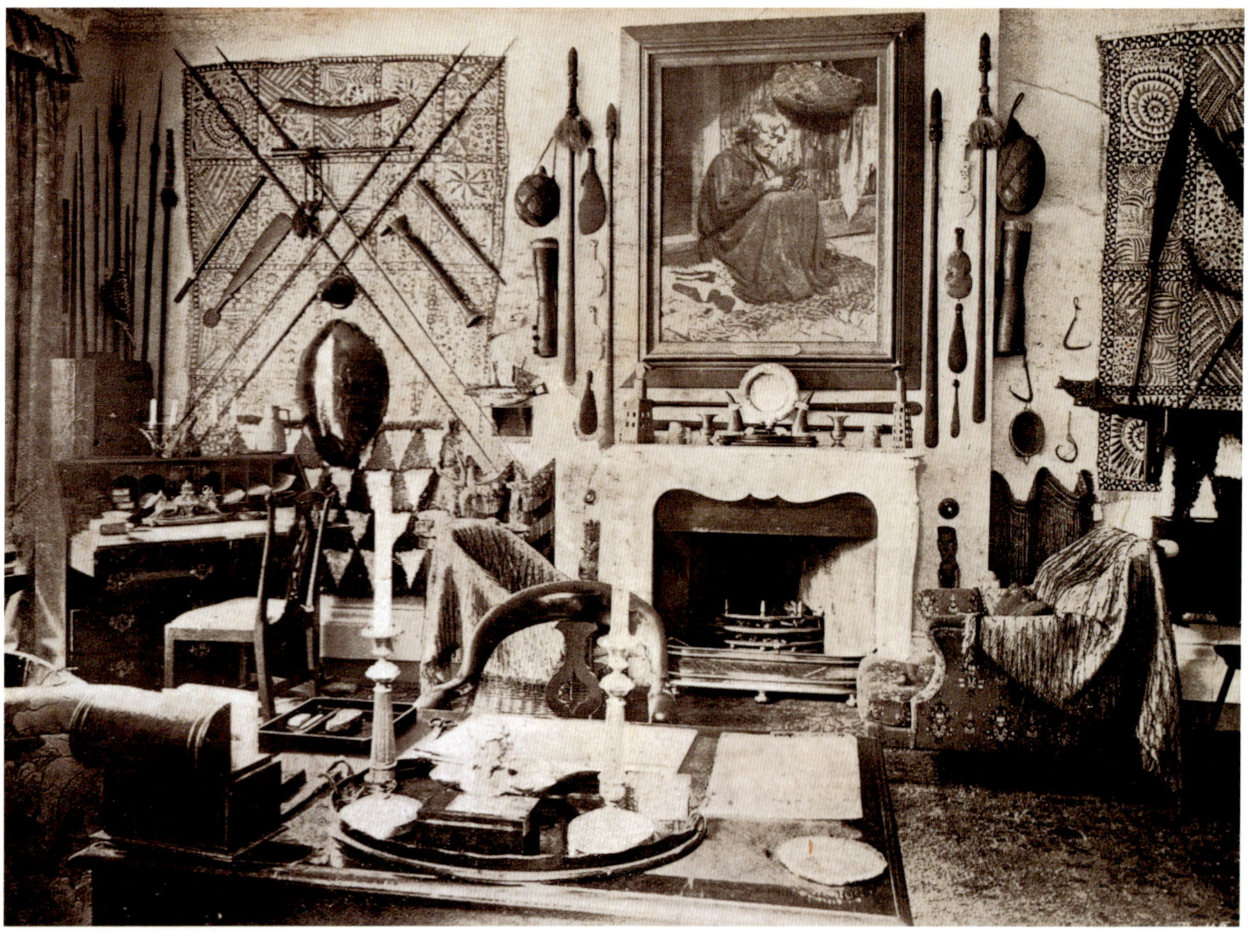

European New Zealanders in the early twentieth century, of a distinct Māori people and culture as bound to die out, either literally or through eventual complete assimilation into European culture. Thus the dying embers in the whare in *The Widow*. Whether 'dying Māori' constituted a fiction or a credible prognosis is not difficult to determine. By the early 1900s the Māori population was increasing.[28] There was plenty of evidence of vigorous activity and vitality among Māori, and resistance, collective and individual, to the colonial programme, particularly over land ownership and usage and parliamentary representation.[29]

While there were, of course, actual elderly Māori, some of whom may well have been unhappy or fatalistic, the image of passive, dejected Māori could not stand either as representative of social actualities or as a metaphor of the prevailing cultural, political and psychological condition of Māori in the early twentieth century. Goldie's representations, however romanticised and nostalgic, were ideologically loaded. Perhaps his standard pictorial type represented a favoured scenario, a wished-for state of affairs among many European New Zealanders. His usual presentation of Māori – in weary old age – suggested that Māori culture belonged to the past, but not to the present or future; that it would be superseded by allegedly more progressive and superior European culture. That is, in the contexts of production and original uses, Goldie's models for *Darby and Joan* and *The Widow* were primarily raw materials to be manipulated; fashioned to fit the artist's and the then European audience's requirements. As such, in 1903, these paintings were not celebrating the autonomy of Māori individuals and their kin.

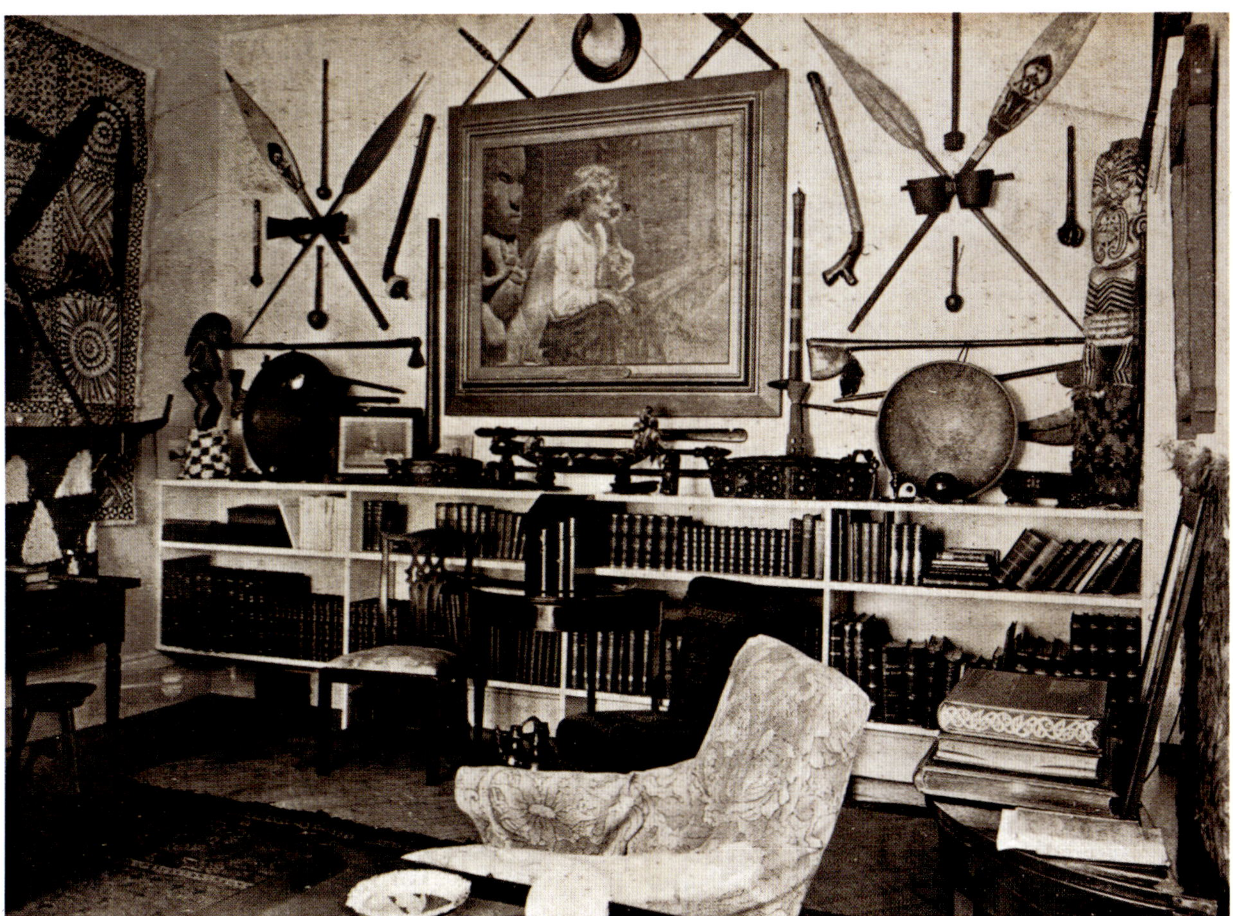

However, the meanings, associations and values of paintings can change over a period of years, according to the cultural, social and institutional contexts in which they are seen and the uses to which they are put. Paintings do not necessarily have closed, fixed meanings and modes of operation. The careers of *Darby and Joan* and *The Widow* are exemplary in these respects. Over nearly ninety years the paintings have been subject to such diverse and conflicting interpretations, responses and uses that in different contexts they have effectively become different pictures. The recent response of Māori kin of the models, Ina Te Papatahi and Harata Tarapata, to the paintings has been noted. Immediately that might suggest that some Māori have internalised the colonialist objectification of the figures. That, though, is not the case. Rather, for some Māori the two paintings portray the authentic, unmediated being of each woman. That is, even while recognising negative features like the original titles and the damaging nature of other Goldie paintings such as Goldie and Steele's *The Arrival of the Maoris in New Zealand* (1898),[30] for Māori the two Goldies can function as embodiments of the spirituality and mana of ancestors. A kind of repossession or reclamation has taken place.

The paintings can also have other values and meanings for Europeans. Goldie's Māori representations generally have been regarded by some anthropologists and museum personnel as ethnologically and historically valuable insofar as they provide a record of physiognomy, moko, dress, ornament and other artefacts. *Darby and Joan* and *The Widow*, despite their original anecdotal function, have more recently been seen and presented by Europeans too as portraits of specific individuals. That is one of their functions in their new National Art Gallery context. They can operate there too as records of certain European attitudes towards Māori culture in the colonial period[31] and as striking examples of turn-of-the-century academic paintings in New Zealand. Yet the National Art Gallery offers a site for Māori to experience the images on their terms also. So radically different meanings, modes of operation and conceptions about visual representation coexist. There is no way the paintings' multiple meanings and functions could be resolved into unitary and homogeneous wholes.

Lest the present institutional re-presentations seem like a form of historical revisionism, it should not be overlooked that aspects of the paintings' colonialist meanings and values no doubt still persist in some social milieux. The two representations could still function as exotic curiosities or as embodiments of that paternalist (or maternalist) and sentimental fiction, the 'old-time Māori' – one that has participated in the less pleasant colonialist and neo-colonialist dimensions of Māori-European interactions. For a variety of reasons and in a variety of ways, then, the former gifts to the Countess of Ranfurly remain highly charged images.

Note: This essay first appeared in *Art New Zealand* 59, Winter 1991, pp.88-92. Since it was published, the National Art Gallery and National Museum have become the joint institution now known as the Museum of New Zealand Te Papa Tongarewa.

DAVID J. WISE

materials and techniques

On his return from Paris, Goldie settled on a method of painting which varied remarkably little throughout his career. This style was firmly based on the principles of drawing and painting from the life model which operated at the Académie Julian. The way in which he posed his figures in portraits, with a dominant light from high on one side and a muted and largely monochromatic background, can be seen in the surviving life studies he brought back from Paris. This method of painting the figure was a system taught in art schools across Europe and formed the basis for numerous artists' treatises published during the nineteenth and early twentieth centuries.[1]

Also related to this training was the notion of painting as an activity based solely in the artist's studio. The search for naturalism and the transient effects of light as pursued by the Barbizon artists and the Impressionists through 'plein air' sketching was the antithesis of the control exercised by the academic artist. Light in the studio was filtered, diffused and organised to delineate the forms. Harsh contrasts between shadow and highlight were avoided through the use of carefully modulated tones and harmonious colours.

Goldie's academic training, his choice of materials and his system of painting is alien to the modern student. In fact, the very concept of an all-encompassing 'system' for the production of paintings has been an anathema for much of this century. These notes review the physical properties of Goldie's paintings and discuss what they can tell us about Goldie's approach to painting and the materials he chose.

supports

While Goldie occasionally made use of wooden panels, by far the largest proportion of his work was executed on canvas. As opposed to earlier centuries when artists undertook preparation of materials themselves, by the end of the nineteenth century most artists bought their canvases ready prepared from artists' suppliers.[2] Even as a student in Paris Goldie purchased his canvases 'off the peg' and he continued this trend throughout his working life. These prepared canvases were stretched on to a fixed frame known as a 'strainer' or on to an expandable frame using wooden keys known as a 'stretcher'. They were primed and ready for painting.

Goldie's preference was for a general-purpose canvas. Even his small paintings are executed on the same medium-weight, plain-weave, linen canvas as his larger works, when traditionally a finer weave with a less apparent texture might have been used. An exception is his copy of Prinet's *Le Bain* [p.67], painted in Paris on a light-weight, fine-weave canvas bearing the stamp of Sennelier, Quai Voltaire. Perhaps, as with many students, Goldie was simply making do with the least expensive option. There is certainly evidence that he re-used canvases while at the Académie Julian, re-priming over less successful paintings.

Goldie's canvases are usually in established portrait-format sizes. A large number of his canvases therefore measure 24 by 20 inches ('Head Size'), 30 by 25 inches ('Three-Quarter Size') and 50 by 40 inches ('Half Length Size'). Smaller and larger paintings exist but these three sizes form a common core in his work. Of those canvases bearing an artist's-colourman stamp, the most commonly occurring are 'Geo. Rowney, London, "Quality A"' canvases and, in the pre-World War I period, those supplied locally by John Leech in Auckland. Whether this was Goldie's choice or an indication of the limited options available in New Zealand is a matter of speculation. Many of the major English firms such as Winsor & Newton and Robersons did have agents in Australia and their products are likely to have been available in New Zealand.

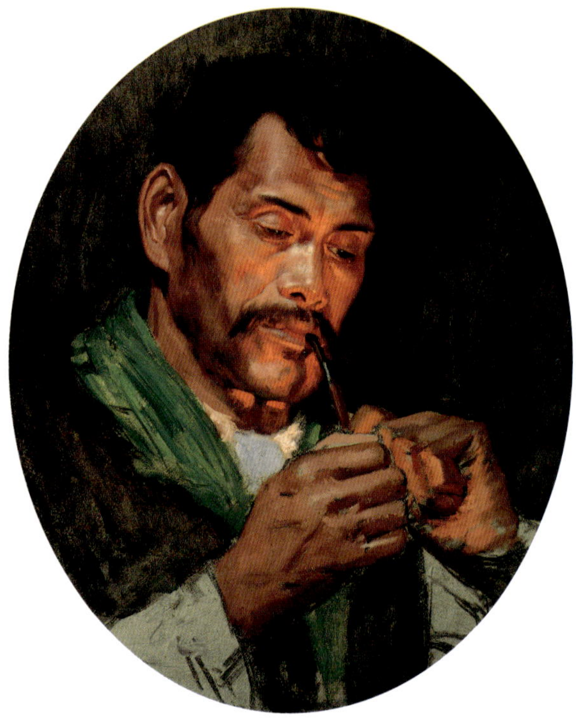

The Rowney canvases were imported into New Zealand fully prepared and stretched on four-bar wooden stretchers in a range of standard sizes. The linen canvas seems to have been of good, even quality and it had a traditional double lead-white oil ground.[3] Although various tints and textures of priming were probably available, including greys and creams, Goldie usually chose a simple white finish.

The John Leech canvases are somewhat more variable than the Rowney product. Although the canvas was again of medium weight, the weave on some examples has a tendency to be more open and the quality of the linen thread was generally poorer. The composition of the ground applied to these canvases was also subject to variation. In some examples studied, the ground is a thin single layer of lead white or a thin, double lead-white ground. In others, the lower lead-white/barytes layer is coated with a thicker layer of zinc white, while sometimes the canvas has a single layer of zinc white and chalk alone. Such inconsistency suggests that the canvas itself was not prepared by John Leech but was acquired from various sources as a roll and simply stretched on to secondary supports by Leech in Auckland.

The use of zinc white in place of lead white in grounds was a matter of debate at the end of the nineteenth century. As lead-white oil paints dry they tend to become yellow in colour and are also liable to sulphide due to atmospheric pollution, discolouring to a dull grey. Zinc white remains unaltered on drying, retaining a brilliant white colour, and it is a stable pigment not usually susceptible to chemical degradation. Its major problem is that, unlike lead-based pigments, zinc white dries poorly in oil and forms a brittle film which cracks easily – a problem which can be overcome with the incorporation of driers.[4] The various formulations on the Leech canvases therefore document manufacturers' attempts to make use of this pigment in grounds. Zinc over lead white, as observed in some of Goldie's grounds, would protect the lead white from atmospheric pollutants, keeping the colour of the priming pure. The lead white might also have been thought to confer some flexibility to the structure. A single layer of lead or zinc white was considered more flexible than a double layer of pigment. The combination of zinc white with a similar proportion of chalk formed what was known as a 'half-ground', dispensing with lead altogether. In addition to reducing the possibility of sulphiding and yellowing, the zinc-chalk combination was an extremely cheap ground layer to manufacture.

An unfinished painting by Goldie, Hohua: matchlight effect *(oil on canvas, 610 x 510 mm, Auckland Museum, gift of Olive Goldie, 1951).*

priming

Goldie's lack of concern over such widely differing surface finishes may be explained by his almost invariable practice of applying his own priming layer over the manufacturer's ground. Goldie's own priming is visible as a series of interlocking, short, diagonally curved brushstrokes at roughly 90 degrees to one another, which form a web under the image layer. The amount of patterning formed by this priming varies quite markedly, from a precise woven net of brushstrokes of almost identical length in the earlier works, to a series of roughly intersecting broad sweeps in the later paintings.

This priming layer was usually composed of pure lead white, occasionally tinted to a blue/grey with charcoal or a slightly warmer grey with the addition of ochre to the lead white/charcoal mixture. The paint was applied in a fairly thick layer, often entirely obscuring the weave of the canvas. It is possible that Goldie used a tube oil paint from which he had leeched out some of the oil medium, as the brushstrokes remain quite prominent. Leeching was a technique widely practised at the time, intended to prevent excessive oil from discolouring the paint on drying and also to speed up the drying time. To apply the textured priming, Goldie used a flat, bristled brush up to 1 inch wide. Such brushes appear in photographs of Goldie's studio.

While this additional priming layer is one of the most immediately recognisable technical aspects of Goldie's practice, its purpose remains something of a mystery. Goldie's work in Paris and immediately following his return to New Zealand is executed on unmodified commercial canvases. While there was a degree of technical experimentation in his student works, academic practice favoured a fairly bland surface, with the ground and canvas likely to be sanded smooth rather than enhanced and any brushstrokes in the painting itself disguised.[5]

The few completed paintings by Goldie which do not have this characteristic additional priming exhibit the degree of flatness and lack of spontaneity with which he painted. The underlying patterning in the priming adds life to what otherwise would be a pedestrian surface, catching the light and breaking up the plane with varnished highlights. It may be that Goldie wished somehow to emulate the 'facture' of the French Naturalist painters such as Jules Bastien-Lepage, with their 'square brush technique', who were so admired by American and British students of the period.

paint layers

It was commonly recommended that only a limited range of oil paints was required for academic figure painting, with all the necessary colours and tones achieved by careful mixing.[6] Nevertheless, in the copies and personal work completed in Paris, and in some of the paintings begun during the early years of his return to New Zealand, such as *The Child Christ in the Temple* [p.79], Goldie experimented with some of the wide range of pigments introduced during the nineteenth century.[7] Passages in these paintings include such vibrant pigments as Emerald Green, Cobalt Violet, Cadmium Orange and the Chrome Yellows (Lead and Strontium Chromates). However, once he decided to adopt a formulaic approach to the painting of his portraits, Goldie dropped these bright colours from his vocabulary and returned to the limited palette he would have used in life painting at the Académie Julian.

For the rest of his career, Goldie largely relied on a palette of Lead White, Carbon Black (including Bone Black), Yellow Ochre, Raw Umber, Red Ochre, Vermilion, Madder, Cobalt Blue, Prussian Blue and Viridian. Charcoal was sometimes used to tint the lead-white priming and it is common to find many of the other brown-earth pigments in his backgrounds. French Ultramarine is also occasionally included to strengthen the Cobalt Blue.

A detail showing the textured priming and margin area of Te Hau-Takiri Wharepapa, a Chieftain of the Ngapuhi Tribe.

Unusually, even in an academic regimen, Goldie does not employ a strong yellow. He seems to rely totally on Yellow Ochre mixed with Lead White to achieve his effects.[8] During the period there was widespread suspicion of the new pigments, especially among traditionally trained artists. Despite the manuals published by colour chemists, which aimed at helping artists choose the most permanent colours among the new pigments, artists' treatises commonly recommended a range of colours similar to Goldie's, heavily biased towards the tried and trusted ingredients.[9]

Once the painting had dried thoroughly, Goldie would begin by briefly sketching out the basic design in charcoal directly on to his white priming. The drawing was relatively free with only rudimentary indications of form and areas of shadow. Charcoal, being coarse, splintery and easily friable, allowed alterations to be readily made to the design. Later in his career, during the 1930s when there was a loosening of his standards, it is common to find the canvas 'squared up' for the transfer of a pre-prepared drawing. In these cases, pencil replaced charcoal as the drawing medium on the canvas. After completing the charcoal outline, Goldie sometimes applied a thin wash of Prussian Blue oil paint. This fairly transparent paint would seal the charcoal while allowing the drawing to remain visible. While similar procedures were taught in the academies and recommended by artists' manuals, Goldie's choice of a blue sealing wash is slightly eccentric. The paint of choice was usually a transparent brown, which added a richness to the thinly painted shadows.[10]

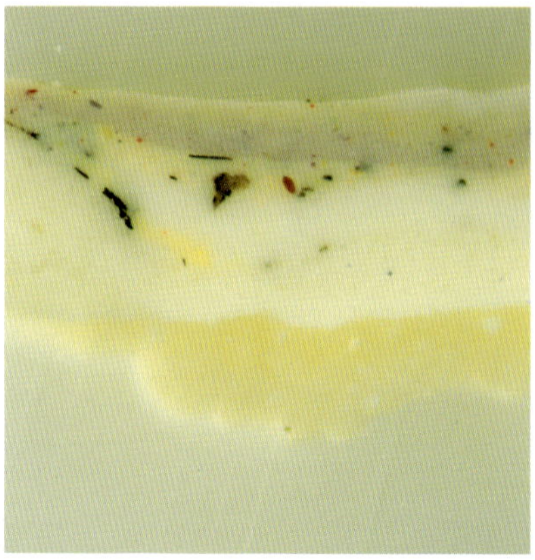

Cross-section (normal light, x200) from the area of Christ's sleeve in The Child Christ in the Temple *1898-1911. The layers from the bottom are: 1. John Leech zinc white/chalk priming. 2. Thick layer of lead white applied by Goldie. 3. Thin layer of charcoal drawing over a brushstroke in the ground. 4. Two fairly thin, pale paint layers.*

Once the drawing was completed to his satisfaction, Goldie proceeded to paint the major areas with a dilute paint that roughly corresponded to the final intended colour. There would be little attempt at this stage to indicate modelling in the forms, the paint simply establishing a middle tone with some indication of lights and darks. In the academic tradition this layer has various names, but is commonly called the 'dead colouring'. The dilution of the paint with spirit of turpentine ensured that the layer dried quickly to a matte finish while remaining slightly absorbent.[11]

This first layer was usually applied with a wide brush, causing the charcoal drawing to become partially incorporated into the paint. The fluidity and relative looseness of Goldie's dead colouring can be observed in many of his oval portraits, once unframed, where it remains in the margin areas without the final finishing layers [p.149]. *The Child Christ in the Temple* can be seen at this early stage in a photograph taken in Goldie's studio in 1900 [p.16]. In the later phase of his career, Goldie seems to have foregone this stage and instead gave the whole canvas a single monochromatic wash, generally composed of ochres. Sometimes this included large amounts of Viridian, giving the strong greenish tint evident in *Reverie: Pipi Haerehuka* 1939 [p.171]. This technique gave an approximate mid-tone over which the final image was then painted. Such a short cut was less than satisfactory and perhaps indicates the deterioration of Goldie's previous technical perfectionism.

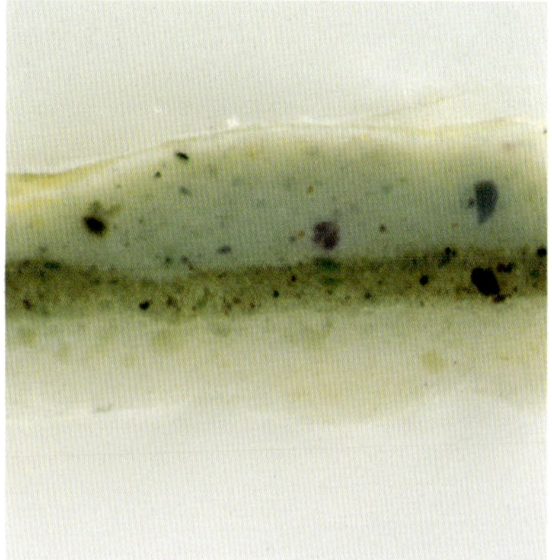

Cross-section from the shirt in Tamehana, from Life *1900 (normal light, x200). This shows Goldie's early, simple sketching style. White ground with two paint layers.*

It is probable that if Goldie adhered strictly to the academic technique, the background of the painting would have been completed before any work on the figures began. The non-descriptive washes of colour which are often seen in his portraits are composed simply of several glazes of paint over the lead-white priming. This transparent structure allows light to bounce back off the white priming, providing a luminous quality. The more specific backgrounds featuring carvings and other details are built up with thicker layers of opaque paint, although a muted tone is achieved by the addition of lead white which prevents the background details from competing visually with the portrait subject.

The painting of the figure began with laying on thicker, more opaque paint over the dead colouring. Work progressed from the general to the specific, beginning with wide hog-hair brushes and finishing with fine sable brushes for detailed work. In accordance with his training, Goldie laid carefully mixed tones of colour next to one another which, working wet paint into wet paint, he then blended to give a smooth transition of light across the forms. Care was taken at this stage to keep the surface of the painting relatively smooth and the brushstrokes not too obvious. While there is very little impasto, even in the finished work, Goldie never aimed for the almost mirror-like surface of many academic practitioners. This can partly be explained by the fact that, unlike many academic artists, Goldie does not seem to have used a resinous medium in his paints but preferred to paint with oil paints straight from the tube, thinned with turpentine when necessary.

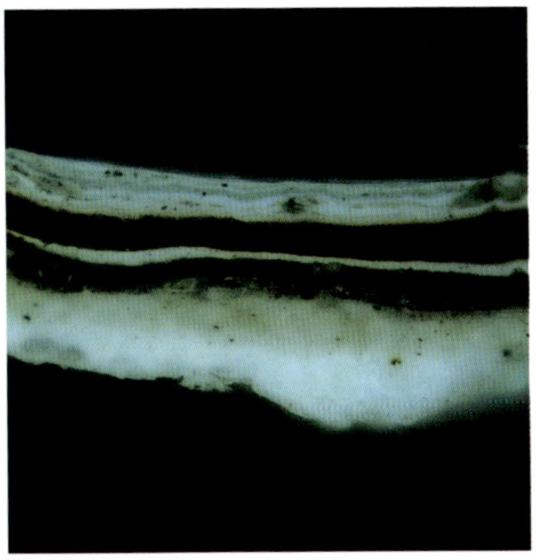

Cross-section (ultra-violet light, x200) from a typical dark background area in The Old Lion *1910. 1. The bright, white line in the centre of the section is Goldie's 'retouch varnish'. 2. The thin, bright top layers are Goldie's original varnish, together with six different restorers' varnishes.*

Cross-sections of Goldie's paintings, however, usually reveal several thin layers of varnish between the various upper paint layers.[12] Their presence suggests that Goldie frequently applied a dilute layer of natural-resin varnish over semi-dried oil paints. This was a common practice at the time, speeding up the progress of a painting. Although this 'retouch varnish', as it was known, prevented the various layers of oil paint from inter-mixing during painting, as the whole structure continued to dry there would be a tendency for the various paint layers to contract independently and cause cracks to appear between layers. Such cracks can frequently be seen in the faces of Goldie's sitters, where the layers are the thickest. The backgrounds of many of the later paintings, in which sound technique was sacrificed to speed of execution, also show cracking. In early portraits, Goldie used bitumen to some extent, especially to attain the final depth in the shadows around the eyes. This transparent pigment, which was popular with many nineteenth-century artists, unfortunately never fully dries. The bitumen continues to move on the surface of the painting, disrupting the paint structure, lowering the tone of the other paints in the shadows and causing cracking and crawling of the paint layers.

Once the general features were established and the forms modelled to his satisfaction, Goldie started work on the finishing layers. This included the addition of details using fine, pointed brushes – for example in the areas of tassels and their shadows on cloaks – and the final highlights and shadows to the facial wrinkles. It was also at this point that Goldie painted the models' hair, building it up with an interwoven mat of increasingly finer brushstrokes over the top of the basic dead colouring. The finishing touches also saw the modification of tones and the strengthening of shadows by the use of scumbles (light colour oil paints, diluted very thinly with turpentine) and glazes (transparent pigments mixed with resin varnishes).

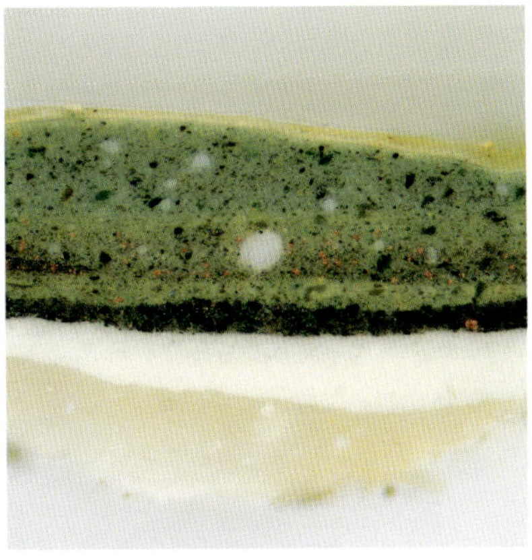

Cross-section from the area of green skirt in Memories *1906 (normal light, x200). The layers from the bottom are: 1. Ground and priming. 2. Dark underpaint, mostly charcoal, some lead white. 3. Goldie repainted the green on four occasions, altering the hue slightly each time.*

varnish layer

Only a few of Goldie's paintings remain with what might be the original, unaltered finish. Most have had at least several additional varnishes applied during restorations and often attempts have been made to remove any original varnish layers which might be thought to have discoloured. The untouched paintings reveal that Goldie did varnish his paintings as a matter of course with a natural resin spirit varnish, probably based on either Mastic or Dammar resins. He seems to have brushed on the varnish thinly and somewhat unevenly, probably giving the painting only a slight surface sheen rather than a heavy gloss. It is possible that Goldie used the varnish to try to compensate for areas of paint which had sunk (become matte) during drying, working slightly more varnish into the matte areas. The semi-glossy nature of his thin varnish would tend to emphasise the effect of his brushed priming layer, whereas a heavy gloss with its strong light-reflective properties would obliterate it.

changes in goldie's paintings

In addition to the normal problems associated with paintings as they age, many of Goldie's paintings have suffered considerably from poor restoration over the fifty to a hundred years since they were painted. A large number of his paintings have cracked and flaked, either through the presence of zinc grounds beneath his own lead-white priming or from the sheer physical thickness of the priming he applied. Those paintings on canvases supplied by John Leech have deteriorated due to the poor quality of the linen cloth and perhaps also as a result of oversizing by the manufacturer. To combat these inherent faults in technique and materials, an easy solution for restorers has been to impregnate stricken paintings with wax/resin mixtures and to attach the original supports to new textile supports or hardboard panels. The considerable heat and pressure involved in this operation, especially in adhering the original canvas to hardboard, causes the paint to soften and flattens the brushwork, particularly in the textured priming layer. The flattening of the impasto significantly alters the appearance of the whole painting, smudging carefully delineated details and decreasing the impact of the specular reflections from the highpoints – that is, deadening the entire painted surface.

The use of wax/resin mixtures can saturate the thinly varnished paint layers, darkening and increasing the depth of colour and strengthening contrasts throughout the painting.[13] In transferring a canvas to a hardboard support, the painting is usually cut off the stretcher by the restorer. As well as destroying the original appearance of the painting, fundamentally altering its nature, much valuable historical information is lost. Goldie often left inscriptions on his stretcher bars as well as attached paper labels, giving titles and sometimes biographical information about the sitter. The inscriptions on the stretchers disappear with the loss of the stretchers, and it is seldom that the trouble is taken to retrieve the labels.

Attempts at cleaning Goldie's paintings, often with excessively strong solvents, has led to the loss of the glazes and modifying layers he applied during the finishing of his works. Solvents can also penetrate between layers, attacking the retouching varnish and undercutting overlying paint layers. This has led to the loss of details and even, in extreme cases, the main body of whole sections, leaving only the dead colouring or the priming. Such major losses of paint have usually been crudely repainted by the restorer and, as a consequence, age poorly and are no substitute for Goldie's own work.

As mentioned, few original varnish layers remain intact on Goldie's paintings. At its most basic, restoration will frequently involve giving a painting a fresh coat of glossy varnish over existing coats of varnish, to resaturate the surface. Between each of these varnish layers, which have usually discoloured to some extent, surface dirt remains trapped. The whole structure acts as a strong filter, darkening and yellowing the underlying paint. A thick layer of varnish will obscure original brushwork, something which Goldie, by his choice of finish, was obviously keen to preserve. It is common to find paintings by Goldie with four or five different varnish layers of various ages, although the record presently stands at thirteen such layers.

Goldie was an artist working within the boundaries of an academic tradition. The implications of the technical complexities resulting from this tradition cannot be understood simply from viewing a painting's surface. Instead, its structure must be microscopically dissected and recorded, with any potential fragility recognised, before the impact of intended restoration work can be assessed. Sensitive conservation and restoration of Goldie's paintings requires a full understanding of the nature of the materials and techniques he employed.

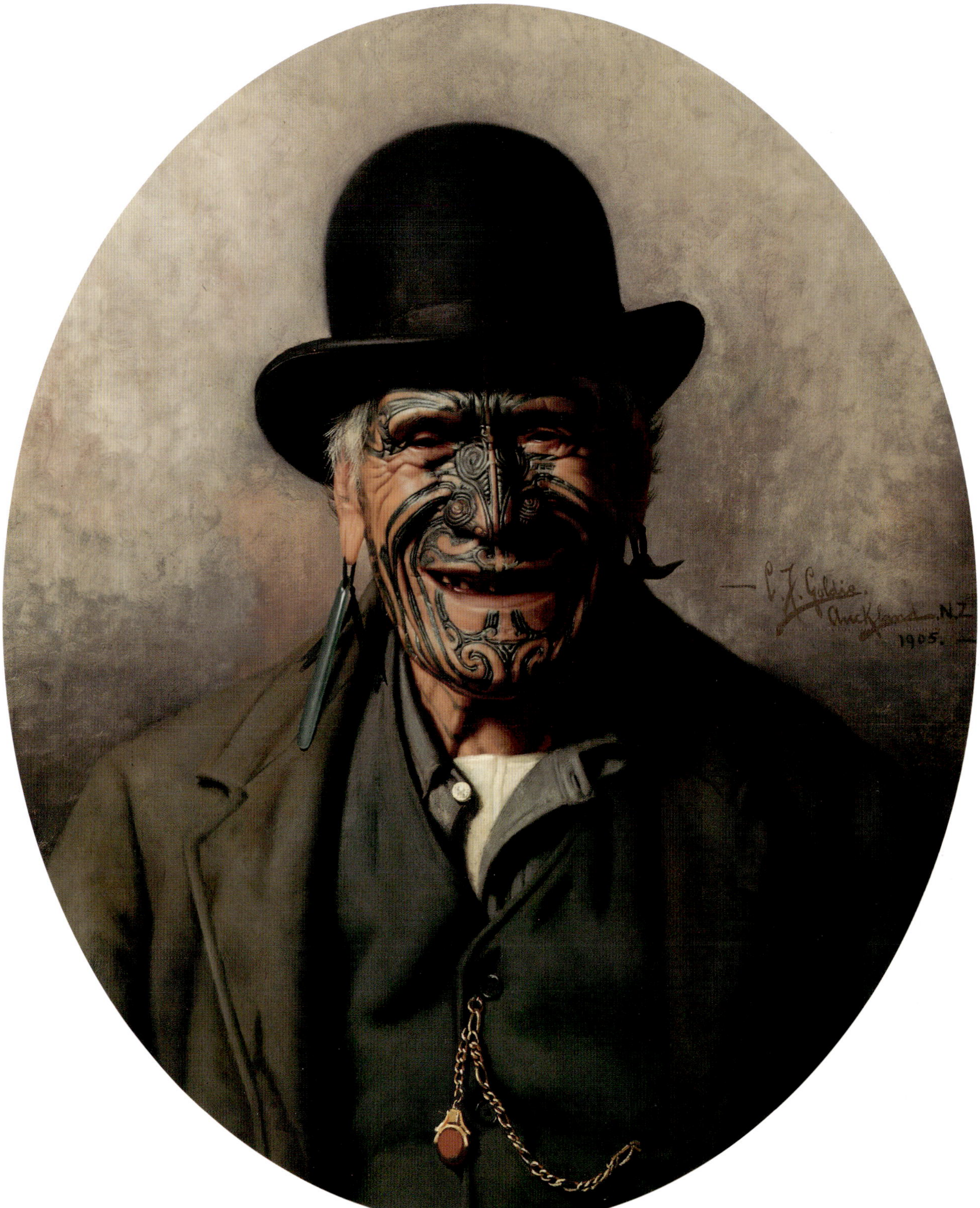

'All 'e Same t'e Pakeha' 1905
Te Aho-o-te-Rangi Wharepu, Ngāti Mahuta
oil on canvas, 715 x 595 mm
Dunedin Public Art Gallery, gift of Sir George Wilson, 1936

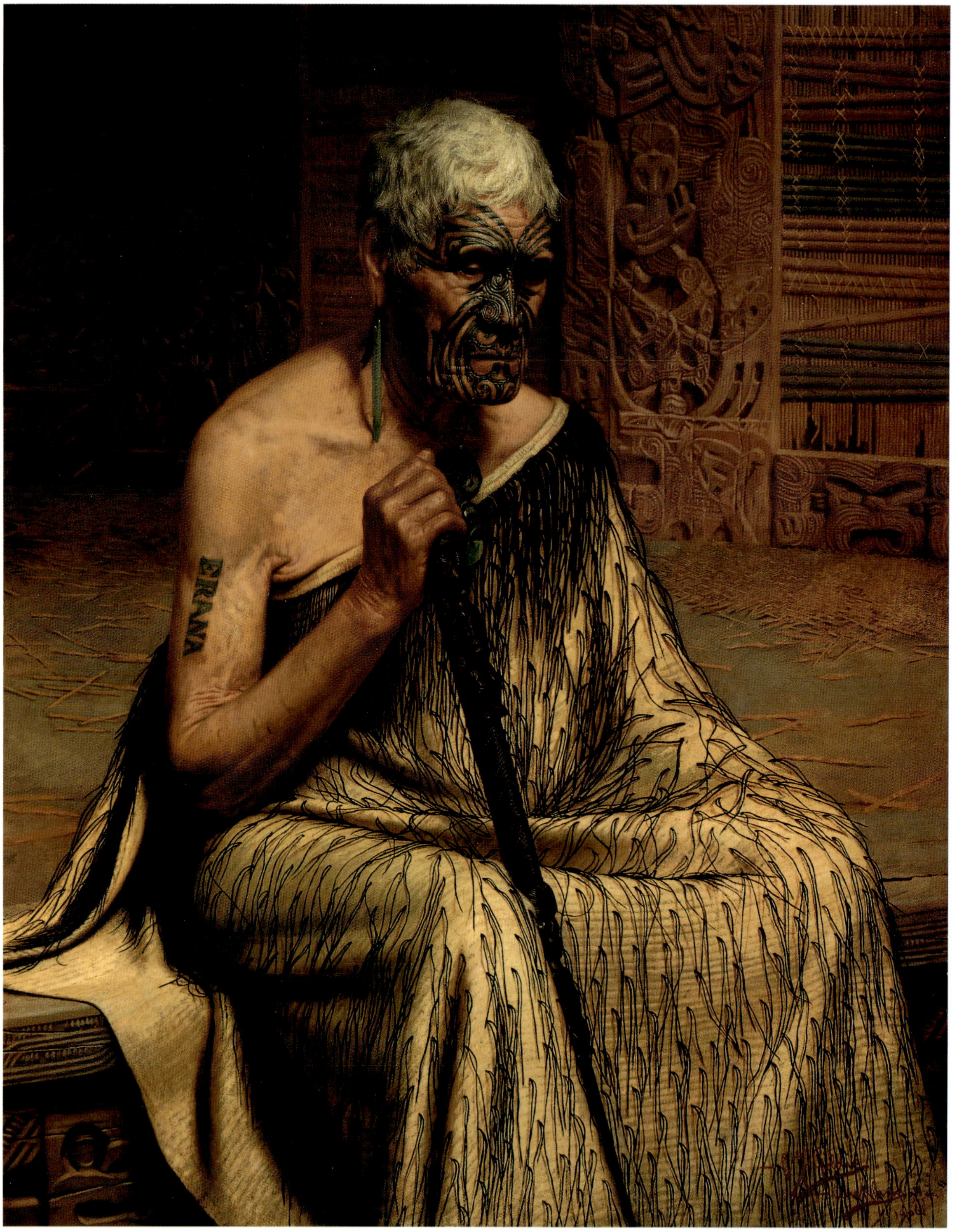

The Calm Close of Valour's Various Day:
Te Aho, a Noted Warrior 1906
Te Aho-o-te-Rangi Wharepu, Ngāti Mahuta
oil on canvas, 1275 x 1015 mm
Auckland Art Gallery Toi o Tāmaki,
bequest of Alfred and Emily Nathan, 1952

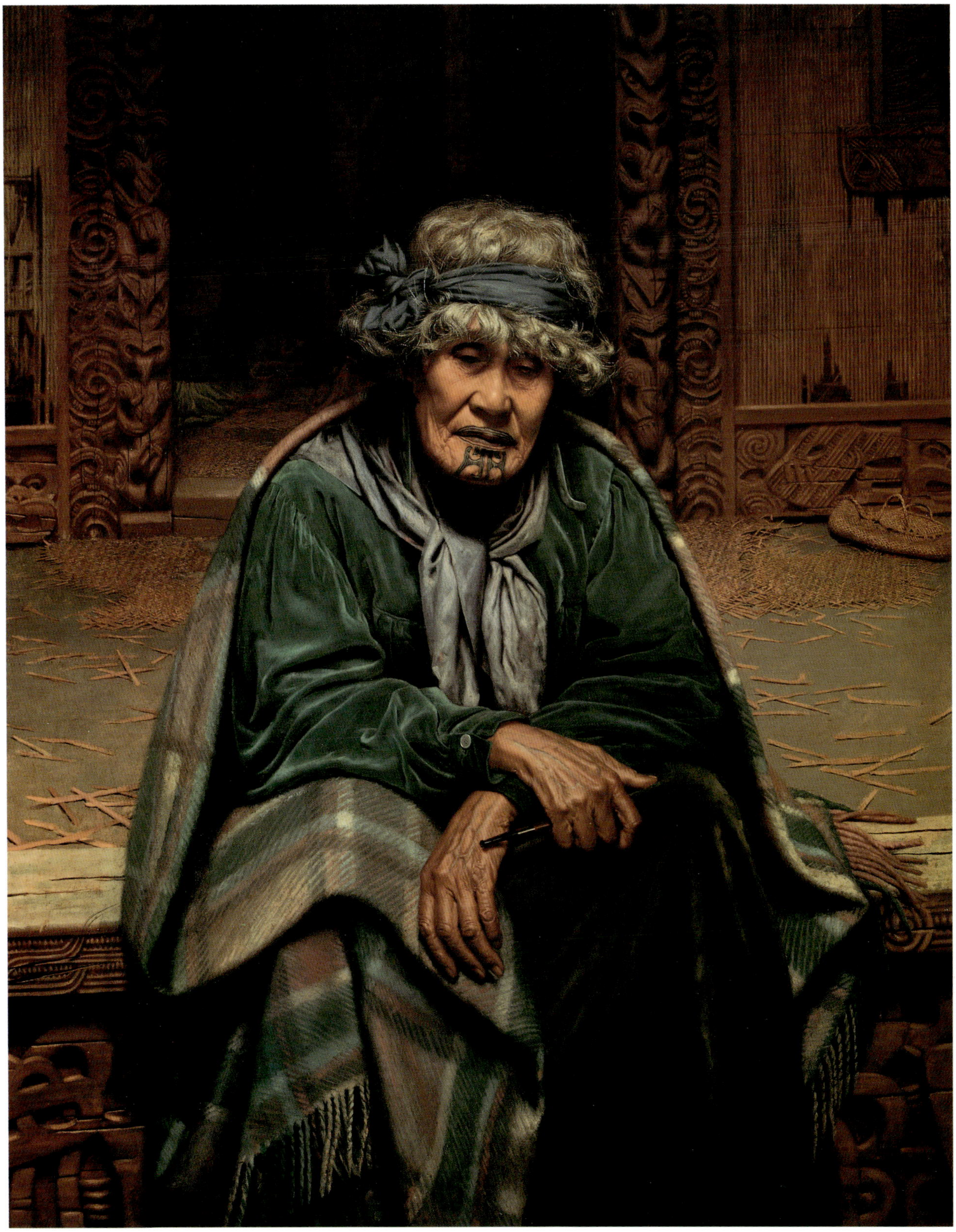

Memories: Ena Te Papatahi,
a Chieftainess of the Ngapuhi Tribe 1906
Ina Te Papatahi, Ngā Puhi

oil on canvas, 1275 x 1015 mm
Auckland Art Gallery Toi o Tāmaki,
bequest of Alfred and Emily Nathan, 1952

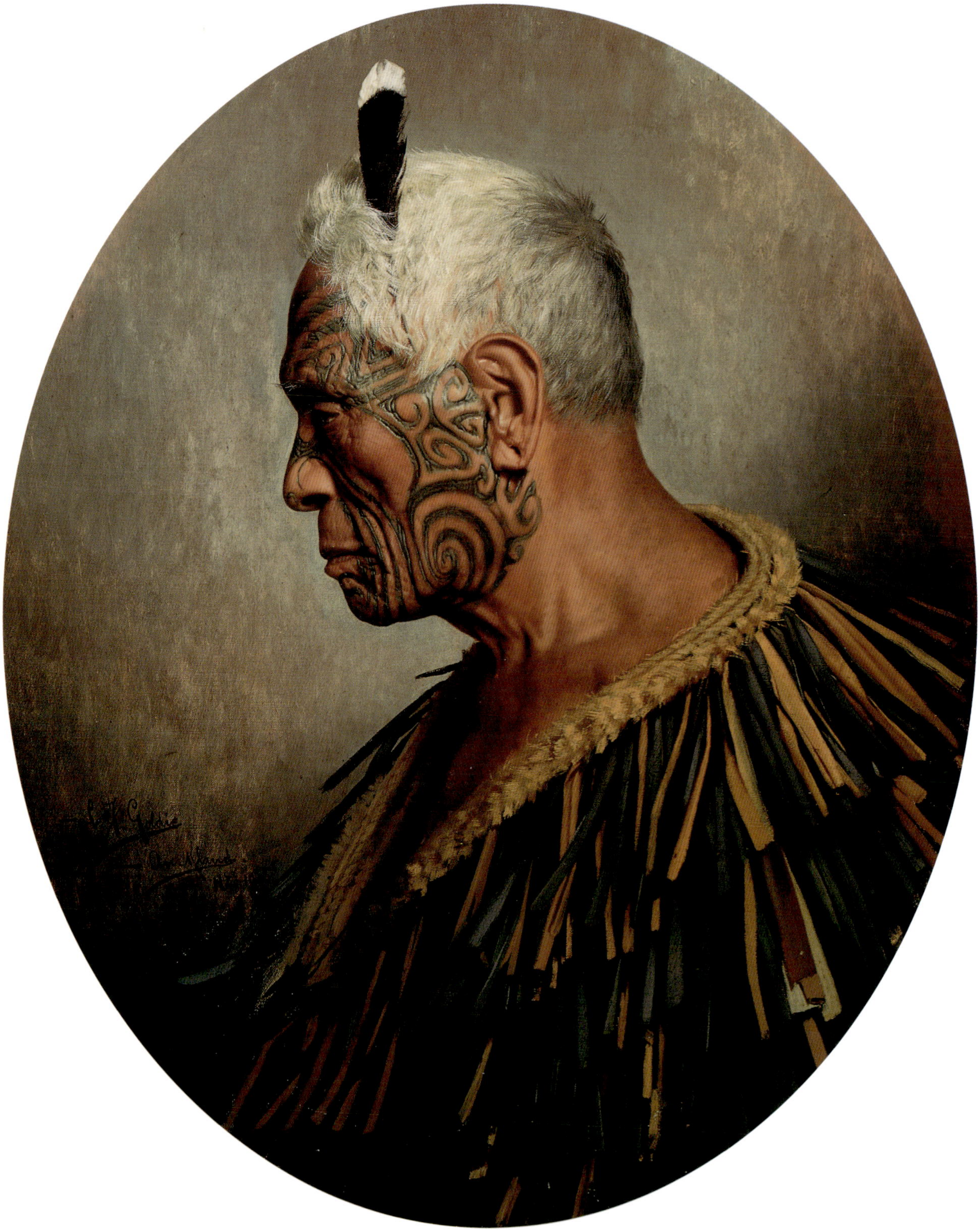

A Noble Relic of a Noble Race 1907
Kamariera Te Hau-Tākiri Wharepapa, Ngā Puhi
oil on canvas, 770 x 640 mm
Auckland Museum, gift of Olive Goldie, 1951

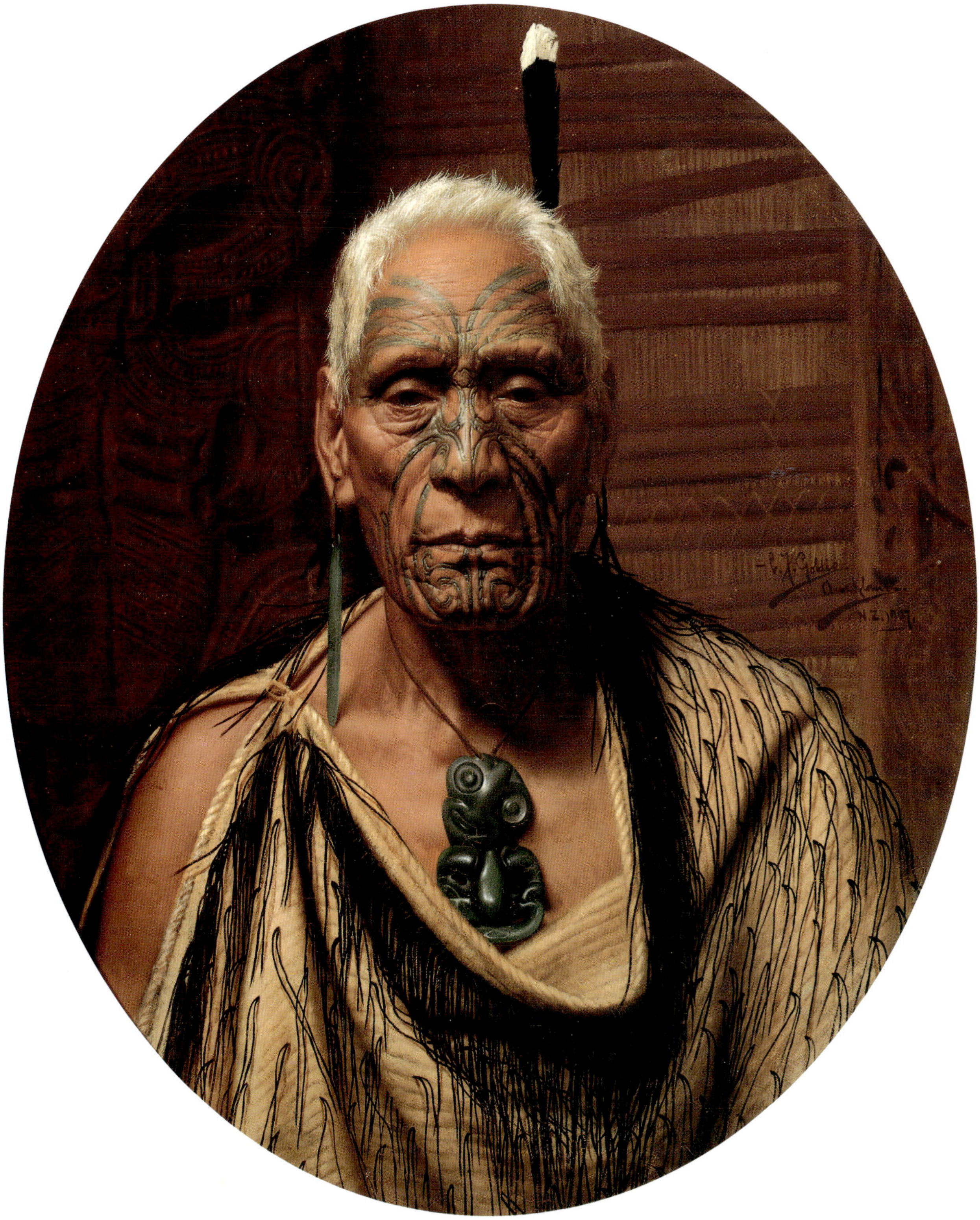

Te Hau-Takiri Wharepapa,
a Chieftain of the Ngapuhi Tribe 1907
Kamariera Te Hau-Tākiri Wharepapa, Ngā Puhi
oil on canvas, 760 x 635 mm
Auckland Museum, gift of Olive Goldie, 1951

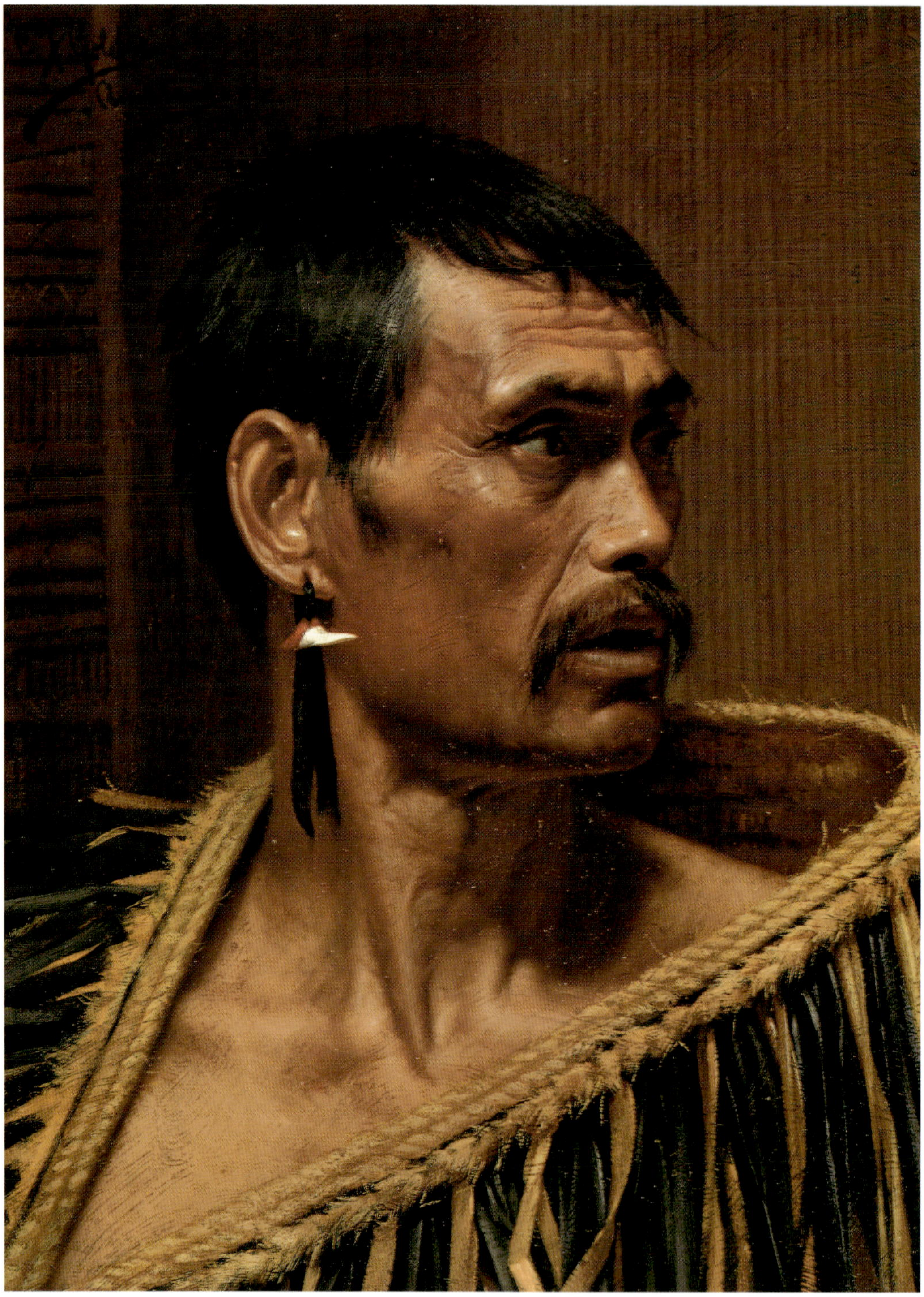

A Study 1906
oil on panel, 350 x 265 mm
private collection

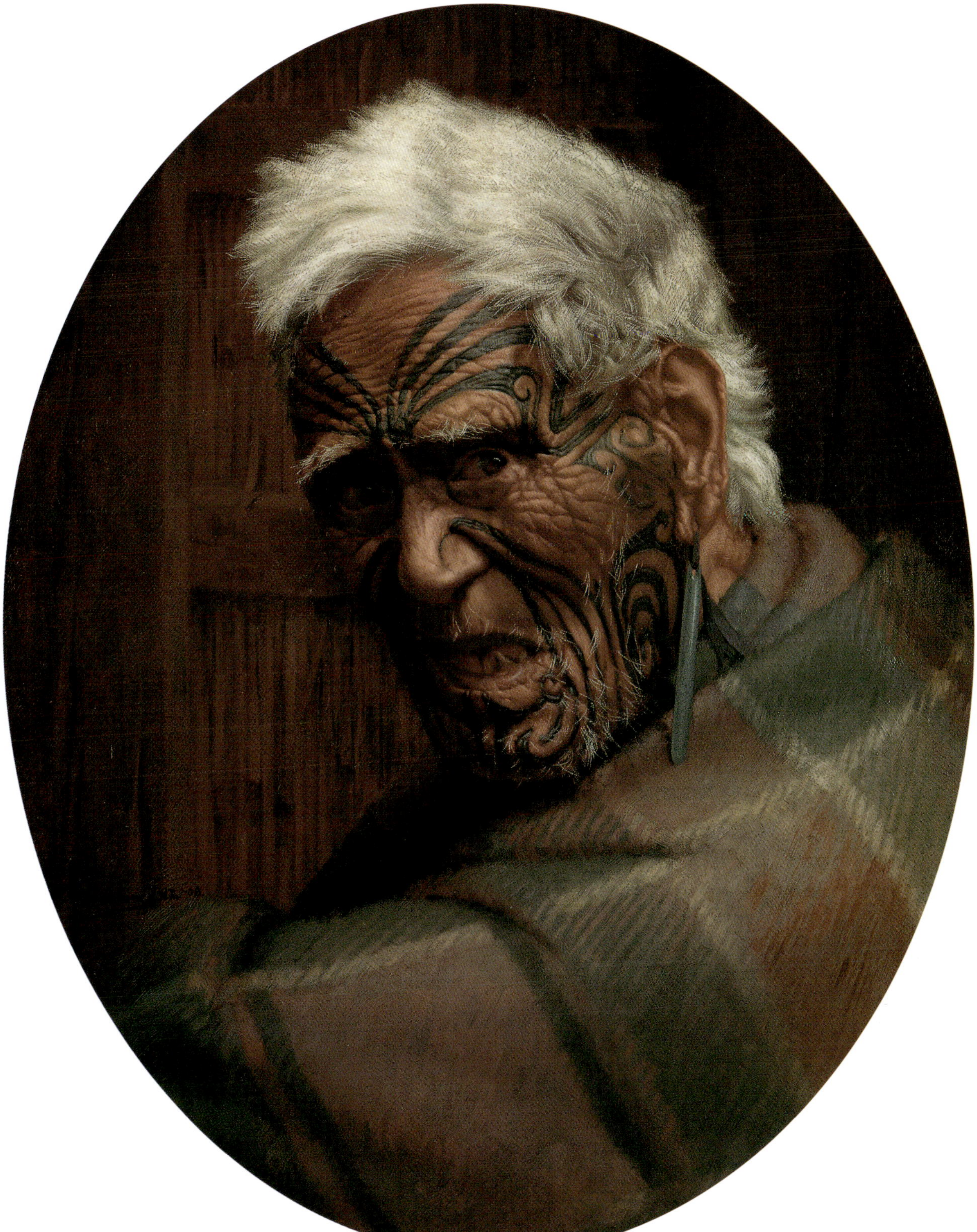

A Centenarian: Aperahama, aged 104 1908
Aperahama Rairai, Ngāti Te Ata
oil on canvas, 610 x 510 mm
private collection

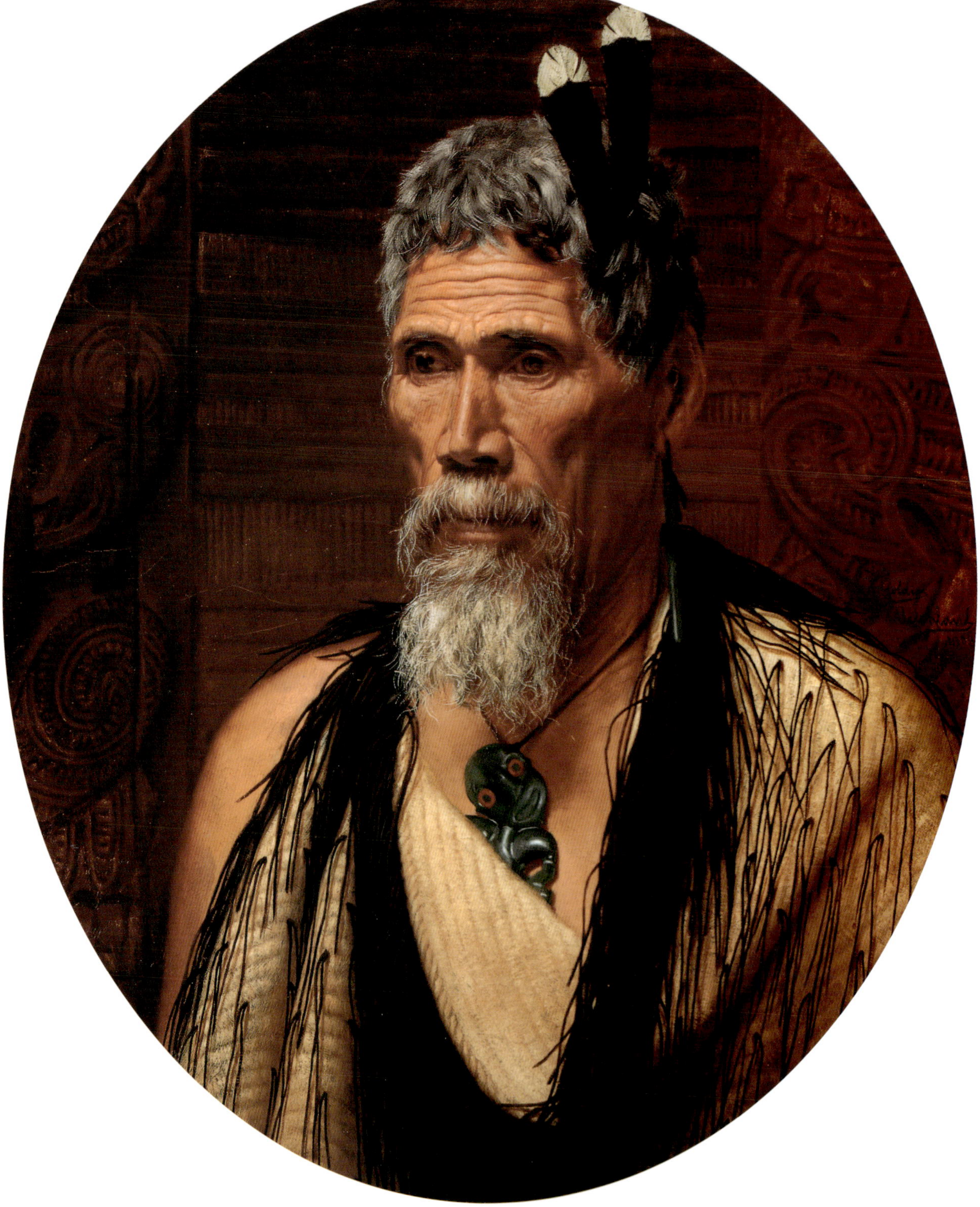

Anaha Te Rahui, the Celebrated Carver of Rotorua 1908
Anaha Te Rāhui, Ngāti Tarāwhai
oil on canvas, 765 x 640 mm
Auckland Museum, gift of Olive Goldie, 1951

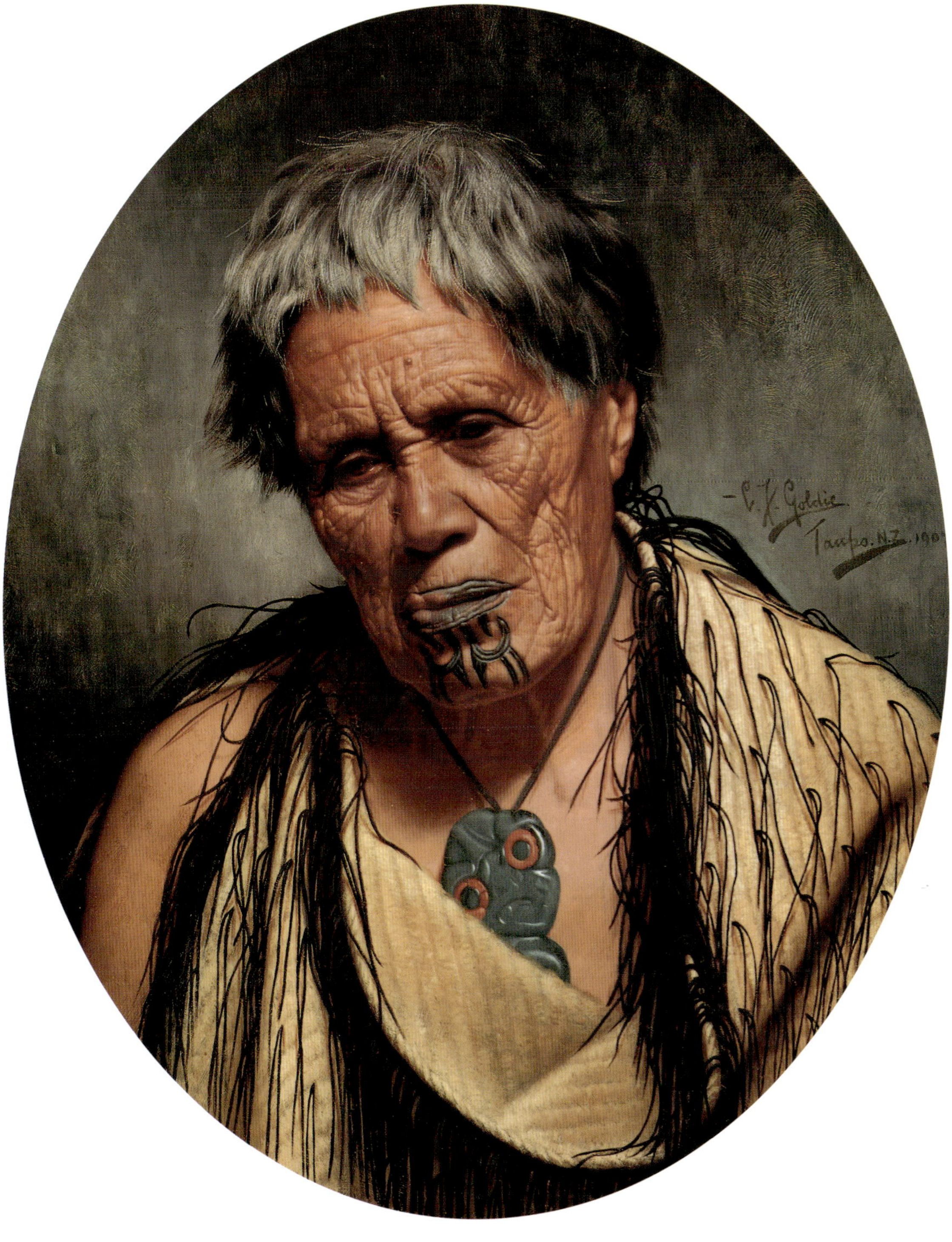

Te Hei, Ngatiraukawa 1907
Te Hei, Ngāti Raukawa
oil on canvas, 615 x 510 mm
Auckland Museum, gift of Olive Goldie, 1951

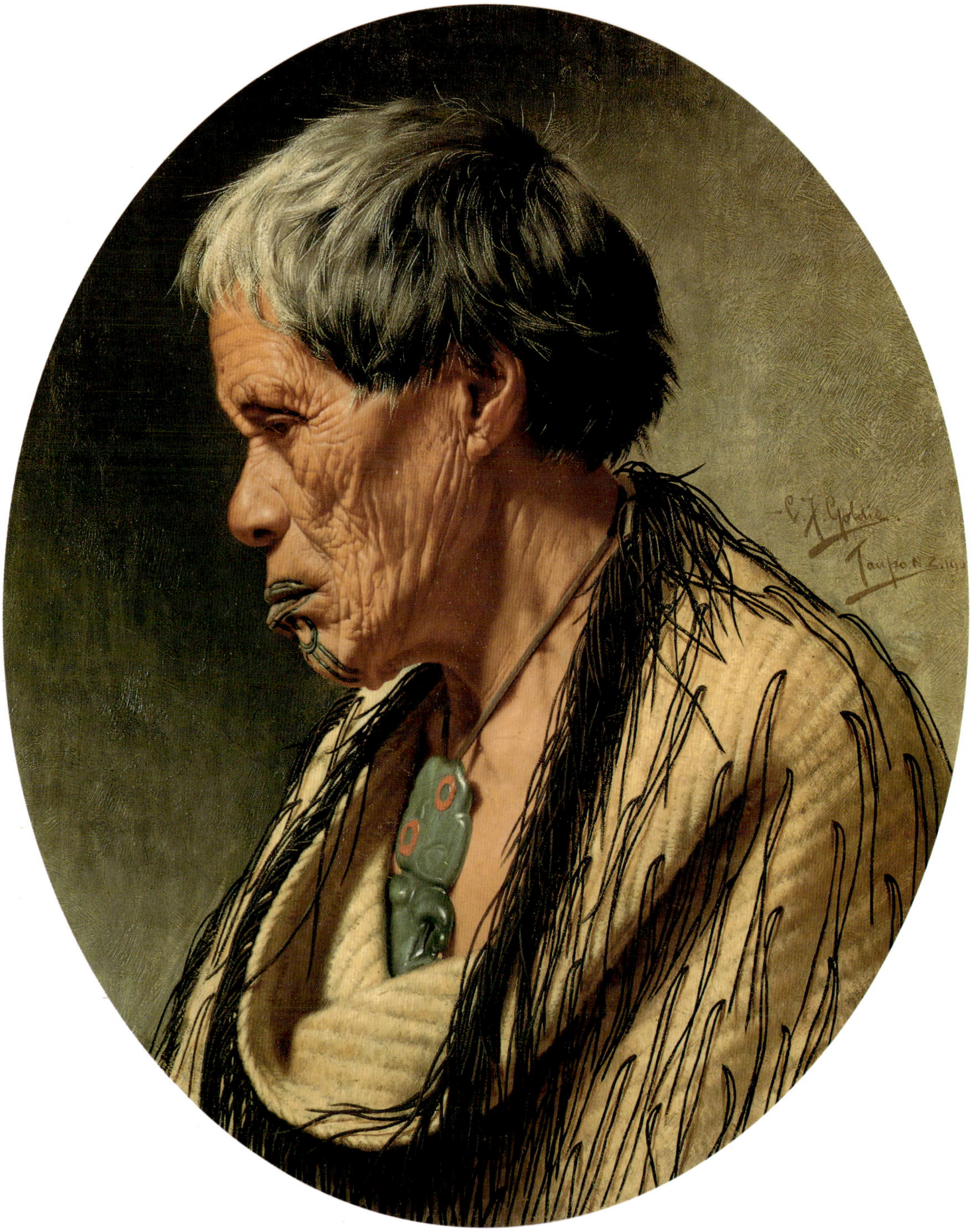

Touched by the Hand of Time 1907
Te Hei, Ngāti Raukawa
oil on canvas, 610 x 510 mm
Auckland Museum, gift of Olive Goldie, 1951

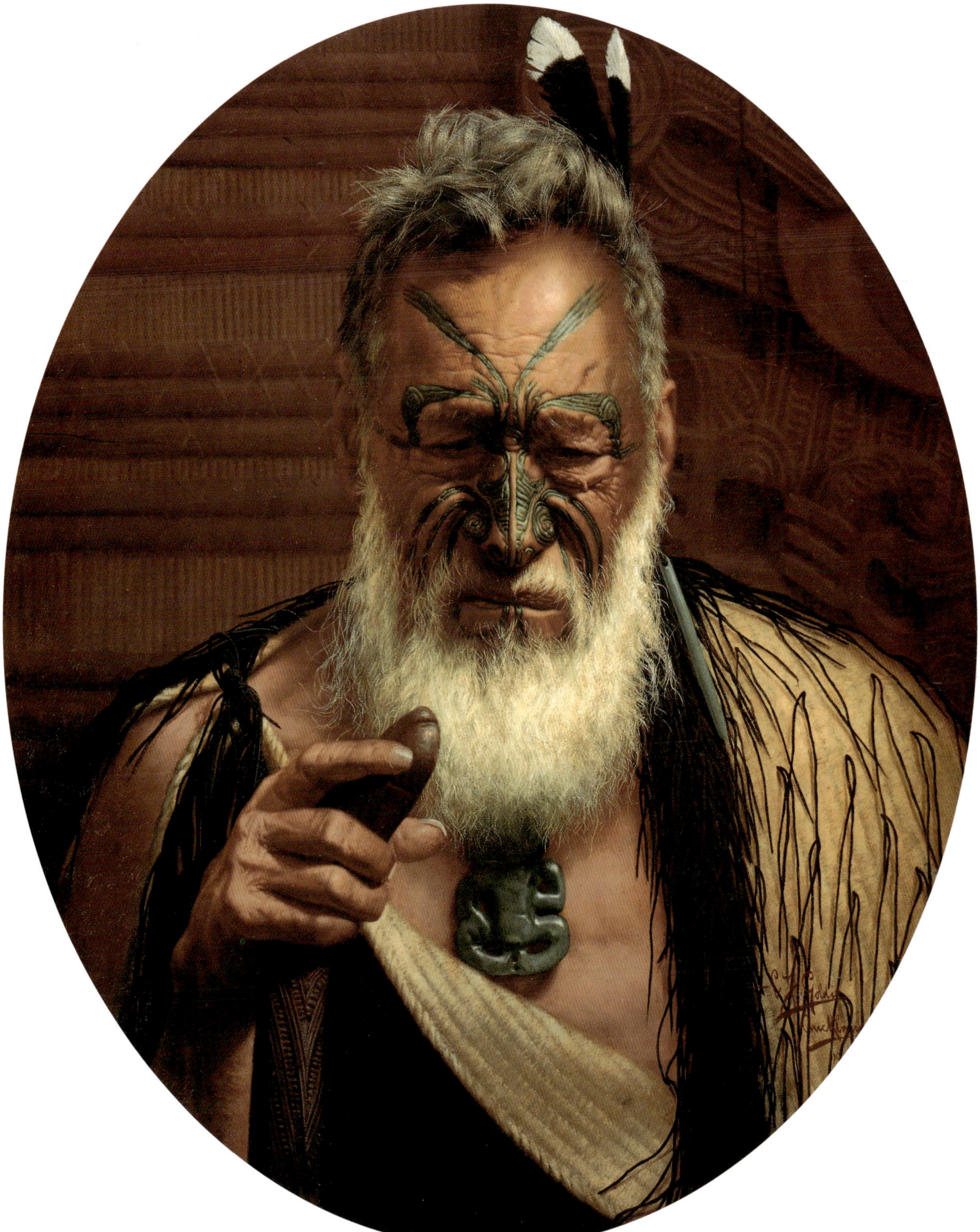

Tikitere Mihi, a Noted Chieftain of the Ngatiuenuku 1908
Tikitere Mihi, Ngāti Uenukukōpako
oil on canvas, 765 x 640 mm
Auckland Museum, gift of Olive Goldie, 1951

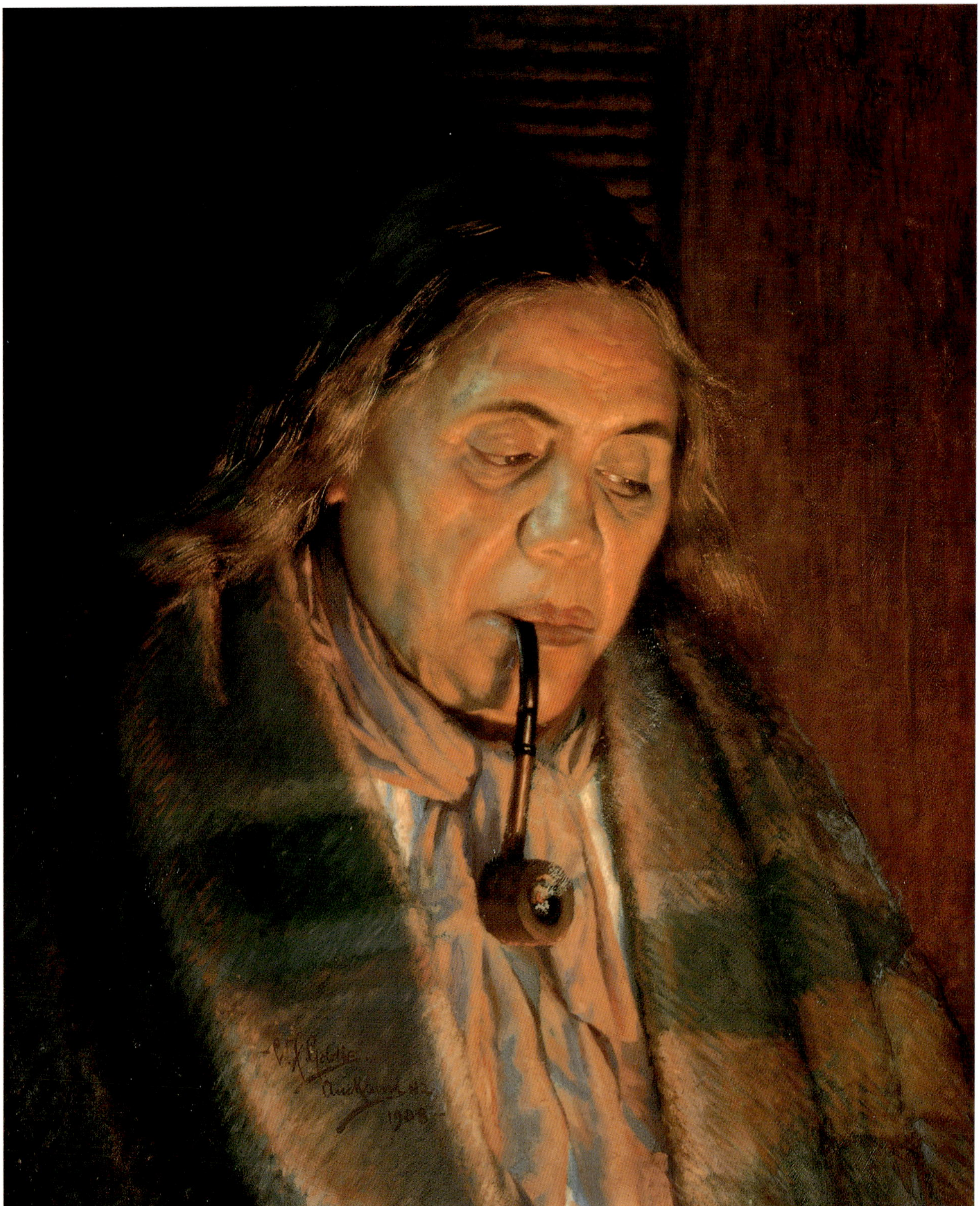

Fire and Smoke 1908
Nikorima
oil on canvas, 615 x 510 mm
private collection

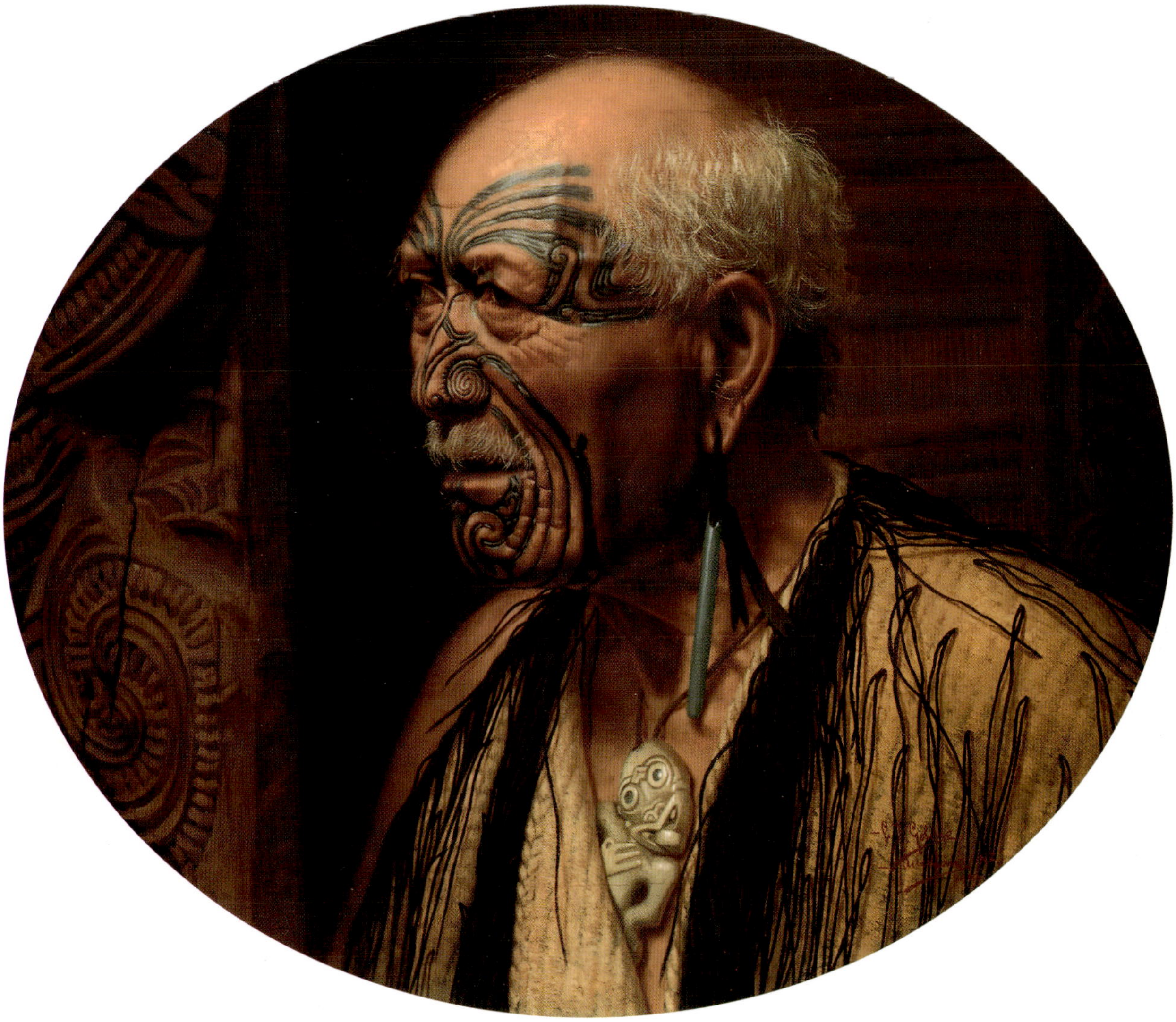

Patara Te Tuhi 1908
Pātara Te Tuhi, Ngāti Mahuta
oil on canvas, 510 x 610 mm
Auckland Art Gallery Toi o Tāmaki,
Auckland Picture Purchase Fund, 1908

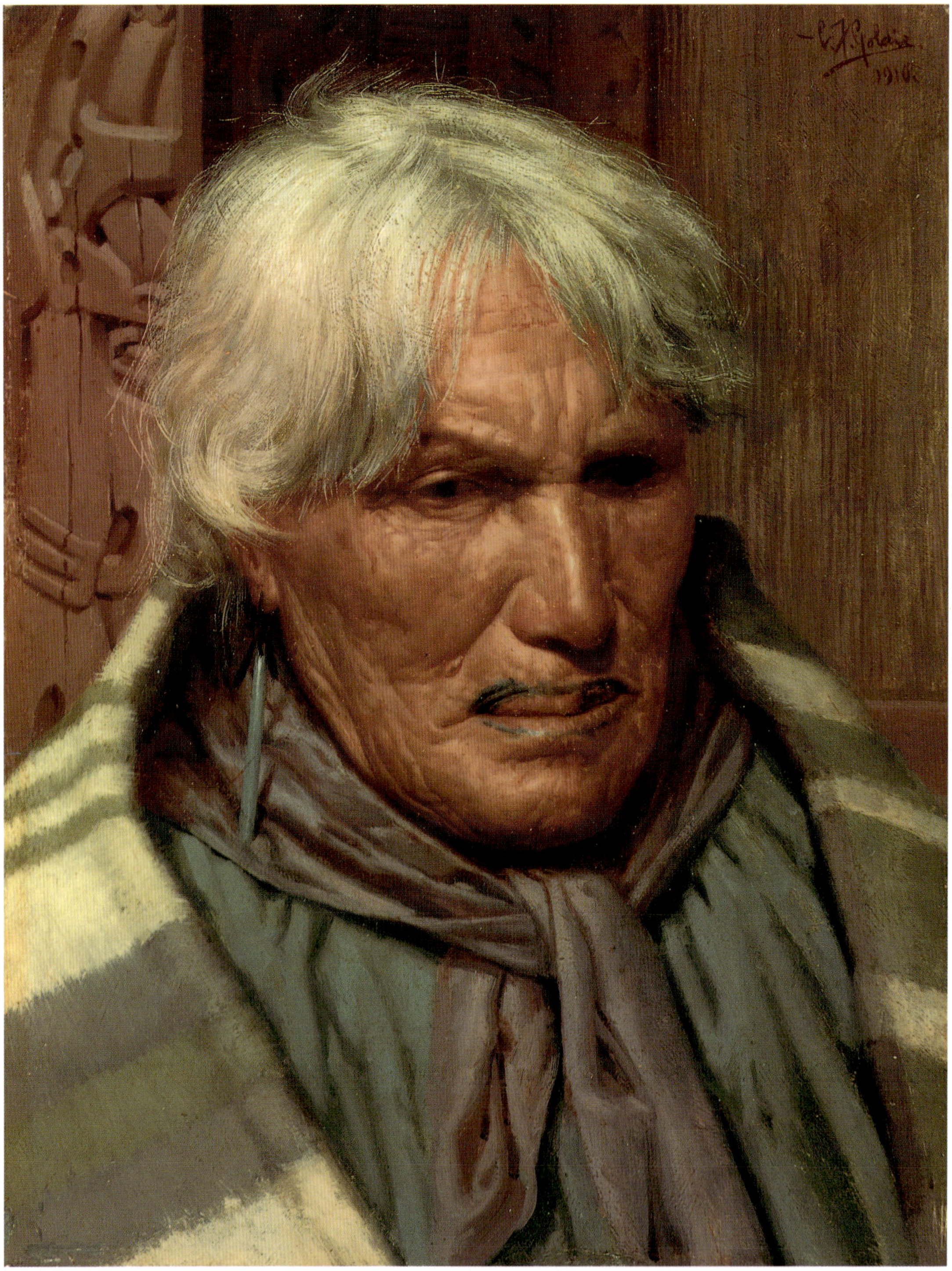

Sophia, the Heroine of Tarawera 1910
Sophia Gray, Te Paea Hinerangi, Ngāti Ruanui
oil on panel, 203 x 153 mm
Auckland Art Gallery Toi o Tāmaki,
presented by Lincoln N. Astley, 1987

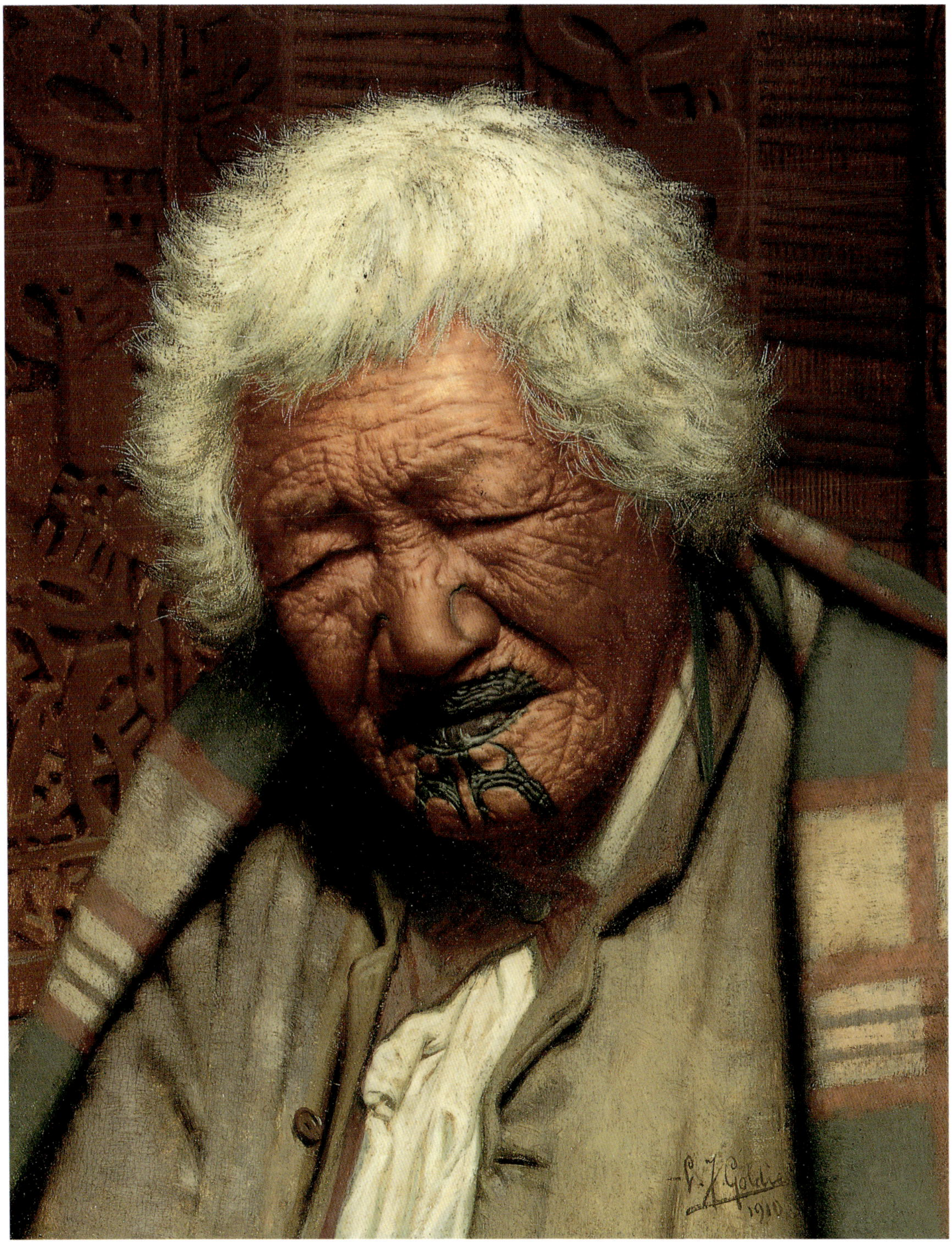

Kapi Kapi, aged 102, a Survivor of the Tarawera Eruption 1910
Ahinata Te Rangitautini (Kapekape), Tūhourangi
oil on panel, 267 x 203 mm
Auckland Art Gallery Toi o Tāmaki,
Auckland Picture Purchase Fund, 1910

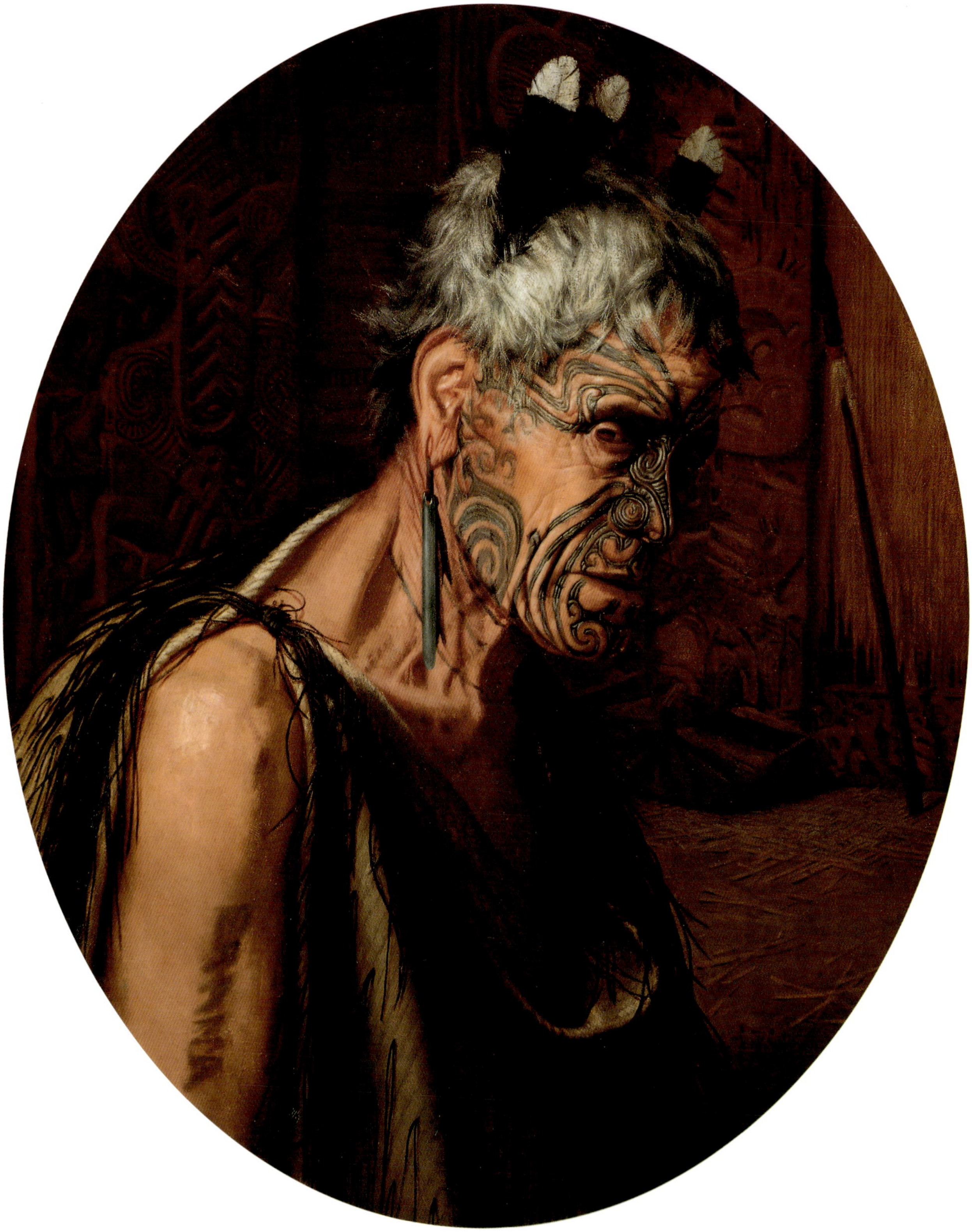

The Old Lion 1910
Te Aho-o-te-Rangi Wharepu, Ngāti Mahuta
oil on canvas, 767 x 635 mm
private collection

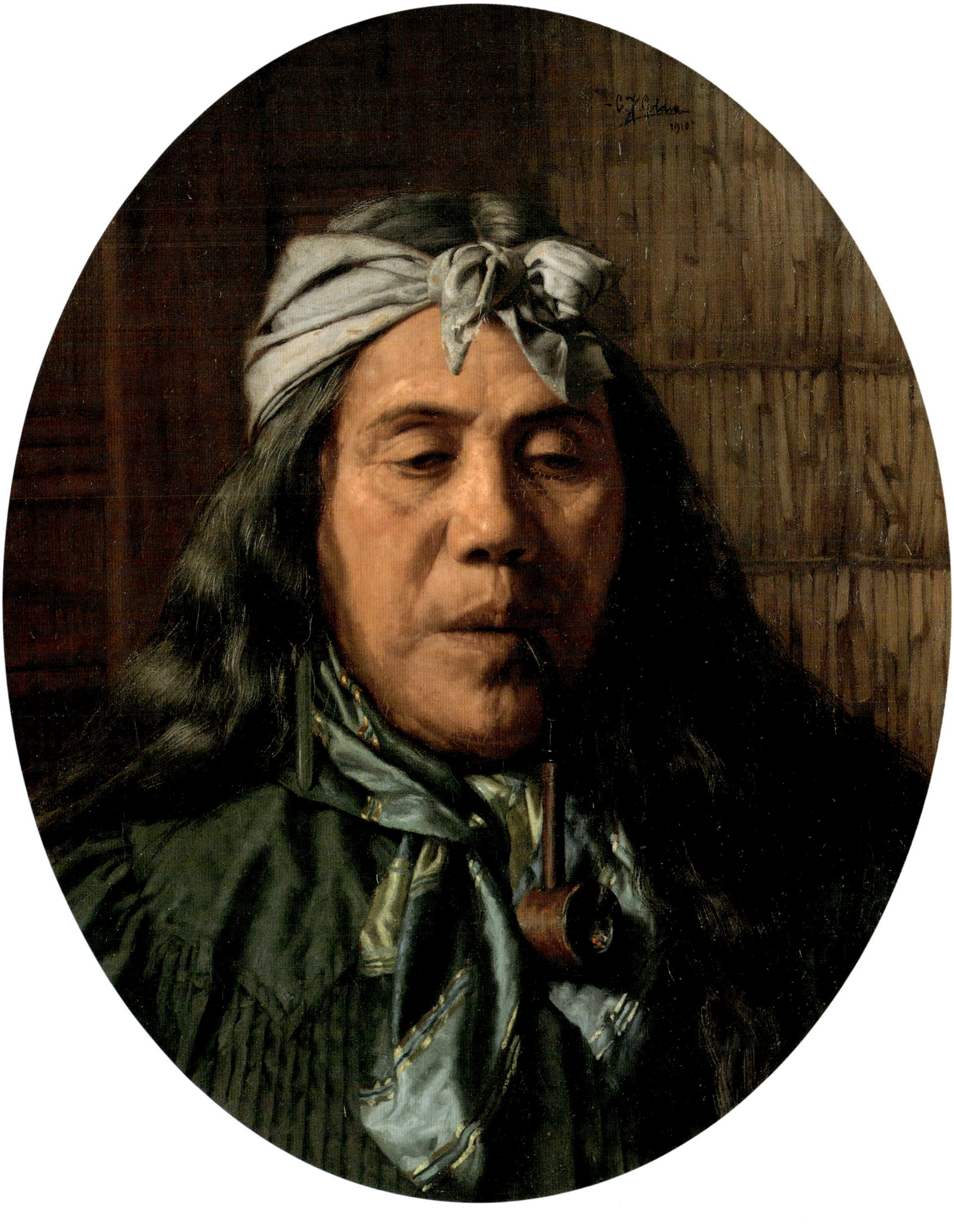

Nikorima and Nicotina 1910
Nikorima
oil on canvas, 610 x 510 mm
collection of Solitaire Lodge, Lake Tarawera

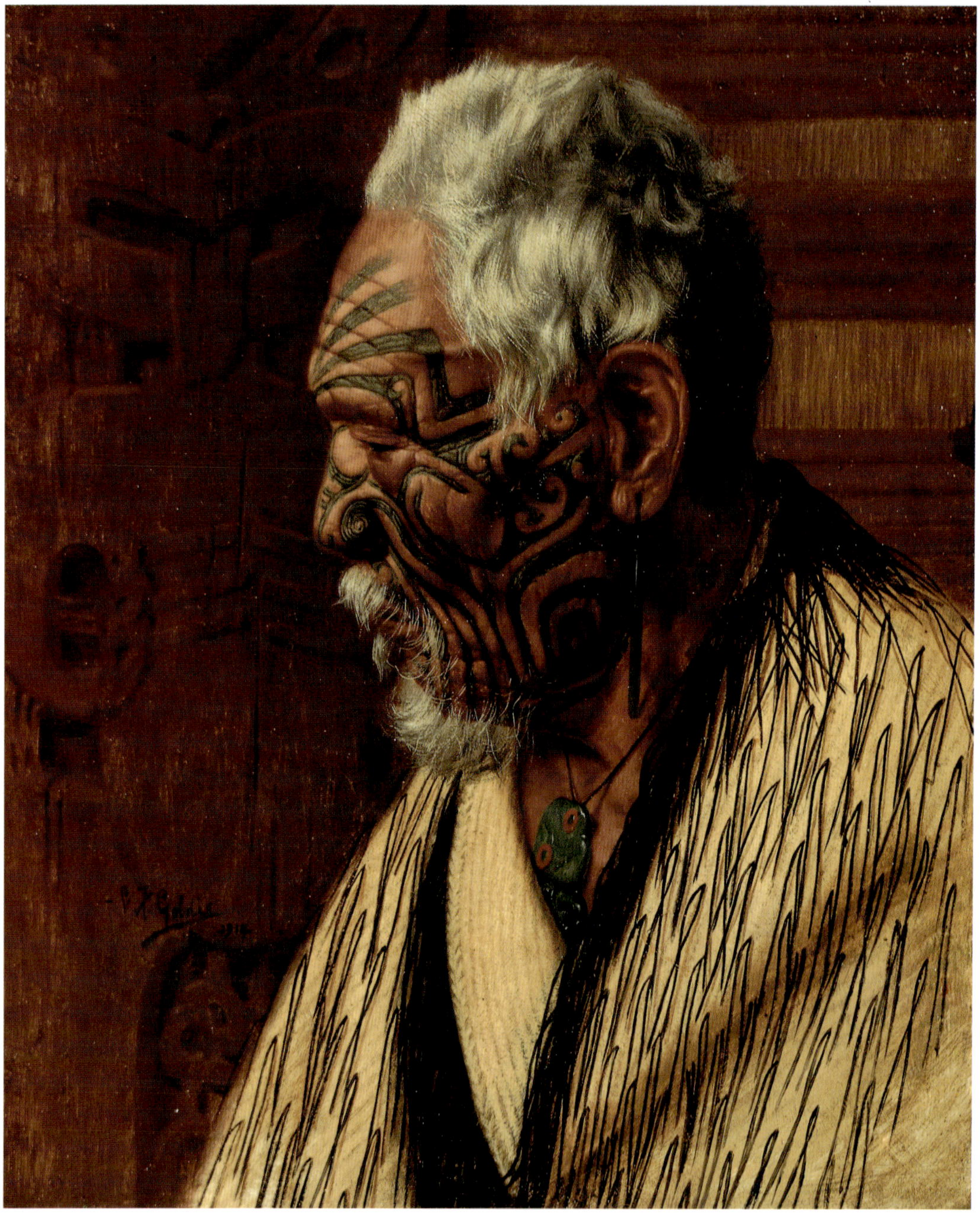

The Whitening Snows of Venerable Eld 1914
Te Wharekauri Tahuna, Ngāti Manawa
oil on canvas, 305 x 255 mm
Auckland Art Gallery Toi o Tāmaki,
bequest of Martin Trenwith, 1929

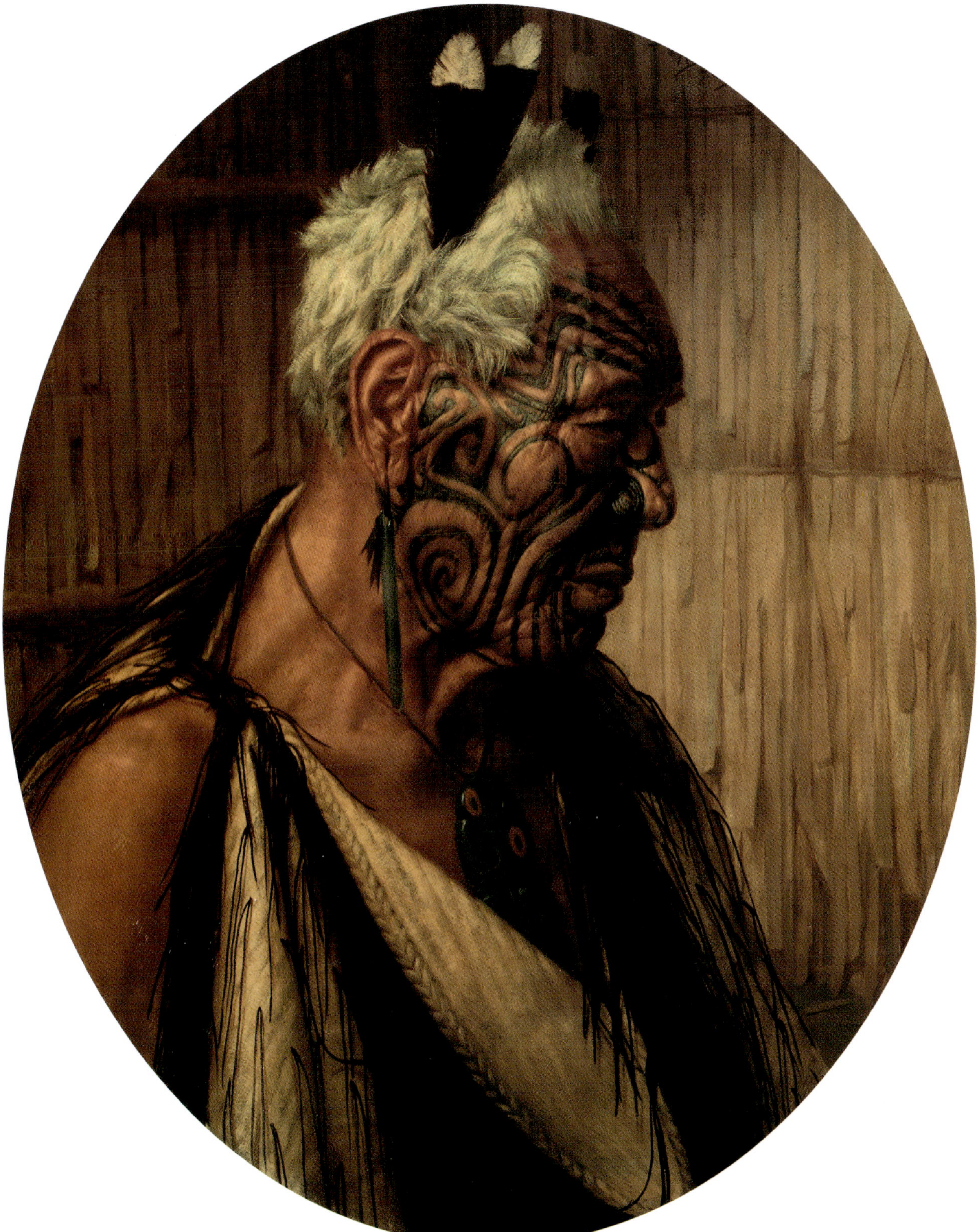

A Noble Relic of a Noble Race: Wharekauri Tahuna, a 'Tohunga' or Priest of the Tuhoe Tribe 1910
Te Wharekauri Tahuna, Ngāti Manawa
oil on canvas, 775 x 645 mm
Auckland Art Gallery Toi o Tāmaki,
Auckland Picture Purchase Fund, 1911

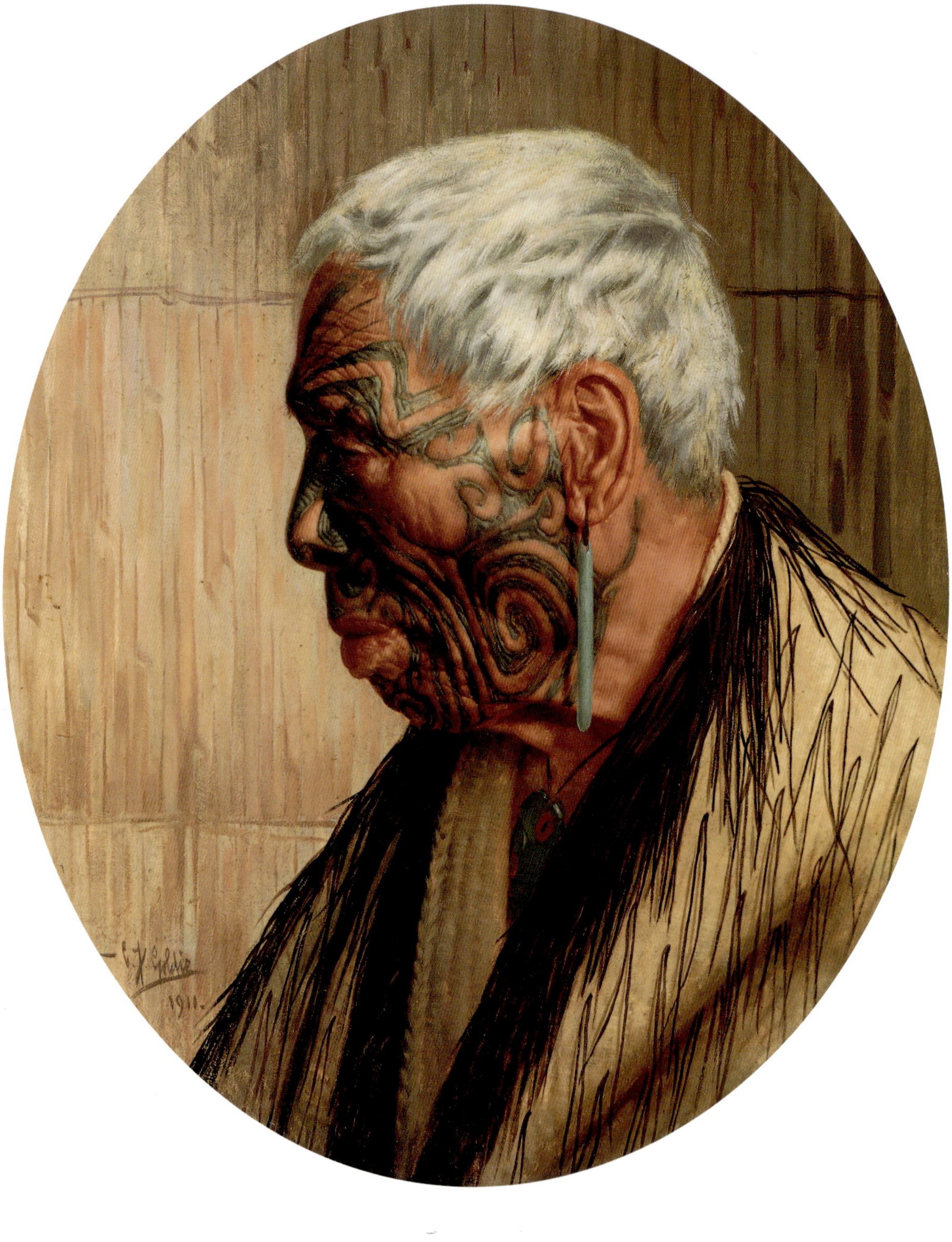

The Last of the Cannibals 1911
Tūmai Tāwhiti, Ngāti Raukawa, Te Arawa
oil on canvas, 610 x 510 mm
Auckland Museum, gift of Olive Goldie, 1951

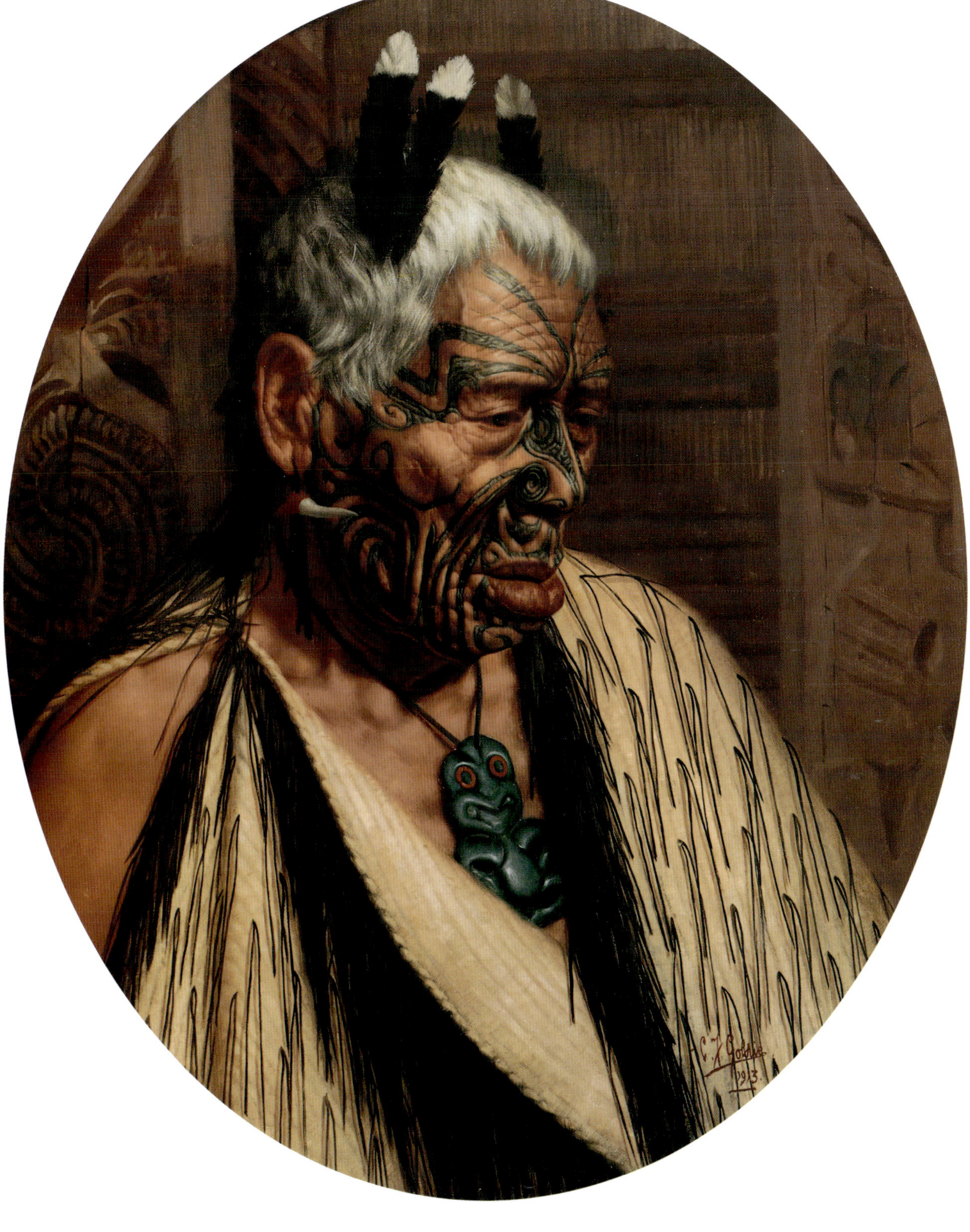

The Last of the Cannibals: Tumai Tawhiti 1913
Tūmai Tāwhiti, Ngāti Raukawa, Te Arawa
oil on canvas, 750 x 620 mm
Aigantighe Art Gallery, Timaru

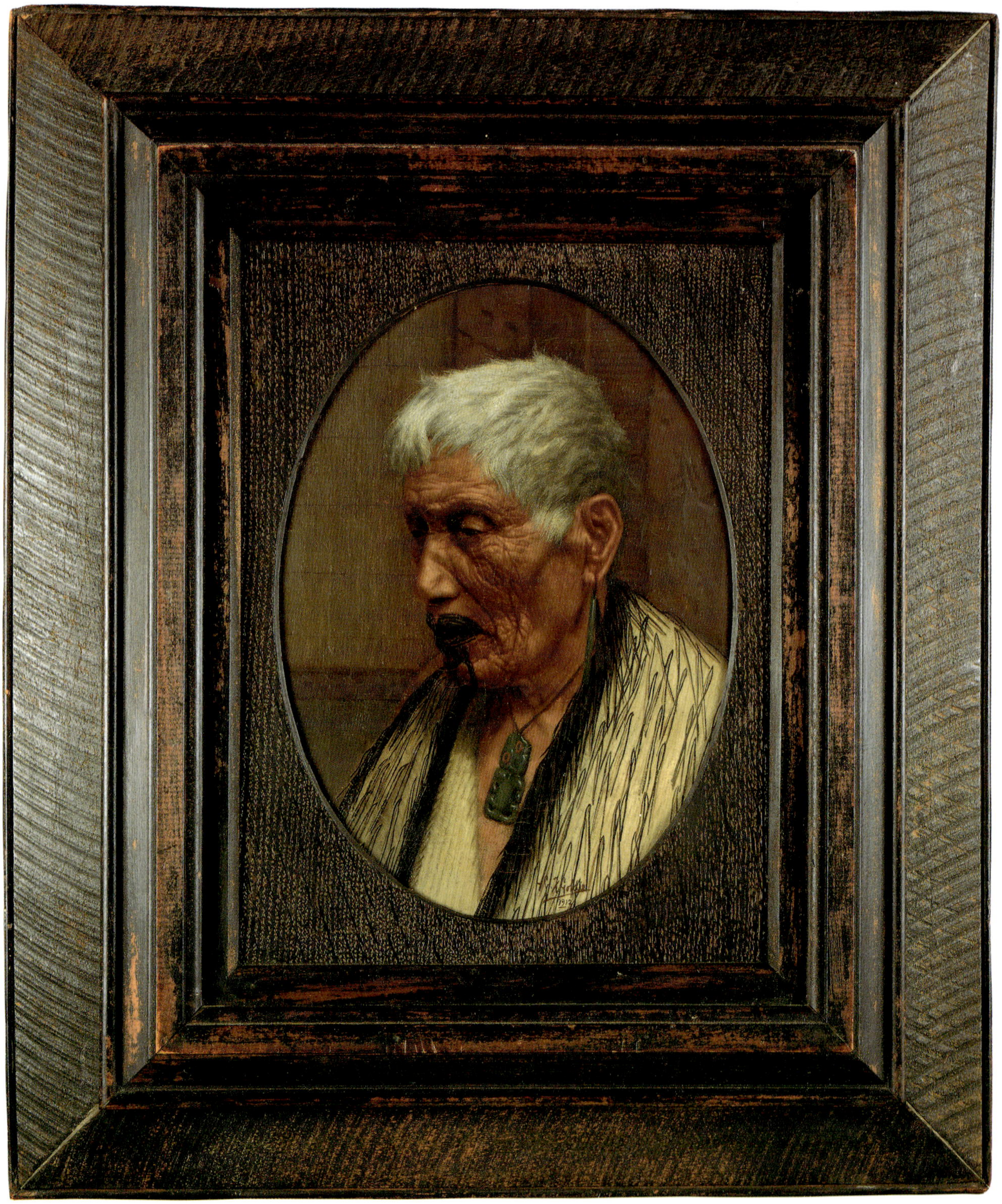

One of the Old School: Wiripine Ninia, a Ngatiawa Chieftainess 1912
Wiripine Ninia, Ngāti Awa
oil on canvas, 290 x 215 mm
Museum of New Zealand Te Papa Tongarewa (neg. no. B038609)

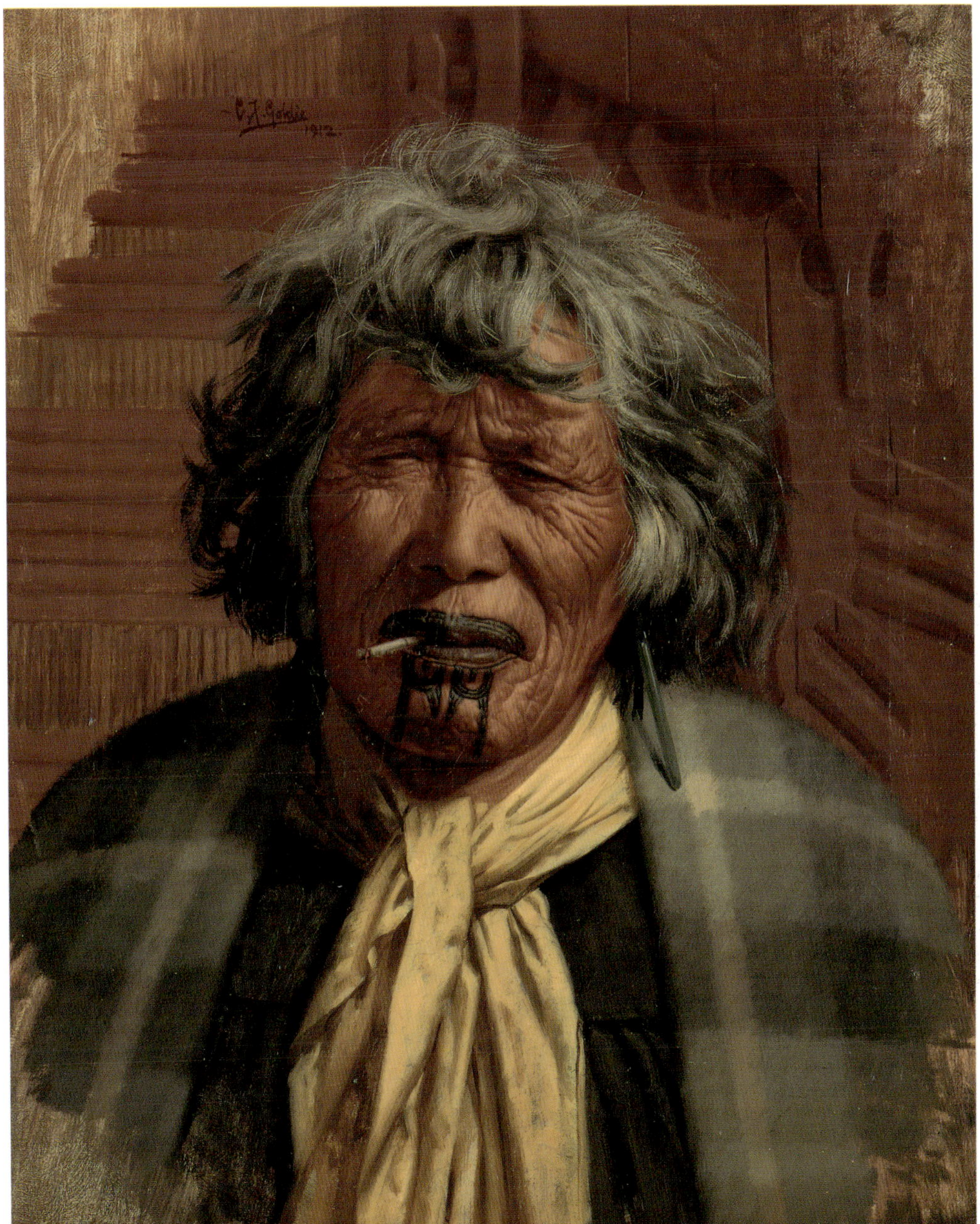

'No Koora te Cigaretti' 1912
Mihipeka Wairama, Tūhourangi
oil on canvas, 381 x 305 mm
Art Gallery of South Australia, Adelaide,
bequest of Sir Lloyd Dumas, 1973

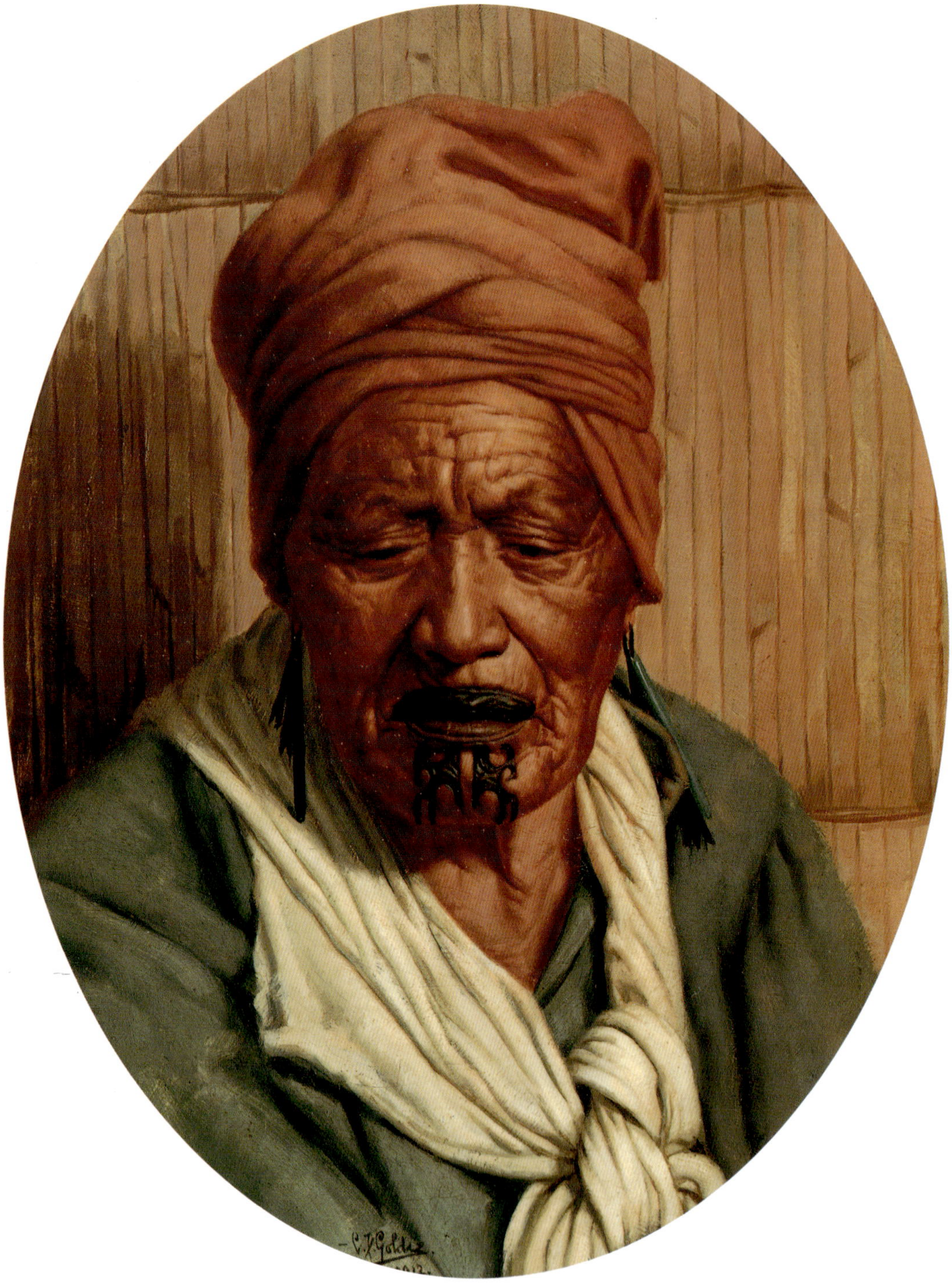

Te Aotiti Tumai 1912
Te Aotiti, Te Arawa, Ngāti Tūwharetoa
oil on canvas, 348 x 270 mm
private collection

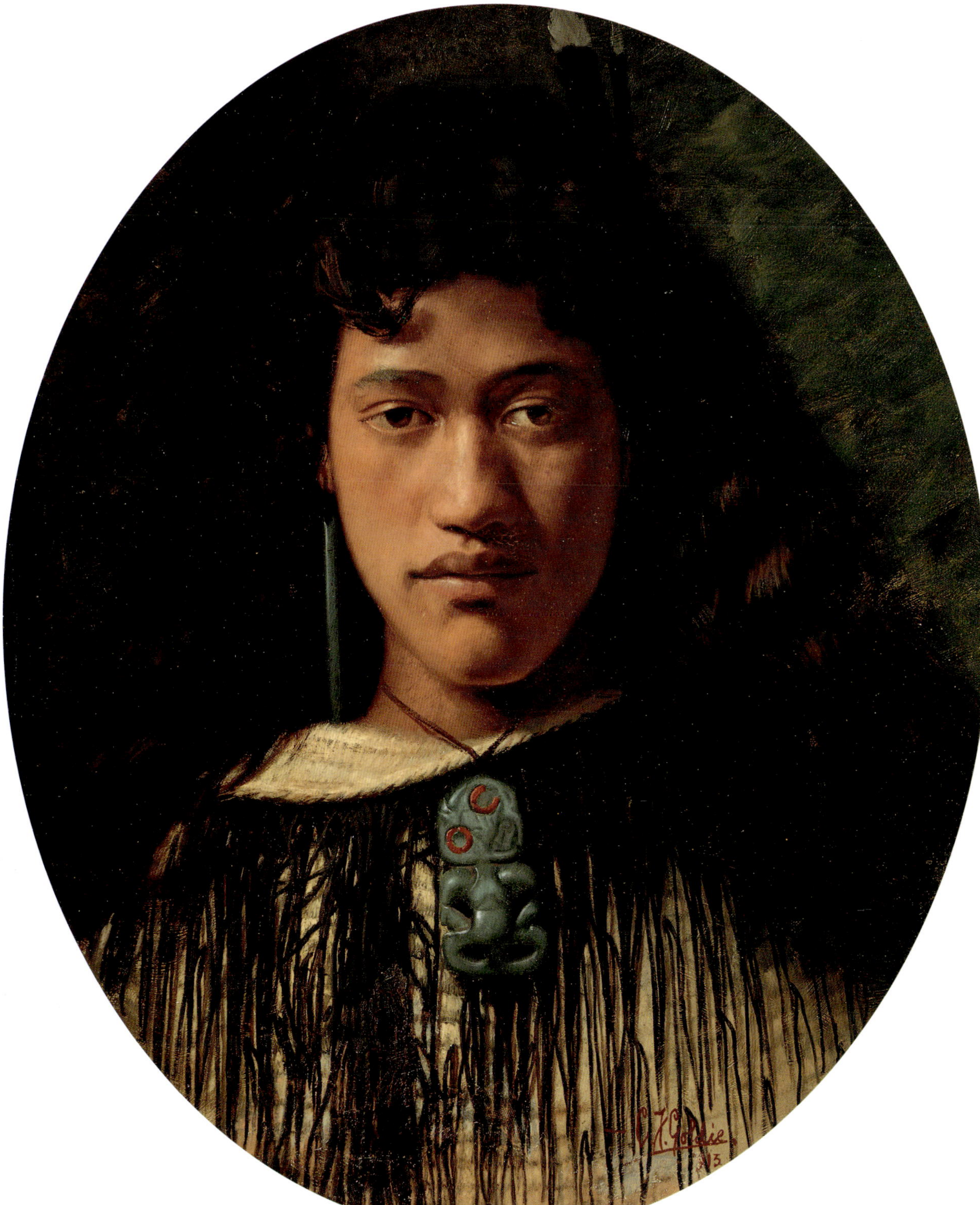

Hinemoa, the Belle of the Kainga 1913
Hinemoa, Te Arawa
oil on canvas, 640 x 545 mm
Auckland Museum, gift of Olive Goldie, 1951

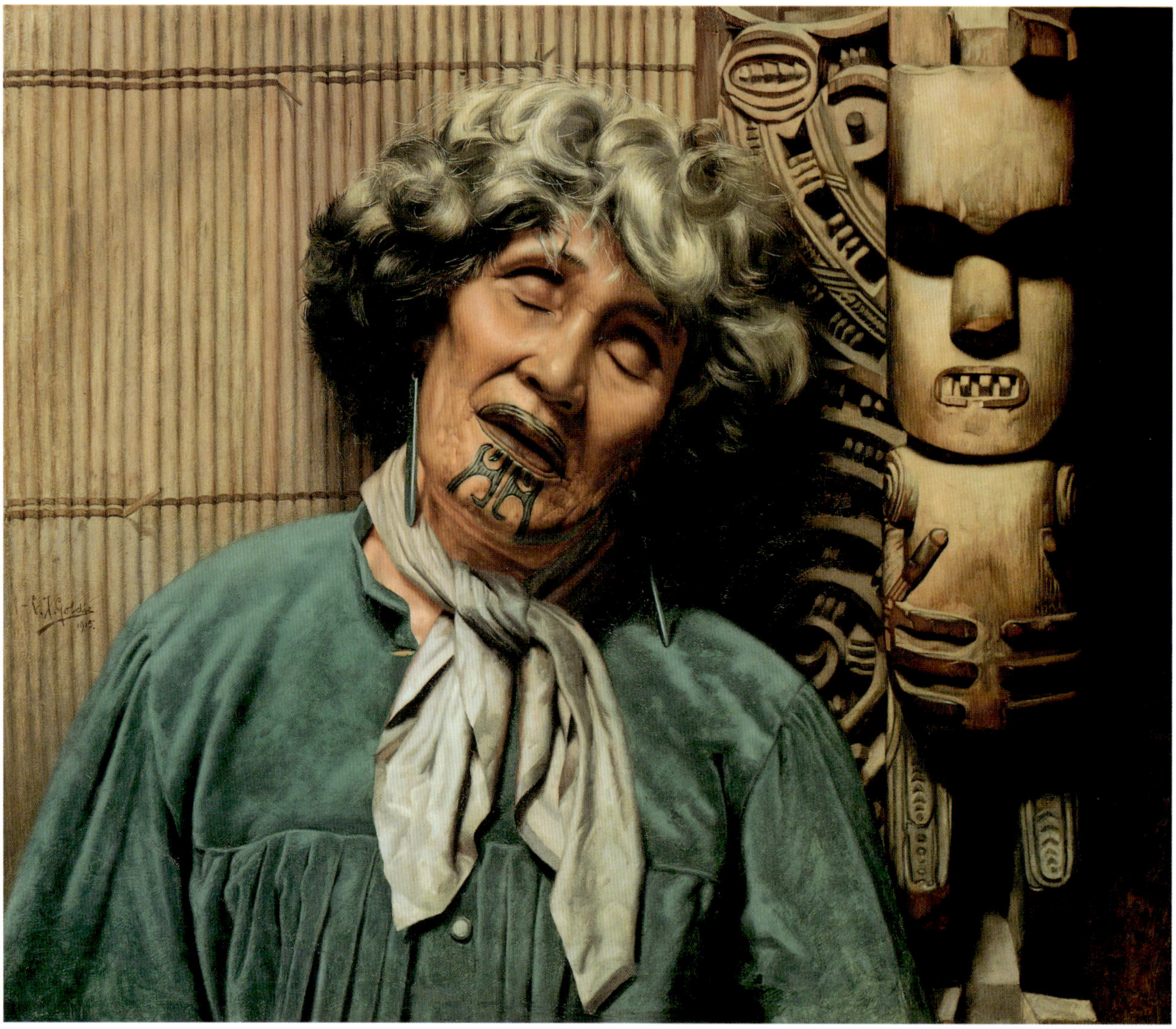

Forty Winks 1915
Ina Te Papatahi, Ngā Puhi
oil on canvas, 625 x 755 mm
private collection

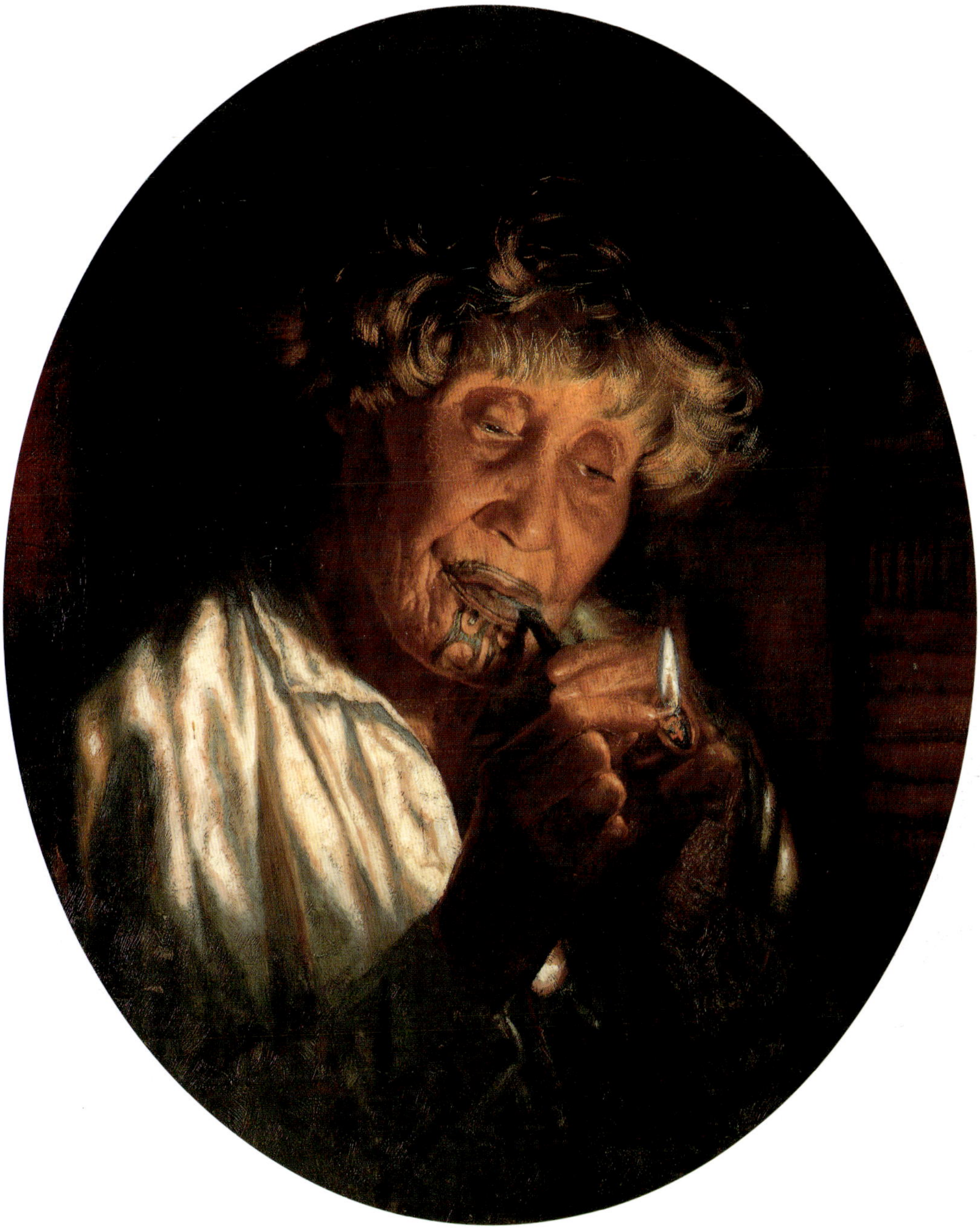

Night in the Whare 1912
Ina Te Papatahi, Ngā Puhi
oil on canvas, 638 x 533 mm
Auckland Art Gallery Toi o Tāmaki,
Auckland Picture Purchase Fund, 1912

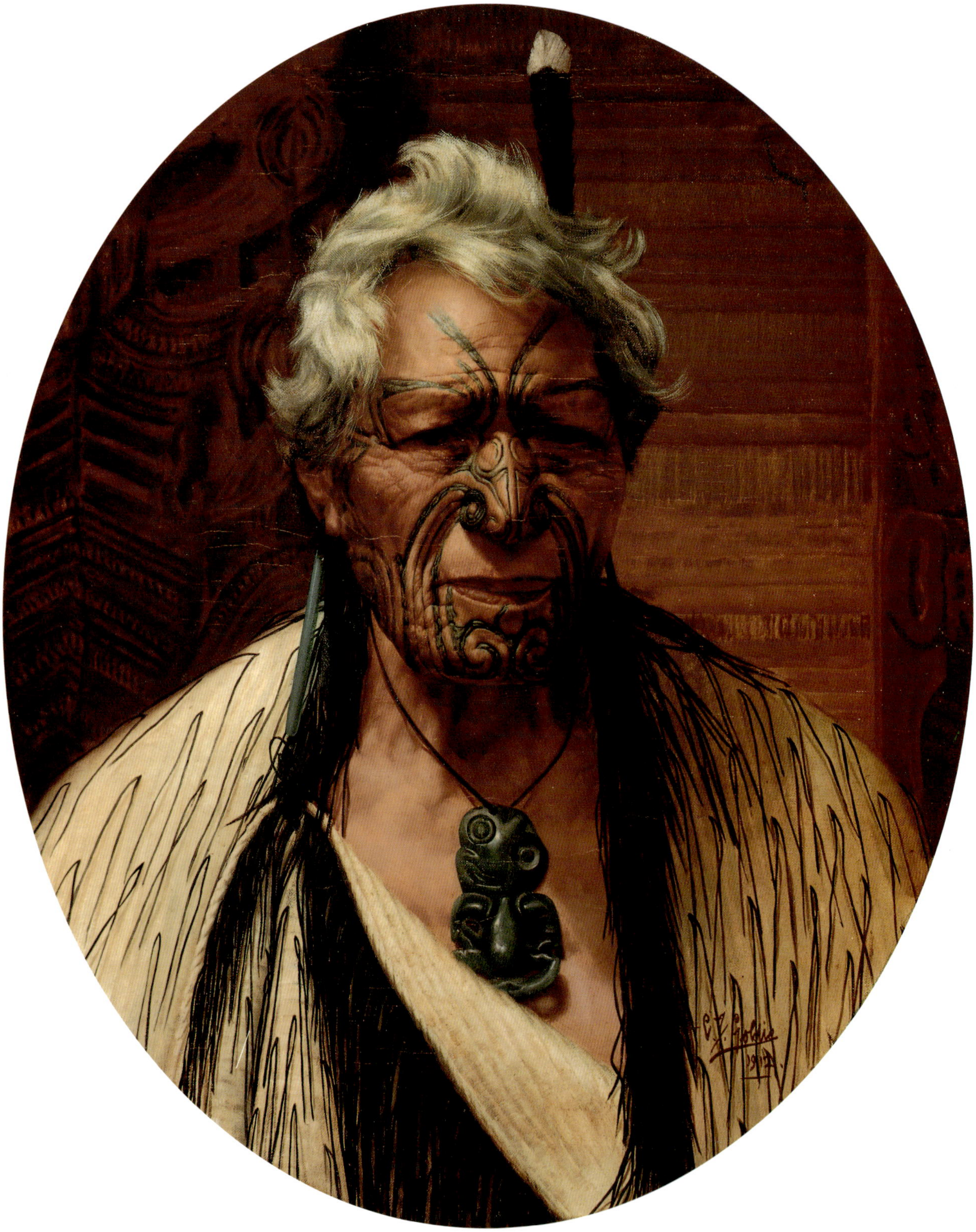

A Noble Northern Chief: Atama Paparangi 1912
Atama Paparangi, Te Rarawa
oil on canvas, 765 x 640 mm
Auckland Museum, gift of Olive Goldie, 1951

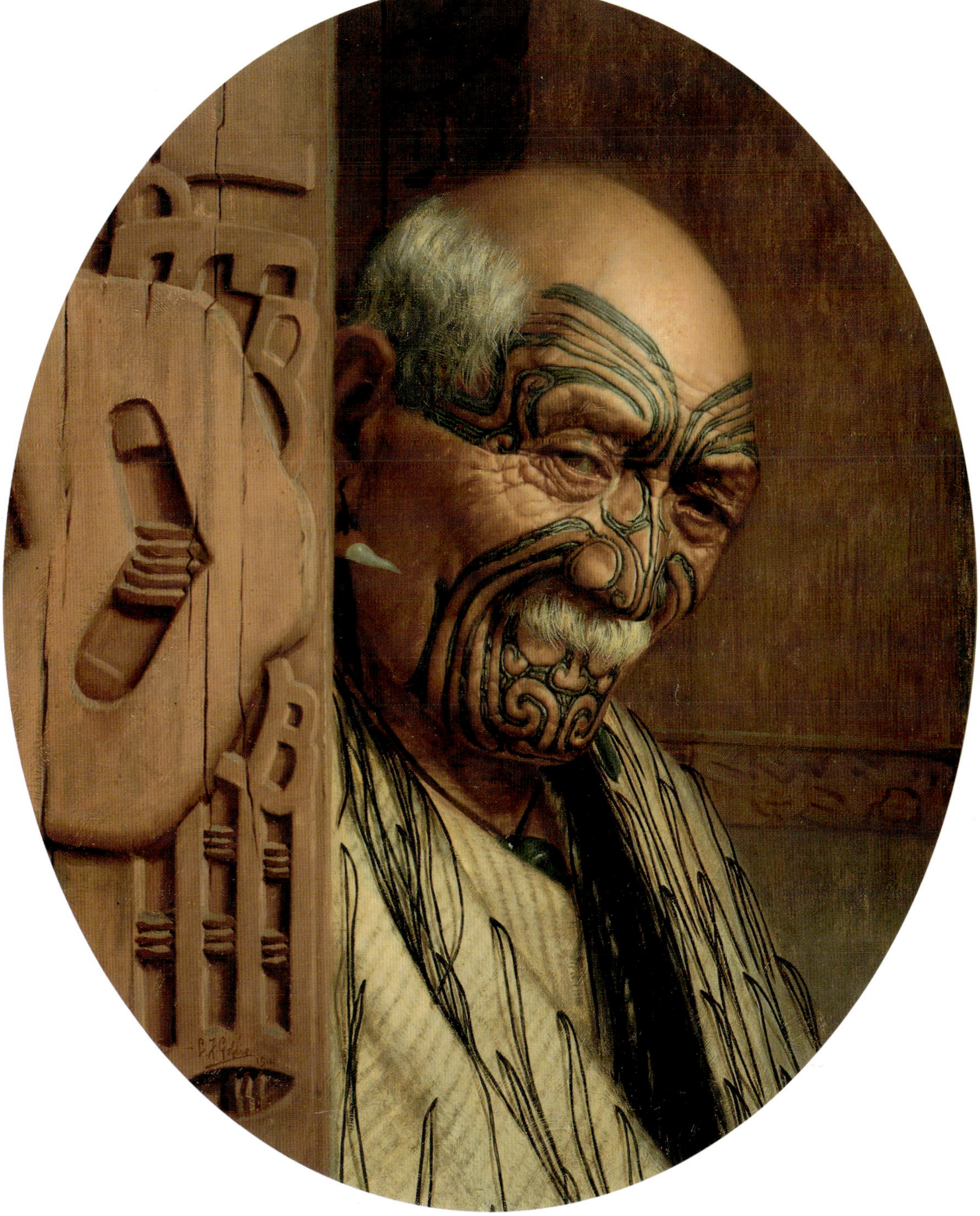

Peeping Patara 1914
Pātara Te Tuhi, Ngāti Mahuta
oil on canvas, 610 x 510 mm
Auckland Museum, gift of Olive Goldie, 1951

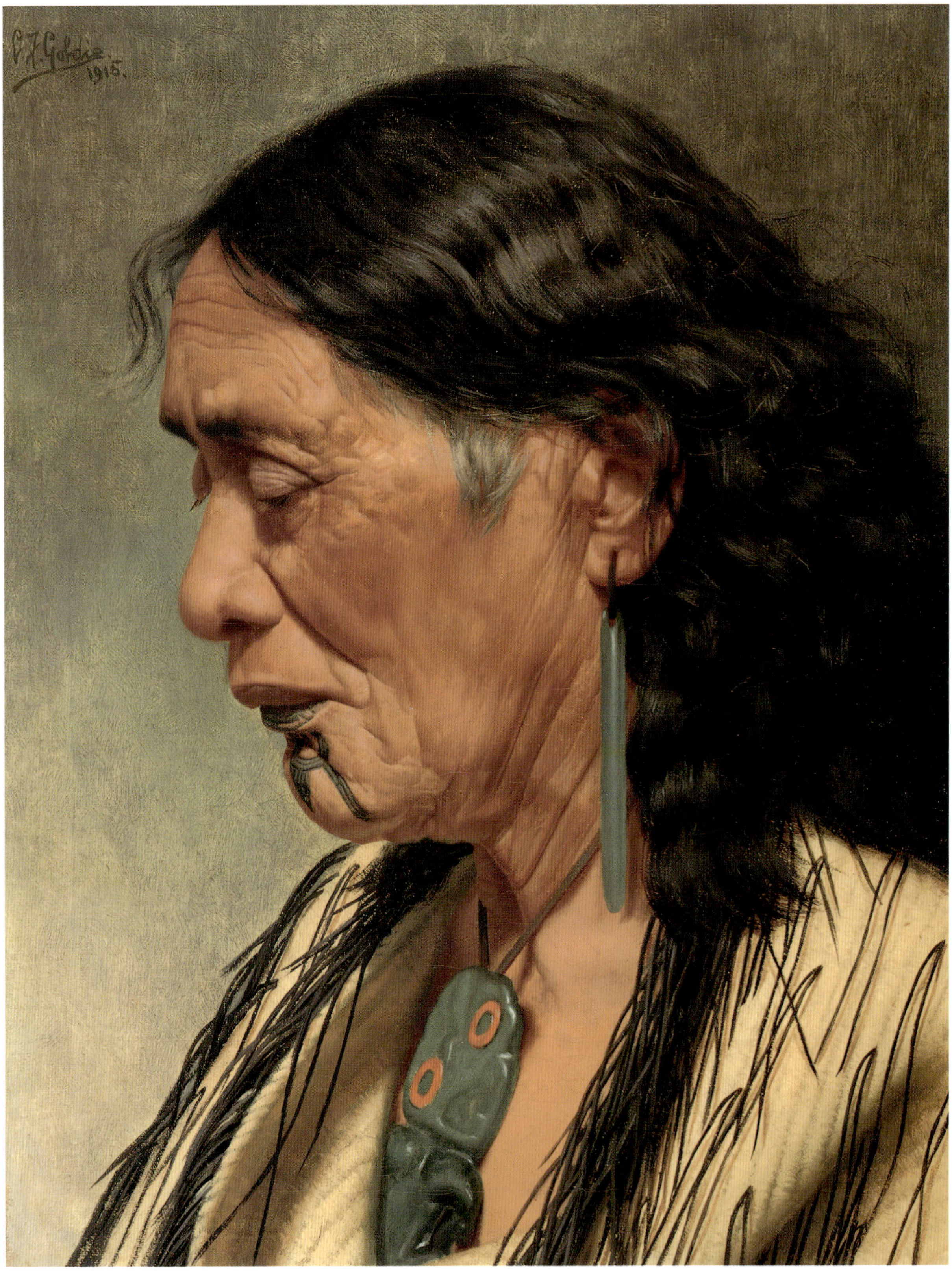

The Widow 1915
Pirira Te Kahukura (Ngāheke),
Tūhourangi, Ngāti Whakaue
oil on canvas, 380 x 305 mm
private collection

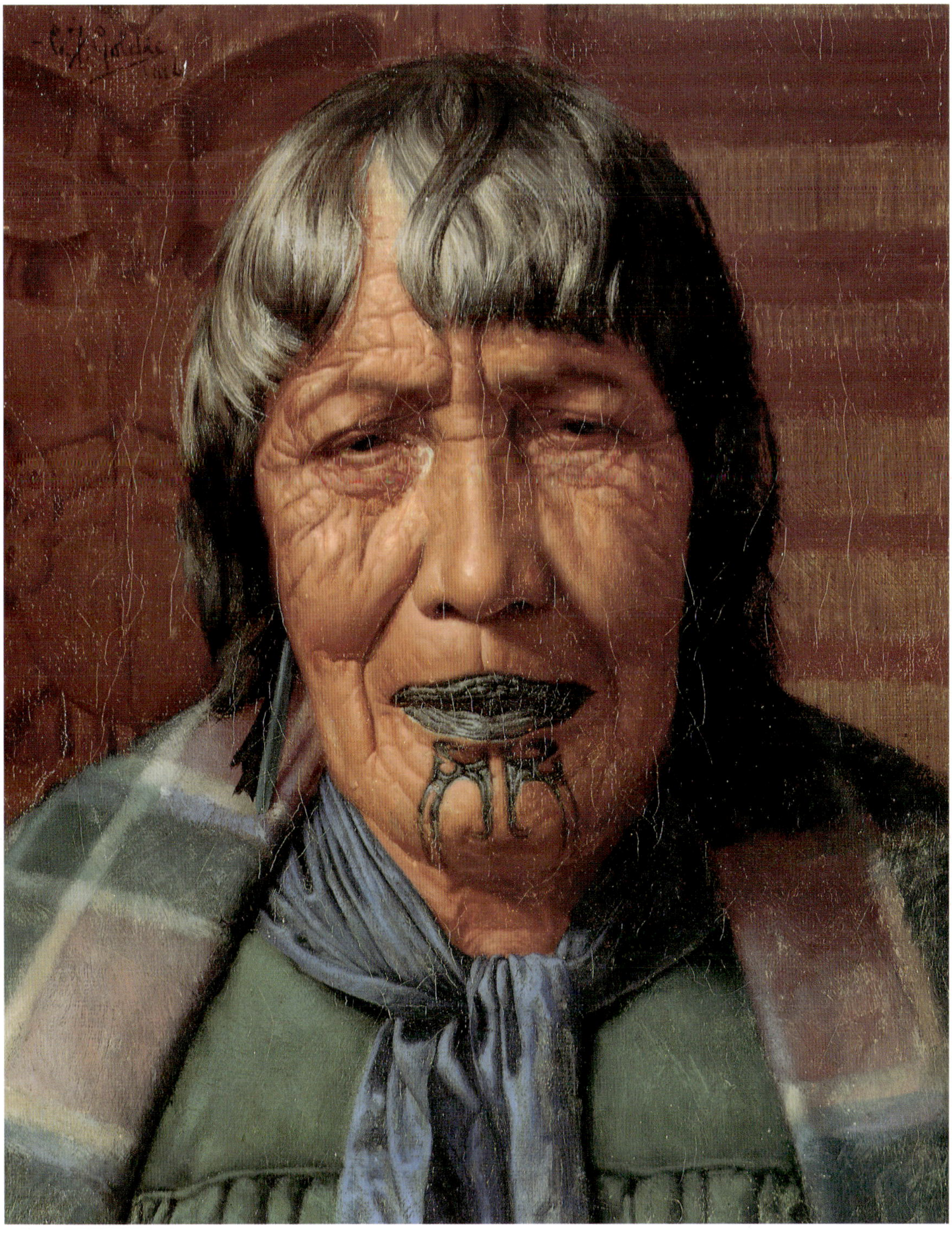

Te Aitu Te Irikau, an Arawa Chieftainess 1916
Te Aitu Te Irikau, Te Arawa
oil on canvas, 260 x 205 mm
private collection

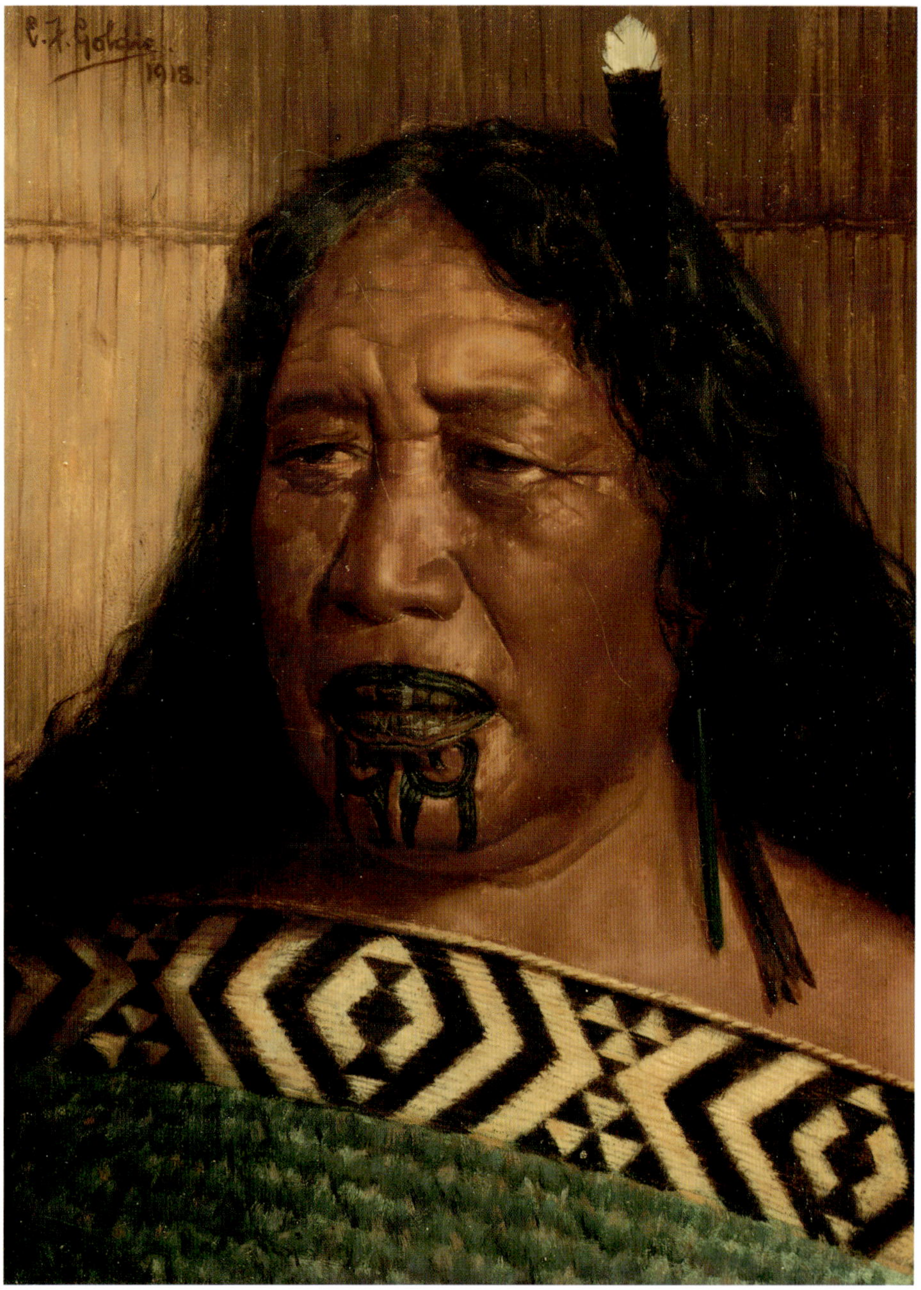

A High-born Lady 1918
Kiri Mātao, Ngāti Whakaue
oil on canvas, 230 x 180 mm
private collection

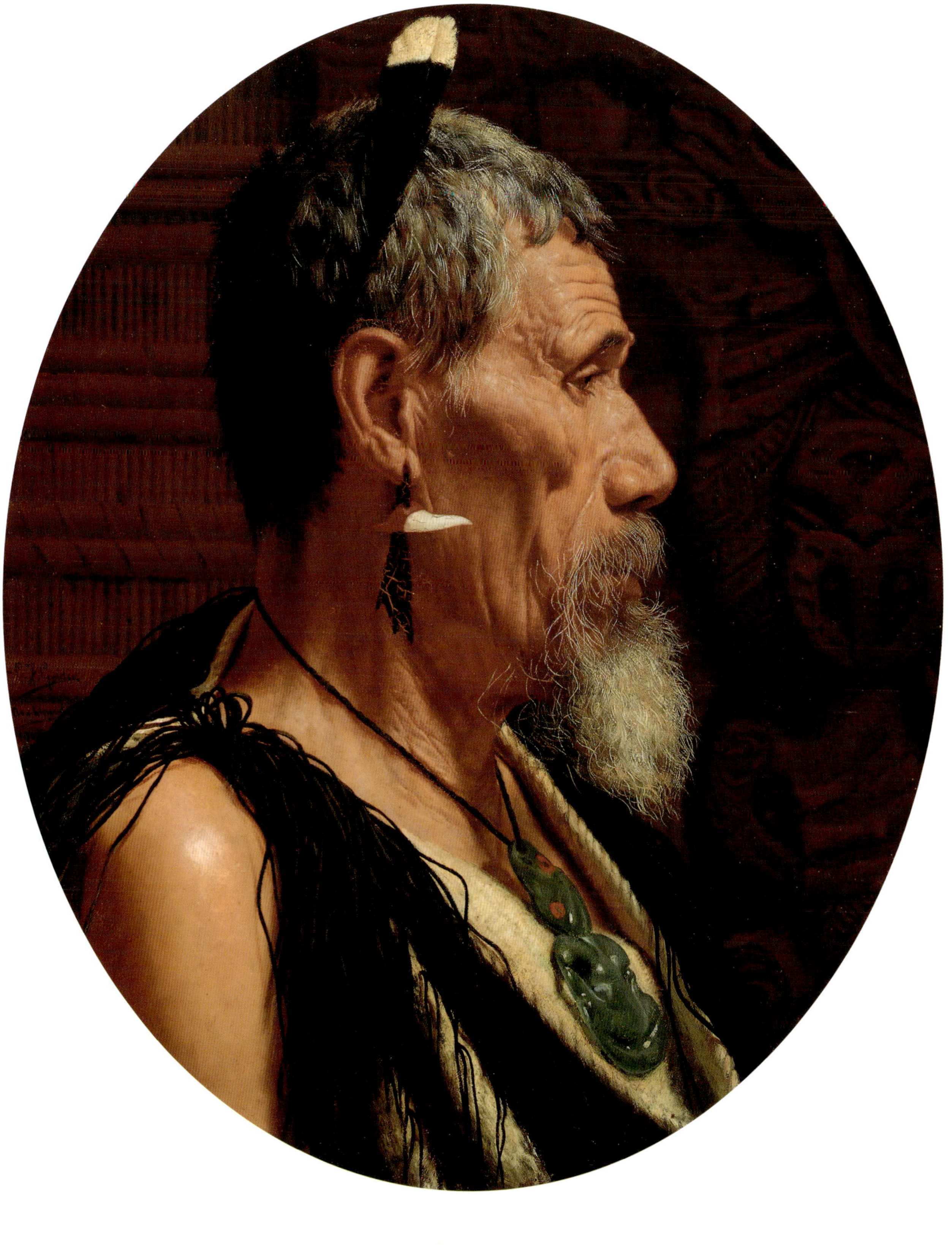

Anaha Te Rahui 1916
Anaha Te Rāhui, Ngāti Tarāwhai
oil on canvas, 615 x 510 mm
Auckland Museum, gift of Olive Goldie, 1951

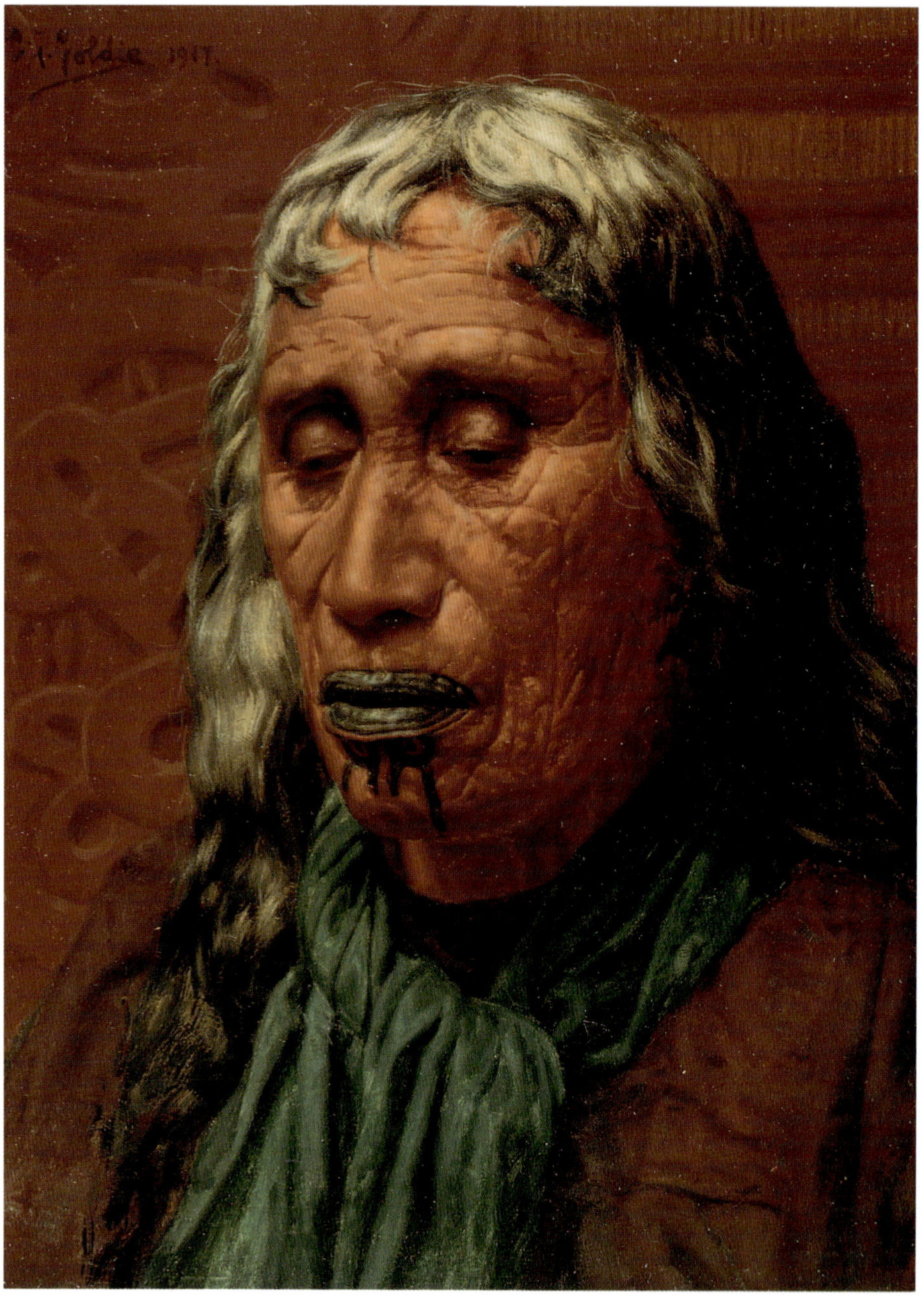

Memories of a Heroine: Hera Puna, widow of the late noted chieftain Hori Ngakapa of the Ngati Whanaunga Tribe 1917
Hera Puna, Ngāti Whanaunga

oil on canvas, 230 x 180 mm

Auckland Museum, bequest of Gertrude Edith Bell, 1985

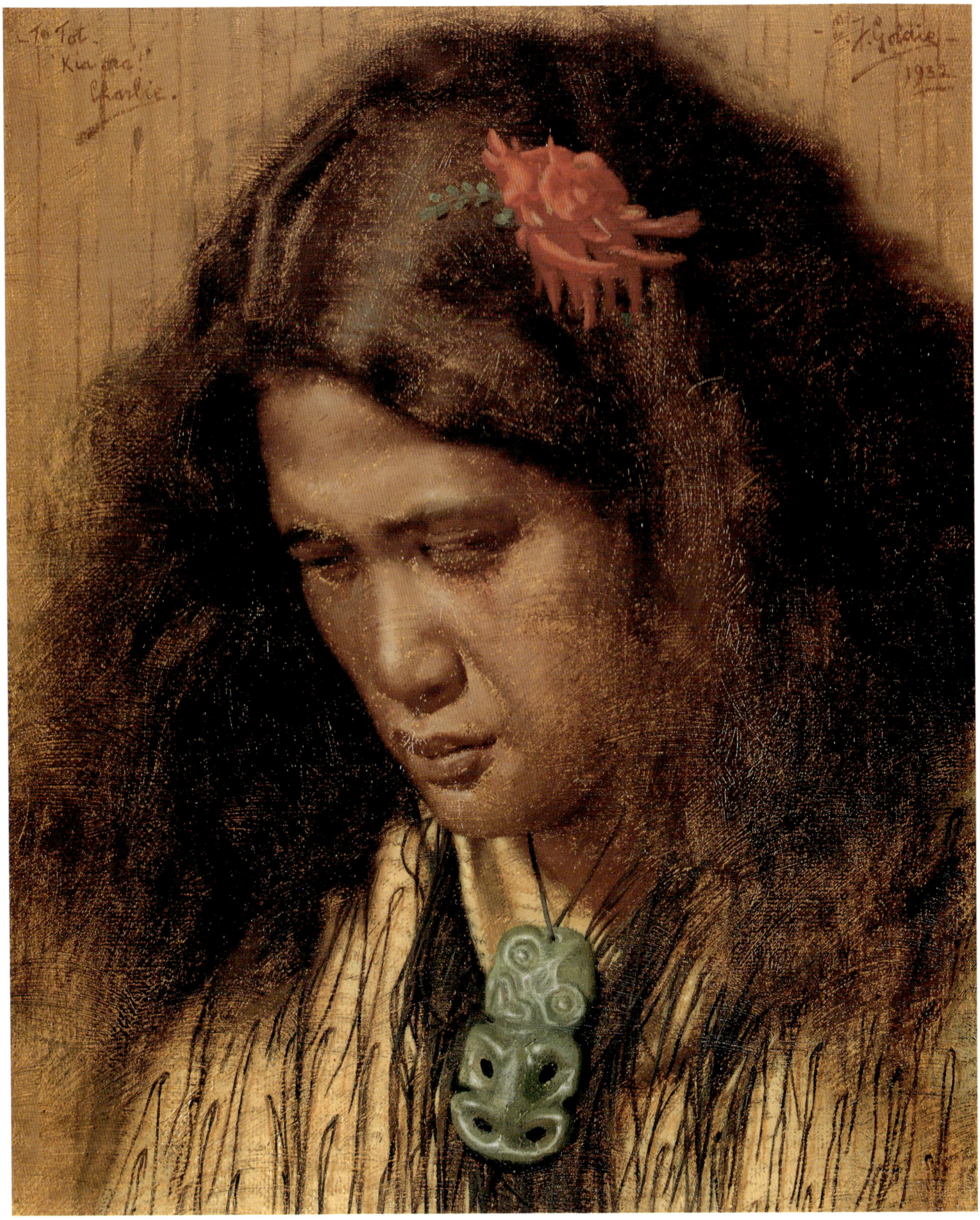

Reverie 1932
Hinemoa, Te Arawa
oil on canvas, 307 x 256 mm
private collection

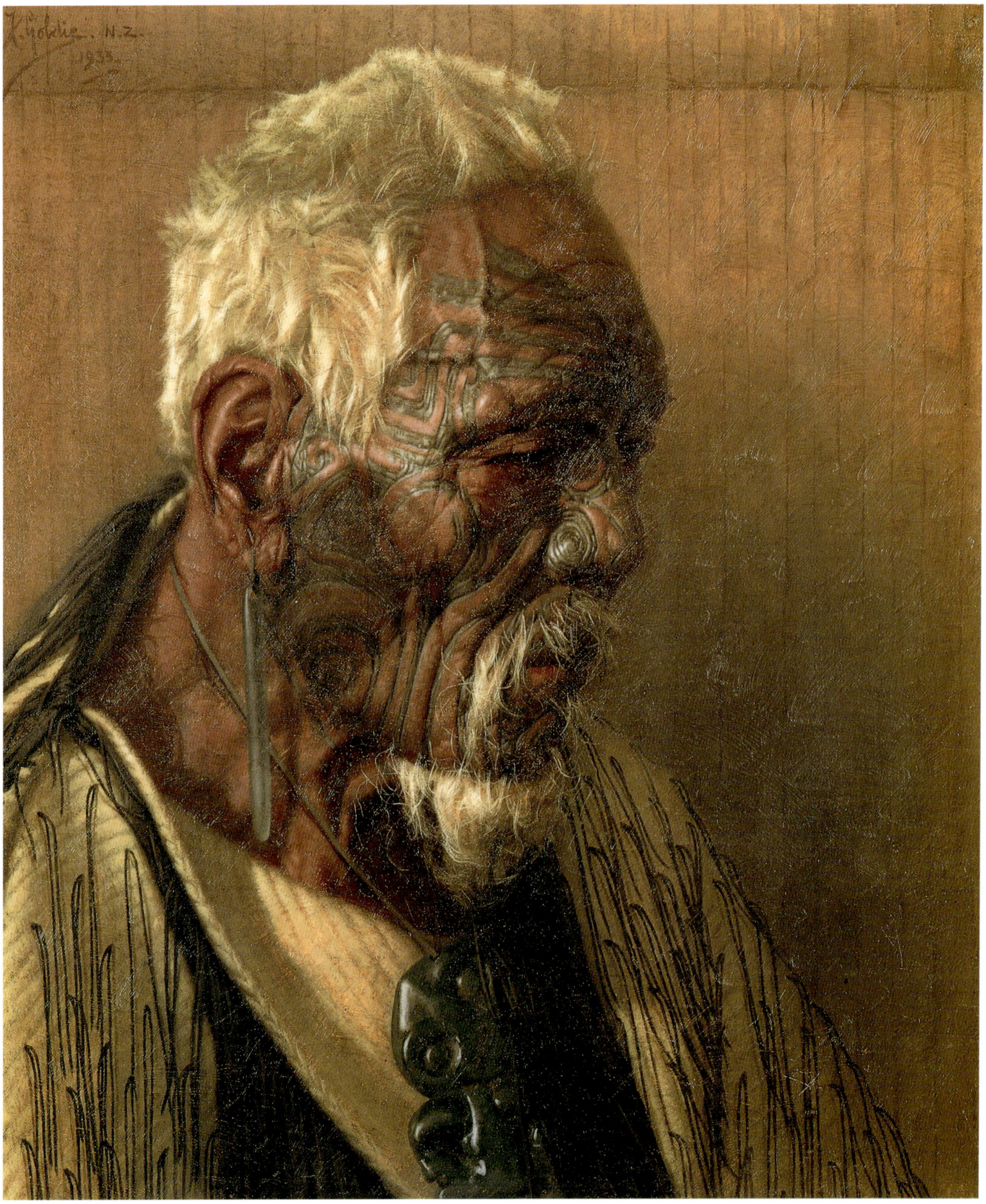

Thoughts of a Tohunga: Wharekauri Tahuna 1933
Te Wharekauri Tahuna, Ngāti Manawa
oil on canvas, 495 x 443 mm
Museum of New Zealand Te Papa Tongarewa (neg. no. B41012)

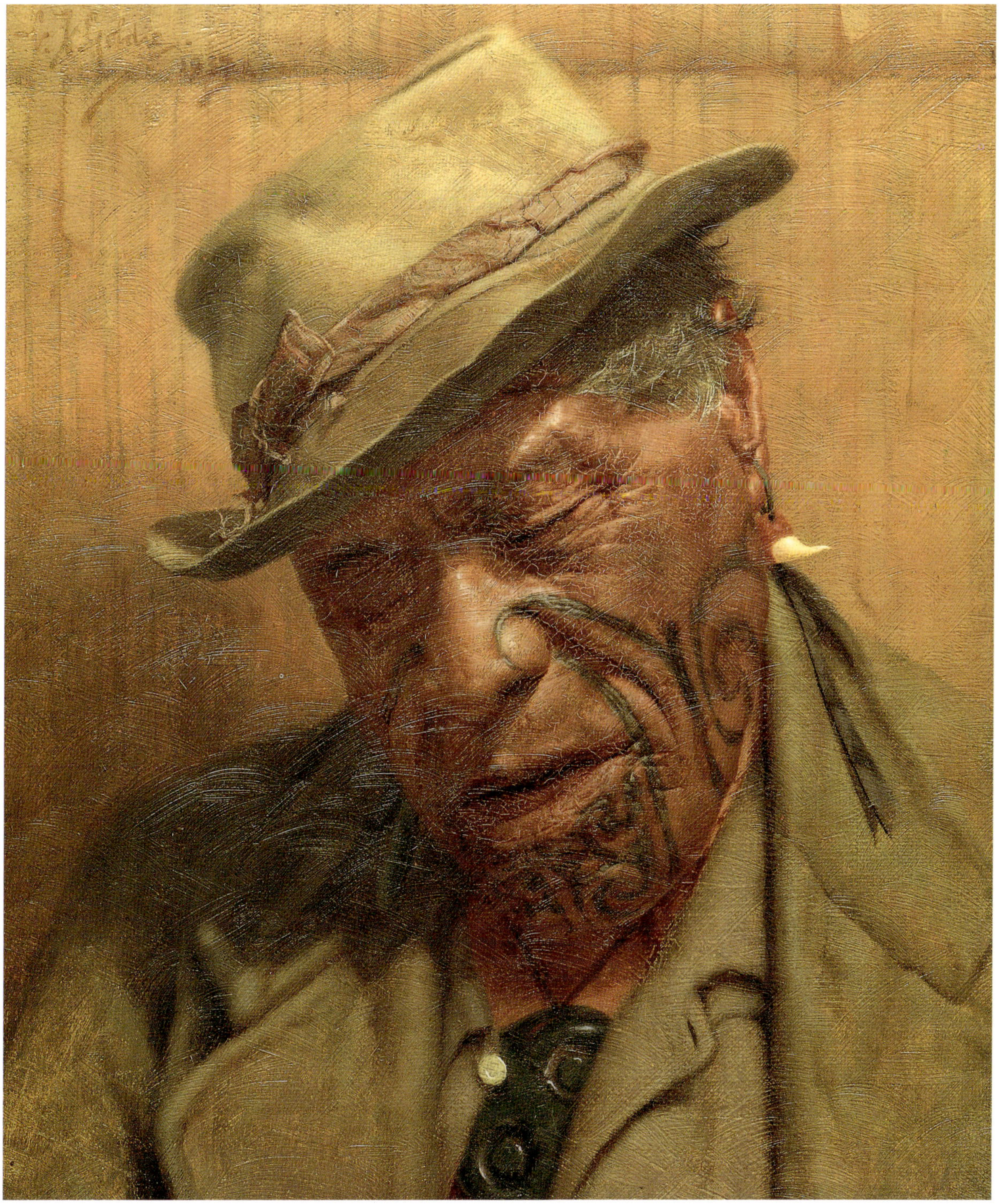

Sleep, 'tis a Gentle Thing:
Pokai, a Warrior Chieftain of the Ngatimaru Tribe 1933
Hōri Pōkai, Ngāti Maru, Ngāti Pāoa
oil on canvas, 405 x 357 mm
private collection

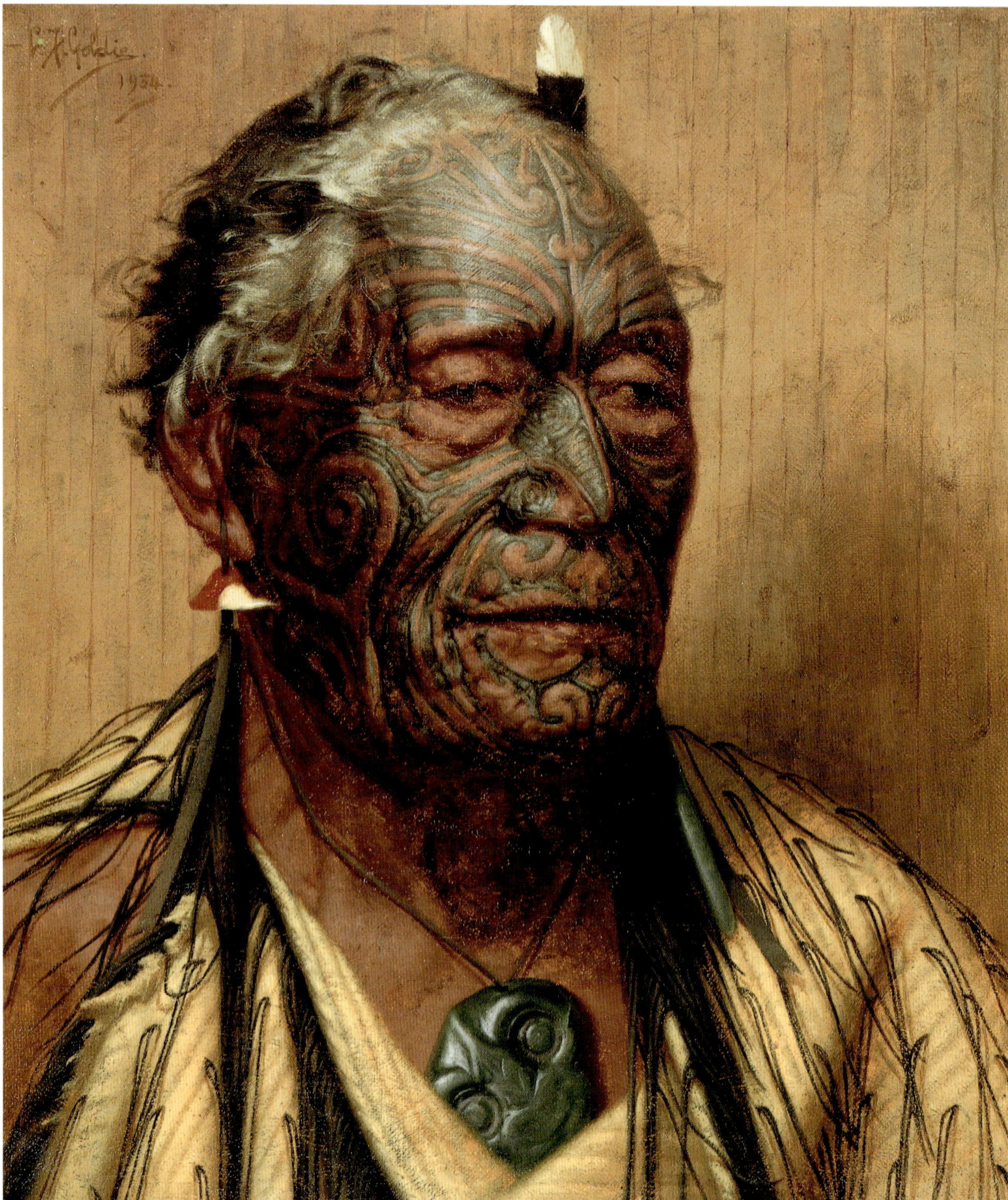

Tamati Waaka Nene 1934
Tamati Wāka Nene, Ngā Puhi
oil on canvas, 455 x 405 mm
Waitangi National Trust, on loan to Auckland Art Gallery Toi o Tāmaki

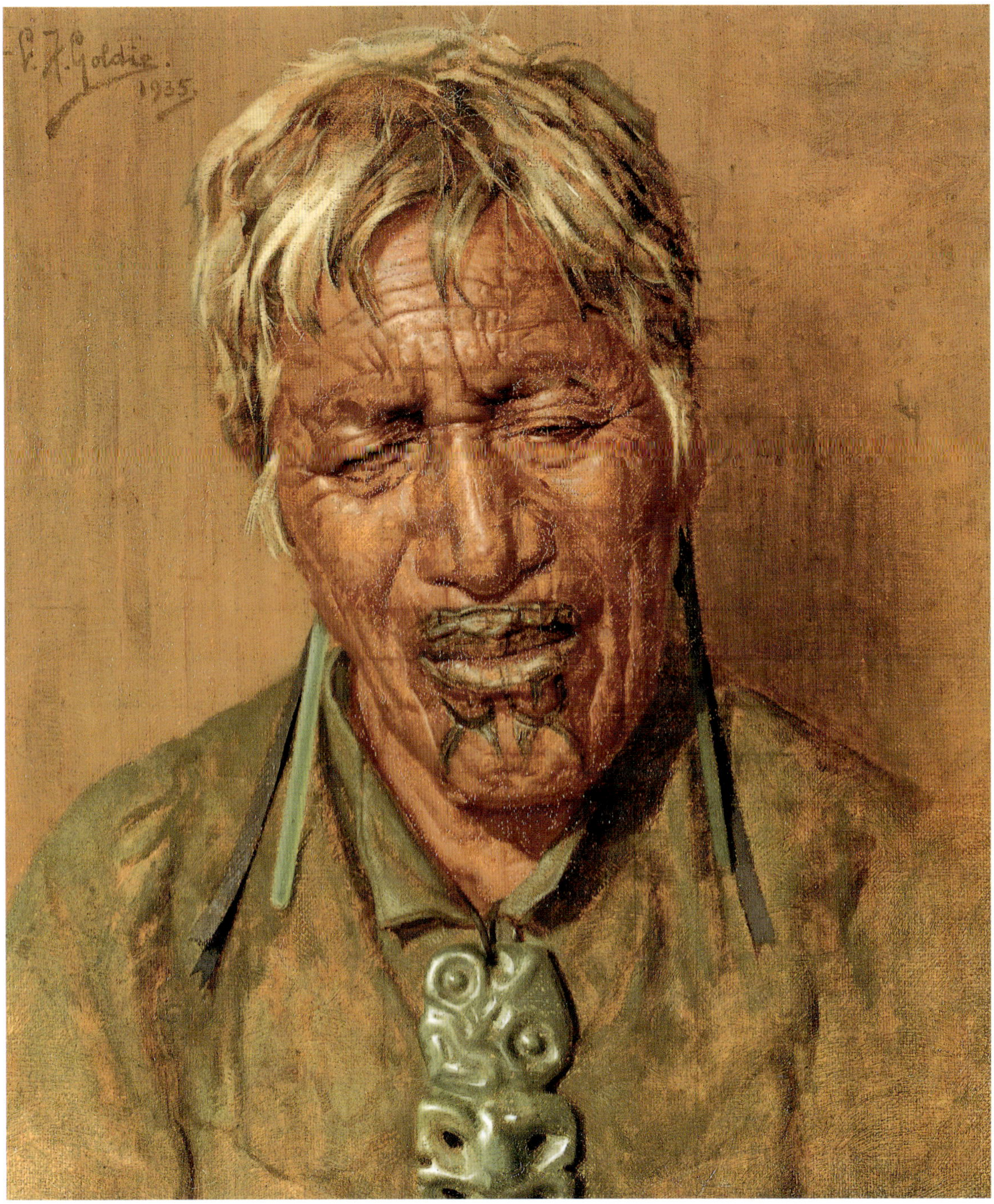

Sweet Idleness: Rahapa, an Arawa Chieftainess 1935
Rahapa Hinetapu, Ngāti Whakaue
oil on canvas, 405 x 350 mm
private collection

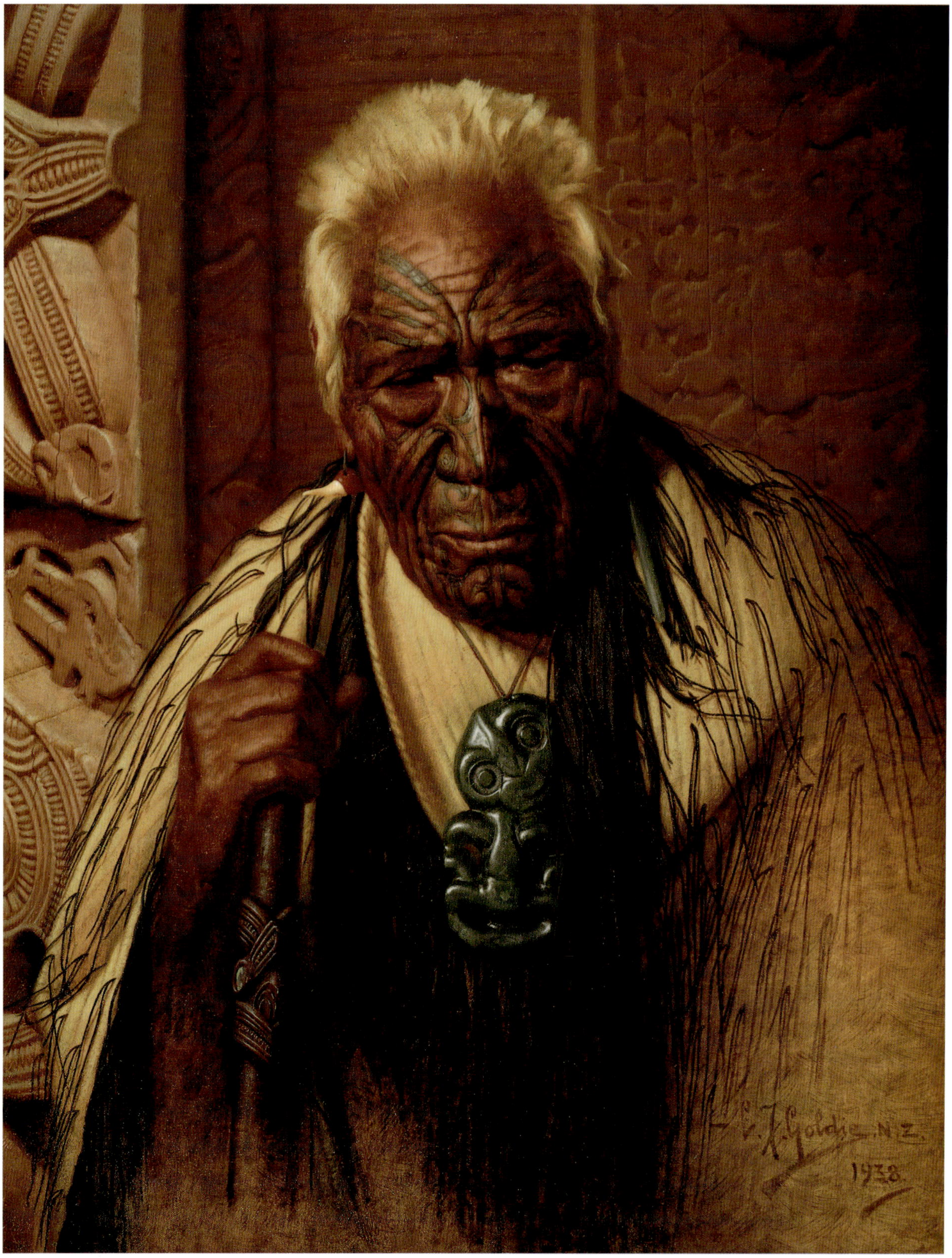

Thoughts of a Tohunga: Wharekauri Tahuna, a Chieftain of the Tuhoe Tribe 1938
Te Wharekauri Tahuna, Ngāti Manawa
oil on canvas, 765 x 612 mm
collection of Huka Lodge, Taupō

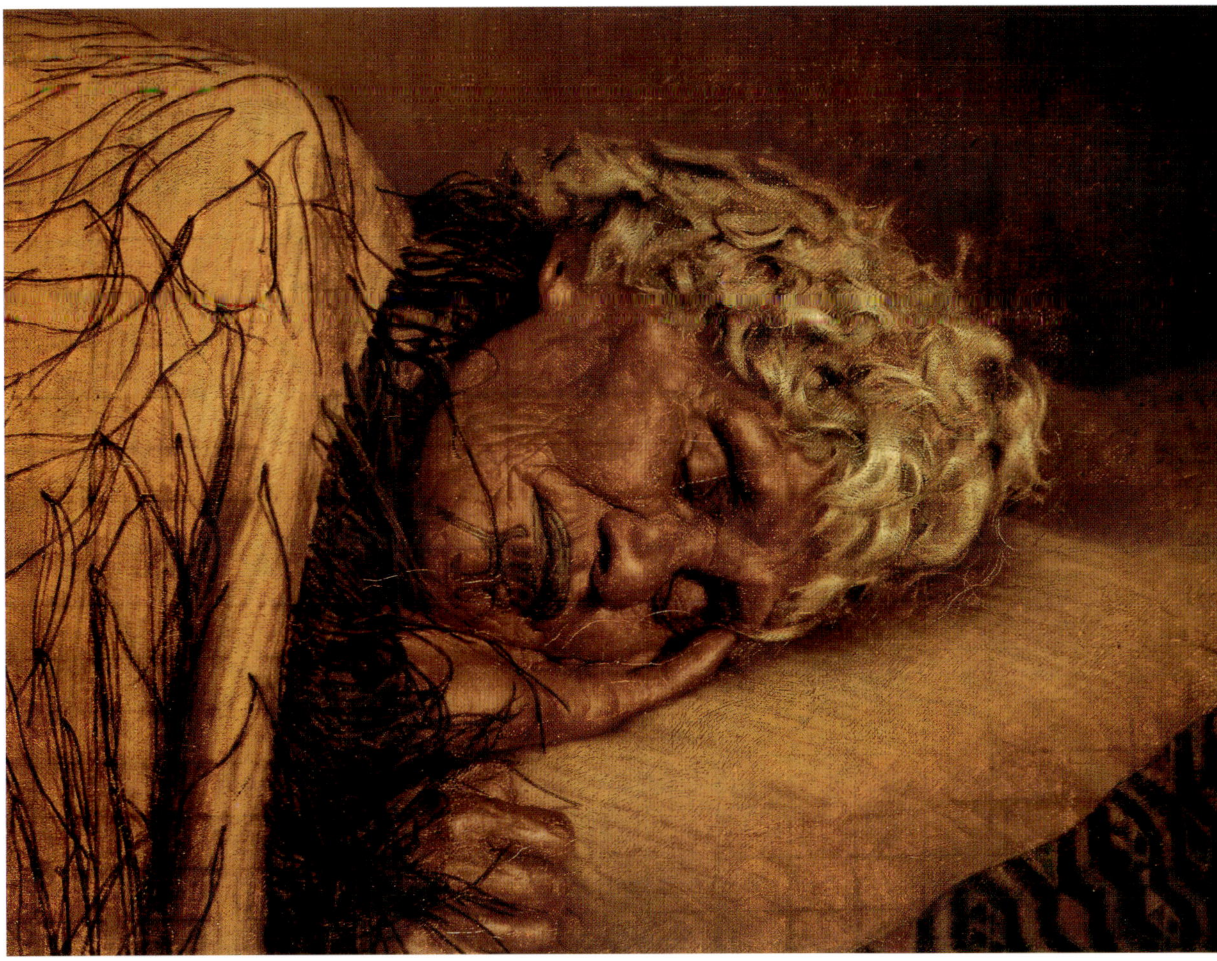

In Dreamland: Ena Te Papatahi,
A Chieftainess of the Ngapuhi Tribe 1937
Ina Te Papatahi, Ngā Puhi
oil on canvas, 380 x 505 mm
private collection

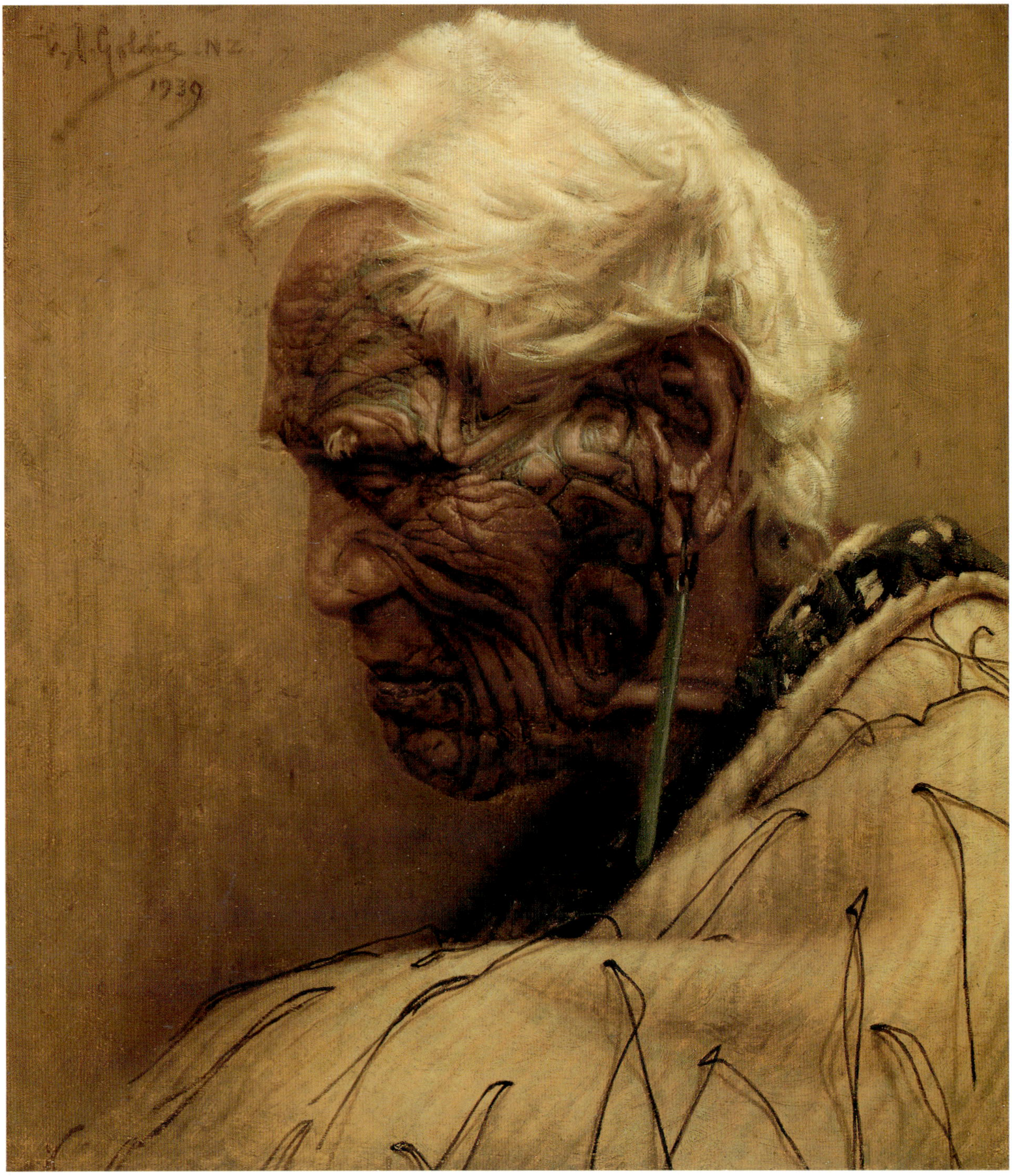

Weary with Years: A Waiuku Chieftain 1939
Aperahama Rairai, Ngāti Te Ata

oil on canvas, 460 x 410 mm

Auckland Art Gallery Toi o Tāmaki, gift of Harold T. Thomas, in memory of his wife, May Elizabeth Thomas, 1989

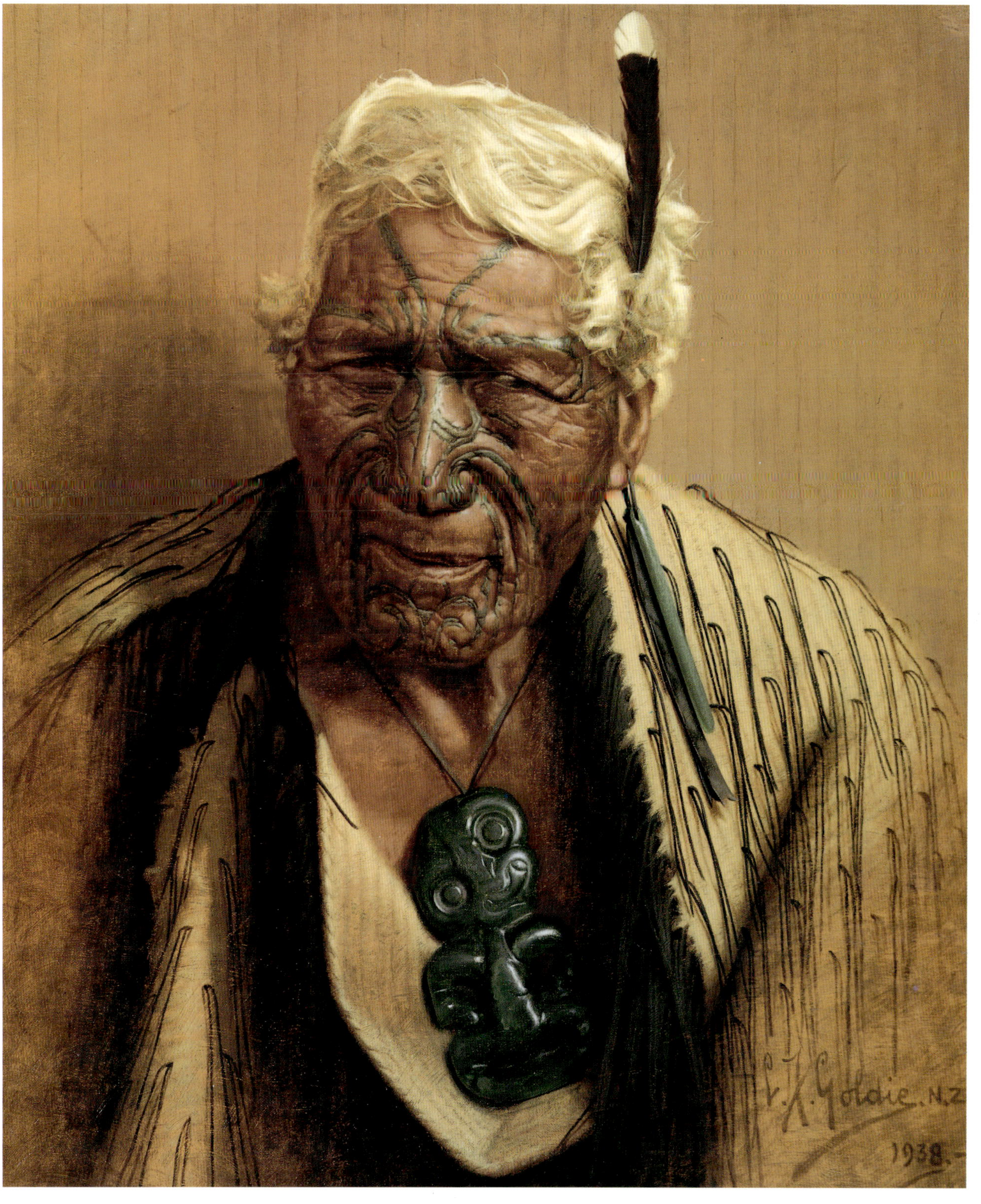

In Doubt 1938
Atama Paparangi, Te Rarawa
oil on canvas, 590 x 510 mm
Dunedin Public Art Gallery

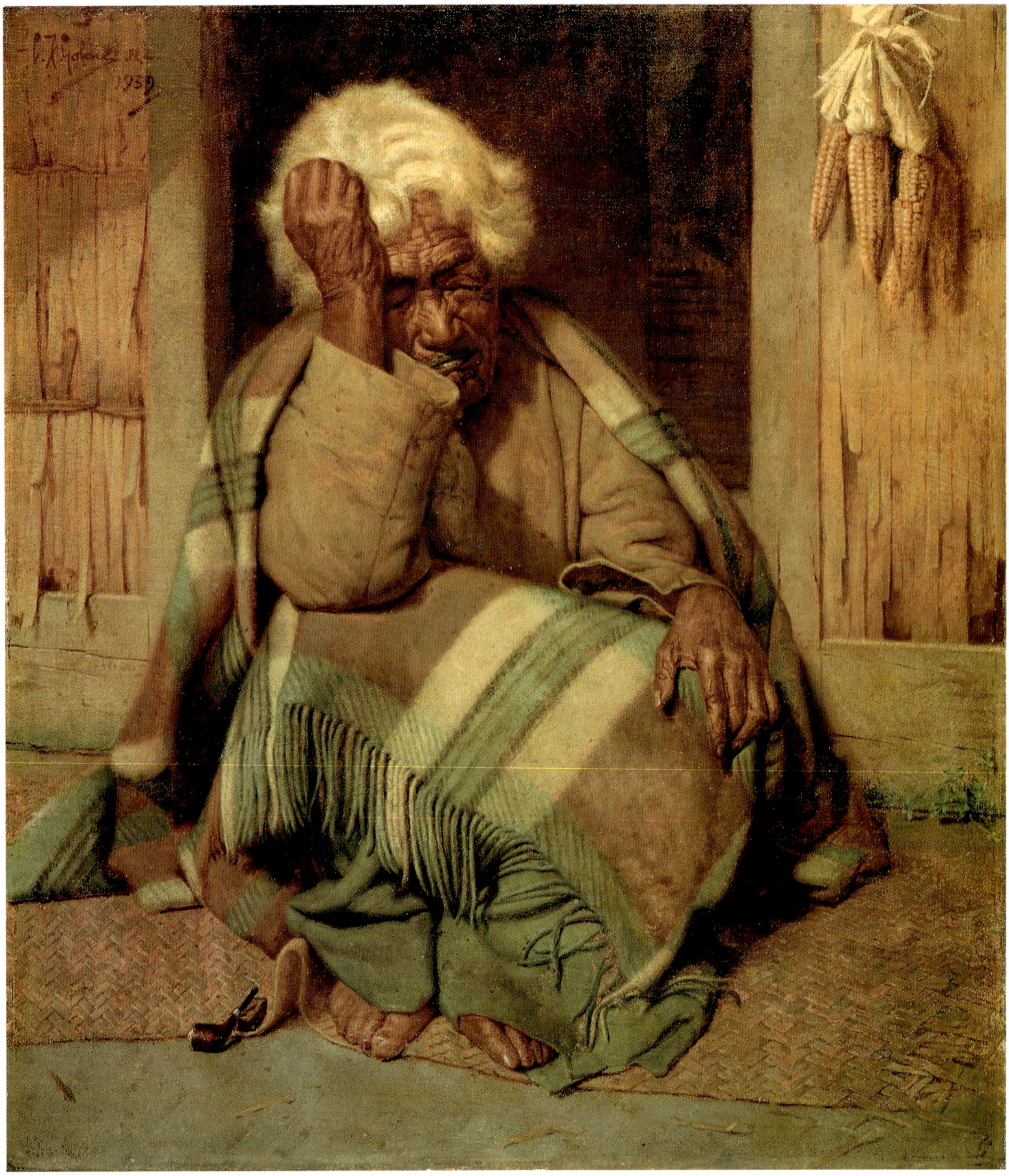

A Hundred Years Have Passed: Kapi Kapi, a Chieftainess of the Arawa Tribe 1939
Ahinata Te Rangitautini (Kapekape), Tūhourangi
oil on canvas, 460 x 410 mm
Auckland Art Gallery Toi o Tāmaki,
gift of Charles F. Goldie, in memory of his mother, 1939

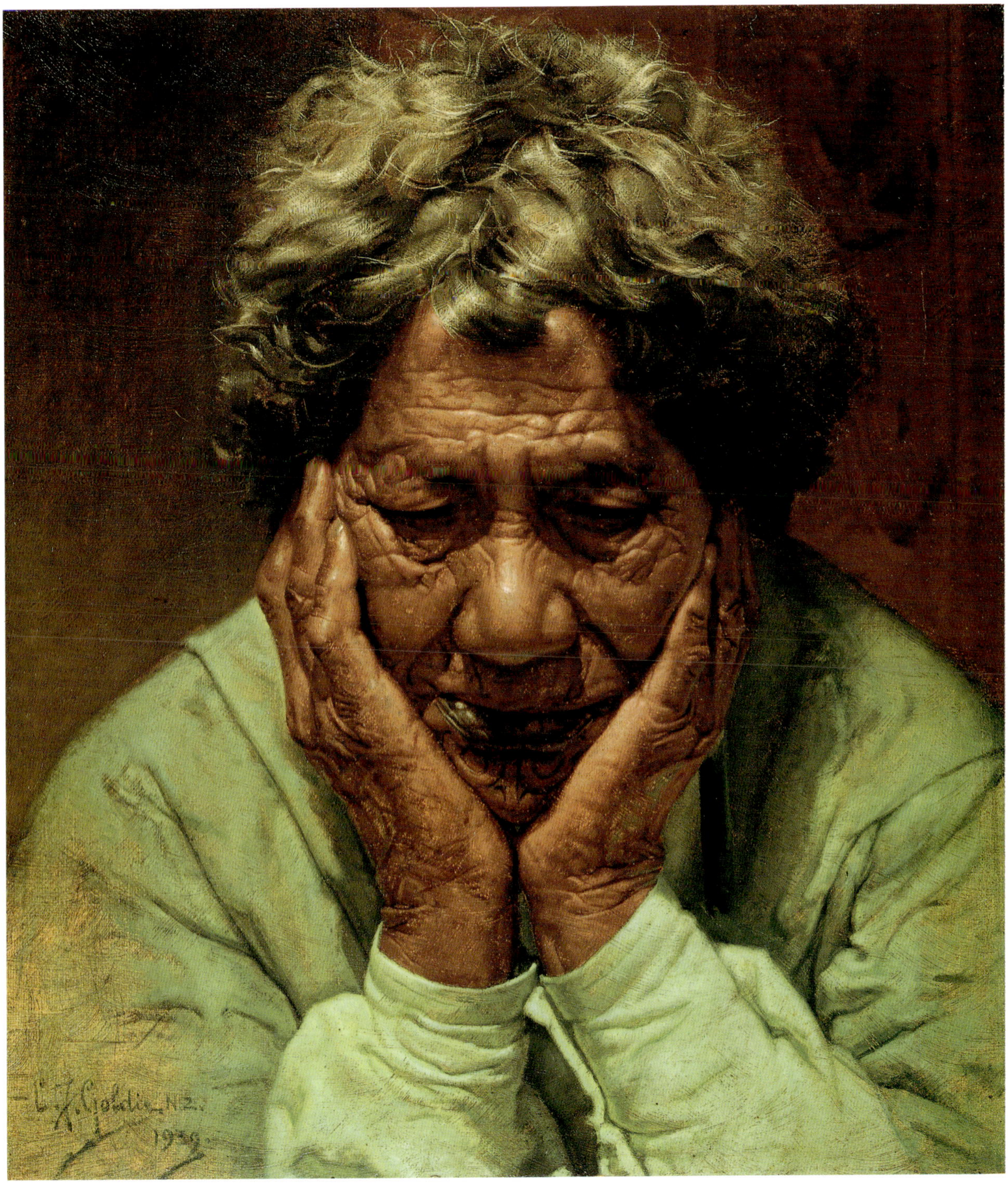

Reverie: Pipi Haerehuka, A Famous Chieftainess of the Arawa Tribe 1939
Pipi Haerehuka (Te Ārani), Ngāti Whakaue

oil on canvas, 460 x 410 mm
Auckland Art Gallery Toi o Tāmaki,
gift of Charles F. Goldie, in memory of his mother, 1939

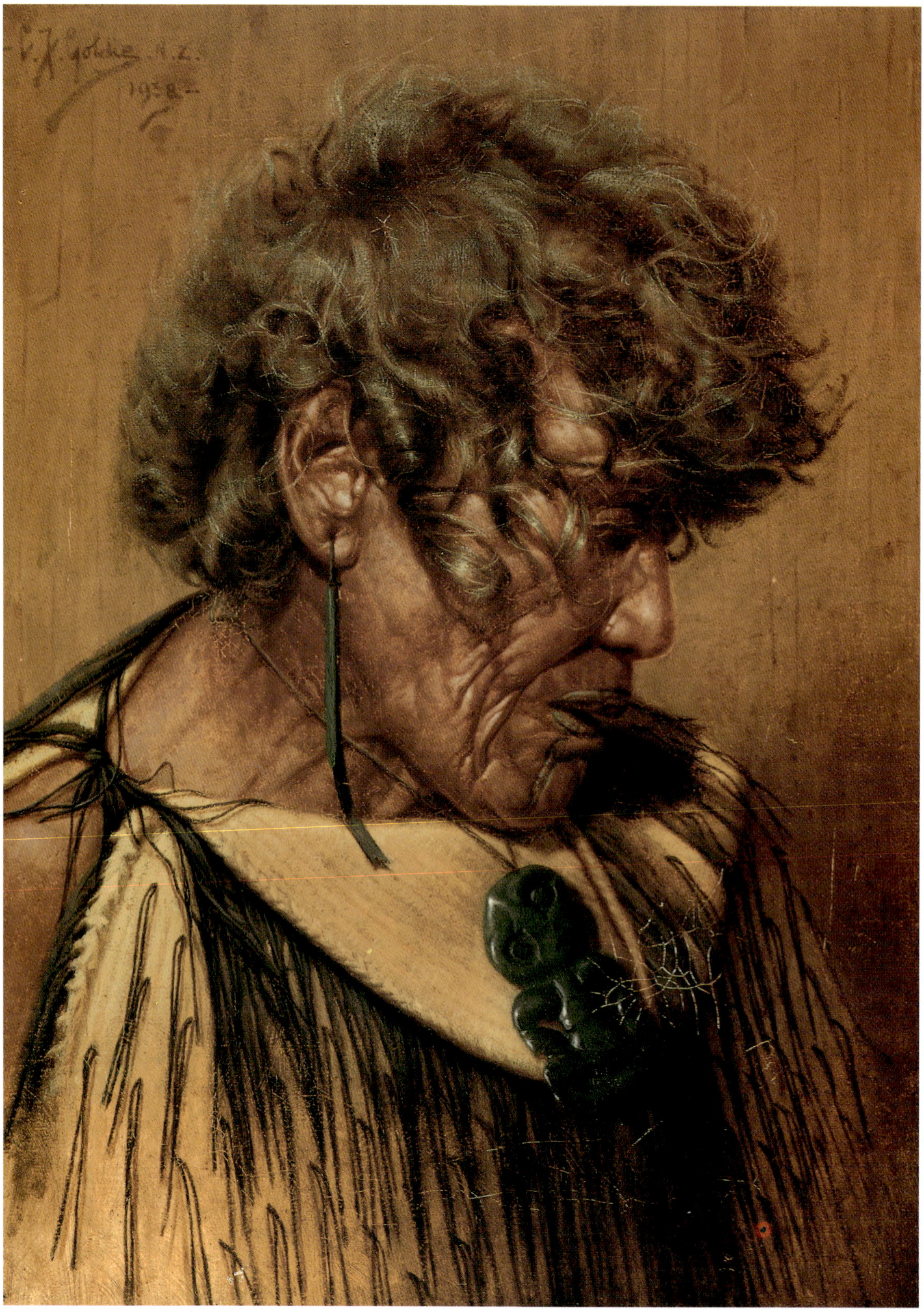

Grief (at a tangi): a Ngatimaru mourner 1938
oil on canvas, 405 x 307 mm
private collection

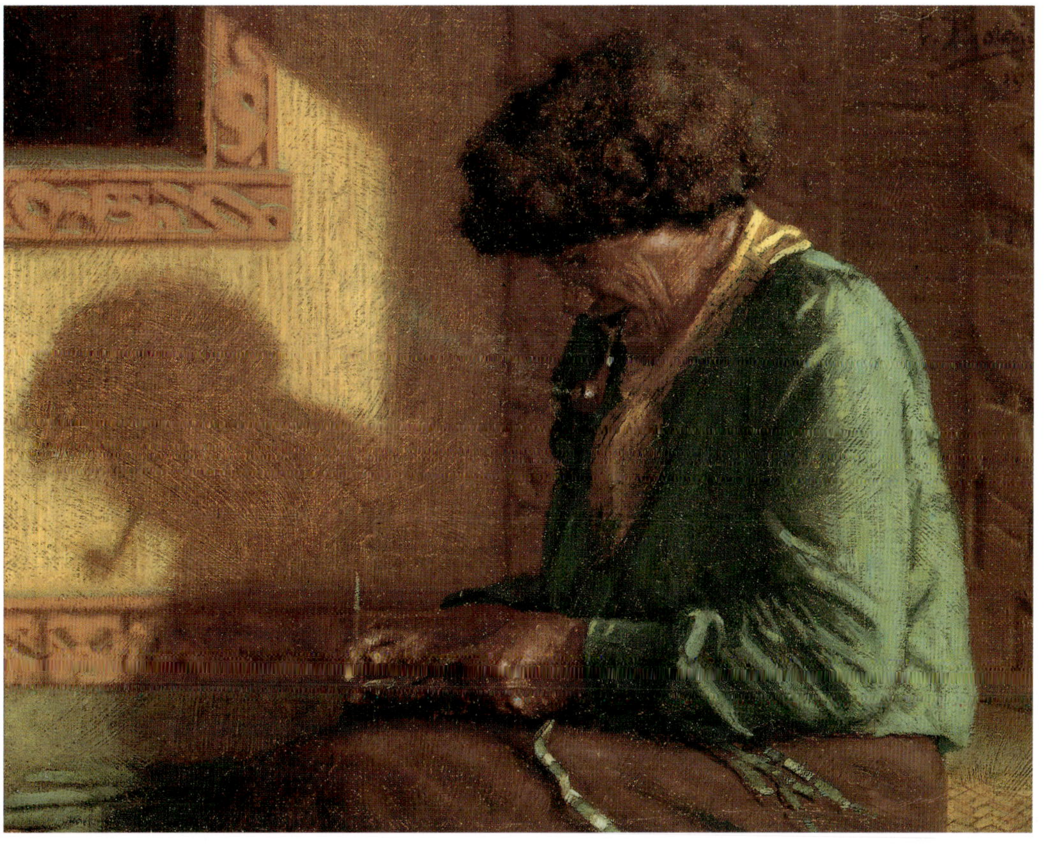

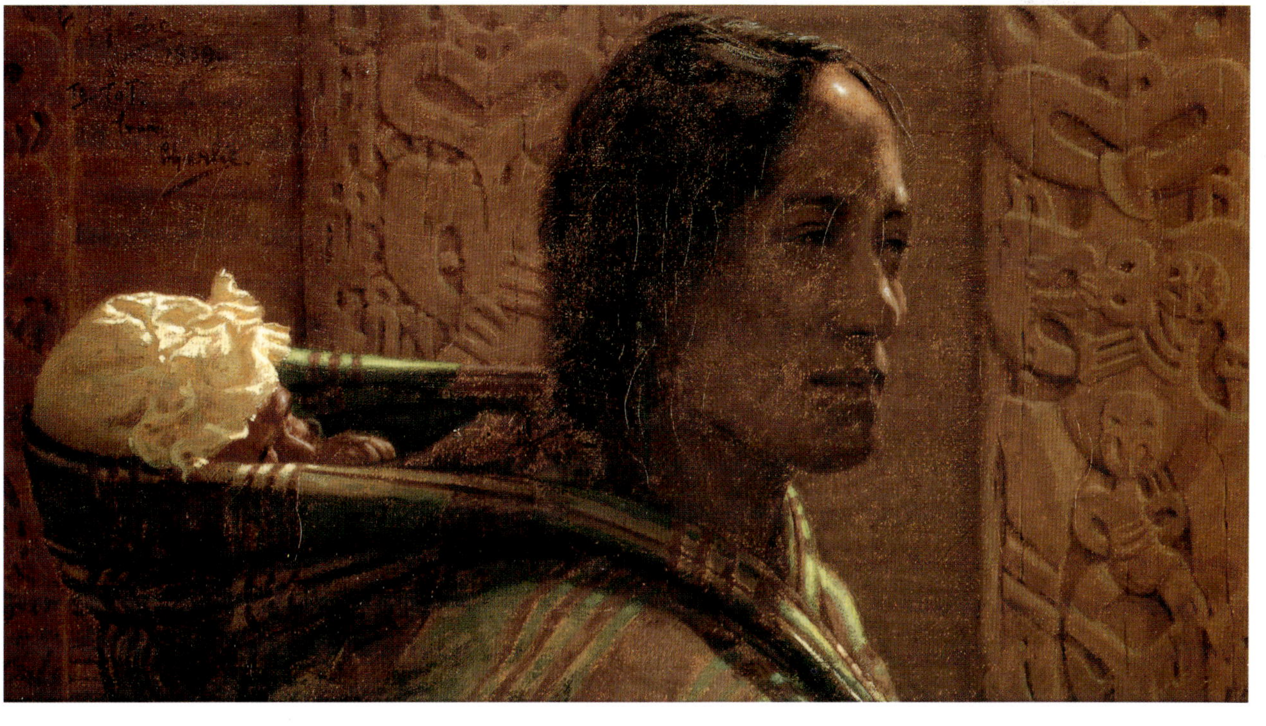

[above]
Solitude, Smoke, Smiles and Shadows 1939
oil on canvas, 210 x 255 mm
private collection

[below]
Ancestors and Descendants 1939
oil on canvas, 205 x 360 mm
private collection

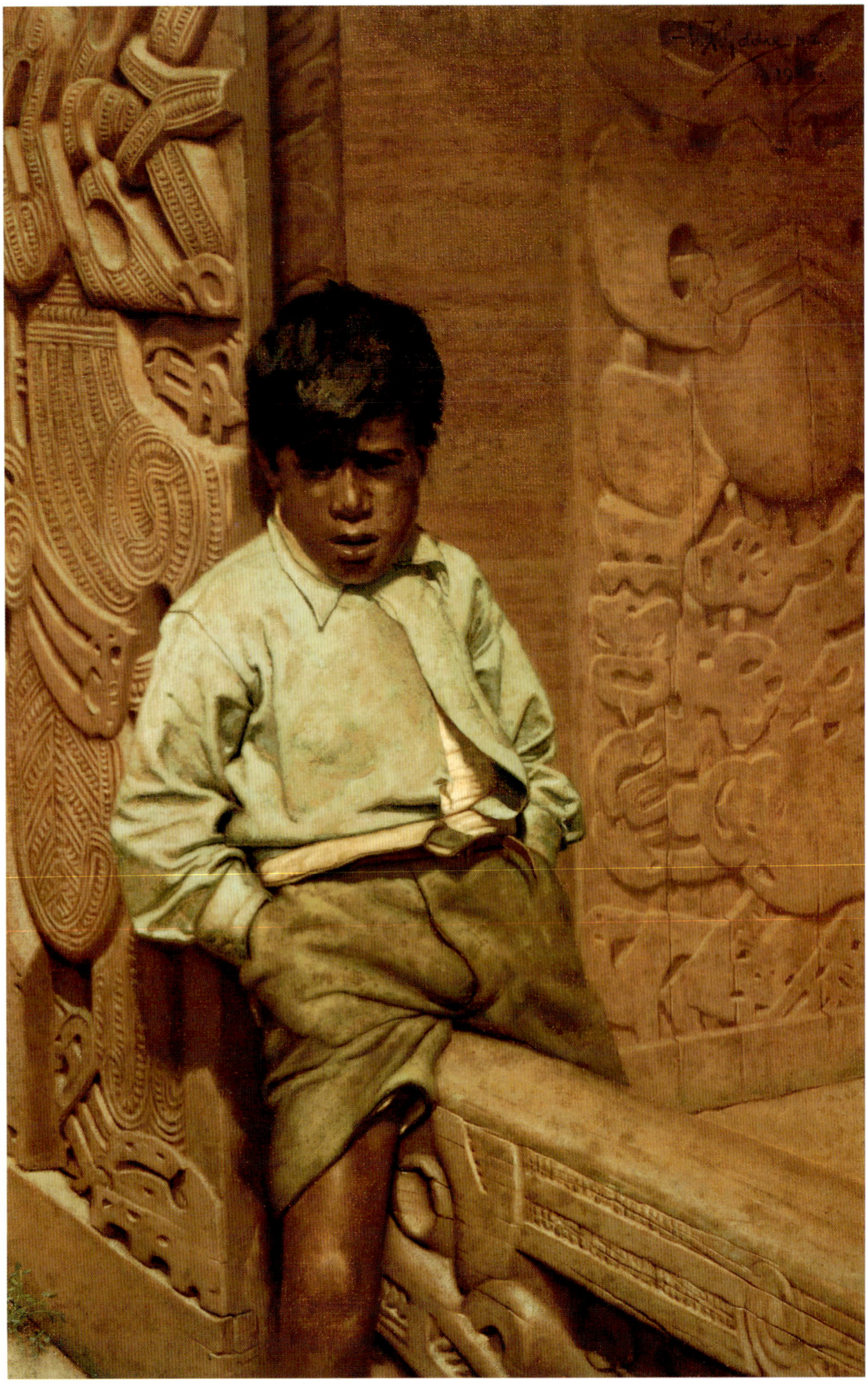

The Heir Apparent, Ohinemutu, Rotorua 1939
oil on canvas, 610 x 405 mm
private collection

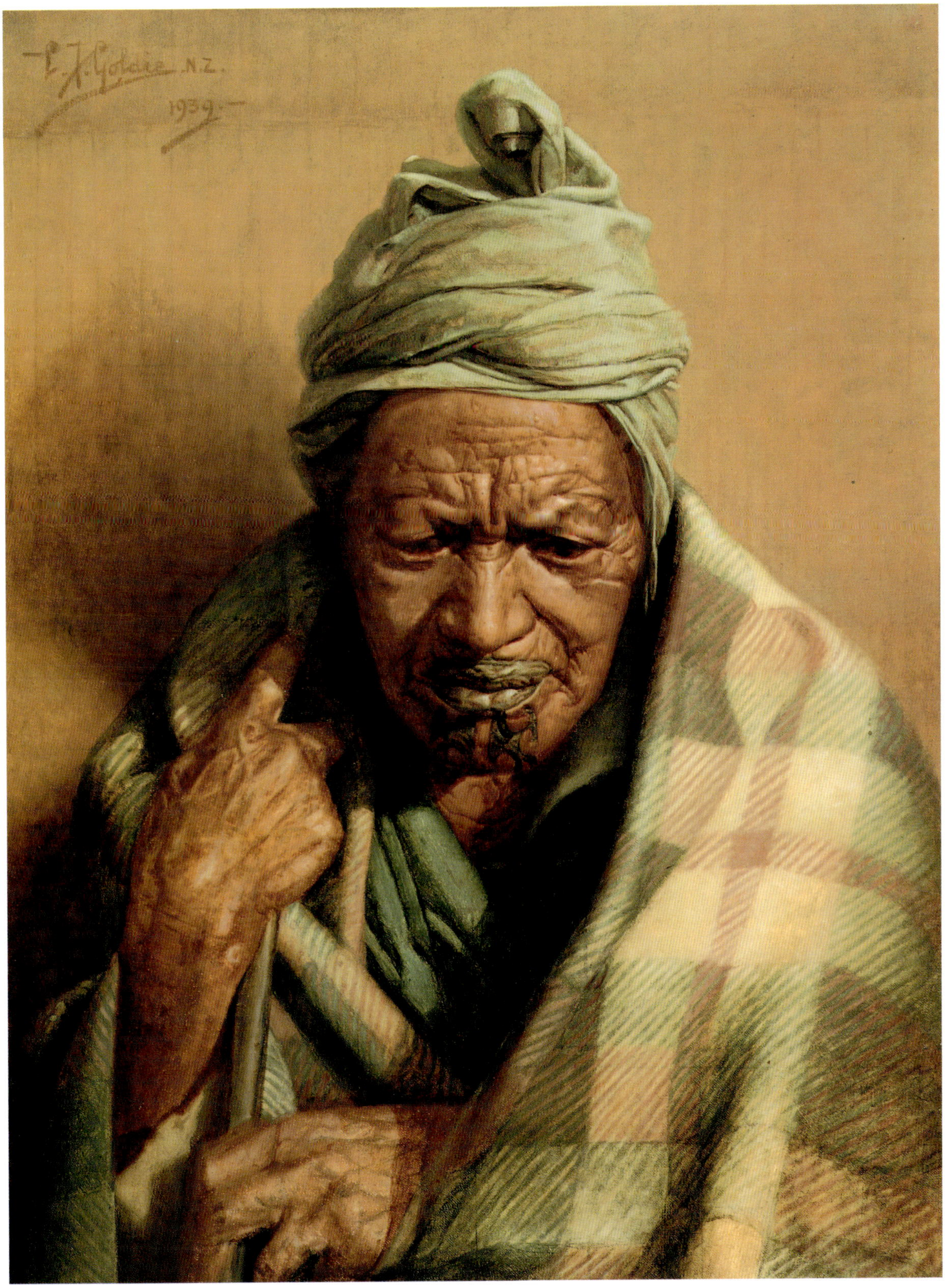

Wife of Tumai Tawhiti, living at Tarukenga, Rotorua 1939
Te Aotiti, Te Arawa, Ngāti Tūwharetoa
oil on canvas, 660 x 510 mm
private collection

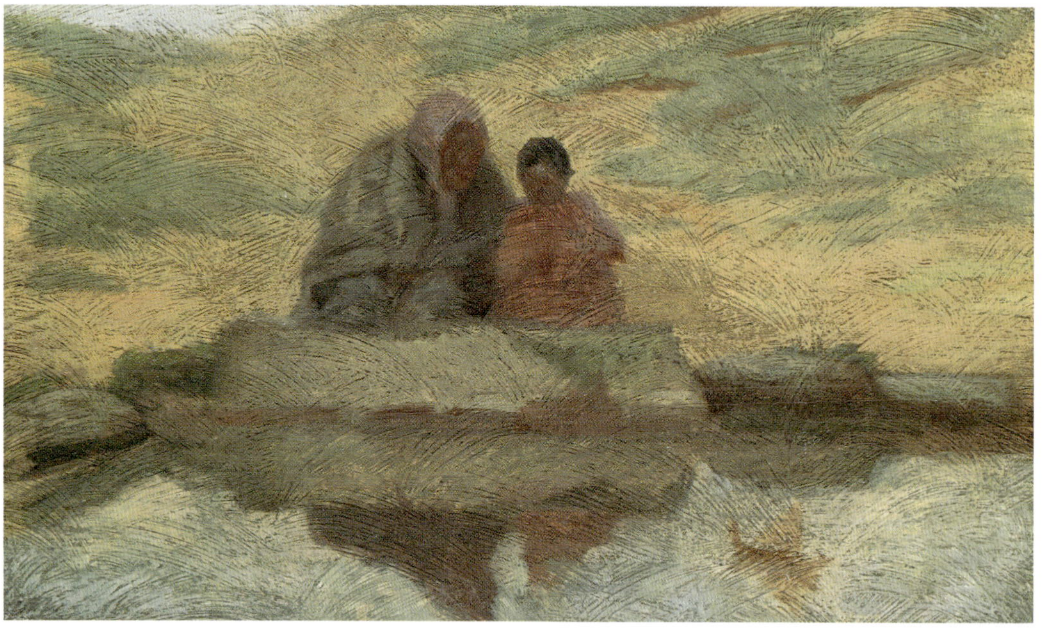

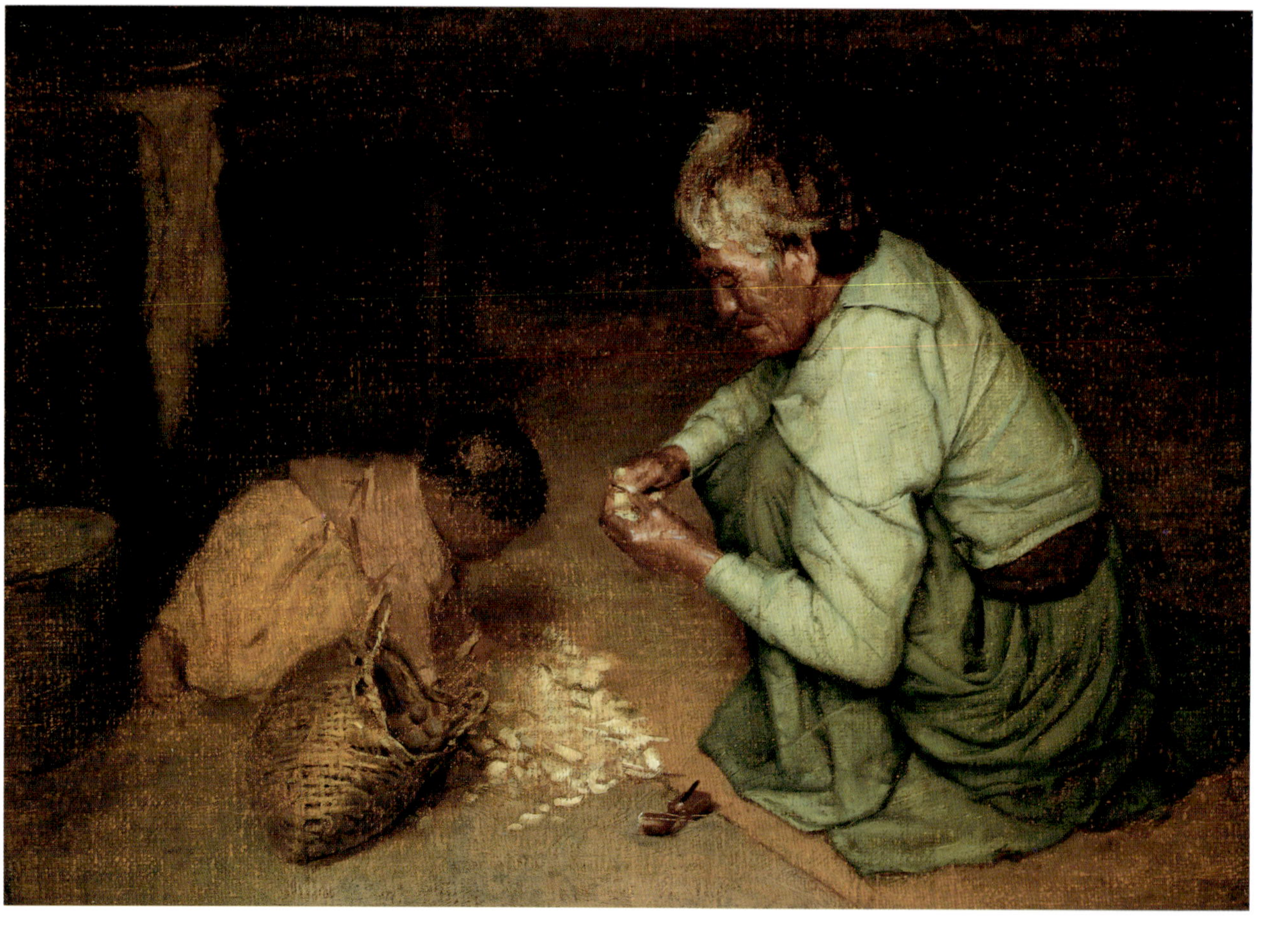

[above]
The Story of the Arawa Canoe c.1940
oil on panel, 115 x 197 mm
Auckland Art Gallery Toi o Tāmaki

[below]
Rahapa, Ohinemutu 1941
oil on canvas, 240 x 345 mm
private collection

selected historical writings

H. P. SEALY
: L'Académie Julian in Paris (1901)

RICHARD ARNOLD SINGER
: Mr C. F. Goldie and his Pictures (1903)

TAKAHI ATAMA PAPARANGI
: Ki a Te Koori, Mr 'Goldie' (1914)

TE HEUHEU TŪKINO
: Kia Mōhio Ngā Tāngata Katoa (c.1935)

CHARLES F. GOLDIE
: The Art Crisis. Auckland Gallery. Battle of the Schools. Modernism Condemned (1934)
: Letters to James Cowan regarding collaborative publications (1935)

JAMES COWAN
: Goldie's Collection. Last of the Rangatiras. Tattooed Chiefs and Kuias. Some Famous Old Maoris (1920)
: A Vanished Art. The Maori Moko. Last of the Tattooed Men (1935)
: The Art of C. F. Goldie: A Great Painter and Interpreter of a People (1941)

H. P. SEALY

H. P. Sealy is an enigmatic figure in New Zealand art history. He seems to have been a favourite pupil of L. J. Steele, in whose Auckland Academy of Art he was the first secretary. This role passed to Goldie in 1891, when Sealy left for two years of study at the Académie Julian. Although still in Paris when Goldie arrived, Sealy was then on the point of returning to Auckland. His lively description of the Académie provides a vivid insight into the Parisian milieu in which Goldie trained as an artist.

L'Académie Julian in Paris (1901)

When a man decides to study Art in Paris, it is quite unnecessary for him to have any qualifications for the purpose. All he requires to do is to call on the Secretary at the 'Académie Julian', lay the matter before him, and, if he decides to study there, he is immediately installed without any preliminaries at all. He is told that if he comes on Monday morning he had better be in good time, and secure a place near the model. This precaution is only necessary, however, in winter, as during the summer months there is only a sprinkling of students and the 'Nouveau', as he is called for the first week or two, can sit where he likes. He will also find that, whereas in summer amongst the few his presence will attract some attention, and he will be the butt of the presiding wits for the time being, in the winter months the new chum, unless perchance he happens to be over shy and self conscious, can make his *début* on Monday morning without molestation. Perhaps during the quarter of an hour's rest, which takes place once in every hour, some of his French critics will inform him that his drawing is *très chic*, and that he is well dressed, and if his work is exceptionally weak, he may be questioned as to whether he is studying for the 'Prix de Rome', which is considered the 'Blue Riband' of the Art World in France. Probably it will be suggested that he shall forthwith pay up his ten francs, being the contribution that each student is taxed for the use of 'fixatif', for the preservation of his charcoal drawings or for turpentine for the mixing of paints. Usually the money, which is collected by the 'Massier', or head student, and which is termed the 'Masse', amounts to a considerable sum in winter, when the studios are full of new arrivals, and if the Massier happens to be in a thirsty mood, he will stand up at the eleven o'clock rest, and shout, 'Messieurs, there are now eighty francs in the Masse; we go to drink!' The cry, *Nous allons boire!* is instantly universal, and the whole school makes a rush for the street, and takes possission of the nearest *café*, where a scene of indescribable confusion takes place, verily a 'Babel of many tongues'. What do we hear? Mostly French, good, bad and indifferent; English, German, Italian, Spanish, Polish, even Japanese, though at the time of which I am writing, only one student represented the land of strange pictures, and he invariably spoke English, flavoured with a strong American accent, for he had lived some years in the States, and was the politest and most amiable of Art students.

The casual observer would be amused to notice, long after the first mad rush is over, the English 'Nouveau', spotlessly clad in check suit and high collar, with his slow, dignified stride, half shy of joining in, and yet feeling it is the proper thing to do. If he should find another of his own sort, to whom he has been duly presented, he will probably take him to another *café*, where each will, as in duty bound, 'shout' solemnly for the other. And how different will be the ways and appearance of both after the 'shaking up' of a month in a French Art School!

At the time of which we write there was, one Monday morning, a fresh arrival, who, though possessing something of the English 'Nouveau's' shyness, had considerable ability as a comic singer, and this having got about, he was promptly 'bluffed' into believing that it was the proper thing to sing on his first day at the school. Having quite made up his mind that he was bound by the unwritten laws of the students to go through some more or less terrible ordeal, he was pleased at being so easily let off, and in a most good natured and affable manner got up, and sang an English comic song. The Frenchmen were delighted at this new departure on the part of 'Les Anglais', and, amid cheers (and jeers) he was informed that, in singing the second verse of a song, it was usual to mount his stool, which, being higher than his waist, made his position a trifle ricketty. However, with the courage of his race, he battled manfully through. When he had finished the last verse, and was struggling along with his piece of charcoal, looking all the time as if he didn't know whether to laugh or to swear, his discomfiture was completed by a well-meaning little man from Lancashire, who informed him that, instead of being the only 'Nouveau' on that particular Monday morning, he was one of about a dozen, and gave him to understand, in short, that he had been 'doing the proper thing' business to death, and worst of all, *making an exhibition of himself*, to the intense amusement of the whole room.

Thus it is that the student with dignity gets it knocked off the first week, and, having no further use for it, lays it aside till he goes home. Unless, by the way, his mother and sister come over for a holiday, in which case he may be seen sneaking about the fashionable neighbourhood of The Arc de Triomphe or the Rue de Rivoli, and some would even go so far as to mount an eye-glass and a silk hat for a few days.

The amicable arrangement of seats for some eighty or a hundred men and boys of all nationalities, and of any age from sixteen to sixty, naturally entails the settling of a variety of disputes amongst so mixed a congregation, and, to simplify matters, a system of regulation by the 'Esquisse', or composition, of the week before is gone through.

The 'Esquisse' is a rough sketch in oils, illustrating a given allegorical subject. The best works are placed in order of merit by the Professor on Saturday morning, the most successful student having the priority of seats on Monday morning, when they can chalk their names on the floor as near the model as they please. The best place would usually be a seat about as high as an ordinary chair, the stools varying in height from less than a foot to four or five feet, the smallest being close to the model's stand and therefore having the disadvantage of giving a violent perspective to the figure. The highest chairs are, of course, out in the middle of the room, being managed like the spokes of a wheel, with the model's platform for the axle.

On Wednesday morning about ten o'clock, the 'Nouveau' would notice a sudden lull in the uproar, the insolent boy in front of them has ceased to whistle and throw bread, the light banter at the model's expense has dropped to a whisper, and that flighty individual herself has ceased to giggle and wriggle to the disgust of the severe American German, who doesn't see why those darned Frenchmen want to go fooling around with the model. He is at least outspoken, and acts as a moral censor.

The cause of this unusual behaviour is probably the kindly warning of the secretary, '*Le Professeur est là*,' wafted in a loud stage whisper from the door, or perhaps the arrival of that important individual himself, in which case all noises instantly cease, the model becomes a statue, and everyone is hard at work.

There can be no possible mistake about which professor it is that attends that morning. A student would know with his eyes shut. M. Ferrier enters quickly, energetically, full of life and action. M. Bouguereau, a fatherly old gentleman, and looking as much like a hearty Scotsman as anything else, comes slowly up behind the nearest student, and gives his opinion in the kindest manner. He hails from the North, and has the more phlegmatic temperament of the Norman. M. Ferrier, on the other hand, comes from the South of France, is more demonstrative, and generally ends by seizing the charcoal if the drawing is hopelessly out, and putting it right in a few touches.

Upstairs the professors are Messieurs Benjamin Constant (the Queen's portrait painter) and Jean Paul Laurens; thus the student in Paris can have the highest talent in France to come and look at him twice a week for a mere trifle. They work in the interests of Art, the pay is merely nominal.

The professor comes on Monday and Saturday; he stays two hours, and goes liberally and conscientiously through his work. The students like him, and believe in him.

A sly tear trickles down the youthful cheek as the great man hurls the naked truth at the luckless offender. He needn't cry, nobody is listening, there is no jealousy at Julian's, no ill feeling. Nobody cares. The only competition is at the monthly 'Concours', where medals are given for the best work in colour or charcoal.

You are looking at a canvas; the model's head is pretty. The artist has beautified it. The study of perhaps two days is now a picture you would value for your drawing-room.

The workman stops as you watch him. He raises his palette knife—one quick slash, and your picture is wiped onto a dirty rag, as mass of meaningless paint. He is out of conceit with his study, he turns his canvas upside down, lights his cigarette, and strolls away.

Next to him is such a nice young man, with a fair moustache and a big nose. He also has painted the same head. If he would only take his palette knife and—but he won't. He is satisfied, there is the difference.

The man that scraped off two days' work knows when he is wrong. The other man leans back with a pleased smile, turns his head from side to side, and—is happy.

Side by side they peg away—bald heads and curly heads, the duffer and the genius, the beggar and the Count, the Australian and the Parisian. No part of the world is too remote, no social state too humble, no incapacity too glaring. Everyone is welcome at the 'Académie Julian' in Paris.

Even New Zealand, farthest probably of all countries, being almost the Antipodes of Paris, had at one time three representatives in one studio. This was in the early nineties, when Messrs T. Ryan, C. F. Goldie and the writer, all from Auckland, were at Julian's, while on the walls, among the compositions, may be seen the signature of S. Begg, now well known as an illustrator, who hails from Napier. This and Mr Goldie's pronounced success as a medalist at the Académie, speak well for our future in the World of Art.

New Zealand Illustrated Magazine,
October 1901, pp.17-22.

RICHARD ARNOLD SINGER

Richard Arnold Singer (1878?-1961) later practised as a solicitor in Auckland. He wrote poetry, a collection of which was published in 1908 as Dreams in Exile, *as well as occasional essays.*

Mr C. F. Goldie and his Pictures (1903)

ART in New Zealand! Verily one would expect to find it in a country so full of sights that are the springs of inspiration to the artist, but experience teaches one to harbour little hope of meeting it in this land. Yet, mount to the top of the extremely prosaic Hobson's Buildings, in the extremely prosaic Shortland street, Auckland, and there will be found a studio full of brilliant studies in oil and chalk, of most delightful curios from all parts of the world, hung and laid with the quaintest mats and carpets, all disposed in the ordered disorder that speaks of a true artist's touch, and above all, adorned with pictures that but little knowledge will convince to be the work of a man who will one day be famous in lands where not alone art, but history also, has an appeal. For Mr C. F. Goldie is an artist by genius and by training. Born a New Zealander, and it appears with an artistic trend in his ancestry, Mr Goldie worked as a young man in Auckland, until he appreciated the fact that, to achieve a mastery in the art for which he was chosen by nature, he must study in the greatest school in painting in the modern world. To Paris, therefore, the Mecca of students of every nationality, Mr Goldie proceeded some ten years ago, and there he studied for six years, starting from the beginning and working up in a gradual course of successful effort, till he took rank with the best students of the studios of Julian in which he was studying. His record in Paris shows that he was placed second, third, and second for three consecutive years in the competition among the United Studios, open to three hundred students for a five and a half days' time study. Besides this, he obtained a medal for a study from life, and the work which gained this medal hangs today upon the walls of the school in Paris in which he studied. Among his masters in Paris are numbered Mons. Bouguereau, Ferrier, Constant, Doucet, Baschet, Schommer, and Bramtot. He made studies from the old masters in the great picture galleries of France, and travelled through Italy and Belgium and other Continental countries, always studying, always observing, always gaining in power and knowledge.

About four years ago Mr Goldie came back to New Zealand, and commenced almost immediately the work upon which he has been engaged ever since, and at which he has made a name for himself, the name of the master-painter of Maori life and character. As a portrait painter, in the usually-understood meaning of those words, he has given us some very fine work, for example his living presentment of the Hon. William Swanson, and the delightful Gainsborough-like 'Portrait of a Young Lady'; but it is in his Maori work that he stands supreme. He has long been a deep student of Maori history and custom. Wherever there has been an opportunity he has gathered knowledge of the life, the habits, the rites, the history and idiosyncrasies of this dying race, and in the wonderful pictures of Maoris, faithful portraits filled with marvellously executed detail, though never losing the breadth essential to a true picture, and stamped with a splendid individuality, the artist has given us work which no other artist who has worked in New Zealand can approach either in point of technique or of sympathy with and understanding of his subject. Maori pictures by other well-known artists possess the defect of being painted from photographs, and though they are interesting and include some magnificent models, they are all too flat and too smooth, and bear too much the impress of the photographs from which they are worked to be classed high artistically, or even, for that matter, historically; for the poses of the models are the poses of the photographer, and such attitudes are emphatically unreal with the Maori. One can, to a certain extent, gather an idea as to the customs and habits of the Maori from these artists; from Mr Goldie one obtains a true and a brilliant impression not only of the habits and customs, but of the very character, the very life, the idiosyncrasies of nature and of feature of the Maori—characteristics that in a few short years it will no longer be possible to represent, for the old chiefs and chieftainesses, and the old warriors whom this artist chooses as his models, are the last of their race; the tattooed man is dying out—the Maori of the new generation is not the majestic warrior of the past; and in devoting himself to the work he has now in hand Mr Goldie is doing an immense, though hardly, at present, sufficiently appreciated, service to the country of his birth and to the causes of art and of history. Such work has never been truly and rightly attempted by any other artist, and there is no other artist living who has the power and ability of Mr Goldie for the task.

Indeed, the ultimate aim of this artist is to undertake larger work in the representation of Maori life and character on a big scale, for which enterprise his more ambitious Maori pictures, such as 'Darby and Joan', exhibit the very highest promise. His intimate studies of the Maori, his careful and voluminous notes, and the many sketches he has already collected, will be of the greatest assistance to him in this respect.

After all, Maori relics can always be obtained for a price, and though the Government are not too solicitous in making collections of relics, still New Zealand possesses several fairly representative Museums. But the old Maori chiefs, and their old time historic race, is dying out all too quickly, and in a decade from now it will be too late to hope for the preservation of the type on canvas for all time. Should not steps be taken, therefore, at once to encourage this work, and to assist New Zealand's finest and truly representative artist in the labours which he has undertaken?

Mr Goldie has been recognised very fittingly by the presentation to Lady Ranfurly of two of his best Maori pictures. Lady Ranfurly and the Governor are ardent admirers of his work, and it is the desire of Lady Ranfurly that Mr Goldie should become well known in the old country where his work is bound to awaken the keenest interest.

As regards the figure in the picture 'Darby and Joan', one of the works presented to Lady Ranfurly, it may be interesting to many to know that the model for this figure, whose name is Ena te Papatahi, is a chieftainess of the Ngapuhi tribe and a younger relation of the one time celebrated Northern chiefs, Tamati Waka and Pateone [sic]. As a girl she was present, in the year 1843, at the inter-tribal battle at Oruru between the Ngapuhi and Rarawa tribes, and she also went through Heke's war in 1845 with Tamati Waka's men, who fought on the British side. She and other women were the food carriers for the men, the pikau being the receptacle for the supplies borne by these Maori vivandières. The old man asleep, portrayed in the well known picture in the Christchurch Art Gallery, was one of the four chiefs who accompanied Tawhiao, the Maori King, when he went to England to visit Queen Victoria. His name is Patara te Tuhi (Patara the Scribe), and he once edited a Maori paper in Waikato, and held the position of private secretary to Tawhiao. The picture 'The Widow', which was also presented to Lady Ranfurly, is full of interesting detail. The old lady portrayed is Harata Rewiri Tarapata, widow of the late chief Paul Tuhaere of Orakei. She is shown in the picture as a lonely dweller in a whare, scanning the relics of her dead husband. The fire inside the dwelling is dying out, the widow having finished her midday meal. In her hands is a greenstone Tiki, and at her side are grouped a dogskin mat, a greenstone mere and a huia feather, together with the silk handkerchief in which the relics were cherished. The picture gives a typical Maori scene to the life, and as a piece of painting constitutes one of Mr Goldie's masterpieces.

It is interesting to learn that Mr Goldie is a firm believer in the Semitic origin of the Maori, a belief he bases upon the characteristics of the Maoris at Rotorua, a district which he knows so well and which he has often chosen as the scene of his artistic labours, thus supporting many other present day authorities on this ethnological conjecture.

To turn, for one moment, from the artist to the man: one finds an interesting personality, an animated conversationalist, a travelled and broad-minded Englishman. Mr Goldie lives for his art, and it will be agreed by those who look at the reproductions of his work in this month's TRIAD that his devotion is attended by admirable—nay, almost magnificent—results.

Triad, vol.11, no.9,
1 December 1903, pp.10-12.

TAKAHI ATAMA PAPARANGI

Atama Paparangi (1817-1917) was chief of Te Taomāui, a hapū of Te Rarawa, based at Mitimiti. Goldie may have met Atama Paparangi when the chief visited Auckland in 1901 for the welcome to the Duke and Duchess of Cornwall and York, although he did not paint him until 1912. Atama's letter acknowledges the receipt of a photographic copy of the portrait now in the Auckland Museum [p.154].

Ki a Te Koori, Mr 'Goldie' (1914)

Mitimiti, Hokianga, Ākuhata 3rd 1914

Ki a Te Koori, Mr 'Goldie', Kai Tango Ahua, Ākarana

E tama, tēnā koe. He pukapuka whakapai atu tēnā ki a koe mō taku whakaahua kua taemai i ngā rangi kua pāhure ake nei. He nui te mīharo o toku iwi ki wāu mahinga pai. Kāti rā kia mihi atu ahau ki a koe.

Kua tioro mai te reo ki runga i te rangi nei; he pipi wharauroa, ko te karere o te Tau. Kua kahu te ngahere i ōna kahu raumati Kua uranga te moana i ngā pohutukawa nei. Kua puāwai ngā pua wānanga o ngā ngahere, ātaahua ana mai, kua awhi ōna tini hoa o ngā ngahere nei. Anō he hunga mārena e tatari nei, kia arahina rātou e te rōpū ārahi o te hunga mō ake nei whiwhi ki te haringa mutunga kore.

Koiana ngā hiahia o tōku ngākau mōu. He maha ngā mahara ātaahua papai. Oti rā, kotahi anō te kupu kaha mai i rite ai ngā mihi aroha me te pai.

Anei kia ora koe me ōu nei hoa aroha.

—Takahi Atama Paparangi

Translation by Te Rangihīroa (Dr Peter Buck),
District Health Office, Auckland

To Mr Goldie, The Painter of Portraits, Auckland
Oh, Son! Greetings!
This letter is to thank you for my picture, which arrived a few days ago. Great is the admiration of my tribe at the beauty of your work. Enough! I will now express my feelings towards you.

A voice from the skies makes music to the ear; it is that of the shining breasted cuckoo, the harbinger of spring. The trees of the forest have bedecked themselves in their summer raiment. The sea is red with the blossoms of the pohutukawa. The clematis in the forest glades have burst into flower, creating vistas of beauty. The myriad graceful trees of the woods augment the scene. They are like unto a bridal pair with their retinue, awaiting the guides who will lead them to the perfect happiness which knows no end.

Such are the feelings of my heart for you. Many are the wishes beautiful and good that I would wish you, but words fail. The sum of the words of greeting, of love and of good fellowship is expressed in this phrase: 'May health and prosperity attend you and all whom you love.'

—Takahi Atama Paparangi

Goldie Scrapbook XIII, pp.105-107,
Auckland Museum Library (MS 438).

TE HEUHEU TŪKINO

Hoani Te Heuheu Tūkino VI succeeded in 1921 as paramount chief of Ngāti Tūwharetoa. This undated letter, written under the letterhead of the Club Hotel, Palmerston North, is intended to assist Goldie in obtaining consent from prospective models. Te Heuheu Tūkino VI died in 1944.

Kia Mōhio Ngā Tāngata Katoa (c. 1935)

Kia mōhio ngā tāngata katoa, he hoa nōku a Kōri, arā (Goldie). Ko te tangata tino mōhio tēnei o te ao, ki te whakaahua (peita) i te kara o te Māori, a nō Niu Tireni nei ia. Ko Ākarana tana kāinga, ā, kei a ia ngā whakaahua a ngā rangatira katoa kua mate. Nā, e hiahia ana ia ki te tango i ngā whakaahua o ngā rangatira, kaumātua, taitamariki e ora nei, kia purutia ēnei whakaahua, hei tohu mō ngā Māori i roto i te whakatupuranga. Ā, ka haria e ia i te whakakitekitenga o ngā āhua katoa o ngā iwi o te ao ki te ekipihana i Parihi, te whenua o te Wiwi. Ko te hiahia kia puta te iwi Māori i taua whakakitekitenga—he taonga nui tēnei, me manaaki e tātou katoa, a, ka mau tō ingoa mō ake tonu atu.

—Te Heuheu Tūkino

So that everyone knows, Goldie is a friend of mine. He is world-renowned, particularly for his paintings of Māori people. He is a New Zealander, living in Auckland, and has many portraits of chiefs who have died. He wishes to paint the portraits of chiefs, elders and children now living, so that these paintings will remain as icons for Māori of future generations. He will take these paintings to France for the Paris exhibition, which will display depictions of peoples of all nations. The desire is that Māori be represented in this exhibition—this is a great gift, which we should all support so that your name will be remembered forever.

—Te Heuheu Tūkino

Goldie Scrapbook XIII, p.141,
Auckland Museum Library (MS 438).

CHARLES F. GOLDIE

Goldie spent many hours of 1934 writing denunciations of 'modern' art, behaviour typical of an older practitioner alarmed by contemporary developments. The 'Art Crisis' Goldie perceived in 1930s Auckland reminded him of the controversy raging when he was a student in Paris, over Gustave Caillebotte's gift to the State of his unrivalled collection of Impressionist paintings. He found a yellowing 1894 copy of the Journal des Artistes *and translated the scandalised outpourings of his Pompier masters. The final tag, 'published by arrangement', suggests that Goldie may have paid for the publication of his essay.*

The Art Crisis. Auckland Gallery. Battle of the Schools. Modernism Condemned (1934)

Your correspondent V. H. Kernot, in a letter of September 5, says: 'Mr Goldie expresses a wish that when the pictures of the Auckland Art Gallery are re-hung, no "modernists" or "self-impressionists" are allowed to creep in.' 'What Goldie means only Mr Goldie knows—or probably doesn't—for he has apparently coined a meaningless phrase just to amuse himself.'

I did coin the phrase 'self-impressionist'. This is my first lapse into 'modernism'. Are not all the 'ism schools' inventions and the appellation of each a coined one? When referring to these 'Modernists', 'Fauvists', 'Cubists', 'Dadaists' and the whole 'ist' family of the future (to save space) I will dud them 'Farcists', another coined word. To say that the phrase 'self-impressionists' is meaningless, is, of course, absurd. Too full of meaning would be more correct, hence V. H. Kernot's annoyance.

Now to the really serious part of the business! Would I keep all 'modernist stuff' out of the gallery? Most emphatically, yes!—for three excellent and irrefutable reasons. Firstly, such rubbish will impress students to the student's detriment. Secondly, it will never impress the general public, who may (if the modernists hold sway) have to pay for these 'banalities', which would occupy valuable wall space which otherwise might be filled with works that would impress the public. Thirdly, modernist products are a very bad investment from every point of view.

It is true that the works of some of the early and 'less mad' 'modernists' such as Manet, Monet, Renoir, Pissarro and others are commanding fairly high prices today, not on account of any little 'art' there might be in them, but on account of the artfulness of the art dealers. Durand Ruel, of Paris, the world's principal dealer in modern art, launched the works of the above-mentioned artists on the art market between 40 and 50 years ago. The 'high-brows', silly snobbish collectors, were his patrons. These people had very little taste, and what they had was 'bad'. This art was made the 'vogue' by the dealer. The dealers bought at a low price from the artist and sold at a high price to the 'highbrows', his clients. The artist was pleased to get his 'experiments' off at any price.

The dealers of London and New York saw the money in the 'farce', and made it tasteful to the less intelligent of their clients. It was an exceedingly profitable deal, so far as the dealer was concerned, and it was his business to keep the prices as high as possible, and he has been fairly successful in this respect.

But the dealer may change his taste at any time, and will if it 'suits his pocket' to do so. 'Victorian art' is at a discount today, and no doubt the dealer is 'cornering' all that is available, and when convenient to himself will make it again the vogue. Once the farcical art 'modernism' goes under, it will never rise again, and possessors of examples of this 'school' will be unable to give them away.

Due to modernism, we are at a very critical stage today in the process of art development in this Dominion, a position similar in every respect to that which faced France in 1894, namely, 'The Battle of the Schools'. I was in Paris at the time, so can speak with knowledge of the subject. A man named Caillebotte donated to the State a collection of works of the leaders of the 'Impressionist' school, including Manet, Monet, Renoir, Pissarro and others, on condition that the collection be exposed permanently in the Luxembourg Public Gallery. The world-renowned artists of France (leaders of the 'sane' school), seeing that serious consequences to French art would arise if this 'rubbish' was hung, publicly and permanently, immediately took the matter up and expressed their opinions in the 'Journal des Artistes', as follows:—

Gerome said: 'We are in a period of decay and imbecility. I do not speak of art alone. No! but of society in general.' Ah! 'Many times have I wished to take a pen and tell the people the truth, but we cannot do so; they will accuse us of jealousy. There are there the works of Manet, Renoir, Pissarro and others. It is not so? I repeat it, for the State to accept such filth (ordure) will be a great disgrace.' 'Go to the Journalists, fear nothing.' 'Now is the time to state the facts boldly.' 'It is anarchy, and nothing has been done to suppress it.' 'Believing in an article by Octave Mirbeau, I risked going to an exhibition of Pissarro's works.' 'Nothing! Nothing! There is no possible expression that will describe such a disorder.' 'There was madness at any price; there were some who painted like this, others like that, in little points, in triangles.' 'I tell you, they are anarchists, they are lunatics.' 'The Italian decadence came about in the same way, encouraged and applauded.' 'Italy plunged as we unavoidably will do.' 'People say it is a hoax.' 'It is nothing of the kind.' 'It is the finish of the nation.' 'It is the finish of France.' 'It is necessary to cry with a loud voice.' 'But Mirbeau, who was once a friend of mine, he must have some particular interest in these people that he extols them.' 'Do you understand, a solid pen is necessary to sustain our campaign.' 'Tell them to their faces. You are all mad speculators!'

Tony Robert Fleury said: 'You ask my advice.' Here it is! 'That which surprises me today will be the painting of tomorrow!' 'Impressionism is in its infancy today, but when a man of robust constitution and solid education adopts it, we will perhaps have a new art.'

Benjamin Constant said: 'Protest vigorously, these people are nothing but experimentalists.' 'If they accept that painting at the Luxembourg.' 'Take down the very honourable works.' 'Take the lot down.' 'Close the Louvre! Do not send any more students to Rome or Holland to study!' 'The Great Masters have lied!' 'Protest by every possible means. Make a campaign! But it is sad to have to deal with such people.'

Gabriel Ferrier said: 'I do not know these people (Impressionists). I do not want to know them!' 'When I see examples of their work I get away quickly.' 'When I go down the Rue Lafitte on the side on which the blue shop is (a reference to the shop of Durand Ruel, art dealer in impressionists' work) I cross quickly to the other side of the road.' 'Then it will not finish with the "Impressionists", there are already a number of under groups of this "school". Cormon (a famous artist) told me a few days ago that they are going to institute more of these "tricksters". It is very unfortunate for France.' 'I see it among my pupils (Julian's Academy).' 'The foreign students are not so stupid as ours, they do not fall into these errors.' And they are going to put that 'stuff' in the galleries, they are going to place Pissarro's works in the Luxembourg, while as yet they have not got a 'Roybet' (a noted artist). 'We see this with sadness, we who have been nourished with the work of the Great Masters at Rome.' 'I do not believe in these artists, I do not believe in the sincerity of the people who extol them.' It is all a question of shop. And my square advice is to turn the lot out; that is the only way to treat them.

Lecomte de Nouy said: 'The Impressionists are not to blame when they are sincere, but the critics who flatter them are worthy of our severity.' 'To put in the Luxembourg the pictures of which you speak will be a deplorable example, for the young people will be turned from serious work. We cannot, we who have worked so hard and are still studying, approve of a tendency which is characterised by absence of study.'

Marchand said: 'Hanging these pictures in the Luxembourg seems to say to the public, "This is good art". To the young artists, "This is what you must do".' 'The advice is easy to follow.' 'An art which has neither draughtsmanship nor execution is too easy to imitate.' 'An amateur could learn to do that in eight days, and, they come to us, we, who have gone to so much trouble to learn to paint (from nature) a female head (for never will they be able to paint a female head), that it should be well painted and resemble the model.' 'We who have arrived after much patient study.' 'They come to tell us.' 'You are old, it is we who know how to paint.'

The foregoing are the opinions of a few of the several famous artists who were interviewed by a representative of the 'Journal des Artistes' in 1894, and I may say that there is not an artist living today of the calibre of the men whose opinions are quoted above. The 'ism' schools are solely responsible for this state of affairs. Things have gone from bad to worse since then. Yet we were told by an Auckland art teacher who lectured at the loan exhibition, such nonsense as: 'Painting in the present day has never been in a more healthy state.' 'Modern painting was not a direct revolution of art, but an evolution of it.' The dictionary definition of the word evolution is 'a gradual development from simplicity to complexity; a gradual advance from a simple or rudimentary condition to one that is more complex and of higher character.' I will leave it to the public, more especially to those who visit the loan exhibition of contemporary art, to say whether it is 'revolution' or evolution that is affecting art so seriously today.

As in Britain, and on the Continent, there was in New Zealand infinitely superior art produced forty years ago than that of today. This goes to prove my contention that the world's art has deteriorated enormously of late years. Therefore, in the interests of art students and the public, we must not allow our galleries to become 'dumping grounds' for this 'vulgar', 'meaningless', modern 'rubbish' that is hawked about the world today labelled 'Art'.—(Published by arrangement.)

New Zealand Herald,
28 September 1934, p.15.

Very little of Goldie's personal correspondence seems to have survived. Taylor & Glen (1979) published the 1933-1937 letters to his London-based nephew T. T. (Terry) Bond, which Bond presented to the National Art Gallery (now the Museum of New Zealand Te Papa Tongarewa). The following correspondence from 1935 discusses an unrealised collaborative publication with an old friend, the writer James Cowan, then based in Wellington. The original manuscripts are among the Eric Ramsden papers at the Alexander Turnbull Library (MS Papers 196), with the exception of the first and final letters which are held in the Research Library at Auckland Art Gallery Toi o Tāmaki.

Letters to James Cowan regarding collaborative publications (1935)

94 Upland Road/Remuera SE2
Jan 2nd–35

Dear Cowan

Many thanks for your letter of Dec 21st & also for a previous one, re prints. I am delighted to have the signed copy of 'Hero Stories' for which best thanks. I have ordered a copy to be sent to Lord Bledisloe by Monday's mail. I am sure that he will be pleased to have it. Very sorry to hear that you are not feeling 'much good'. I am not 'up to much' myself: the weather here has been very hot & humid, Easterly & N.E weather knocks me right out. Regarding the prints, the specimens you sent were returned to you some considerable time ago. I trust that you received them in good condition. I did not send you my opinion of them earlier as I knew that nothing further would be done until after the holidays. Candidly I do not think that they are a great success. In the first place they are smaller than the size I stipulated. Secondly they are too yellow in colour, in No 1 the colouring is patchy & the hair too white. You say that Tombs intends altering the tone etc. but until I see what alterations he is going to make I cannot give a definite opinion. I have asked Breckon to send you a glossy print of 'Memories' Pipihaerehuka, which is the picture that you said you would have liked Tombs to have made a print of. I think it better that he should send me a finished print of the picture (the size I stipulated). White hair as in Wharepapa, is always difficult to reproduce & we may have to cut some of them out. If Tombs cannot (through not having the necessary machinery) give me satisfactory reproductions I'm afraid that we shall have to drop the affair & concentrate on your book 'Moko'. Breckon is sending you a print of the picture that was mentioned in the 'Post' you may use it in your book.

Kindest regards/Yours sincerely/C.F. Goldie

94 Upland Road/Remuera/Auckland SE2
May 27th–34 [35]

Dear Cowan

I read in the 'Star' that you had not received 'The King's Jubilee Medal'. If such is the case 'its a *damned shame*'. I can only put it down to an inexcusable oversight on the part of the compiler of the 'eligibles' in the Wellington province. I rang up the Editor of the 'Herald' forthwith and asked him whether he knew that it was so & asked him whether something could not yet be done in the matter?

He said, 'Cowan should certainly have been honoured' & that he would look into the matter. Whether he has done so or not I cannot say.

I was on very intimate terms with Lord Bledisloe & just before he left my place when standing at the front door, on his last visit I said 'Lord Bledisloe. I should like to see Cowan honoured.' He was very sympathetic & said 'I know Cowan's work. Cowan's work will live.' (I had at different times sent him copies of your books but was sorry that I was unable to procure a copy of 'the Maoris of New Zealand'.) Whether it is in Lord Bledisloe's power to do anything in the matter I cannot say, but am hoping for the best.

Trusting that you are feeling better than when you last wrote, with kindest regards to Mrs Cowan and yourself

Yours sincerely/C.F Goldie

P.S. You will remember that Illingworth the Australian Sculptor was commissioned by the Govt to make ten (10) busts of Maori types. I saw them on pedestals in the Dominion Museum Library. Could you find out for me for certain whether they are in *bronze* or *plaster of paris*? From my observations they appeared to me to be in plaster. CFG

94 Upland Road/Remuera SE2/Auckland
June 10th–35

Dear Cowan

Many thanks for congratulations & good wishes. I cannot understand why Andersen and Elder should be honoured and yourself overlooked. In my opinion & that of many other [sic] you stand out pre-eminently for an honour. Can you account for it, has there been some 'pull' do you think? Bishop Bennett in an address given recently at Hawke's Bay said that 'Cowan, Best, and Percy Smith should have received some recognition long ago' or words to that effect. Your stuff is mainly, if not all, original whereas that of Andersen & Elder is pirated from the 'Old Masters' that I think sizes up the position. It is original data that counts & that is what we want. The whole thing is on a par with an artist who copies 'Old Masters' in the Galleries all his life (as some do) & gives nothing fresh to the world at all. What use has his life's work been?, none whatsoever.

However, now that Art & Literature are beginning to come 'into their own' due mainly I think to the thought & influence of Viscount Bledisloe and perhaps Bernard Shaw's criticism or the two combined, we cannot allow you to be forgotten when the New Year's Honours are handed out. I must keep Viscount Bledisloe furnished with reminders if need be, so you must notify me when your two books now in the publisher's hands are available to the public & I will forward copies to Viscount Bledisloe.

In your book on Tattooing, you may use reproductions of any of the pictures I sent you with the exception of Tamati Waaka, the copyright of which I have given to the Waitangi Trust, & that of Atama which is the property of Viscountess Bledisloe. I will also send you photographs, if you wish of any pictures in my private collection in the Auckland Art Gallery (about 35 slides in all). If you will let me know which ones you would like? I will not allow anyone else to have them. In the collection is a study of Te Aho with the head foreshortened in order to show the tattooing under the chin & on the neck also on the upper eyelids (the only study of its kind in existence, & made specially for the purpose above stated). You are welcome to a print of it if of any use to you.

Later, when I get a little more time I will suggest a scheme to you by which we might collaborate viz. an artistic & well-gotten up book of say six chosen studies of my work either direct photographs similar to those you already have or the best of reproductions for purposes of sale to the best class of tourist (something much needed at present) to be sold say at half a guinea or more (they'll pay if it's good). It will be for you to write up the subjects & I will attend to the artistic part of the production, designing the cover etc. I do not want any of the proceeds, the whole may go to yourself and the publishers. I want as little as posssible to go [to] the publishers, at the same time we must not stint in any way the quality of the work, it must be the best possible. If you fall in with the idea, I will give it much more thought. Tourists are keen on my 'stuff' and will pay a good price provided that we give them what they want, & I think I know their requirements.

What do you think of the idea?

Kindest regards to Mrs Cowan & self

Yours sincerely/C.F. Goldie

94 Upland Road/Remuera SE2
July 1st–35

Dear Cowan

Yours of June 26th duly received. Immediately on receipt of your former letter I instructed Breckon the Weekly News photographer (who took the photos you already have) to make negatives of such studies in my collection that I thought would be useful for your purpose. I have not heard from him since and do not want to hurry him with the work as I told him to get the best results possible giving special attention to detail of tattooing & colour values. I enclose herewith a few details of some of the photos I am sending to you.

Now, as to funds have you sufficient for your requirements? I am holding 'pretty good' at present and can sell all I paint at my own price.The last 3 studies I sold, the largest of which was 16½ inch x 18½ inch, the prices paid respectively were 250 guineas, £350 & 150 guineas.

I should like to help you in this very important matter & will be very pleased to remit to you. *You need not return the money until you have made your fortune*. I like yourself am keenly interested in everything Maori. My experience has been that it is impossible to do good work if one has any worries. I know too well the feeling, it's damnably nerve wracking! Do not hesitate for a moment to give me a hint. It will be a great pleasure to me to do anything in my power to assist you to be able to give of your best.

With kindest regards to Mrs Cowan & yourself

Believe me/Yours sincerely/CF Goldie

94 Upland Road/Remuera SE2
July 15th–35

Dear Cowan

Yours of July 11th duly received. The 3 last photos you mention, were not from Breckon. I asked my sister to send them to you after giving Breckon what I considered to be ample time to do justice to the work I asked of him, I rang him on Sunday & found that he had had the flu', but will commence the work this week. You were right with regard to the Tarukenga Warrior, his name is Tumai Tawhiti. He was a boy on Mokoia at the time of Hongi's raid, but escaped with another boy to the mainland in a canoe. The old woman you speak of at Tarukenga must have been *Tumai's* wife I have a photo of her. *Hamupara te Arahori* was the wife of Haumiti, a finely tattooed man who lived at Tokaanu.

Regarding the matter of finance, as you insist I will withold the money for the present but you must understand that it is at your disposal whenever you wish it.

I have not felt much inclined for writing lately as I have had indigestion pretty badly & writing is torture to me at all times.

Will write more fully when I get photos from Breckon.

Kindest regards to Mrs Cowan and self

Yours sincerely/C.F. Goldie

94 Upland Road/Remuera SE2
July 23rd–35

Dear Cowan

Yours of 19th now duly to hand. Regarding the proposed 'deluxe' book of reproductions of my pictures. I suggest that on the first say 10 or 15 pages, before the reproductions are introduced, that you write up some general notes on the maori [sic] more especially on tattooing, ornaments, dress etc that would be applicable to the studies which come later in the book & intersperse in the writing reproductions from photographs of ornaments such as tiki, peka-peka ear-drops etc. Photographs could be made at the Dominion Museum if you have not already got such in your collection. This would add additional interest to the publication. I have found that tourists are keen to obtain all possible information regarding these things, more especially the Americans. They do not like to appear ignorant on these points when questioned by their friends & explanations by an authority will appeal to them. I have in my possession the first copy of 'Art in N.Z.' published by H. Tombs. It is gotten up in a good style but my wish is to accentuate its good points, do something better. I am giving the matter a great deal of thought, which is essential if the book is to be the success that I hope for it. I am jotting down ideas as they come to me & will advise you more fully later. The 'Thing' must not be rushed, it has simply got to, & will be a success. I have seen a good deal of this sort of publication in my travels & have a pretty good idea of what appeals to the tourist It must be a 'souvenir' book, in every sense a book that will be placed on the tables in their salons & not stuck away in a book case. A book that the wealthy will buy several copies of to distribute amongst their friends. I have pleasure in including my cheque for 60 guineas, it being crossed, it of course will have to go through a banking account. If you have not got such a thing about, perhaps Mr Tombs or some other friend will oblige.

In the present 'kia ora'

Kindest regards to all

Yours sincerely/C.F. Goldie

94 Upland Road/Remuera SE2
Aug 14th–35

Dear Cowan

I must apologise for not having written to you before this, to thank [you] for the photographs of Wahanui & his wife which you kindly sent me. As a matter of fact I have not felt up to the mark lately. I bought a 'Spencer' negative of Wahanui which is similar in every respect to the print you sent me, the negative of which I thought you said was in the possession of a surveyor friend of yours. I thought that mine was the original & that therefore I held the copyright but evidently it is not so.

Regarding the books! You appear to have misunderstood me, I do not suggest that you should combine your 'moko' work with the 'souvenir' book: just a few general remarks on tattooing only, together with ornaments & dress, something applicable, to answer any question tourist purchasers might be asked by their friends regarding these details. If you do not think that you have sufficient material to make a fair sized volume on 'Moko' combine it with carving etc. under the title of 'Maori Art' or some such title. I am getting together material, as to size of book, paper & cover etc for the 'tourist' book of prints. I have several very fine 'deluxe' editions, on 'Art' & the 'Lives of Artists' some of them published at £5 a copy & there is a fund of artistic material in the 'get up' of some of them which is of great value to me. The size of the book (which will not be very thick) should be at least 12" x 10" in order [to] give sufficient margin for the prints.

Breckon will be sending you (in a few days time) 11 additional prints of some of my gallery pictures. With the exception of 2 or 3 of them, all will be on glossy paper, which gives the detail of tattooing very plainly. This is essential for your work on 'moko'.

The reproductions in the 'Souvenir' will be on rougher paper brown in tone to give an artistic effect. We must decide how many prints are to be inset in the Tourist book. I think that at least 2 or 3 of Breckon's latest should be included with those you have & I would like a suggestion from you, as to which.

I was awarded a diploma or medal at this year's salon for my picture 'Thoughts of a Tohunga' Wharekauri Tahuna. I do not know yet what it was. Will hear further shortly.

Kindest regards to Mrs Cowan & self

Yours sincerely/CF Goldie

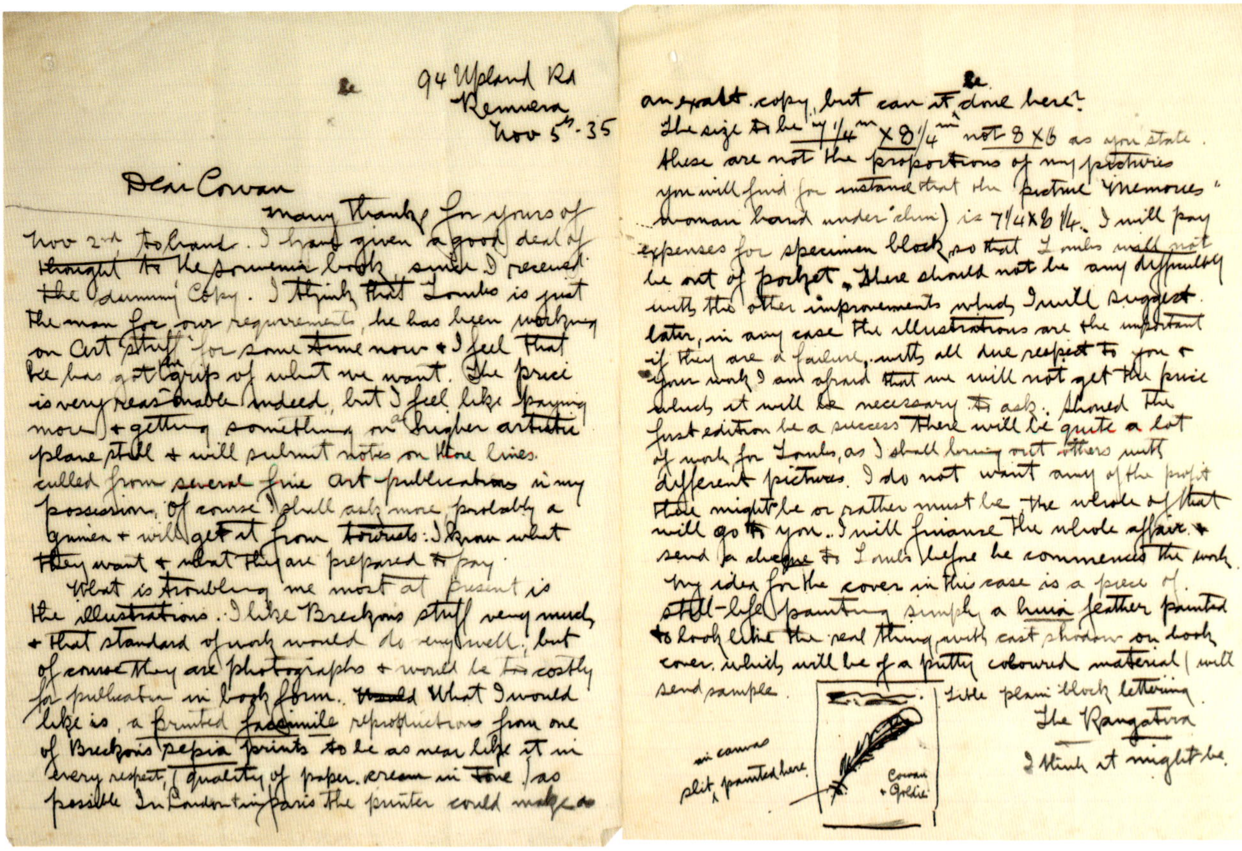

94 Upland Rd
Remuera
Nov 5th-35

Dear Cowan

Many thanks for yours of Nov 2nd to hand. I have given a good deal of thought to the souvenir book since I received the 'dummy' copy. I think that Tombs is just the man for our requirements, he has been working on art stuff for some time now & I feel that he has got the grip of what we want. The price is very reasonable indeed, but I feel like paying more & getting something on a higher artistic plane still & will submit notes on those lines culled from several fine art publications in my possession. Of course I shall ask more probably a guinea & will get it from tourists: I know what they want & what they are prepared to pay.

What is troubling me most at present is the illustrations. I like Breckon's stuff very much & that standard of work would do very well, but of course they are photographs & would be too costly for publication in book form. What I would like is, a printed facsimile reproduction from one of Breckon's sepia prints to be as near like it in every respect, quality of paper, cream in tone as possible. In London or Paris the printer could make an exact copy, but can it be done here?

The size to be 7¼" x 8¼" not 8 x 6 as you state. These are not the proportions of my pictures you will find for instance that the picture 'Memories' (woman hand under chin) is 7¼ x 8¼. I will pay expenses for specimen block so that Tombs will not be out of pocket. There should not be any difficulty with the other improvements which I will suggest later, in any case the illustrations are the important if they are a failure, with all due respect to you & your work I am afraid that we will not get the price which it will be necessary to ask. Should the first edition be a success there will be quite a lot of work for Tombs, as I shall bring out others with different pictures. I do not want any of the profit that might be or rather must be – the whole of that will go to you. I will finance the whole affair & send a cheque to Tombs before he commences the work. My idea for the cover in this case is a piece of still-life painting simply a huia feather painted to look like the real thing with cast shadow on dark cover, which will be of a pretty coloured material (will send sample. Little plain block lettering. The Rangatira I think it might be.

in canvas slit, painted here

Cowan + Goldie

Charles F. Goldie to James Cowan, 5 November 1935 (Research Library, Auckland Art Gallery Toi o Tāmaki).

94 Upland Road/Remuera SE2
Sep 30th [1935]

Dear Cowan

Many thanks for your letter of 25th. From your previous letter I gathered that you were going to have a chat with Tombs regarding the souvenir book. I suppose that Tombs is the best man available for printing a 'deluxe' edition & would not be more expensive than others, in any case he is close at hand to you, which is a great advantage. Before we can do much more, we must decide on the size the book is to be & Tombs should be helpful to us in this matter. It is important that the reproductions should have a fair margin of background & I am of the opinion that the page of the book should be at least 10" x 12¼ full. The book will not be very thick so that we can afford to give it some length & breadth. Kindly talk this matter over with Tombs & let me know what dimensions you decide on & I can then get on with the cover of the book, which I shall paint in oils on a canvas of the size of the agreed dimensions. Then there is the question of *title for the book*, perhaps: 'Noble Relics of a Noble Race' Rangitiras of Ao-tea-roa. Tombs and yourself could better fix this up than I.

Then again how many reproductions should be included in the book? As to the selection from the photos you have I think it advisable that preference be given to 'subject' portraits rather than to 'straight' portraits for instance the profile of Wharekauri Tahuna 'Thoughts of a Tohunga' & 'Memories' Pipihaerehuka in modern costume, hand under chin are what I term subject portaits. There is another 'Life's Long Day Closes' Te Aho, head raised, gasping. I do not know whether this one appeals to you or not, but I rather like it, it is somewhat poetic in treatment. The profile of Te Aho with taiaha 'A Hero of Many Fights' should I think go in. However, have a chat with Tombs regarding the prints mentioned & let me know what he suggests. The size of the cover is the important [issue] at present, what about 10 x 12¼ page? [sketch of book cover dimensions]

With kindest regards to Mrs Cowan & self

Yours sincerely/C.F. Goldie

94 Upland Road/Remuera
Nov 5th–35

Dear Cowan

Many thanks for yours of Nov 2nd to hand. I have given a good deal of thought to the souvenir book since I received the dummy copy. I think that Tombs is just the man for our requirements, he has been working on art stuff for some time now & I feel that he has got the grip of what we want. The price is very reasonable indeed, but I feel like paying more & getting something on a higher artistic plane still & will submit notes on those lines culled from several fine art publications in my possession. Of course I shall ask more, probably a guinea & will get it from tourists: I know what they want & what they are prepared to pay.

What is troubling me most at present is the illustrations. I like Breckon's stuff very much, & that standard of work would do very well; but of course they are photographs & would be too costly for publication in book form. What I would like is *a printed facsimile* reproduction from one of Breckon's *sepia* prints to be as near like it in every respect (quality of paper, cream in tone) as possible. In London & in Paris the printer could make an exact copy, but can it be done here? The size to be $7\frac{1}{4}$ in x $8\frac{1}{4}$ in *not 8 x 6* as you state. These are not the proportions of my pictures[,] you will find for instance that the picture 'Memories' (woman hand under chin) is $7\frac{1}{4}$ x $8\frac{1}{4}$. I will pay expenses for specimen block so that Tombs will not be out of pocket. There should not be any difficulty with the other improvements which I shall suggest later, in any case the illustrations are the important [thing,] if they are a failure, with all due respect to you & your work I am afraid that we will not get the price which it will be necessary to ask. Should the first edition be a success there will be quite a lot of work for Tombs, as I shall bring out others with different pictures. I do not want any of the profit there might be or rather must be, the whole of that will go to you. I will finance the whole affair & send a cheque to Tombs before he commences the work. My idea for the cover in this case is a piece of still-life painting, simply a *huia* feather painted to look like the real thing with cast shadow on book cover, which will be of a putty coloured material (will send sample). Title plain block lettering. *The Rangatira* I think it might be.

[thumbnail sketch of proposed cover]

If the specimen of illustration is satisfactory we can proceed with the work immediately. I think you will agree with me that the illustrations must be of the quality of Breckon's photographs.

How do you like my idea for the cover. I want something simple. The colouring will of course be black, white & putty or *old raupo* coloured ground. Miss Lysnar used a somewhat similar design on the wrapper of the book she published but it was at my suggestion & it was not very well carried out. The original idea is mine absolutely.

For the present/In haste/Yours sincerely/C.F. Goldie

JAMES COWAN

James Cowan (1870-1943) is known for his writings on Māori and colonial history. One of his earliest publications was a 1901 catalogue of Gottfried Lindauer's Māori portraits collected by Henry Partridge, which he expanded into a full-scale monograph in 1930. When Goldie's personal collection went on display in 1920, joining the Partridge Collection that had entered the Auckland Art Gallery five years earlier, Cowan wrote an effusive description for publication in the Auckland Star. *Although his authorship went unacknowledged, annotated clippings survive in Cowan's personal copy of his 1901* Maori Biographies *(Alexander Turnbull Library).*

Goldie's Collection. Last of the Rangatiras. Tattooed Chiefs and Kuias (1920)

Auckland possesses the finest collection in existence of Maori weapons, greenstone ornaments, canoes and carvings. The city also possesses the only two collections in the world of Maori portraits and studies. One is the fine series of pictures by Lindauer, which became the property of the citizens through the generosity of the collector (Mr H. E. Partridge). The other is a valuable collection of originals by Mr C. F. Goldie, which has been loaned to the city, and has now been hung in the City Gallery.

There are in the 27 portraits that comprise the collection some very interesting personalities. The picture of a thoughtful-looking ancient is that of Anaha, the last of the old-time carvers. He used to live in a small whare near the steaming pools of Ohinemutu, just below Lake House. He could often be seen sitting outside in the sun, with a blanket tied round his waist like a kilt, crooning some 'karakia' (incantation) as he tapped away with mallet and chisel and carved the rich red wood of the totara into the likeness of fearsome god, with protruding tongue, eyes of iridescent pawa [sic] shell, and the mystical three-fingered hands. He was a tall man of spare frame, and in his old age much bent, but in spite of the fact that his hand in his latter days trembled like a leaf, he did some wonderful carving almost up to the time that he was called away to join the ancestors he loved to figure.

A different sort of Maori altogether was Te Aho, who served Mr Goldie as a model for a long while. He hailed from Mercer, and belonged to the Ngati-mahuta. It is Te Aho in a bowler hat and pakeha costume, who smiles from hundreds of homes in a reproduction called 'A Good Joke'. The old chief shared with Queen Elizabeth a taste for accumulating large and varied wardrobes. Te Aho's taste ran mainly, however, to caps and hats, of which he had dozens, and seems to have spent in this way a considerable portion of the money he earned in being a model. In his younger days this kindly old soul from the banks of the Waikato was a famous canoe-builder and a fighter.

Another fine picture, called 'A Hero of Many Fights', is a profile portrait of Te Aho. A third study of Te Aho is a unique one, with the head thrown back and eyes closed, to show the tattooing under the chin and on the eyelids.

The rangatira of the old school was a gentleman, even if he had a few habits that might not pass muster in a drawing-room. You will find examples in such books as Sir John Logan Campbell's 'Poenamo' and Maning's 'Old New Zealand'. Of such a type was Kamariera Wharepapa, who belonged to Mangakahia, North Auckland, and was connected with both the Arawa and Ngapuhi tribes. Born in 1823 he lived to the latter part of 1919. As a young man he and some other natives were taken on a visit to England on the ship Ida Ziegler in the year 1862. They had a most eventful stay in London, and were presented to Queen Victoria. Kamariera was a handsome man even in his old age, and one can well understand that he must have been a singularly fine-looking brave before the fires of youth burned low. An English girl was captivated by the stalwart tattooed New Zealander, and after changing her name to Mrs Wharepapa came out to the colony with her dusky spouse. Kamariera looks in Mr Goldie's picture exactly what he was—an aristocrat. Even judged by our own standards he was a man of singularly lofty ideals, and had as chivalrous a code of honour as many a belted knight of the brave days of long ago.

There must be Aucklanders who will remember a tall tattooed Maori who used to appear in Queen Street occasionally and attract attention by his singular rigout—a koti roa (long black coat) and black belltopper—which suggested in cut and colour that it was a legacy from one of the very early missionaries. This was Atama Paparangi, of the tribe of Rarawa, and he hailed from the banks of the Hokianga, the home of heroes and fighters. Atama was a famous warrior, and had used his 'tupara' (double-barrelled gun) with much effect at the fight against the white man at Kororareka and in the battle of Okaihau, two famous incidents in Heke's war of 1845-6. Atama died some time in 1917.

Tikitere Mihi, who lived at the sleepy lakeside kainga of Te Ngae, was a chief of the Arawa. He stood 6ft 2in on his bare feet, and was proportioned accordingly—a Hercules of a man. It was Tikitere whose classic features were perpetuated in the bust by the Australian Illingworth, who executed several commissions for the New Zealand Government. For the bust he shaved off his flowing beard, which in Mr Goldie's picture gives him a patriarchal appearance, and it is one of the few Maoris the artist has painted with a beard. Like the old Romans, the Maori of high-caste was invariably shaven, the principal idea being, of course, to show off the beauty of the blue tattoo executed by the tohunga with much ceremony and ritual.

'The Majesty of Death' is a portrait of Ina Te Papatahi, a woman who figures in several of Mr Goldie's pictures. She was closely related to those noted chiefs who were such firm friends of the pakeha—Tamati Waka Nene, who stood by us so loyally in the wars of the turbulent Heke, and Patuone, who lived across the Waitemata for many years, and now lies buried in the cemetery on the slopes of Mount Victoria. Ina was a very old lady indeed, and many may remember her venerable figure at the Maori Hostelry at the foot of Constitution Hill, where she passed the evening of life. She had a very likeable nature, and was the womanly counterpart of aristocratic Kamariera mentioned above. She had a keen sense of humour, like most of the Maori dames, and used to take a great interest in the painting of her portrait. In this canvas, she is seen laid out for the tangi, robed in a valuable mat of blue iridescent pigeon feathers, and with her greenstone tiki laid on her breast. The foreshortening of the face used to puzzle Ina very much, and when she saw it she shrugged her shoulders and said, 'Ach, too much like the bulldog.'

Auckland Star, 6 November 1920, p.17.

Goldie's Collection (CONTINUED)

In 'The Last of the Cannibals' we have a really diabolical old gentleman, whose strenuous life went back to the slaughterous descent of Hongi and his savage Ngapuhis on the Arawas who took refuge on the tribe's most sacred ground, Mokoia, the mountain islet that lies in the middle of Rotorua. That was away back in the early days of the eighteenth [sic] century, when the Ngapuhis had just learned the value of musket and powder and started on their terrible raids on their enemies, who were mostly still armed with the old-fashioned Maori weapons, the mere and the patu. Tumai Tawhiti was the name of the ill-favoured chief in the picture. He managed to escape from the clutches of the Northern berserkers by escaping from Mokoia with a couple of other lads in a canoe and getting across the lake in the midst of the confusion of the fight. They found refuge on the bush-clad sides of dark Ngongotaha, a sacred burying ground of the Lake people. Tumai took part in the bloody struggle at Te Tumu, south of Maketu, in the Bay of Plenty, which was fought in 1836. He played a conspicuous role in the slaughter, accounting for quite a number of the enemy, and he did not shirk his share in the horrible cannibal feasts that followed. Every line of Tumai's well-tattooed face speaks of the 'kaitangata' (man eater).

Kapikapi was the only woman Mr Goldie found with the tattooed spiral on the nostril, and she also had some uncommon marks on the shoulder, to show which the mat was arranged in the manner in the portrait, although it is not the native style of wearing that article of clothing. She belonged to the Tuhourangi, a branch of the Arawa, living at Whakarewarewa, and was one of those saved from the appalling eruption of Tarawera in 1886, mainly through the exertions of Sophia, the famous guide. Kapikapi was 102 when she died about seven or eight years ago, and although she was bent and shrunken she used to work right up to the end. She was a splendid specimen of the Maori matron. The upper part of her body was much marked with dark scarred weals—the evidence of the sincerity of her mourning in the days when women of her tribe showed their grief by scoring their brown bosoms and arms with sharp pieces of tuhua, or obsidian. Truly a Spartan race, the old-time Maori!

Waiuku was the home of Aparahama (Abraham) Rairai, and his characteristics are well hit off in the title Mr Goldie has chosen, 'The Old Lion'. He was 104 years of age when the picture was painted in 1908, and his legs were not much thicker than sticks. Aparahama was one of the last of the Maoris to possess that much-admired ornamentation of the chieftain, the 'rape' or elaborately tattooed spirals on the buttocks. Those who were present at the great hui to the present King at Rotorua in 1901 will remember the pride of a Ngapuhi ancient who was 'mokoed' in the same manner, and the proud and deft way in which the old fellow flicked aside his mat to show this mark of his high lineage as he stalked back to his tribe after presenting his offering to the royal guests.

Perema Te Pahau, known as 'The Bone Scraper', belonged to the Tuhourangi, and hailed from the village of steam-holes and geysers, Whakarewarewa. He is painted in a dog-skin mat worth about £80, the most prized 'kakahu' (clothing) that Maoridom possessed in the pre-Pakeha days. Perema was extremely tapu on account of his calling, which consisted in preparing the bones of the departed after they were dug up from their temporary grave, and before they were placed in the tribal burying place, usually a cave in some rocky cliff, or other natural orifice in the 'wahi tapu' (sacred place).

Near this picture is a portrait of a noted chief who was very familiar about Auckland some few years ago, Patara te Tuhi, or 'Patara the Scribe'. This picture is called 'Peeping Patara' and shows him looking round the corner of a carved door post. There is a better one of him further along on the same wall. This is Patara to the life; a shrewd, discreet old chap, well-fitted to take the helm in political matters and be the private secretary of kings, for those were Patara's roles in his prime. Patara was also an editor, and Mr Goldie suggests slyly that is perhaps the reason he is bald—Patara being the only bald Maori the artist came across during his intercourse with the remnants of the race.

Patara was private secretary of King Tawhaio when that potentate was a power in the land, and during the Maori war he edited the 'Hokioi' (the name of a bird) which cackled pungent 'kingite' opinions during the Maori wars of 1860-70. Its rival, a sheet run by the late Sir John Gorst, and called by the name of a rival bird, was supposed to chirp loyal sentiments to combat the influence of Patara's production. Which of the rival editors got the best of it editorially does not matter at this late date, but our dusky journalist scored eventually for the office of the pakeha journal was well raided by the opposition, the press was tossed into the Waikato—Ngaruawahia being the scene of the journalistic trial of skill—the editor had to take to his heels, and the unkindest cut of all, the type was melted down into bullets which were probably more effective than Patara's paragraphs. Patara certainly had a keen sense of humour, and if he had been with a white skin instead of a brown one there would probably be a tablet to his memory in some Valhalla of the nation's famous men.

All the portraits but one are of the elders of the tribe, and the exception is a charming picture called 'Hinemoa', a pretty Maori girl who belongs to Whakarewarewa. Her wonderful hair is admirably treated, and there is something very captivating about the half-wild beauty of the sitter. She is not quite a full-blooded Maori, and the suggestion of the merging of the two races in her features makes it a very fitting and rather pathetic pendant to Mr Goldie's collection of the last of the chiefs and chieftainesses of her people.

Auckland Star, 13 November 1920, p.17.

A Vanished Art. The Maori Moko. Last of the Tattooed Men (1935)

The disappearance of an ancient and beautiful form of primitive artcraft is always a matter for regret. One of these branches of skill practised by the craftsmen of Polynesia, and of the Maori in particular, is the art of tattooing the face and body. New Zealand was once pre-eminently the land of 'moko', the general Maori term for the design of tattoo. The symmetrically moko'd warrior face has long been a distinguishing badge of this country with the kiwi and the fern tree. We have long had it on our banknotes, on our tourist posters, in many of our books, and many a traveller has come to this country expecting to see, among other strange and wonderful sights, Maori warriors with black-scrolled faces stalking the city streets. Indeed that spectacle was once familiar enough, but not within the last quarter of a century or so. Only on the women's chins and lips can the blue-black lines of tattoo be seen nowadays; and they are becoming a rare sight in most districts.

The great assemblage of tribes at Rotorua in 1901 to greet the empire's Royal couple was the last large congress of the native race, the last parade at which the tattooed men of the old generation were seen. To see them after that was an increasingly rare incident. The benevolent, shrewd old face of Patara te Tuhi, made famous by Mr C. F. Goldie in his paintings of tattooed types, was one of the last seen frequently in Auckland. Patara survived until 1911. Another of Mr Goldie's subjects, Kamariera Wharepapa, of Mangakahia, a Ngapuhi chief with a romantic history, was one who outlived Patara. But the dark-chiselled face of the old New Zealander was after that period only to be seen in the outer parts of the land, here and there—the Waikato, on Taupo's shores, and in the Urewera Country. That was where the ancient art last lingered. The last three tattooed warrior faces I saw were at Ruatoki, Waimana and Ruatahuna, in 1921; venerable guerilla bush fighters of the Urewera, old scouts and mountaineers, lone relics of a wild and thrilling past that survived into the beginning of a new era for the Maori.

The last tattooed male Maori has gone; never again will living man gaze upon his face, so splendidly, so heroically carved with the classic chisel of Mataora. The last survivor to my knowledge was Ngakuru Pana, a fine-looking chief of the Hokianga sections of Ngapuhi; his home was at Waimamaku. He told me that he was born, he estimated, five years before the signing of the Treaty of Waitangi. When he visited Wellington on native land business many years ago I took him to the Government photographer, as was usually my way when a tattooed acquaintance of mine came to town. The old-timers were pleased to be photographed on such occasions. There was a time when the camera, like the surveyor's theodolite, was an object of suspicion in the kainga. No photographer was ever allowed to obtain a picture of Te Kooti or of Te Whiti. Their sacred mana was jealously hedged about by their followers. But there were many I have known who were very willing to have their deeply-trenched lines of facial decoration gone over with a fine brush and black colour in order so that the photograph should reproduce the moko fully and clearly. King Tawhaio's cousin, the old Ngati Mahuta chief Mahutu te Toko, was one of those whom I conveyed to a studio for the purpose of a portrait. We very carefully heightened his handsome moko with black paint; with the result that when he looked in the mirror he was so delighted that he declared he would not wash his face for a month; his youth had been renewed; he looked as if he had just been tattooed (without pain this time) and coloured with the black Ngarehu pigment from the soot of burning kauri gum.

For many years the study of moko and its details and variations has been one of my pet interests, in the course of researches into matters Maori. There were often small differences in patterns followed by the various tribes which only close study would reveal. To the casual eye one face-suit of moko would exactly resemble another. Very often this was the case; but the tohunga-ta-moko, the artist who plied the bone or steel chisel and the little tapper or mallet, would occasionally vary his design, in accordance with his hereditary teaching or the suggestions of his client—or patient. When I made a careful pencil drawing of the tattoo that stood out like a fierce black mask on the features of Netana Whakaari, one of the last Urewera chiefs of the old brigade (the scene was on the banks of the Waimana River), I saw that the tattooer had made a curious break in the two middle rows of curved 'tiwhana', the arch-like moko on the forehead. This interruption, of an inch or so, is peculiar, I think, to the Urewera and Arawa districts. I have very seldom seen it broken in that manner and then continued in a symmetrical zigzag to the side of the head. The only example I can recall just now besides old Netana (who sat very patiently for me and talked of his bush warfare days while I copied his face-picture) is not a living figure but a wood carving, the Hou-taiki effigy, at the foot of the Ngati-Whakaue flagstaff in front of the carved house Tama-te-Kapua at Ohinemutu.

Netana told me that he was tattooed at Taurau, Ruatoki, before the beginning of the Taranaki war, 1860; the artist-operator was a hunchback man whose fathers before him had been tattooers and carvers. Comparatively few men were tattooed after that period; in the King Country there was a revival of the art about 1865, by King Tawhaio's order, in keeping with the revival of other olden practices. Netana's moko gave him a singularly fierce appearance; it was very black, and his glittering eyes looked as from a closely-fitting mask of curves and spirals, varied by the straight lines down the nose.

I have read many an erroneous account of moko by those who knew nothing about the subject at first-hand. It has been asserted, for example, that no two patterns of tattoo on men's faces were alike; and that elaborate tattoo was the prerogative of a chief; that it was his exclusive badge. Obviously it was impossible that there should be tens of thousands of different designs. Of the many hundreds of tattooed faces I have seen there were a great many which as far as I could discover exactly resembled each other. There were, of course, many variations, due to the artist's taste or the tattooed one's fancy, or inability to endure a complete moko operation. So far from the decoration being exclusive, anyone could be tattooed fully and artistically, whatever his status in the tribe, provided he could recompense the artist well.

The old-time moko artists I knew, the grand old moko'd faces we used to see, have all passed to the Reinga. But the art could readily enough be revived. An expert wood carver could also practise tattooing. We have all the old designs, preserved in pictures and on the figures in carved houses. All that is needed is the olden spirit that admired and endured. Will any of the Young Maori Men's Party volunteer and submit their lamentably smooth faces to the beautifying touch of the 'Uhi-a-Mataora', in the noble joint cause of science and art?

The women, as a class, are more conservative than the young men. Now and again a tattoo of the modern type punctures and pigments the chin of brown beauty; and very handsome those 'kauwae' patterns are. But, alas, the paleface lipstick and powder dab have the preference; the Maori is losing the olden sense of the artistic fitness of things.

Auckland Star, 9 November 1935, magazine section, p.12.

from The Art of C. F. Goldie: A Great Painter and Interpreter of a People (1941)

[...] Before long he secured as a subject for his brush a grand old tattooed chief who in those years was a friend of mine and one of my most valued tutors in Maori lore, the venerable Patara te Tuhi, who lived at Mangere on the Manukau Harbour. It was not merely a matter of paying a model for sittings; the importance of preserving for future generations the best examples of the Maori rangatira whose class was fast disappearing had to be explained to him. Patara quickly appreciated the position; he agreed to sit for Goldie, and sit he did, faithfully coming from Mangere on the appointed days—a benevolent-looking aristocratic sage, whose deeply-tattooed face has become familiar to thousands through Goldie's portraits.

Patara had a brother, Honana Maioha, who like him had been a councillor deep in the confidence of the Maori king. Honana was a keen lawyer-like man, a tattooed business man; he scolded Patara for sitting to the pakeha artist for five shillings a sitting of an hour when that artist was going to make pictures that would sell for thousands of pounds. But good old Patara only smiled his wise old smile, and went on sitting with his accustomed benevolent patience. One day in midsummer the ancient nodded and fell asleep, overcome by the heat; and Goldie, delighted with the natural pose, produced his first really great portrait.

Then from his studio, where he worked away steadily, with intervals every now and again when he went into the Maori districts, there came a procession of wonderful studies of the tattooed men and women of the race—glorious works, preserving with the utmost fidelity the features and flesh colouring and the closest detail of tattooing.

[...] In New Zealand he came to know numerous tribes, and many old pakeha residents, who helped him to secure subjects for his brush. Several men in particular, with fine features, beautifully tattooed, were from the Ngapuhi tribe, of the North. They were famed in their younger days for their chieftain-like looks and their deportment, and there were some who made history in their day. Further south, there were greatly contrasting types; one was a dour old bushman who lived near Tarukenga, overlooking Rotorua: he was of a small tribe of vassals to the lordly Arawa, who aforetime provided human sacrifices at the launching of new war canoes or the opening of a new carved house.

Another, whose portrait by Goldie was a revelation to the art world in Paris and London, was the ancient warrior and tohunga Wharekauri, whom Goldie found at Whirinaki, on the border of the Urewera Country. He was at least a hundred years old—not the only centenarian in the artist's sitters—he had been a cannibal like many of his contemporaries. By contrast, there are beautiful portraits of Maori women, in gentle, retrospective mood. The artist sees them with their thoughts fixed on the past, the days never to return.

New Zealand Magazine, March-April 1941, pp.8-12.

goldie's exhibitions

Like most artists, Goldie failed to create an inventory of the works that left his studio. For this reason, the records of paintings exhibited over the first 25 years of his career are a valuable indication of the original output. Titles of works are given *as they appeared in printed catalogues*, even though some are misspellings of the titles that Goldie invariably supplied on labels fixed to the reverse of the frame. It should be noted that several of the forged Goldie paintings that have appeared in recent years come complete with such a label, itself a forgery of Goldie's distinctive script.

Goldie's handwritten list of Maori studies, which accompanied their loan to the Auckland Art Gallery in 1920, record the collection which (mostly) ended up in the Auckland Museum.

In the absence of John Leech's sales records, the true extent of Goldie's later *œuvre* remains unknown. Nevertheless, the record of works exhibited during this period can be supplemented by the paintings remaining with the artist and his dealer at the end of Goldie's life. These are listed in the official valuation of Goldie's collection, which also includes the loan collection at Auckland Art Gallery. The complete valuation document is given, for the values placed on the works in 1947 differ considerably from the blanket insurance cover of £150 per item in the original loan document of 1920.

All of these lists overlap, frustrating any attempt to place an absolute figure on Goldie's output.

new zealand art students' association

1885 Drawing (second prize, letter of commendation)
1886 Still Life: Maori carvings, mere, baler, matting, and tui-bird (watercolour, bronze medal)

auckland academy of art

1890 34 Still Life, Souvenirs from the Battle Field (first prize)
1891 23 A Study of Native Birds (bronze medal)
34 Group of Schnapper with Goldfish in Bowl
1892 4 Study of New Zealand trees (silver medal)
– Kawhena (silver medal)

auckland industrial and mining exhibition

1898–1899 5 Portrait (after Rembrandt)
16 The Last Supper (after Tiepolo)
35 Solitude £5-5-0
40 Study of an Old Man (after Rembrandt)
51 Portrait of Simon de Vos (after de Vos)
102 Portrait (after Bailly)
103 A Study from Life
105 A Martyr £10-10-0
109 Portrait of a Dutch Burgomaster (after Rembrandt)

auckland society of arts

1885 Shaded Study from the Round—Ornament (certificate of merit)
1886 Study of Still Life, in Oils (third certificate)
1887 Shaded Study from the Round—Ornament
Study of Still Life, in Oils [roses] (one guinea prize)
1888 56 Still Life Study
Painted plaque [convolvulus on gilt background]
1889 57 A Quiet Spot, Waitakerei
1890 – Souvenirs from the Field of Battle
– Study of a tree fern (watercolour; honourable mention)
1891 111 Still Life [fish] (honourable mention)
1894 "Shaded Study of a Head, from the Antique" (Bronze medal)
Two drawings sent from Paris
1895 34 Defiance
65 Head of Italian
1899 8 (with L. J. Steele)
Arrival of the Maoris in New Zealand £200-0-0
1900 13 Portrait of C. L. Kerry, Esq.
27 Study from Life
110 Of making many Books there is no end, and much Study is a weariness of the Flesh
114 Study from life
120 Tamehana (from life)
1901 13 Sammy's Smile £14-14-0
19 Portrait (Hon. W. Swanson, Esq., M.L.C.)
34 Portrait
44 Kai Paipa £15-15-0
57 "Aperahama" (Te Arawa Tribe)
77 Caught Napping £12-12-0
70 Patara te Tuhi (an old warrior)
93 A Study from Life
109 Hamiora Haupapa (Te Arawa Tribe)
130 Suspicion £10-10-0
1903 18 One of the "Old School"
38 Darby and Joan (unfinished)
45 Ena te Papatahi, a chieftainess of the Ngapuhi Tribe £26-5-0
60 Ahinata te Rangitautini, Tuhourangi Tribe
94 The Widow
1904 11 Portrait J. R. Hooper, Esq.
19 Memories £31-10-0
47 Meditation £26-5-0
1905 20 A Hero of Many Fights
36 Te Aho (a noted Waikato Warrior)
67 "All 'e Same 'te Pakeha"
82 A Study
100 Perema Te Pahau (the Bone Scraper), Tuhourangi Tribe £31-10-0
104 Portrait, T. W. Leys, Esq.
123 Portrait
137 "The Memory of what has been and never more will be" (picture unfinished)
151 Forty Winks £35-0-0
1906 136 "The Calm Close of Valour's Various Day" (Te Aho, a Noted Warrior)
177 "Sophia"
211 Suspicion
1907 8 Te Hau-Takiri Wharepapa, a Chieftain of the Ngapuhi Tribe
28 A Noble Relic of a Noble Race
81 A Study
88 Suspicion
99 Touched by the Hand of Time
113 Te Hei, Ngatiraukawa Tribe
1908 12 A Study
17 The Last Sleep
19 Harata Rewiri Tarapata (widow of the late Chief Paul Tuhaere, of Orakei)
46 Tikitere Mihi (a noted Chieftain of the Ngatiuenuku)
57 Anaha te Rahui (the celebrated Carver of Rotorua)
191 Ahinata te Rangitautini (a chieftainess of the Tuhourangi Tribe)
292 A Study
297 Patara te Tuhi
342 A Centenarian
1909 2 Ahinata te Rangitautini, a chieftainess of the Tuhourangi Tribe £18-18-0
11 A Centenarian, Aperahama, aged 104 £73-10-0
31 Weary with Years £63-0-0
46 Patara (The Scribe)
48 Kapi Kapi (Rotorua)
79 Treasured Dreams of Times Long Past
1910 23 The Old Lion £105-0-0
87 Nikorima and Nicotina £45-0-0
312 Kapi Kapi (aged 102); A Survivor of the Tarawera Eruption £15-0-0
1911 22 The Last of the Cannibals
48 Memories, Rakapa. An Arawa Chieftainess £14-14-0
56 Sophia, the Heroine of Tarawera £14-14-0
80 A Noble Relic of a Noble Race, Wharekauri Tahuna, a 'Tohunga' or priest of the Tuhoe Tribe £78-15-0
124 Hiamoe (Drowsy), Sophia the Heroine of Tarawera £16-16-0
138 The Child Christ in the Temple, questioning with the Doctors, found by His parents £250-0-0
1912 2 Maramena Uiari. A Chieftainess of the Tuhourangi Tribe £12-12-0
12 Memories. Rakapa, an Arawa Chieftainess £14-14-0
64 The Widow £63-10-0
69 Night in the Whare £47-10-0
99 A Noble Northern Chief, Atama Paparangi £84-0-0
137 The Model's Dilemma £47-10-0
317 No Koora te Cigaretti £14-14-0
324 The Late Sophia, the Heroine of Tarawera £12-12-0
1913 6 No koora te Cigaretti £20-0-0
18 The Cannibal £78-15-0
43 Hinemoa, the Belle of the Kainga £31-10-0
49 The Whitening Snows of Venerable Eld, Otama Paparangi £16-16-0
71 Rakapa, an Arawa Chieftainess £14-14-0
75 A Centenarian, Kapi Kapi (a survivor of the Tarawera Eruption) £14-14-0
100 One of the old School, Wiripine Ninia (a Ngatiawa Chieftainess) £14-14-0
104 "Memories," the Last of her Tribe £68-15-0
1914 15 Peeping Patara £73-10-0
38 The Last of the Tohungas (or Priests), Wharekauri Tahuna £95-0-0
97 The Whitening Snows of Venerable Eld £19-19-0
111 Sad Memories £14-14-0
123 Te Aitu te Irikau, an Arawa Chieftainess £12-12-0
132 Memories £21-0-0
139 Supplication £55-15-0
1915 22 The Widow £14-14-0
40 Memories—"Wiripine Ninia, a Ngatiawa Chieftainess" £13-13-0
45 No Koora te Cigaretti £14-14-0
82 Wiripine Ninia, a Ngatiawa Chieftainess £21-0-0
121 Rakapa, an Arawa Chieftainess £13-13-0
148 Memories—Ena te Papatahi (a Ngapuhi Chieftainess) £14-14-0
161 Drowsy—Pipihuka (a Ngatiwhakane Chieftainess) £14-14-0
1916 36 Memories: Wiripine Ninia (a Ngatiawa Chieftainess) £13-13-0
102 Tamaiti Tukino, an Arawa Chieftainess £8-8-0
119 Kai Paipa £13-13-0
130 Te Aitu te Irikau—An Arawa Chieftainess £13-13-0
138 Reverie: Ena Papatahi, a Ngapuhi Chieftainess £26-5-0
144 Kapai te Torori, Kiri Matao £14-14-0
154 Wharekauri Tahuna (The Last of the Tohungas), Tuhoe Tribe £21-0-0
1917 7 "Memories" Mihipeka Wairama (an Arawa Chieftainess) £13-13-0
43 "Sad Memories", Ngaheke (an Arawa Chieftainess) £15-15-0

63 No Koora te Cigaretti—Kapi Kapi (aged 102 years) £10-10-0
68 In Doubt. Maramena Wiari (an Arawa Chieftainess) £14-14-0
70 "Life's Long Day Closes". Atama Paparangi (a Rarawa Chieftain) £18-18-0
77 Grief. Perira te KahuKura (an Arawa Chieftainess) £10-10-0
88 "No koora te cigaretti". Te Hune (a Touhorangi Chieftainess) £13-13-0
117 Te Hei (a Ngatiraukawa Chieftainess) £10-10-0
119 Memories. Te Aitu te Irikau (an Arawa Chieftainess) £10-10-0
1918 25 Memories of a Heroine—Hera Puna (widow of the late chief, Hori Ngakapa) £17-17-0
28 One of the Old School—Wiripine Ninia (a Chieftainess of the Ngatiawa Tribe) £17-17-0
75 The Whitening Snows of Venerable Eld—Kamaka (a Chieftain of the Maniapoto Tribe, aged 90 years) £18-18-0
90 Weary—Harieta (an Arawa Chieftainess) £18-18-0
117 A High-born Lady—Kiri Matau (an Arawa Chieftainess) £14-14-0
128 A Woman of High Degree—Te Aitu te Irikau (an Arawa Chieftainess)
131 Life's Long Day Closes—Kapikapi (an Arawa Chieftainess, aged 102 years)
149 Reverie—Rakapa (an Arawa Chieftainess) £14-14-0
172 Ninety Years Have Passed—Tamaiti Tukino (a Chieftainess of the Tuwharetoa Tribe) £18-18-0
1919 6 Pipi Puzzled. Pipihaerehuka (a chieftainess of the Ngatiwhakaue Tribe) £15-15-0
11 Sophia (the Heroine of Tarawera aged 85 years) £12-12-0
30 A Warrior Widow Wiripine Ninia (a chieftainess of the Ngatiawa Tribe) £16-16-0
32 Planning Revenge. Pokai (a warrior chieftain of the Ngatimaru Tribe) £21-0-0
73 A Centenarian. Kapikapi (an Arawa Chieftainess aged 102 years) £16-16-0
116 "A Noble Relic of a Noble Race". Atama Paparangi (a Chieftain of the Rarawa Tribe) £26-5-0
125 "Reverie"—Te Aitu Te Irikau (an Arawa Chieftainess) £10-10-0
127 "Memories"—Tamaiti Tukino, aged 95 years £8-8-0
137 "Memories of a Heroine"—Hera Puna (widow of the noted Chief Hori Ngakapa) £18-18-0

wanganui society of arts and crafts

1903 115 Harata Rewiri Tarapata, widow of the late Chief Paul, of Orakei £27-10-0
174 I Looked Far Back into Other Years £27-10-0

new zealand academy of fine arts, wellington

1900 21 The Morning Call, Venice £14-14-0
24 "Elaine" £12-12-0
48 There is a rapture on the lonely shore There is a society where none intrude (Byron) £6-6-0
1902 162 Kai Paipa £22-0-0
172 Portrait, the Hon W. Swanson, M.L.C.
183 Patara Te Tuhi, an old Warrior
1903 127 Harata Rewiri Tarapata, (widow of the late Chief Paul of Orakei) £27-10-0
128 Portrait, Lord Northland
155 "I Looked Far Back into Other Years" £21-10-0 [Hera Puna]
1909 153 A Centenarian £68-5-0
159 Weary with Years £63-0-0
171 A Centenarian, Kapi Kapi, Rotorua £63-0-0
208 Tihiteri Mihi, Polorua £84-0-0
251 Ahinata Te Rangatautiui £15-15-0
263 (Memories) Te Hei £10-10-0
287 The Majesty of Death £47-5-0
1910 201 Nikorima and Nicotina £38-10-0
220 Wharekauri—A Noble Relic of a Noble Race £84-0-0
221 Memories—Rakapa, an Arawa Chieftainess £15-15-0
222 Sophia, the Heroine of Tarawera £15-15-0
254 The Old Lion (Te Aho te Rangi) £84-0-0
255 Ahinata (aged 102 years)—A Survivor of the Tarawera Eruption £12-12-0
258 A Ngatiraukawe Joke £12-12-0
1911 233 Rakapa, an Arawa Chieftainess £15-15-0
249 Sophia, the Heroine of Tarawera £15-15-0
256 Ena, Te Papatahi "Memories" £16-16-0
262 Te Aho te Rangi (a noted warrior of the Ngatimahuta tribe) £18-18-0
273 Wharekawi Tahuna (a Tohunga of Tuhoe Tribe, Age 100 years) £18-18-0
293 Uripine Ninia (a Chieftainess of the Ngatiawa Tribe) £16-16-0
307 Te Aitu te Irakau, an Arawa Chieftainess £12-12-0

canterbury jubilee industrial exhibition

1900 5 A Portrait, after Rembrandt
11 "Arrival of the Maoris in New Zealand", C. F. Goldie and L. J. Steele, lent by Art Gallery, Auckland
23 A Burgomaster, after Rembrandt
34 Study from Life
70 "The Four Evangelists", after Jordaens
274 "Elaine" £12-12-0

canterbury society of arts

1901 59 "Of Making many Books there is no End, and much Study is a Weariness to the Flesh" £17-17-0
61 One of the Old School £17-17-0
1902 1 A Hot Day £26-5-0
57 Patara te Tuhi, an old Warrior £60-0-0
83 Caught Napping £16-16-0
84 "Sammy", Rotorua £18-18-0
1903 10 Hon. Swanson £80-0-0
16 Harata Rewiri Tarapara
36 Ena Te Papatahi £26-5-0
51 The Sentry £9-9-0
97 Sad Thoughts £18-18-0
1904 47 Memories £27-10-0
55 Harata Rewia Tarapata £27-10-0
1905 11 Meditation £26-15-0
53 The late Perema te Pahau, "The Bone Scraper" £38-10-0
69 "40 Winks" £38-10-0
382 Sad Memories (lent by Mr Roper)
1908 24 Te Hau Takiri Wharepapa £105-0-0
89 Touched by the Hand of Time £63-0-0
101 A Centenarian £68-5-0
1909 45 A Centenarian. "Aperahama," aged 104 years £68-5-0
57 Fire and Smoke £47-5-0
353 The Last Sleep £47-5-0
1910 8 Tikitere Mihi (an Arawa Chieftain) £73-10-0
178 The Smile of a Ngatiraukawe £14-14-0
181 Kapi Kapi (102 years) a Survivor of the Tarawera Eruption £14-14-0
191 Memories, Ena te Papatahi, a Chieftainess of the Ngapuhi tribe £14-14-0
275 Weary with years, Te Aho (a famous Warrior) £63-0-0
1911 2 "A Noble Relic of a Noble Race", Wharekauri Tahuna, A Tohunga or Priest of the Tuhoe Tribe £78-15-0
25 Hiamoe (Drowsy) Sophia, the Heroine of Tarawera £18-18-0
35 Ena te Papatahi—A Ngapuhi Chieftainess £16-16-0
38 Rakapa—An Arawa Chieftainess £14-14-0
41 Sophia—The Heroine of Terawera £16-16-0
43 Te Aitu te Irikau—An Arawa Chieftainess £14-14-0
44 Memories, Rakapa—An Arawa Chieftainess £14-14-0
1912 69 Wiripine Ninia (a Chieftainess of the Ngati-awa tribe) £16-16-0
70 Rakapa (An Arawa Chieftainess) £16-16-0
71 The late Sophia (The Heroine of Tarawera) £15-15-0
72 Wharekauri Tahuna—a Tohunga (or priest) of the Tuhoe Tribe £18-18-0
73 Te Aitu te Irikau (An Arawa Chieftainess) £12-12-0
394 The Widow £52-10-0
1914 306 In Doubt £12-12-0
321 Te Aitu te Irikau; An Arawa Chieftainess £12-12-0
322 No koora te Cigaretti £13-13-0
327 The Widow £13-13-0
328 Sulks £13-13-0
1916 273 The Widow "Ngaheke" £18-18-0
277 Memories £17-17-0
287 Drowsy, Pipihaerehuka, an Arawa Chieftainess £13-13-0
288 Kapai te Torori £14-14-0
293 Te Aitu te Trikau, an Arawa Chieftainess £13-13-0
1917 15 Lost in Thought, Ngahetze [sic], An Arawa Chieftain [sic] £15-15-0
16 Distrust, Maramina Wiara £14-14-0
24 Memories—Waripine Ninia £13-13-0
25 "The Memory of what has been and never more will be". Harieta (An Arawa Chieftainess) £16-16-0
311 No koora te cigaretti. Te Hume (Chieftainess of the Touhourangi Tribe) £13-13-0

south canterbury art society (timaru)

1913 163 When Mild Evening Comes in Mantle Grey £8-8-0
164 One of the Old School, Wiripine Ninia, a Ngatiawa Chieftainess £14-14-0
169 Reverie (lent by Mrs Wm Grant)
215 Rakapa, an Arawa Chieftainess £13-13-0
274 Memories. The last of her Tribe £68-15-0
312 The Last of the Cannibals, Tumai Tawhiti £84-0-0
332 No Koora Te Cigar £12-12-0

otago art society

1902 14 "Kai Paipa" £22-0-0
21 Patara Te Tuhi (an old Warrior)
41 Caught Napping £12-12-0
73 "Kai Paipa" £26-5-0
89 Ena Papatahi, a Chieftainess of the Ngapuhi Tribe £31-10-0
1904 85 Meditation £26-15-0
99 Harata Rewiri Tarapata (Widow of the late Chief Paul Tukaere of Orakei) £31-15-0
1908 15 Amaha te Rahui (the Noted Carver of Rotorua) £52-10-0
31 A Centenarian £63-0-0
61 Fire and Smoke £52-10-0
181 The Last Sleep £57-15-0
234 Ti Hau Takiri, Wharepapa, a Noted Chieftain of the Ngaputu Tribe
1909 29 Tikitere Mihi £84-0-0
65 Weary with Years £63-0-0
83 A Centenarian, "Apirahama" (aged 104 years) £68-5-0

145 The Old Sentinel £12-12-0
149 "Ahinata" (A Chieftainess of the Inhourangi Tribe, aged 102 years) £12-12-0
1910 27 *Hiamoe* (Sleepy), *Ena te Paputahi* (a Chieftainess of the Ngapuhi Tribe) £14-14-0
34 Wharekauri (a Noble Relic of a Noble Race) £84-0-0
112 The Old Lion (Te Aho te Rangi) £84-0-0
127 Patara (the Scribe), a noted Chieftain of the Ngatimahuta £16-16-0
169 Memories, Rakapa, an Arawa Chieftainess £10-10-0
173 No Koora te Higaretti, Kapi, Kapi, (A Survivor of the Tarawera Eruption, age 102.) £14-14-0
1911 120 Te Aitu te Iri Hau, an Arawa Chieftainess £12-12-0
130 Memories, Wiripine Ninia, a Chieftainess of the Ngatiawa Tribe £16-16-0
145 Memories, Ena te Papatahi, a Ngapuhi Chieftainess £16-16-0
151 Sophia, The Heroine of Tarawera £15-15-0
155 Whare Kauri-Tahuna (A Tohunga of the Tuhoe Tribe, aged 100 years) £18-18-0
161 Te Aho Te Rangi (A noted Warrior of the Ngatimahuta Tribe) £18-18-0
1912 61 A Noble Northern Chief, Atama Paparangi £22-10-0
67 Memories, Wiripine Ninia, An Arawa Chieftainess £13-13-0
68 The Widow £52-10-0
76 The Model's Dilemma, "Don't move, it's only a fly" £42-10-0
85 In Doubt, Haratu-Tunapatu, a Ngapuki Chieftainess £12-12-0
89 "One of the Old School." Tamaiti Tukinu, an Arawa Chieftainess £10-10-0
115 Mara Mena Wiari, a Tuhourangi Chieftainess £14-14-0
1913 19 When Mild Evening comes in Mantle Grey £8-8-0
87 Rakapa, an Arawa Chieftainess £13-13-0
1915 12 The Widow £21-0-0
15 Memories, Winpine Ninia, a Ngatiawa Chieftainess £18-18-0
67 A Centenarian, Kapi Kapi Au Kawa, Chieftainess, aged 102 years £13-13-0
70 No Koora te Cigaretti £13-13-0
143 Winpine Ninia, a Ngatiawa Chieftainess £12-12-0
146 Drowsy, Pipihaerehuka, a Chieftainess of the Ngatiwhakane Tribe £13-13-0
1916 4 A Chieftainess of the Tuhourangi Tribe £13-13-0
11 Lost in Thought £15-15-0
35 Memories £13-13-0
63 A Chief of the Ngatimahuta Tribe £16-16-0
75 An Arawa Chieftainess £13-13-0
102 An Arawa Chieftainess £17-17-0

royal academy of arts, london

1934 371 Memories: Te Arani, a Chieftainess of the Arawa tribe of Maoris, Rotorua
376 Thoughts of a Tohunga: Wharekauri Tahuna, a Priest of the Tuhoe tribe of Maoris, Rotorua
591 An Aristocrat: Atama Paparangi, a Chieftain of the Rarawa tribe of Maoris, New Zealand
1935 514 Pokai, a warrior chieftain of the Ngatimaru Tribe, N.Z.

société des artistes français, paris

1935 1045 Les Pensées d'un prêtre: Wharekauri Tahuna: Un prêtre indigène de la Nouvelle Zélande
1936 1129 Le sommeil
1130 Il fait lourd
1938 716 In Dreamland [illustrated in catalogue]
717 A Midsummer's day
1939 1324 Thoughts of a Tohunga
1325 In Doubt (Atama Paparangi)

māori studies deposited at auckland art gallery, october 1920

1 Te Aho te Rangi (full face)
2 Kamariera Te Hautakiri Wharepapa (full face)
3 Tikitere Mihi
4 Anaha te Rahui
5 Wharekauri Tahuna
6 Atama Paparangi
7 Te Hei ¾ face
8 The Majesty of Death
9 Tumai Tawhiti (The Last of the Cannibals)
10 Ahinata te Rangitautini
11 Apcrehama (The Old Lion) *
12 Perema te Pahau (The Bone Scraper)
13 A Noble Relic of a Noble Race
14 Perema te Pahau
15 Te Aho (Study showing tatooing under chin etc)
16 "Memories" Te Hei
17 Anaha (profile)
18 "Napping" Ena te Papatahi
19 Patara te Tuhi (The Scribe)
20 "A Hero of Many Fights"
21 Peeping Patara
22 "Life's Long Day Closes"
23 The Model's Dilemma
24 Hinemoa (The Pride of the Pah)
25 "The Widow" Tamaiti Tukino
26 Hohua Matchlight effect unfinished study
27 Perema small study

* This picture was withdrawn from the Collection by instructions of the Town Clerk, it have [sic] been purchased from the artist with the purpose of being presented to Lady Jellicoe. See Town Clerks Minute dated 15 Nov. 1924.
[Insurance:] 1-25: £150; 26,27: £75.

c.f. goldie picture valuation 1947

Paintings at John Leech Ltd

1	Te Hei Ngatiraukawa Tribe "Kapai te Kai paipa"	£150
2	The Blind Woman of Taupo	£183.15
3	"Suspicion" Mihipeka Wairama Tuhourangi Tribe Whakarewarewa Rotorua	£183.15
4	A Gray Day (Child Study)	£ 40
5	As Rembrandt would have painted the Maori	£157.10
6	Day Dreams Ngataria Haupapa Arawa Tribe	£145
7	Complacency Takarea Te Heu Heu A Chieftainess of the Arawa Tribe	£95
8	Perira Te Kahukura or Ngaheke Ohinemutu	£135
9	"A Midsummer Day" Maoriland Pokai	£345
10	Perira Te Kahukura or Ngaheka [sic]	£290
10A	Wharekauri Tahuna	£75
10B	Unfinished Canvas	£10

Paintings at the Goldie Residence

11	"Pokai Perturbed" Ngatamaru Tribe Thames	£120
12	"In Dreamland" Ina Te Papatahi of Ngapuhi Tribe	£100
13	"Thoughts of a Tohunga" Wharekauri Tahuna of Galatea Chief and Tohunga of Tuhoa Tribe	£230
14	"In Doubt" Atama Paparangi A Chief of the Rarawa Tribe	£210
15	Tumai Tawhiti An Arawa Chief	£180
16	Head of Te Aho te Rangi (Foreshortened to show under chin)	£70

Paintings at the Auckland Art Gallery: Maori Studies

17	Memories	£100
18	Hohua — A Study	£40
19	Hinemoa The Pride of the Pah	£40
20	Peeping Patara	£30
21	Te Aho te Rangi	£160
22	Anaha te Rahui (full face)	£100
23	Patara te Tuhi	£200
24	A Noble Relic of a Noble Race	£185
25	A hero of Many Fights	£150
26	Parema [sic] te Pahau	£175
27	The Majesty of Death	£20
28	The Model's Dilemma	£15
29	Te Aho te Rangi	£60
30	Anaha te Rahui (profile)	£80
31	"Life's Long Day Closes"	£60
32	Tikitere Mihi	£175
33	Atama Paparangi	£160
34	Kamariera Wharepapa	£160
35	Apcrehama	£40
36	Te Hei	£100
37	"Napping" Ena Te Papatahi	£45
38	The Widow	£20
39	Aninata Te Rangitautiri [sic]	£95
40	Tumai Tawhiti The Last of the Cannibals	£80
41	"Grief" Ngaheke A Chieftainess of the Tuhourangi Tribe	£150
42	Wharekauri Tahuna	£130
43	Parema [sic] Te Pahau (The Bone Scraper)	£40
44	"A High-born Lady" Hamapara Teurahori	£130
45	Mita Taupopoki	£60

Copies and Original Studies: Auckland Art Gallery

46	Rembrandt Portrait of the Artist	£2
47	Rembrandt Burgomaster	£10
48	Rembrandt Cavalier	Nil
49	Rembrandt Young Man	£5
50	Rembrandt Old Man	Nil
51	Jordaens The Four Evangelists	Nil
52	Bailly Portrait of a Young Man	£8
53	Tiepolo The Last Supper	£3
54	Millet The Bathers	Nil
55	De Vos Portrait of the Artist	£5
56	Goya Head of Christ	£5
57	Ribera The Entombment	£1
58	Prud'hon The Cricifixion [sic]	£1
59	Original Study An Old Italian (head)	£2
60	Original Study Supplication	£5
61	Fragonard Nymphs	Nil
62	Original Portrait of a Lady	£1
63	Competition Study	£3
64	Competition Study	£3
65	Competition Study	£3
66	R. Gwelo Goodman Landscape	£2
67	Original Study Boy's Head	£1
68	Original Study "The Blind Model"	£1
69	Colour note after Restout St Paul giving sight to Ananias	£2
70	Colour note after Andrea de Sarto The Holy Family and St. John – Louvre	£2
71	Original Composition Death of Virginius	£2
72	The Return of Marcus Sectius Study in Composition after Guerin — Louvre	£2
73	Original Composition "By the Waters of Babylon"	£1
74	Original Study Old Man's Head	Nil
Total Value		*£5570*

notes to the text

References to Goldie's Scrapbooks refer to the volumes held in the Auckland Museum Library.

introduction

1 Florence Roberts, 'Goldie – many know the painter, few know the man', *New Zealand Woman's Weekly*, 20 October 1958, p.9.
2 'The passing show', *Auckland Star*, 5 June 1935, p.6.

early life

1 For further family details refer to the biography in Taylor & Glen, 1977, pp.5-36.
2 G. W. A. Bush, *Decently and in Order*, p.208.
3 Eliot R. Davis, *A Link with the Past*, p.241.
4 The correspondence between Nell Chew and her American lover William Sharp was transcribed by Marge Stacey, who donated a copy to the Auckland City Library. I am grateful to Theresa Graham for bringing these letters to my attention.
5 Nell Chew to William Sharp, 2 December 1887.
6 Nell Chew to William Sharp, 20 December 1891.
7 Nell Chew to William Sharp, 1 April 1892.
8 'Sunday Schools' Industrial Exhibition', *Auckland Evening Star*, 23 November 1886, p.2.

an artist emerges

1 See Roger Blackley, 'The exhibitions of Maori art in Auckland 1884-1885: Documents of the New Zealand Art Students' Association', *Antic* 3, 1987, pp.116-122.
2 See Roger Blackley, 'The Greek statues in the Museum', *Art New Zealand* 48, Spring 1988, pp.96-99; Richard Wolfe, 'Shading from the round: the sketchbooks of Kennett Watkins', *Art New Zealand* 73, Summer 1994-95, pp.73-77.
3 Mick Pendergrast, *Te Aho Tapu, The Sacred Thread* (Auckland, 1987), pp.37, 96. The cloak was formally presented to the Auckland Museum by C. O. Davis in 1887, but may have entered the Museum at an earlier date. For a depiction of the Museum's earliest method of displaying cloaks, see Blackley, 'The Greek statues in the Museum', p.99.
4 *New Zealand Herald*, 18 April 1890, p.5.
5 *New Zealand Herald*, 28 April 1890, p.4.
6 'Academy of Art, the conversazione', *Auckland Star*, 29 April 1890, p.8.
7 Now in the collection of the Museum of New Zealand Te Papa Tongarewa.
8 *New Zealand Herald*, 28 May 1890, p.6.
9 *Auckland Weekly News*, 31 May 1890, p.30.
10 'The art exhibition. Noticeable pictures', *Auckland Star*, 4 March 1891, p.5.
11 *New Zealand Herald*, 16 March 1891, p.5. In fact, the only medal Goldie had won to date was from the Art Students' Association in 1886.
12 'Auckland Academy of Art', *New Zealand Herald*, 10 December 1891, p.5.
13 *New Zealand Herald*, 12 December 1891, p.5.
14 'Auckland Academy of Arts', *New Zealand Herald*, 14 December 1891, p.6.
15 A year earlier, L. J. Steele exhibited a portrait of Kawhena, 'Academy of Arts', *New Zealand Herald*, 12 December 1891, p.5.
16 'Auckland Academy of Art exhibition', *Auckland Star*, 12 December 1892, p3.
17 *Australian Star*, 26 November 1892, p.2.
18 See *Catalogue of the National Art Gallery of New South Wales*, Sydney, 1888.
19 See *Victorian Olympians*, exhibition catalogue, Art Gallery of New South Wales, 1975, p.25.

the académie julian, paris

1 Archives de l'Académie Julian, Archives Nationales, Paris. The relevant volumes are 63 AS 1, 'Livres de comptabilité des élèves, 31 rue du Dragon, atelier de gauche, Bouguereau et Ferrier'.
2 Archives Nationales, Paris, 63 AS 4, '31 rue du Dragon, atelier de droite, J. P. Laurens et B. Constant'.
3 Catherine Fehrer, *The Julian Academy, Paris, 1868-1939*, p.iv.
4 Alfred Nettement, writing in the journal *L'Académie Julian* in 1909, translated by Catherine Fehrer in *The Julian Academy*, cat. no.5.
5 Sealy, 'L'Académie Julian in Paris', reprinted later in this book. When he exhibited with the Salon of the Société des Artistes Français in 1935, Goldie listed his masters as Bouguereau, Ferrier, Constant, Doucet and Baschet. The following year he dropped Doucet from the list.
6 *Journal des Artistes*, 29 December 1895, p.1291.
7 *Auckland Weekly News*, 22 February 1896, p.18.
8 *Journal des Artistes*, 27 December 1896, p.1708.
9 Listed at the time of their loan to Auckland Art Gallery in 1920 (Research Library, Auckland Art Gallery Toi o Tāmaki).
10 Donated to the Luxembourg in 1895, the original is now in the Musée Petiet, Limoux. It measures 750 x 850 mm, only fractionally larger than Goldie's first copy on a canvas bearing the Senellier stamp (Auckland Art Gallery Toi o Tāmaki).
11 Goldie's 1934 article quotes extensively from 'Enquête à propos de la Donation Caillebotte', *Journal des Artistes*, 8 April 1894, p.1.

life in paris

1 Thomas Evans, 'In the Latin Quarter of to-day', *The Quartier Latin, Journal of the American Art Association of Paris*, vol.II, no.11, June 1897, p.360.
2 'The Quat'z'Arts Ball: extracts of a letter from Bill Hill to his friend Allan Jonson', *The Quartier Latin*, no.1, July 1896, p.19.
3 Several undated newspaper clippings quoting from such letters were pasted into Goldie's and his family's scrapbooks (eg. Scrapbook XI, p.56, concerning pictures Goldie admired at the Royal Academy in 1893).
4 Alexander Turnbull Library, A252/10-13.
5 Ibid, A 252/12. Another of these drawings (A252/11) is reproduced in Taylor & Glen, 1977, p.12.
6 Ibid, A 252/10.
7 'Artists and photographers', *Cyclopedia of New Zealand* (vol.2, Auckland), Christchurch, 1902, p. 321.
8 'M. Gabriel Ferrier au milieu de ses élèves', reproduced on the front cover of *L'Académie Julian*, November 1902 (Bibliothèque Nationale JO 50038). The portrait must have been taken before the summer of 1896, when Kirkpatrick left the school.
9 H. P. Sealy, 'In the studio, Mr C.F. Goldie's work', *New Zealand Illustrated Magazine*, November 1901. Kirkpatrick, an occasional runner-up in the Académie Julian prizelists, is a complete unknown in English art history.
10 *Cyclopedia of New Zealand*, (vol.2, Auckland), Christchurch, 1902, p.320.
11 *The Quartier Latin*, vol.III, no.15, October 1897, p.493.
12 Goldie himself never listed Guthrie as one of his teachers. The information appears to have been supplied to Taylor & Glen, via the Aigantighe Art Gallery, by a niece of Sir James Guthrie.

plans for the future

1 Undated newsclipping, Scrapbook XI, p.24.
2 Scrapbook XI, p.56: circa March 1897. The portrait competition took place in February 1897 (*Journal des Artistes*, 7 March 1897, p.1787).
3 C. F. Goldie to Grace Hesketh, Alexander Turnbull Library (A252/10).

the arrival

1 *Auckland Industrial and Mining Exhibition, Official Handbook and Catalogue*, Auckland, 1898.
2 'French Academy of Art exhibition', *New Zealand Graphic*, 4 November 1899, p.832.
3 'French Academy of Art exhibition', *Auckland Weekly News*, 3 November 1899, p.22.
4 'Society of Arts Exhibition', *Auckland Star*, 9 November 1899, p.2.
5 *The Wanderings of a Spiritualist*, London, 1921, facing p.208.
6 Gunn's memories are reported under 'Painting of picture', identified as *Auckland Star*, 22 May 1956 (Gallery Scrapbook, Research Library, Auckland Art Gallery Toi o Tāmaki).
7 James Cowan, 'The Art of C. F. Goldie: A Great Painter & Interpreter of a People', *New Zealand Magazine*, March-April 1941 pp.8-12.

launching a career

1 'Auckland Society of Arts exhibition', *New Zealand Graphic*, 27 October 1900, p.782.
2 'Auckland Society of Arts', *Auckland Star*, 22 October 1900, p.2.
3 'In the studio, Mr C.F. Goldie's work', *New Zealand Illustrated Magazine*, November 1901, p.146.
4 *Auckland Star*, 2 November 1900, p.4.
5 Taylor & Glen, 1977 and 1979. A different Goldie painting has hung for years in the Auckland Museum, labelled as Wiremu Tāmihana of Ngāti Hauā. According to Goldie's manuscript listing of the 1920 loans to Auckland Art Gallery, it depicts a man named Hohua (see reproduction on page 122).
6 'Auckland Society of Arts. Second notice', *Auckland Star*, 22 October 1900, p.2.
7 An unpublished *New Zealand Herald* photograph of 29 November 1954 shows the old frame, complete with *trompe l'œil* scarf, enclosed within a new white frame (Auckland Museum Library).
8 *New Zealand Herald*, 31 October 1933, p.12. Tautari died at Ōrākei on 29 October 1933, aged 99, several hours after the death of his 92-year-old brother-in-law, Te Hira Pateoro.
9 'The Auckland Society of Arts', identified by Goldie as *New Zealand Photographer*, 7 November 1900 (Scrapbook XI, p.64).
10 Clipping identified by Goldie as *Herald*, 19 October 1900 (Scrapbook XI, p.66).
11 Allen Hutchinson to C. F. Goldie, 18 October 1900 (Scrapbook XI, p.64).
12 For the presence of the 'Roman senator', see 'Christchurch Exhibition gallery of paintings', *Triad*, 1 December 1900, p.12.
13 'Auckland Society of Arts exhibition', *New Zealand Herald*, 1 November 1901, p.3.
14 'Auckland Society of Arts exhibition', *Auckland Star*, 25 October 1901, p.5.
15 'Society of Arts exhibition', *Auckland Star*, 1 November 1901, p.2.
16 'Random Shots', *Auckland Star*, 30 March 1901, supplement, p.4.
17 *Otago Witness*, December 1902, C. F. Goldie newsclippings (MS 6), Museum of New Zealand Te Papa Tongarewa.
18 Minutes, Auckland Society of Arts, MS 19 (A5,6), Auckland Museum Library.
19 For a reference to the factionalised Auckland art scene of the time, see H. P. Sealy, 'Art in an easy chair', *New Zealand Herald*, 26 October 1900, p.6.

noble relics

1 'Auckland Society of Arts exhibition', *New Zealand Herald*, 1 November 1901, p.3.
2 Death of Dr Goldie', *Auckland Star*, 16 June 1904, p.2.
3 William Goldie, 'Maori medical lore', *Transactions of the New Zealand Institute*, 1904, pp.1-120.
4 William Goldie, 'The destiny of the Maori race', *New Zealand Herald* (supplement), 18 May 1901, p.1.
5 'Ki a Ina kei Waipapa', Scrapbook XIII, p.182.
6 The signature is consistent with work from 1912,

which may be the date Goldie *intended* to inscribe. Goldie was not in the habit of 'forging' his own earlier works.

7 Te Aho-o-te-Rangi's invoices to Goldie are in Scrapbook XIII, pages 177-182. An invoice on page 181 states 'I tēnei rā me hōmai ki au ētehi hereni kia £1-0-0 pauna' (Today give me one pound, in shillings).

8 Scrapbook XIII, p.65. The second half of this letter is now missing. For an English translation see Taylor & Glen 1977, p.37.

9 Scrapbook XIII, p.177.

10 Scrapbook XIII, p.178.

11 Alfred Hill to Edward Tregear, 4 October 1904 (private collection).

12 J. M. Thomson, *A Distant Music: the Life and Times of Alfred Hill*, pp.81-82.

13 'Auckland Society of Arts: twenty-second annual exhibition,' *Auckland Star*, 30 April 1903, p.4.

14 *Tattooing in the Olden Time* is reproduced in Bell, *Colonial Constructs*, plate VI, opposite p.209.

15 *Observer*, 20 June 1903 (Scrapbook XI, p.81).

repeat performances

1 'Society of Arts', *Auckland Star*, 17 July 1905, p.2.

2 Lizzie H. Grant to C. F. Goldie (Scrapbook XI, p.80).

3 'Auckland art exhibition', *Auckland Star*, 29 April 1904, p.3.

4 'Society of Arts', *Auckland Star*, 19 July 1905, p.4.

5 A handwritten 'private' letter from Augustus Hamilton to Goldie, dated 30 January 1906, asks Goldie to hurry up with the 'list of pictures & proposed terms for originals & copies' (Scrapbook XIII, p.29). I am grateful to Eamonn Bolger and Ross O'Rourke for locating the original correspondence at the Museum of New Zealand Te Papa Tongarewa.

6 Ibid. Hamilton added: 'If pictures can be bought it is needless to say which ones I want.'

7 'Auckland Society of Arts exhibition', *New Zealand Graphic*, 2 June 1906, p.39.

8 Ibid.

9 Clipping identified by Goldie as *Auckland Star*, 21 February 1907 (Scrapbook XI, p.81).

enlarging the gallery

1 'Auckland Art Society, opening the exhibition,' *New Zealand Herald*, 25 April 1907, p.3.

2 'Auckland Art Society', *New Zealand Herald*, 25 April 1907, p.3.

3 'Auckland Society of Arts', *Auckland Star*, 27 April 1907, p.7.

4 'Purchase of pictures', *Auckland Star*, 20 May 1908, p.3.

5 'The Maori in bronze, a sculptor's trials', *New Zealand Herald*, 19 March 1908, p.6. Illingworth's friendship with Goldie is established by a letter dated 19 March 1908 (Scrapbook XI, p.38).

6 'Our comic artist's impressions of the Auckland Society of Arts' annual exhibition', *Auckland Weekly News*, 21 May 1908, supplement, p.5.

7 'Amongst the pictures. [No. I.]', undated clipping (Gallery Scrapbook, Robert McDougall Art Gallery).

8 'Canterbury Art Society', *Lyttelton Times*, 20 March 1909, p.7.

9 Reported by James Cowan; see 'Goldie's Collection', page 188 in this book.

the other side of fame

1 *Weekly Graphic*, 3 June 1908, p.43.

2 Christmas supplement, *Auckland Weekly News*, 1902.

3 Christmas supplement, *Weekly Press* (Christchurch), 1904.

4 Supplement, *New Zealand Graphic*, 22 July 1905.

5 The first chromolithograph dates from 1905, with another edition produced in England c.1910.

6 'The Auckland Society of Arts', *Triad*, vol.11, no.3, 1 June 1903, p.17.

7 'The Auckland Society of Arts', *Triad*, vol.16, no.4, 1 July 1908, p.10.

8 'Otago Art Society', *Otago Daily Times*, 24 November 1909, p.2.

9 *Evening Post*, 9 October 1911, p.2.

10 'Picture exhibition', *New Zealand Times*, 12 October 1911, p.5.

11 C. F. Goldie to Augustus Hamilton, 29 September 1910 (Museum of New Zealand Te Papa Tongarewa).

12 H. Wardell to C. F. Goldie (Scrapbook XI, p.66).

continuing the career

1 'Auckland Art Society', *New Zealand Herald*, 19 May 1909, p.8.

2 'Auckland Society of Arts', *Auckland Star*, 30 May 1910, p.6.

3 Scrapbook I, p.76.

4 'The picture of the exhibition', *New Zealand Herald*, 9 June 1911, p.7.

5 'Auckland's new pictures', *Weekly Graphic*, 22 January 1913, p.24.

6 'Auckland Society of Arts', *New Zealand Herald*, 22 June 1913, p.5.

7 The deed of settlement was dated 1 April 1913. Its existence is revealed in a court case concerning the estate of David Goldie (150/41, *Harry Tinsley Goldie v. N. A. Duthie and others*).

8 Goldie to Alfred Hill 23 Oct 1916, Hill Correspondence, vol. 2, pp.285-89, Mitchell Library, Sydney. I am grateful to Sarah Shieff for bringing this document to my attention.

elopement to sydney

1 John Barr to C.F. Goldie, 2 March 1921 (Research Library, Auckland Art Gallery Toi o Tāmaki).

2 'Sanity in art. . .Mr Sid Long's return', news clipping from June 1921 (Gallery Scrapbook, Art Gallery of New South Wales).

3 *New Zealand Observer*, 11 August 1923, p.4.

the menace of modernism

1 'Auckland through German eyes. A book by Dr Max Herz', *Auckland Star*, 18 January 1912, p.4.

2 *New Zealand Free Lance*, 10 January 1923, p.10.

3 Iris Wilkinson, 'Where Charles Goldie is supreme', *New Zealand Observer*, 17 January 1935, p.9.

4 Goldie to John Barr, 16 December 1921 (Research Library, Auckland Art Gallery Toi o Tāmaki).

5 'Art in New Zealand. Caustic criticism', *New Zealand Herald*, 24 October 1924, p.10.

6 'Mr Fisher's criticism. Great interest aroused', *New Zealand Herald*, 25 October 1924, p.12.

7 *New Zealand Herald*, 1 November 1924 (supplement), p.5.

8 'British pictures. Decadence in art', *New Zealand Herald*, 21 August 1934, p.12.

9 Eve Vaile, 'The art exhibition', *New Zealand Herald*, 23 August 1934, p.15.

10 'Art export ban: Mr C.F. Goldie's view', *New Zealand Herald*, 24 April 1934, p.8.

11 'The Art Gallery', *New Zealand Herald*, 4 February 1938, p.13, followed by the letter to the Mayor and Councillors, 19 March 1938 (Research Library, Auckland Art Gallery Toi o Tāmaki).

12 Evelyn C. Vaile, 'The Art Gallery', *New Zealand Herald*, 10 February 1938, p.15.

13 John Barr to the Town Clerk, 25 March 1938, attached to Goldie's letter of 19 March 1938.

the late career

1 James Cowan, 'Painting history', *Auckland Star*, 12 October 1933, p.6.

2 Viscount and Lady Bledisloe visited the Goldies on several occasions, extending an invitation to join them on the government yacht *Matai* at the Waitangi celebrations (Scrapbook XIII, p.164).

3 'Noted Maori chief. . . gift of Auckland artist', *New Zealand Herald*, 27 January 1934, p.12.

4 For reproductions, see Taylor & Glen 1979, plates 22 and 26.

5 Nelle M. Scanlan, 'Art as she is. This year's Academy', *Auckland Star*, 14 June 1934, p.6.

6 Now in the Auckland Museum, presented by Olive Goldie.

7 C. F. Goldie to T. T. Bond, 5 January 1936. Goldie's letters to Terry Bond, now in the archives of the Museum of New Zealand Te Papa Tongarewa, are reprinted in full in Taylor & Glen 1979, pp.17-23.

8 For the prices, see C. F. Goldie to T. T. Bond, 10 December 1935.

9 The price to Lady Bledisloe is confirmed in a letter from Cecil Day to C. F. Goldie, 26 February 1934 (Scrapbook XIII, p.50).

10 'Pictures at a guinea', *New Zealand Herald*, 6 September 1935, p.14.

11 Letter dated 31 August 1936 (Alexander Turnbull Library).

12 Taylor & Glen, 1977, p.35.

13 See Francis Pound, 'Some late signatures of Charles Frederick Goldie', *Art New Zealand* 5, 1977, p.16.

14 'Maori paintings, souvenirs for destroyer', *New Zealand Herald*, 15 July 1941, p.6.

goldie's posthumous fortunes

1 E. B. Gunson, 'Goldie paintings', *New Zealand Herald*, 29 January 1948, p.6.

2 Juan Les Pins, 'Goldie paintings', *New Zealand Herald*, 14 February 1948, p.8.

3 John Bell, 'Art for the people, shrewdly gathered', *Auckland Star*, 30 July 1951, p.4.

4 'Improvements at City Art Gallery', *Auckland Star*, 4 November 1954, p.4.

5 'Goldie's pupils tell restorer of his methods', *Auckland Star*, 24 March 1955, p.4.

6 Peter Tomory, Introduction to *New Zealand Painting*, exhibition catalogue, Auckland City Art Gallery, 1956, p.[5].

7 Art Lover, 'Art of Goldie', *New Zealand Herald*, 9 May 1956, p.10.

8 'Art of C. F. Goldie', *New Zealand Herald*, 11 May 1956, p.10.

9 J. D. Savage, 'Art of C. F. Goldie', *New Zealand Herald*, 18 May 1956, p.10.

10 A. Bryan, 'Lindauer and Goldie', *New Zealand Herald*, 29 August 1960, p.6.

11 Eric Lee-Johnson, 'Goldie and Lindauer', *New Zealand Herald*, 17 August 1960, p.6; Daniel Hay, 'Lindauer Collection', *New Zealand Herald*, 24 August 1960, p.8.

12 E. R., 'Goldie portraits proudly displayed in Wellington', *Evening Post*, 21 July 1960, p.28.

13 'Petition to Council on Goldie works', *North Shore Advertiser*, 6 August 1963, p.3.

breaking the records

1 'Pictures at a guinea', *New Zealand Herald*, 6 September 1935, p.14.

2 John Barr to George E. Buzza, 25 January 1944 (Research Library, Auckland Art Gallery Toi o Tāmaki).

3 Scrapbook XIII, p.144. The posthumous material in this scrapbook was inserted by Olive Goldie.

4 Scrapbook XIII, p.158. The sale at Elloughton Grange, home of the late William Grant, included a total of 45 paintings.

5 Harry Dansey, 'Why is there gold in the Goldies?', *Auckland Star*, 8 March 1969, p.7.

6 Dansey, ibid.

7 Sue Cornwell, 'Is it for the gold' in a Goldie – or for the art?', *New Zealand Woman's Weekly*, 15 May 1972.

8 'Top Goldie', *New Zealand Herald*, 10 December 1988, section 4 (Business Report), p.1.

theft, vandalism and forgery

1 'Two Goldies taken from auctioneers', *New Zealand Herald*, 24 July 1969, p.5.

2 'Goldie harm "malicious"', *New Zealand Herald*, 29 July 1969, p.6.

3 *Dominion Sunday Times*, 9 September 1973.

4 'The missing Goldies', *Dominion*, 13 September 1973.

5 'Have you seen these paintings', Goldie file, Research Library, Auckland Art Gallery Toi o Tāmaki.

6 'Two stolen Goldie paintings recovered', *New Zealand Herald*, 23 November 1973, p.1.

7 'School's Goldie painting is stolen off wall', *Auckland Star*, 30 October 1973, p.1.

8 Reference in John McDonald, 'Artist Goldie – is he really all that good?', *Auckland Star*, 3 November 1973, Weekender section, p.3.

9 '$10,000 Goldie stolen from Dowse museum', *Evening Post*, 22 December 1981, p.1.

10 'Paintings damaged. Vandalism at art gallery', *New Zealand Herald*, 5 December 1944, p.4.

11 'Staff find hole in NZ art treasure', *Auckland Star*, 26 June 1985, p.1.

12 Ian Gordon, 'A curse on you', *Auckland Star,* 1 July 1985, p.8.
13 'Painting of Maori', *New Zealand Herald,* 31 August 1938, p.15.
14 'Not an original', *New Zealand Herald,* 2 September 1938, p.15. The photograph and enquiry from the *New Zealand Free Lance,* with Goldie's inscribed opinion, are in Scrapbook XII, p.82.
15 '"Exciting" work sold to gallery', *New Zealand Herald,* 7 May 1985. Van der Velden's authorship was verified by curator Anne Kirker and van der Velden scholar Rodney Wilson.
16 'Goldie v Goldie: you decide', *New Zealand Herald,* 19 August 1993, sec.2, p.2.
17 'More out there, says art forger', *North Shore Times Advertiser,* 23 October 1992, p.51.

the 'ranfurly' controversy

1 A comprehensive account of the saga was contributed by Rosemary McLeod: 'There's no brawl like an art brawl', *North & South,* April 1991, pp.52-63.
2 Alister Taylor, 'Digging for Goldie', *NBR Weekly Magazine,* 7 December 1990, p.27.
3 Rosemary McLeod: 'There's no brawl like an art brawl', p.62.
4 'Debate degrading', *Northern Advocate,* 7 December 1990.

goldie in the māori world

1 A. G. Stephens, 'Art in Australia, the Archibald Prize', *Auckland Star,* 13 March 1926, p.34.
2 'Literature and art. Nature in New Zealand', *Auckland Weekly News,* 3 July 1902, p.10.
3 George Graham, 'Maori customs. Faults in historical pictures', *Auckland Star,* 3 August 1934, p.6. Watkins's *Legend of the voyage to New Zealand* was exhibited from 1912, when it was purchased by Samuel Vaile and Sons for the Auckland Art Gallery.
4 James Cowan, 'Coming of the Maori', *Auckland Star,* 13 August 1934, p.6.
5 D. R. Simmons, 'C. F. Goldie – Maori portraits', *AGMANZ News,* vol.3, no.2, May 1974, p.38.
6 'Goldie painting irks Tu Tangata teacher', *Waikato Times,* 27 February 1980, p.1.
7 For the historical context of *The Arrival* see Leonard Bell, *Colonial Constructs,* pp.165-173. Bell argues that part of the appeal for Pākehā audiences related to the underlying message: 'they too were immigrants'.
8 Others have regarded this image as one of exploitation. Alan Taylor described the interpretation presented here as 'contemptible' (*Kia Hiwa Rā,* March 1996, p.2).
9 'The Maori in bronze', *New Zealand Herald,* 19 March 1908, p.6.
10 'Goldie unlimited', *New Zealand Herald,* 28 October 1978, sec.2, p.8.
11 Taylor & Glen, 1979, p.151.
12 Theo Schoon to Michael King, undated letter [early 1970s], Alexander Turnbull Library. I am grateful to Damian Skinner for alerting me to Schoon's comments on Goldie.
13 'Maori portraits. . . Paris Salon entries', *New Zealand Herald,* 10 February 1938, p.8.

trouble with reproductions

1 Michael King, 'Some Maori attitudes to documents', *Tihei Maori Ora,* Auckland, 1978, p.15.
2 Scrapbook XIII, p.177.
3 'Not an original', *Auckland Star,* 2 September 1938, p:15.
4 *New Zealand Herald,* 17 April 1996, p.12.
5 'Goldies home after 66 years', *Dominion,* 9 January 1984, p.1.
6 'Dealer refused Goldies offer', *Dominion,* 3 May 1985, p.5.

smoothing the pillow

1 'Society of Arts,' *Auckland Star,* 13 July 1905, p.3.
2 'The passing show', *Auckland Star,* 5 June 1935, p.6.
3 'Are the Maoris decreasing?', *Auckland Star,* 5 April 1884, p.3.
4 See Ross Galbreath, 'Images of colonisation: native rats and dying pillows', *Turnbull Library Record,* vol.26, nos.1&2, 1993, pp.33-42.
5 'Where the white man treads: Some more concerning the Treaty of Waitangi', *New Zealand Herald,* 22 July 1905 (supplement) p.1.
6 Quoted in M.P.K. Sorrenson's introduction to *Na To Hoa Aroha. . . The correspondence between Sir Apirana Ngata and Sir Peter Buck* (Auckland, 1986), p.17.
7 Edith Searle Grossman, 'The native schools of Auckland', *New Zealand Illustrated Magazine,* June, 1903, p.201.
8 Ken Gorbey, 'Charles Frederick Goldie', *AGMANZ News,* vol.5, no.2, May 1974, p.36.

pākehā 'history'

1 See Leonard Bell, *Colonial Constructs,* pp.166-173.
2 'Society of Arts', *Auckland Star,* 13 July 1905, p.3.
3 *New Zealand Illustrated Magazine,* August 1905, p.352.
4 Lay Figure, 'Picture exhibition', *New Zealand Times,* 12 October 1911, p.5.
5 'Painting history', *Auckland Star,* 12 October 1933, p.6.
6 Reproduced in Taylor & Glen, 1977, plate 38.
7 D. M. Stafford, *The New Century in Rotorua,* Rotorua 1988, p.152.
8 E. S. G., 'The Aucklanders', *Otago Witness,* 5 November 1902, p.69.
9 Florence Roberts, 'Goldie – many know the painter, few know the man', *New Zealand Woman's Weekly,* 20 October 1958, p.9.
10 'Art in Auckland', *Auckland Star,* 21 May 1913, p.7.
11 W. Baucke, *Where the White Man Treads,* Auckland, 1928, p.143-144. *Kapai te Torori* is reproduced in Taylor & Glen, 1979, p.103.
12 Ray Watchman, 'Painter of portraits', *New Zealand Listener,* 11 September 1976, p.20.

goldie's legacy

1 Eileen Cowan to Eric Ramsden, 15 July [1947], Alexander Turnbull LIbrary.
2 'Fine 1902 Goldie portrait up for sale', *New Zealand Herald,* 28 September 1965.
3 Ray Watchman, 'Painter of portraits'.
4 Scrapbook XIII, p.157.
5 'Among the Pictures', *Lyttelton Times,* 7 April 1916, p.8.
6 *Evening Star,* 13 November 1902, p.6.
7 'Otago Art Society', *Otago Daily Times,* 17 November 1908, p.2.
8 'The Auckland Society of Arts', *Triad,* vol.11, no.3, 1 June 1903, p.17; *New Zealand Graphic,* 20 June 1903, p.1709.
9 See David W. Forbes, *Encounters with Paradise, views of Hawaii and its people, 1778-1941,* exhibition catalogue, Honolulu Academy of Arts, 1992, p.221.
10 'New Zealand Art' by G. S., *New Zealand Illustrated Magazine,* June 1903, p.165.
11 Ray Watchman, 'Painter of portraits'.
12 Confusion exists among curators and dictionary compilers regarding Goldie's appropriate working name as an artist. His almost invariable signature, both in paint and ink, was *C. F. Goldie.* Yet museum labels and auction catalogues usually describe him in baptismal fashion, *Charles Frederick Goldie.* We have decided to honour the wishes of the elderly artist, who in 1936 wrote to his nephew: 'give my name as Charles F. Goldie'.

tā moko: māori tattoo

1 The following works have been consulted in the preparation of this essay:

Ngahuia Te Awekotuku, Roger Neich, et al., *MAORI: Art and Culture,* British Museum Press / David Bateman, 1996.

J.C. Beaglehole (ed), *The Endeavour Journal of Joseph Banks 1768-1771,* 2 vols., Angus & Robertson, 1963.

James Cowan, *The Maori Yesterday and Today,* Whitcombe & Tombs, 1930.

Te Rangihiroa (P. H. Buck), *The Coming of the Maori,* Maori Purposes Fund Board, 1949.

Michael King & Marti Friedlander, *Moko: Maori Tattooing in the Twentieth Century,* Alister Taylor, 1972.

Isabel Ollivier & Cheryl Hingley (eds & translators), *Early Eyewitness Accounts of Maori Life I: Extracts from the Journals of the Ship St Jean Baptiste 1769,* National Library of New Zealand, 1982.

Horatio G. Robley, *Moko and Maori Tattooing,* Southern Reprints, 1987.

two paintings by C. F. Goldie

1 Dalkey Archive Press, Elmwood Park, Illinois, 1988, p.92.
2 Jim Barr, art critic and curator, quoted *Evening Post,* 12 December 1990, p.9.
3 W. A. Sutton, painter and former National Art Gallery trustee, quoted *Dominion,* 5 December 1990.
4 Quoted *New Zealand Herald,* 1 December 1990, p.3.
5 Margaret Austin in conversation with Leonard Bell, 11 February 1991.
6 Quoted *National Business Review,* 20 December 1990, p.6.
7 Ibid, 7 December 1990, p.26.
8 Quoted *Dominion,* 30 November 1990, p.3.
9 Quoted *Evening Post,* 12 December 1990, p.9.
10 Quoted *New Zealand Herald,* 12 December 1990, p.24.
11 e.g. *New Zealand Graphic,* 20 June 1903, p.1709.
12 Ibid, 9 May 1903, p.1323.
13 Ibid, 20 June 1903, p.1709.
14 Ibid, 27 June 1903, p.1779.
15 *Observer,* 16 November 1901.
16 *Auckland Star,* 23 June 1903.
17 *New Zealand Free Lance,* 8 October 1910.
18 e.g. *New Zealand Free Lance,* 21 November 1903.
19 *Auckland Star,* 28 July 1932, p.7.
20 *Observer,* 20 June 1903.
21 *Auckland Star,* 28 July 1932, p.7.
22 *Observer,* 20 June 1903.
23 Letter: Earl of Ranfurly to Mr Mitchelson, Chairman of the Ranfurly Veterans Home, reprinted in the *New Zealand Herald,* 9 August 1905, p.4.
24 *Auckland Star,* 28 July 1932, p.7.
25 eg. *New Zealand Herald,* 13 July 1905, p.6, and *Auckland Star,* 2 September 1904.
26 *Oxford English Dictionary,* Clarendon Press, Oxford, 1989, vol.IV, p.247.
27 *Auckland Star,* 9 June 1903.
28 See D. I. Pool, *The Maori Population of New Zealand 1769-1971,* Auckland University Press, Auckland, 1977.
29 See, for instance, J. A. Williams, *Politics of the New Zealand Maori, Protest and Co-operation, 1891 - 1901,* University of Washington Press, Seattle and London, 1969, and R. Walker, *Ka Whawhai Tonu Matou: Struggle Without End,* Penguin, Auckland, 1990.
30 As noted by Irihapeti Ramsden, panellist, in 'Sentimental Parlour Pieces of Great Works of Art? A discussion on the cultural and artistic significance of paintings by C F Goldie', Wellington City Art Gallery, 3 April 1991.
31 Jenny Harper, reported in the *Evening Post,* 12 December 1990, p.9.

materials and techniques

1 A. Boime, *The Academy and French Painting in the Nineteenth Century* (London, 1971).
2 D. Bomford, J. Kirby, et al, *Art in the Making, Impressionism* (National Gallery, London, 1990) pp.44-50.
3 A double ground usually consists of a coarse first layer of pigment mixed with fillers such as chalk and barytes, followed by a thinner coating of purer pigment. The top layer might be left fairly smooth or, alternatively, textured to give a distinctive tooth.
4 I would like to acknowledge the assistance of Dr Lesley Carlyle at the Canadian Conservation Institute for information on zinc white from her research into nineteenth-century artists' materials.
5 Personal communication, Jo Kirby, Scientific Department, National Gallery of London.
6 Carolus Duran, the French academic artist and teacher, is quoted in J. Collier's *A Manual of Oil Painting* (London, 1892) as recommending a palette of only eight pigments: black, viridian, raw umber, cobalt

blue, red lake, light red, yellow ochre and white. Other authors reduced this list to as few as five pigments.

7 The range of pigments available to the artist roughly doubled during the nineteenth century, with many bright and permanent colours introduced to replace older pigments from mineral sources which had a poor reputation for reliability. Not all the pigments introduced were particularly stable and artists and teachers often treated them with a good degree of suspicion.

8 Identification of pigments was carried out using Polarised Light Microscopy, Ultraviolet Fluorescence Microscopy and micro-chemical tests. Identification of the commercial grounds and Goldie's primings was carried out using EDX (Energy Dispersive X-Radiography) facilities at the University of Auckland Geology Department. I would like to thank Dr R. Simms for his assistance in carrying out the EDX analysis.

9 Books such as *The Chemistry of Paints and Painting* by Sir Arthur Church, first published in 1896, were exhaustive in their testing of the full range of artists' pigments. Artist/teachers such as William Muckley in his *A Handbook for Painters and Art Students* (4th edition, 1893) were equally convinced that the real knowledge of how pigments behaved came from experience of their use and not from how they performed in the laboratory.

10 See Solomon J. Solomon, *The Practice of Oil Painting and Drawing* (London, 2nd edition, 1911) pp.105-110

11 Ibid, p.115.

12 Cross-sections are minute flakes of paint, usually taken from an area of damage. The fragments are set in a polyester resin block and polished to reveal the strata of the ground and paint layers. The polished section is examined under an optical microscope at magnifications of between x100 and x400. Cross-sections were taken from works painted throughout Goldie's career. Approximately 30 paintings were examined and samples taken for cross-sectional analysis. A further 10 paintings were examined and sampled for pigment analysis.

13 D. Bomford and S. Staniforth, 'Wax-resin lining and colour change', *National Gallery Technical Bulletin*, vol.5, 1981, pp.58-65, National Gallery, London.

bibliography

manuscript sources

Goldie family scrapbooks, private collections (Auckland, Dunedin).

Goldie Scrapbooks, Auckland Museum Library.

Goldie papers, Research Library, Auckland Art Gallery Toi o Tāmaki.

Goldie papers, Museum of New Zealand Te Papa Tongarewa.

Eric Ramsden papers, Alexander Turnbull Library.

Alfred Hill papers, Mitchell Library, Sydney.

Robert McVeagh papers, private collection (Hawke's Bay).

published texts by charles f. goldie

'The Grey Statue', *New Zealand Herald*, 26 October 1900, p.6.

'Art Export Ban. Mr. C. F. Goldie's View. Not Unmixed Calamity. Trend of Modern Painting', *New Zealand Herald*, 24 April 1934, p.8.

'British pictures, a painter's survey, the menace of "isms", decadence in art', *New Zealand Herald*, 21 August 1934, p.12.

'Art Gallery, re-hanging of pictures, modernist propaganda, Mr C. F. Goldie's views', *New Zealand Herald*, 3 September 1934, p.6.

'The art crisis. Auckland Gallery. Battle of the Schools. Modernism condemned', *New Zealand Herald*, 28 September 1934, p.15.

'Fine Arts Block', *New Zealand Herald*, 15 November 1935, p.17.

'Art in New Zealand', *New Zealand Herald*, 19 December 1935, p.15.

'A tribute', *Auckland Star*, 24 February 1937, p.6.

'The Art Gallery', *New Zealand Herald*, 4 February 1938, p.13.

secondary sources

'Artists and Photographers,' *Cyclopedia of New Zealand* (vol.2, Auckland), Christchurch, 1902, pp.318-321.

Aspects of New Zealand Art. Exhibition catalogue, National Art Gallery, Wellington, 1984.

Barr, Jim. 'The Goldie rush', *New Zealand Listener*, 18 February 1978, p.28.

Bell, Leonard. 'Life and death at sea: L. J. Steele and C. F. Goldie's *The Arrival of the Maori in New Zealand*, 1898', *Bulletin of New Zealand Art History*, vol.3, 1975, pp.2-8.

Bell, Leonard. *The Maori in European Art, a survey of the representation of the Maori by European artists from the time of Captain Cook to the present day*, Wellington, 1980.

Bell, Leonard. 'Two Paintings by C. F. Goldie: Their Brilliant Careers', *Art New Zealand* 59, Winter 1991, pp.88-92.

Bell, Leonard. *Colonial Constructs: European Images of Maori 1840-1914*, Auckland, 1992.

Bell, Leonard. 'The colonial paintings of Charles Frederick Goldie in the 1990s: the postcolonial Goldie and the rewriting of history', *Cultural Studies*, vol.9, no.1, 1995, pp.26-42.

Bell, Leonard. 'Looking at Goldie: Face to face with "All 'e Same t'e Pakeha"', *Voices*, National Library of Australia, Summer 1996-97, pp.52-77.

Blackley, Roger. 'The exhibitions of Maori art in Auckland 1884-1885: Documents of the New Zealand Art Students Association', *Antic* 3, 1987, pp.116-122.

Blackley, Roger. 'Goldie, Charles Frederick', *Dictionary of New Zealand Biography*, vol.3, 1996.

Brown, Gordon H. and Keith, Hamish. *An Introduction to New Zealand Painting, 1839-1967*, Auckland, 1969.

Brown, Gordon H. *New Zealand Painting, 1900-1920: Traditions and Departures*, exhibition catalogue, Queen Elizabeth II Arts Council of New Zealand, Wellington, 1972.

Brown, Gordon H. 'Charles Frederick Goldie: The Artist and his Age', *AGMANZ News*, vol.5, no.2, May 1974, pp.38-40.

Bush, G. W. A. *Decently and in Order, the Centennial History of the Auckland City Council*, Auckland, 1971.

Cornwell, Sue. 'Is it for the Gold' in a Goldie – or for the Art?', *New Zealand Woman's Weekly*, 15 May 1972, pp.8-11.

Cowan, James. 'Goldie's collection. Last of the rangatiras. Tattooed chiefs and kuias. Some famous old Maoris', *Auckland Star*, 6 November 1920, p.17.

Cowan, James. 'Goldie's collection. On loan to city library. Some of the artist's sitters', *Auckland Star*, 13 November 1920, p.17.

Cowan, James. 'A vanished art. The Maori moko. Last of the tattooed men', *Auckland Star*, 9 November 1935, magazine section, p.12.

Cowan, James. 'The art of C. F. Goldie: A great painter and interpreter of a people', *New Zealand Magazine*, March-April 1941, pp.8-12.

Davis, Eliot R. *A Link with the Past*, Auckland, 1949.

Docking, Gil. *Two Hundred Years of New Zealand Painting*, Wellington, 1971.

Dunn, Michael et al, *Face Value: a Study in Maori Portraiture*, exhibition catalogue, Dunedin Public Art Gallery, 1975.

Dunn, Michael. *A Concise History of New Zealand Painting*, Sydney, 1991.

Eichbaum, Gerda. 'Gericault's *Raft of the Medusa* and Goldie-Steele's *Arrival of the Maoris* – a comparison', *Art in New Zealand*, March 1942, pp.130-134.

Esplin, Thomas. 'Goldie, Charles Frederick, O.B.E. (1870-1947)', in *An Encyclopedia of New Zealand* (ed. A.H. McLinctock, Wellington, 1966) vol.1, pp.825-826.

Fehrer, Catherine. *The Julian Academy, Paris, 1868-1939*, exhibition catalogue, Shepherd Gallery, New York, 1989.

Goldie, William. 'The destiny of the Maori race', *New Zealand Herald* (supplement) 18 May 1901, p.1.

Gorbey, Ken. 'Charles Frederick Goldie', *AGMANZ News*, vol.5, no.2, May 1974, pp.35-36.

Hérold, Martine. *L'Académie Julian a cent ans, 1868-1968*, Paris [1968].

Howe, K. R. *Singer in a Songless Land: a Life of Edward Tregear*, Auckland, 1991.

King, Michael. 'Moko and C. F. Goldie', *Journal of the Polynesian Society*, vol.84, no.4, December 1975, pp.431-440.

King, Michael (ed.). *Tihei Maori Ora: Aspects of Maoritanga*, Auckland, 1978.

Lloyd, L.C. 'Charles Frederick Goldie – the technical aspect', *AGMANZ News*, vol.5, no.2, May 1974, pp.36-37.

Marwick, Ross. 'Charles Frederick Goldie' *Survey*, Robert McDougall Art Gallery, July 1971, pp.4-7.

McCormick, E. H. *Letters and Art in New Zealand*, Wellington, 1940.

McLintock, A. H. *National Centennial Exhibition of New Zealand Art*, Wellington, Department of Internal Affairs, 1940.

Platts, Una. *Nineteenth Century New Zealand Artists, a Guide and Handbook*, Christchurch, 1980.

Pound, Francis. 'Some late signatures of Charles Frederick Goldie', *Art New Zealand* 5, 1977, p.16

Roberts, Florence. 'Goldie – Many know the painter, few know the man', *New Zealand Woman's Weekly*, 20 October 1958, pp.8-9.

Scholefield, G. H. *A Dictionary of New Zealand Biography*, Wellington, Department of Internal Affairs, 1940.

Sealy, H. P. 'L'Académie Julian in Paris', *New Zealand Illustrated Magazine*, October 1901, pp.17-22.

Sealy, H. P. 'In the studio: Mr. C. F. Goldie's work', *New Zealand Illustrated Magazine*, November 1901, pp.144-157.

Simmons, D. R. 'Charles Frederick Goldie – Maori portraits', *AGMANZ News*, vol.5, no.2, May 1974, pp.37-38.

Singer, Richard Arnold. 'Mr. C. F. Goldie and His Pictures', *Triad*, vol.11, no.9, December 1903, pp.10-12.

Taylor, Alister. *C. F. Goldie: Famous Maori Leaders of New Zealand*, Auckland, 1993.

Taylor, Alister and Glen, Jan. *C. F. Goldie: his Life and Painting*, Martinborough, 1977.

Taylor, Alister and Glen, Jan. *C. F. Goldie: Prints, Drawings and Criticism*, Martinborough, 1979.

Thomson, John Mansfield. *A Distant Music: the Life and Times of Alfred Hill*, Auckland, 1980.

Watchman, Ray. 'Painter of portraits', *New Zealand Listener*, 11 September 1976, pp.20-21.

index

Bold entries indicate titles of Goldie's paintings and individuals depicted. Bold numerals refer to the page on which the plate can be found.